The Challenge of Pluralism

The Challenge of Pluralism

Church and State in Six Democracies

Third Edition

J. Christopher Soper, Kevin R. den Dulk, and
Stephen V. Monsma

ROWMAN & LITTLEFIELD
Lanham • Boulder • New York • London

Published by Rowman & Littlefield
A wholly owned subsidiary of
The Rowman & Littlefield Publishing Group, Inc.
4501 Forbes Boulevard, Suite 200, Lanham, Maryland 20706
https://rowman.com

Unit A, Whitacre Mews, 26-34 Stannary Street, London SE11 4AB,
United Kingdom

British Library Cataloguing in Publication Information Available

Library of Congress Cataloging-in-Publication Data
Names: Soper, J. Christopher, author. | Monsma, Stephen V., 1936– Challenge of plural-
ism.
Title: The challenge of pluralism : church and state in six democracies / J. Christopher
Soper, Kevin R. den Dulk, and Stephen V. Monsma.
Description: Third Edition. | Lanham : Rowman & Littlefield, 2017. | Rev. ed. of: The
challenge of pluralism : church and state in five democracies / Stephen V. Monsma
and J. Christopher Soper. 2nd ed. c2009. | Includes bibliographical references and
index.
Identifiers: LCCN 2016043224 (print) | LCCN 2016052427 (ebook) | ISBN
9781442250420 (cloth : alk. paper) | ISBN 9781442250437 (pbk. : alk. paper) | ISBN
9781442250444 (electronic)
Subjects: LCSH: Church and state—History—21st century. | Democracy—Religious as-
pects—Christianity—History—21st century. | Religious pluralism—Christianity—
History—21st century.
Classification: LCC BV630.3 .M66 2017 (print) | LCC BV630.3 (ebook) | DDC 322/
.109051—dc23
LC record available at https://lccn.loc.gov/2016043224

Printed in the United States of America

Contents

Preface to the Third Edition

The first edition of *The Challenge of Pluralism* was published in 1997. It is an understatement to say that the landscape of church-state relations has changed profoundly in the intervening two decades. We have seen growth in the fact of pluralism throughout the world, and particularly in the countries we survey in the book, with overall decline of religious affiliation and activity in western democracies, but also the emergence of new movements and resurgence of older ones. The democracies we examine have increasingly focused on one aspect of this dynamic change—the challenged posed by their growing Muslim populations—and this edition gives some special attention to the resulting complexities and tensions. But in many ways the conflicts over Muslim immigration into Europe and the United States is part of a much longer story of how governments have struggled over questions of religious liberty and assimilation. As in previous editions, this book asks whether the formal institutions and underlying cultural norms that shape the status of religion in western democracies are well designed to carry the weight of religious diversity in its many forms.

Another notable change over these past two decades is the growing interest in the global dimensions of religion and politics among our colleagues. In 1997, few scholars were giving serious attention to the political challenge of religious pluralism in cross-national perspective. Today, the study of religion in global affairs has become something of a cottage industry, and the most recurrent questions and themes have centered on religious freedom. Much of this interest, of course, was driven by new religion-based movements and events, most notably the September 11 attacks and other acts of terrorism. Scholars have also leveraged the data generated by new monitoring regimes for religious freedom within the U.S. State Department, the U.S. Commission on International Religious Freedom, and the U.N. Special Rapporteur on

Religion or Belief, as well as the intensive research of think tanks such as the Pew Research Center. While some scholars have raised doubts about the assumptions that underlie this intellectual work and advocacy, even the skeptics agree that the policy importance of religious freedom is ascendant. This scholarship, however, tends to focus on how states *interact* over questions of religious liberty, particularly through their foreign policies. *The Challenge of Pluralism* continues to take a different tack by asking what we can learn about religious freedom and church-state relations by *comparing* the largely domestic policies that shape the relationship of religion and government.

The Challenge of Pluralism has always focused on only a slice of the vast global experience of religion: western democracies that can trace their democratic experiments to the Enlightenment ideas of the eighteenth and nineteenth centuries. This narrow comparative focus is largely a decision of research design; we wished to hold some factors constant—e.g., democracy, basic commitment to religious freedom, roughly similar intellectual traditions—to learn what we can from a factor that varies, namely, frameworks for church-state relations. We continue to follow that approach in this edition. But we also concluded that there are good reasons to expand this edition with the inclusion of France. One reason is certainly the increasing challenge that France has faced over the past two decades with Muslim immigration, which has sparked debates about the right balance between integration and accommodation. But we have also added France because its model of religion-state interaction presents an illuminating contrast with the other frameworks and political cultures in the book, especially the church-state separationism of the United States. Readers of earlier editions will note that the six countries we survey are now divided into pairs: separation (the United States and France); pluralism (the Netherlands and Australia); and establishment (England and Germany). We hasten to note, however, that these are rough family resemblances; each of the countries in this study differs from all others in significant ways, and that variation is a rich opportunity for comparison.

The Challenge of Pluralism has benefited immeasurably from the insights of both scholars and practitioners over its three editions, including some new additions for this current version. Jérôme Fourquet provided some important data and commentary on the French religious experience. Jolene Vos-Camy's translation work helped the authors deal with their rusty French, and she also strengthened the discussion of religion in seventeenth-century France. Stanley Carlson-Thies confirmed and clarified some of the recent history of state support for faith-based social services in the United States. Matt Kaemingk graciously read and commented on several chapters. We received excellent research assistance through the Henry Institute at Calvin College, especially from Abbie Schutte, Benjamin Ridder, and Ellen Hekman. Susan McEachern, Rebeccah Shumaker, and the rest of the editorial team at Rowman & Littlefield were accommodating partners. Our thanks to these colleagues for their support and encouragement.

Preface to the Second Edition

In the ten years since this book was published, we are tempted to say that everything is the same and everything is different when it comes to church-state issues in the United States, the Netherlands, Australia, England, and Germany. One of our purposes in writing the first edition of this book was to stress that the manner in which the United States resolves religious freedom and religious establishment issues is distinctive when compared to the practices of other political democracies. Like its predecessor, this edition reaches that same conclusion: the United States is exceptional among political democracies in how it approaches such issues as the reach and meaning of religious free exercise rights, the place of religion in public schools, state support for religious schools, and government money going to religious non-profit social service agencies. What also remains the same ten years later is the importance of inherited church-state institutions and practices in resolving contemporary issues. The names of some of the religious groups have changed over time, as have the specific religious freedom and establishment issues in question, but the church-state practices of the past continue to create a powerful stream that shapes the contours of the current debate.

On the other hand, the world of religion and politics in these five countries is radically different from what it was ten years ago. Most notably, the European states and Australia have become more religiously pluralistic than at any time in these countries' histories. This is largely a consequence of immigration, particularly the immigration and settlement of large numbers of Muslims and other religious minorities into the Netherlands, Australia, England, and Germany. Ten years ago, political conflict around religion in Europe seemed to some a thing of the past, a relic of a bygone era when religion had cultural sway and political power, but a factor that would continue to recede as secular forces took over. Secularism remains a powerful force in western Europe and Australia, but the repoliticization of religious disputes in each of the countries in our study negates the naive assumptions that religion would somehow disappear as a political variable. Issues that were barely on the horizon ten years ago, such as state aid to Islamic schools, the teaching of religions other than Christianity and Judaism in public schools, and the meaning of freedom for non-Christian religious minorities are now at the forefront of politics in the Netherlands, Australia, England, and Germany. In this way, Australia and Europe have come to look more like the United States, where religion was and remains an important political variable.

In revising the first edition, we benefited greatly from the advice of various people who read drafts of our chapters and made very helpful comments. In particular, we would like to thank Michael Hogan, Gerhard Robbers, Chris Janse, and Sophie C. van Bijsterveld. We would also like to acknowledge the support of our colleagues at Pepperdine University and the Henry Institute of Calvin College who assumed more than their fair share of administrative tasks while we shut ourselves in our offices working on our manuscript. The book would not have been possible without the numerous interviews we conducted with activists and scholars in each country for this project. In every case, those interviewees were generous with their time, helpful with their insights, and gracious in more ways than we can possibly recount. Finally, we wish to thank the staff at Rowman & Littlefield for encouraging us in this second edition and for being patient when we were running up against, and even past, deadlines. In particular, we owe Susan McEachern a debt of gratitude for her patience and support.

At home, we continue to receive loving support for our efforts, but we also get the necessary encouragement to leave the world of church and state behind in order to involve ourselves in the daily lives of our respective families. Our families richly deserved the dedication to the first edition of the book, and we are happy to rededicate this volume to them as well.

Preface to the First Edition

American society continues to be deeply divided on the question of the proper relationship between the institutions of church and state. Almost every year the Supreme Court is marked by sharp divisions in the church-state cases that come before it, divisions that mirror the disagreements and controversies of the broader American society. It was while we were discussing church-state practice in the United States that it occurred to us that a comparative analysis of how other western pluralistic democracies resolve church-state tensions might shed new light on this enduring issue in American politics. This book, then, is a comparative study of church-state policy in the United States, the Netherlands, Australia, England, and Germany. We do not pretend that this book will resolve a political debate in the United States that is as abiding as it is frustrating to the groups and individuals involved in it, but it is our hope that it will provide a different perspective on it.

As we delved further into the study of these five countries, we were struck at how contemporary church-state practice had much to do with each nation's unique history and cultural assumptions about the proper place of religion in public life. This book is not an apology for the church-state practice in any one of these countries, but we have attempted to be sensitive to each nation's particular history in the story we have told. At the same time, our study has convinced us that sufficient similarities in the church-state experiences of the five countries exist that allow us to make some general conclusions that would apply to each. Democracies, we believe, can and should learn from each other.

The lessons these countries offer are particularly important now. Increasing levels of religious pluralism in the modern world raise tensions among religious groups and challenge the inherited church-state models of the nations in our study. In addition, the growth of the welfare state has led to an expansion of government involvement in almost all aspects of society, including religious life, and threatens to undermine past relations between religious and political institutions.

We are convinced that the answer to these growing conflicts is to be found in a church-state policy that is genuinely neutral among all religious groups and between religious and secular perspectives generally, and that accommodates and promotes the religious pluralism that is a natural feature of each nation. We do not believe that the state can attain genuine neutrality, or evenhandedness among religious and secular groups in society, with a church-state policy that supports only some religious groups and practices but not others, nor through a no-aid-to-religion standard that ends up favoring secular over religious perspectives. Either of these policies would violate the standard of government neutrality that we believe should lie at the heart of a country's church-state policy. It is to the extent that the five nations in our study fall short of this goal that we are critical of their practices, while it is to the degree to which each attains this evenhandedness that they serve as a model from which we hope to draw some lessons.

We have received assistance and cooperation from many people in our research for this book. We would like to thank the dozens of people whom we interviewed in each country for our study. They gave freely of their time and expertise, provided us with invaluable insight about the church-state practices of their countries, and were a constant source of support with the hospitality they extended to us. We also owe a considerable debt to the following people who read portions of the manuscript and gave numerous suggestions that helped us avoid errors and generally strengthened the book: J. P. Balkenende, Sophie van Bijsterveld, Gary Bouma, Stanley Carlson-Thies, Lothar Cönen, Michael Hogan, Cees Klop, Frans Koopmans, George Moyser, Jørgen Rasmussen, Gerhard Robbers, and Jerry Waltman. We also would like to thank Lothar Cönen for his help in arranging for many of the interviews in Germany. The blame for any remaining errors of fact or interpretation is, however, ours alone. Stephen Wrinn, our editor at Rowman & Littlefield, provided just the right combination of encouragement and suggestions to strengthen our manuscript, and he wisely selected an outside reviewer for the book who read the entire manuscript carefully and made very helpful comments. We would also like to thank the American Political Science Association and Pepperdine University for providing us with grant money for travel to each of these countries.

Finally, we would like to thank our families for their constant love, moral support, patience, and interest in our work: our wives, Jane and Mary, and our children, Katharine and David, and Martin and Kristin. They all richly deserve the dedication of this book.

Chapter One

Introduction

It is not surprising that two of the most powerful and longest lasting of human institutions—the church and the state—have often had an uneasy relationship.[1] Religion is such a pervasive, deeply ingrained aspect of human existence that it has played a prominent role in nearly every society in recorded history. Government has been a similarly omnipresent feature of human experience. Both institutions make real claims on the thinking and behavior of human beings; they shape how we order the practical aspects of our life, how we join together with others in community, and even how we understand our basic purposes. Sometimes the claims of both institutions complement and even reinforce each other. But just as frequently they come into conflict, even to the point of violence. As a result of the enduring presence and power of both the church and the state, human societies struggle perpetually with how these two vital spheres of human endeavor should relate to each other. In the most diverse societies that struggle can be quite intense.

This book explores how six western liberal democracies—the United States, France, the Netherlands, Australia, England, and Germany—have sought to deal with the relationship between church and state. All six are economically developed and stable democratic nations, yet they have approached the question of church-state relations in different ways. They are also challenged by their capacity to accommodate and integrate diverse and ever-changing expressions of religion within their borders. The United States has a long history of drawing from its diversity as part of its politics. There are interest groups committed to one side or the other of church-state questions, Congress struggles each year with legislation and constitutional amendments that seek to change the ground rules of church-state relations, parties and candidates for office seek the support of blocs of religious voters,

1

and almost every year the Supreme Court decides church-state cases marked by closely divided votes and at times vitriolic opinions. In the other democracies considered here, changing patterns of immigration are raising new church-state challenges, especially the large number of Muslim arrivals that have struggled to assimilate into countries imbued with a mix of Christian and secular thinking. As political scientist Jonathan Laurence notes, "For host societies like Britain, France, Germany, [and] the Netherlands . . . , Islam in Europe is no longer just a matter of ginger diplomacy with former colonies or current trading partners: the integration of Muslims has become a nation-building challenge of historical significance."[2] But the recent experience of Islam has exposed deeper church-state questions that western democracies have confronted for centuries, including the basic difficulty of recognizing and accommodating newcomers who do not share majority norms. The rise of a small, but real, violence-prone Islamist movement is simply the latest in a long line of challenges to church-state arrangements.

Exploring the issue of church-state relations in these countries has also taken on a new importance because many governments have devolved certain activities and programs previously run by state agencies to private, usually nonprofit organizations, many of which have a religious history or orientation. In the United States this trend is epitomized in the faith-based initiative started during the George W. Bush administration, which continues to foster grantmaking to faith-based social services today. France, the Netherlands, and other countries have large welfare states that have also increasingly relied on local associations to serve human needs. As western governments look to these private and often religiously based organizations to play larger roles in society, questions of church and state have been magnified. Will faith-based groups be pressured to tone down their religious orientations in exchange for state funding? Should they be? Are religiously based agencies that are excluded from governmental funding programs—as is largely the case for elementary and secondary schools in the United States—the victims of a form of discrimination? These questions are not new, but the potential scope of religious social service activity is new.

Our goal in this book is to use comparison to guide democracies—and the United States in particular—in their attempts to relate church and state to each other in a manner that supports the religious freedoms of their citizens and their religious organizations. The "challenge of pluralism" in our title suggests our approach in two ways. In an *empirical* sense of the phrase, we start with the fact that diversity, and sometimes deep difference, characterizes the modern experience of nearly every democracy in the world. In this sense, the challenge of pluralism is how best to live together when members of the political community are driven apart by their heterogeneity, especially when differences are defined by religious faith. In a *normative* sense of our title, we argue that states ought to address many of the conflicts that arise because of religious (and other forms of) diversity by applying a set of principles that honor the importance of that diversity to the common good. As we discuss below, we root these pluralistic principles in a specific concept of "positive" or "substantive" neutrality. In this sense, the challenge of pluralism is a call to states to treat religious diversity with an evenhandedness and an accommodating spirit.[3]

In this introductory chapter we set the context for our study by first considering three basic church-state questions that repeatedly arise in democratic polities. In subsequent chapters we explore how each of the six countries has responded to these questions. We then present a basic religious liberty goal that we use as a standard to evaluate the strengths and weaknesses of the six countries' approaches to church-state issues. The third section describes three models of church-state relationships, and the final section explains why we selected these democracies for study.

THREE QUESTIONS

Questions of church and state have often proven contentious even in stable, successful democracies. More specifically, there are three very basic questions that, at various points in history, have confronted democratic societies. One question is: *How far can a democratic polity go in permitting religiously motivated behavior that is contrary to societal welfare or norms?* There is general agreement that when the exercise of religious freedom by one group has the effect of endangering the health or safety of others or of significantly disrupting the smooth functioning of life lived in society, the claims of religious freedom must yield to the welfare of the broader society. In this sense religious freedom is not an absolute. On this basis, most western democracies require, for example, religious burial practices to meet normal health standards and those organizing religious processions on public streets to obtain the normal permits regulating the timing and size of such processions. But this leaves many questions. How serious must the threat to public health and safety or the normal functioning of society be before the government insists that the right to religiously motivated practices must be curtailed?

There is also the matter of religious groups violating deeply held societal norms. Modern democracies—no matter how committed to religious pluralism—would not allow human sacrifice, even if it were part of a group's sincere religious beliefs. Allowing human sacrifice would so violate such deeply held norms as respect for human life that society would be torn apart if it were allowed in the name of religious freedom. Democratic societies that are fully committed to freedom of religion have decided there are certain norms or values too fundamental to human existence and too deeply held for religion to be used as a basis for their violation. In such cases religion must yield to the claims of the broader society and its values. When religious groups violate those principles the force of law can be brought to bear on them. The political order sometimes outlaws and punishes certain religiously motivated practices.

But here, too, questions arise over where to draw the line between practices that are legally permissible and impermissible in the name of religion. Human sacrifice may be out, but what about polygamy—a toxic issue in nineteenth-century America? Or how should democracies address arranged marriages, a common global practice that is nonetheless anathema in western societies? Or what is to happen when Muslim schools in western societies teach attitudes and values—such as those relating to the role of women in society—that are today rejected by those societies? These are not trivial questions. Religious freedom is a fundamental freedom. Many Americans, when referring to religious freedom as the "first freedom," have more than its location in their Bill of Rights in mind. The horrors of wars in the name of religion and of western societies burning religious heretics at the stake not that many years ago stand as vivid testimonies to the importance of religious freedom. Let no one take it for granted or look lightly on attempts even to nibble away at its fringes.

But societal unity and welfare are also of crucial importance. What binds society together is much more than a conglomeration of persons occupying the same territory. Instead, a society is marked both by cooperative efforts promoting societal welfare that make possible life lived in a complex, interdependent society and by shared values, myths, and memories that lead persons to imagine themselves as a people. It is as persons identify themselves as members of a common society that cooperative tasks, sacrifices for the larger good, and other basics of human civilization are made possible. When common values and beliefs of a fundamental nature are shattered, or when some persons' practices endanger and disrupt the lives of others, society is threatened with disintegration: at best, cooperation is made difficult and, at worst, barbarism and civil war result. The current violence in Syria, Libya, or northern Nigeria stand out as illustrations of the horrors that can result when bonds of respect, trust, and civility are absent.

In addition, something more than societal unity may be at stake. Many theorists have contended that free, democratic government is finally dependent upon a populace with certain internalized values and habits of the mind. Clinton Rossiter once wrote, "It takes more than a perfect plan of government to pursue ordered liberty. Something else is needed, some moral principle diffused among the people to strengthen the urge to peaceful obedience and hold the community on an even keel. . . . [Democratic] government rests on a definite moral basis: a virtuous people."[4] If, in fact, a "virtuous people" is essential for a successfully functioning democracy, any movements—including religious ones—that work to build up a sense of virtue or morality among the public and that teach respect for the welfare of others become crucial for a healthy democracy, and any movements that undercut or subvert a sense of virtue, morality, and consideration for others pose a significant threat to democratic government. Does democratic self-preservation therefore mean religious movements that undercut a sense of public virtue and morality, or that subvert respect for the welfare of others, should not receive religious freedom protection? Germany, France, Australia, the Netherlands, and England are all struggling with this question as they work to balance the religious freedom of their Muslim citizens—a small number of whom seem to be resisting assimilation into the majority culture—with the need for national unity resting on liberal democratic values.

In short, religious freedom, on the one hand, and shared values and beliefs and public health and safety, on the other hand, are enormously important. Political theorist Will Kymlicka highlights this need for balance when he writes that "any plausible or attractive political theory must attend to both the claims of ethnocultural minorities and the promotion of responsible democratic citizenship."[5] The stakes in resolving the question of how far a polity can go in permitting behavior contrary to societal welfare and norms that is justified on the basis of religious beliefs are indeed high.

This leads to the second basic question related to religion and society that confronts democratic polities today: *Should the state encourage and promote consensual religious beliefs and traditions in an attempt to support the common values and virtues that bind a society together and make possible limited, democratic government?* This is the positive version of the first question just raised.

If Rossiter is right and certain shared civic virtues are crucial for societal unity and democratic governance, should government perhaps not only oppose those religious practices and movements that would undercut those virtues, but also encourage them in a positive manner through the promotion of certain consensual religious values and symbols? Social scientists have noted repeatedly the importance of religion within civil society, that set of voluntary associations and organizations—recreational sports leagues, labor unions, charitable groups, houses of worship, etc.—that mediate between the individual and the state. More specifically, religious networks have tremendous potential to foster the norms of trust, efficacy, and reciprocity that form the necessary "social capital" of modern democracies.[6] Should states seize that potential by supporting religious networks directly? We will see many examples throughout this book in which the state has chosen to support certain religious norms and networks as a means to strengthen the virtues of democratic citizens. But when the state supports religion of this sort, does it threaten to co-opt the religious networks it seeks to strengthen? Or does it violate the norm of religious freedom for those citizens whose own networks are left unsupported?

A third basic question emerges from a fundamental fact of life in all industrialized, urbanized western democracies: the expansion of the modern administrative state into almost all areas of life. Whether it is economic regulation and stimulation, health care, education at all levels, care for the elderly, land-use planning and zoning, radio and television licensing and regulation, preservation of historical sites, or regulation of abortion and other health services, the modern administrative state is active in regulating, supporting, and providing services. But almost all the areas just cited as examples of state activity are also areas in which religious communities have been and continue to be active. This leads to the question: *When religious groups and the state are both active in the same fields of endeavor, how can one ensure that the state does not advantage or disadvantage any one religious group or either religious or secular belief systems over others?* If the state, for example, collects taxes from the entire population in order to fund its own schools and to help fund the programs of the schools of the traditional, well-established religions, but does not fund the schools of newer, nonmainstream religions, is it not advantaging some religions and disadvantaging others? Or if the state funds its own secular social service programs and those of secularly based nonprofit agencies, but leaves religiously based groups involved in the same social service programs to struggle on without state help, is not religion disadvantaged? But if the state inserts religion into its own activities or funds the activities of religious groups, does it not run the risk of favoring one religious group over others or of favoring religion over secular perspectives? As the modern state has entered more and more areas to regulate, fund, or provide services, questions of evenhandedness among all religious groups and between secular and religious groups arise.

In the following chapters we consider how six countries whose church-state principles and practices we have chosen for analysis have responded to these three questions.

A BASIC GOAL

In discussing and at some points suggesting answers to the three questions raised in the prior section, we hold to the basic ideal of governmental neutrality on matters of religion. We define neutrality as government neither favoring nor burdening any particular religion, nor favoring or burdening religion as a whole or secular systems of belief as a whole. This neutrality is attained when government does not influence its citizens' choices for or against certain religious or secular systems of belief, either by imposing burdens on them or by granting advantages to them. Instead, government is neutral when it is evenhanded toward people of all faiths and of none. This concept of state neutrality on matters of religion is what the American legal scholar Douglas

Laycock has termed *substantive neutrality* and what Stephen Monsma calls *positive neutrality.*[7] Laycock describes substantive neutrality as being achieved when the government minimizes "the extent to which it either encourages or discourages religious belief or disbelief, practice or nonpractice, observance or nonobservance."[8] In the key areas of education and faith-based social services we consider throughout this book,[9] we contend that the neutrality goal is preferable to other theories or frameworks, such as an established church, a multiple establishment, no aid at all for religion, a wall of separation between church and state, and financial support for a wide range of religious expressions. That is the standard against which specific church-state principles and theories, or specific means to implement those principles and theories, should be judged. It is when this goal of neutrality is fully realized that the moving words of U.S. Supreme Court Justice Potter Stewart take on life and meaning: "What our Constitution indispensably protects is the freedom of each of us, be he Jew or Agnostic, Christian or Atheist, Buddhist or Freethinker, to believe or disbelieve, to worship or not worship, to pray or keep silent, according to his own conscience, uncoerced and unrestrained by government."[10]

This basic goal of governmental neutrality on matters of belief and practice—whether religiously or secularly based—is largely in keeping with the liberal tradition within western society, yet differs in some important ways from that tradition. That tradition emerged on the western scene in the eighteenth-century Enlightenment, received a concrete manifestation in the French Revolution, was a strong social and political movement in the nineteenth century, and is a very active force down to today in all six democracies considered in this book. In fact, in a generalized way one can say that virtually all of western society today is liberal. Individual rights are universally respected (in theory and usually in practice), inherited class distinctions are not in principle supposed to provide special political prerogatives, the principle of "one person, one vote" is the norm, and selecting political leaders by free, competitive elections is fully accepted. In terms of these ideals and practices, all six of the countries included in this book are liberal democracies.

Liberalism can, however, also be seen as a more specific philosophical theory or movement associated with the Enlightenment. Many Enlightenment thinkers reacted with horror to the apparent role of religion in the wars of the seventeenth century; they also rejected the often conservative nature of religious bodies that supported hereditary privileges and authoritarian government and opposed democratic reforms. Liberals placed great faith in human reason, believing that if people were freed from existing economic, political, and religious constraints they could, through the exercise of their reason, reach a consensus on the virtues and institutions needed for a free and prosperous society. Religion in its particular manifestations was seen as rooted in authority and superstitions and—when brought into the political arena—as a dangerous force, since it would work to divide society and become a basis for one group to use the political order to force its will onto others. On the other hand, basic, consensual religious beliefs were both discoverable by human reason and adequate to construct a free, prosperous society. Enlightenment liberals believed religion in its particular manifestations should be banned from the public realm as a dangerous, divisive force; it saw religion in its rational, consensual manifestation as having the potential to unify the public realm.

Enlightenment liberals, therefore, typically called for a strict separation of church and state. They believed such a separation would spare the state from the dangerous divisions particularistic religion posed, yet would not harm particularistic religion, since it would continue to flourish in the private realm. Citizens would be free to express their faith in their private lives, but it would have no relevance to the state. The state would thereby be neutral on matters of religion. It would neither help nor hinder any particular religion. The state would only support and identify with rational, consensual religious themes, such as duty, honesty, responsibility, and respect, on which all religions and even all reasonable nonreligious people agreed. It thereby equated government neutrality on matters of religion and strict church-state separation. This meant Enlightenment liberals also saw religious freedom as being wholly a negative freedom, that is, as consisting of the right to be free from government restrictions or restraints on one's exercise of religion. For the most part, they did not see religious freedom in positive terms, that is, as requiring certain positive governmental actions that would make it possible for people to live out their religious faiths. All that was necessary for people to be fully free was for government to stay out of religious affairs.

Enlightenment liberalism was often at odds with the existing church authorities, since they resisted both the liberals' theoretical assumptions and the practical political consequences of those assumptions. This meant Enlightenment liberalism often had an anticlerical nature. Today it is sometimes forgotten that the French Revolution was as much a revolution against the organized church and social class privileges as it was a revolution against an authoritarian monarchy. All six countries considered in this book had strong Enlightenment liberal movements, and the story of church-state relations in each of them is to a significant degree the story of the varied ways in which the conflict between the Enlightenment liberals and opposing movements played out.

Their liberal assumptions, however, are coming under increasing attack in today's world. As will become clear as this book progresses, the religious communities of all six countries considered are concerned with a wide range of public policy questions and are active in providing education, health care, and other social services. If indeed religion has a strong public relevance and if religious groups, as well as government, are involved in providing educational, health, and social services in each of these countries, the Enlightenment liberal belief in limiting religion to the purely private realm is simply not consistent with the actual experience of religion. That is why earlier in this section we defined government neutrality not in terms of strict church-state separation or any other specific church-state arrangement, but in terms of an evenhandedness among people of all faiths and of none. We view neutrality in terms of government not influencing by its actions its citizens' choices for or against any particular religious or secular system of belief. It should neither advantage nor burden religion. We do not assume that withdrawing all government support for particularistic religion, extending government support for generalized, consensual religion, or merely removing all government restraints on the exercise of religion necessarily equates to neutrality.

THREE MODELS

Even a cursory look at church-state relations in the six democracies to be considered reveals that they all have followed different church-state policies. In thinking more systematically about church-state relations in these countries and in organizing the mass of observations we will be making, it is helpful to think in terms of three basic models of church-state relations that modern, western democracies have followed. None of the six countries under review here follow any one of these models in a pure form, but each country falls within the general framework of one of the three categories. Having those models in mind helps to organize and focus the many observations we make in the chapters that follow.

One model is the strict church-state separation model. Under this model—which traces its roots to the Enlightenment liberal view of society and politics—religion and politics are seen as clearly distinct areas of human endeavor that should be kept separate from each other. Religion is seen as a personal, private matter, best left to the realm of personal choice and action. When religion and politics are mixed—with either the state dictating religious beliefs or practice or religion using the state to advance its cause—both religion and politics suffer. The state should be neutral on matters of religion and this neutrality is assumed to be achieved best by keeping religion and politics separate. Those who support this model point to the religious wars of the seventeenth century and present-day religious strife in the Middle East and elsewhere as examples of what happens when religion and politics mix. Of the six countries under consideration here the United States and France come the closest to following the strict separation model, though in different ways and with varying levels of consistency.

A second model—at the opposite end of the continuum from the church-state separation model—is the established church model. Under this model the state and the church form a partnership in advancing the cause of religion and the state. Church and state are seen as two pillars on which a stable, prosperous society rests. The state provides the church with recognition, accommodation, and often financial support; the church provides the state with an aura of legitimacy and tradition, recognition, and a sense of national unity and purpose. In present-day modern democracies it is usually seen more as a traditional, innocuous, but also helpful holdover from earlier times, than as a living, vibrant church-state model essential in today's world.

Religious establishment can take several different forms. It can, first, be either formal or informal. In formal church establishments the government recognizes and supports one particular church or denomination, and while other religions are tolerated, they clearly do not occupy the favored position the established church does. Religious establishment may also be more informal in nature. Here one particular church is favored by the state, and that church supports the existing political order, but both occur not because of formal, legal provisions, but because of certain informal forces such as those of tradition or the overwhelming numerical or cultural strength of one religion. Church establishment can also be marked either by only one particular established church or by a system of multiple church establishment. Under the latter system, the state seeks to favor and work with two or more favored religious bodies. Here the state may promote a generic "religion-in-general"[11] that is more of a civil religion, supportive of the state and its traditions, than a particularistic faith. Of the six countries considered in this study, England is the only one with a formally established church, although we argue that in Germany there is an informal multiple establishment.

The third church-state model is the pluralist or structural pluralist model.[12] Under this model "society is understood as made up of competing or perhaps complementary spheres."[13] Included among these spheres or realms of societal activities are education, business, the arts, and the family—and religion and government. These spheres have distinct activities or responsibilities, and they are to enjoy autonomy or freedom in their efforts to fulfill them. But it is crucial to note that the pluralist model sees religion not as a separate sphere with only limited relevance to the other spheres as the strict separationists do, but as having a bearing on all of life. Pluralists also stress the existence of secular perspectives or worldviews that play a similar role to religion in society. "Pluralism is a matter of political respect by the state for the many world views held by the different kinds of institutions that fulfill the differentiated needs of a free society."[14] Hence substantive (or positive) neutrality is a key value for pluralists. Government is not to take sides among the plurality of religious and secular worldviews swirling about in society. It is to seek equal justice for all of them, with justice essentially defined as giving them all their freedom and neither advantaging or disadvantaging any of them. The Netherlands is the clearest example of a country that has self-consciously sought to follow this pluralistic model, while Australia also fits comfortably within this framework.

In the following chapters we describe church-state relations in the six countries and seek to classify them in terms of these three models. Each of the three models is represented by two countries. While church-state patterns are never identical between any two countries across the globe, we contend that these three models are broadly representative of what one finds among political democracies around the world.

SIX STABLE DEMOCRACIES

The six countries chosen for our study are particularly well suited for our purposes for three basic reasons. First, they are all stable democracies whose successful commitment to religious freedom is generally recognized. Germany has the Nazi regime in its past and the eastern part of the country emerged from an oppressive communist past only recently, but for sixty years West Germany—into which East Germany was absorbed—has been recognized as part of the family of liberal western democracies. Thus the six countries selected fit our purpose of wishing to explore how polities recognized as mature, successful democracies have dealt with the issue of church-state relations.

Second, all six countries are religiously pluralistic, with predominantly Christian traditions, both Protestant and Catholic, but also with many smaller religious minorities. In the case of Germany and the Netherlands, Protestants and Catholics are today about numerically equal, but in those countries Protestants have been dominant in a social and political sense through most of the modern era, and thus it was the Protestants that set the tone or played the dominant role in working through church-state issues. In all six there is a religious pluralism, characterized by large numbers of both Catholics and Protestants, and the Protestants in turn are divided into a variety of groups. Also, each of these countries has absorbed increasing numbers of adherents of non-Christian faiths—and especially the Muslim faith—and a fast-growing segment of people of no religious faith. Religiously, all six nations are indeed facing the challenge of pluralism.

A third characteristic of the six countries is that, despite their similar cultural, Christian heritages, they have chosen distinctly different approaches to church-state issues. England has an officially established church; the United States has followed a route emphasizing strict church-state separation but with emerging trends in favor of equal treatment; France is committed to its own version of church-state separationism that explicitly requires conformity to a public philosophy; Australia has constitutional provisions very similar to those found in the American Constitution but has interpreted and implemented them in a quite different manner; the Netherlands is known for following a self-conscious policy of religious pluralism; and Germany, although not having an officially established church, has a long history of close cooperation between the state and the church. Thus the six countries are not carbon copies of each other. They offer a rich texture of differences that make them excellent subjects for comparative study.

Each of the following six chapters deals with one of the countries and follows the same basic outline. Each chapter first gives a brief description of some salient characteristics of the nation and next gives a historical summary of church-state relations in that country. Church-state relations have clearly been shaped by the unique history of each country, and this section seeks to explain these unique sets of circumstances and how they have led to certain theories, assumptions, and mind-sets that have guided church-state relations in that nation. Each chapter then considers how—in light of its history and its church-state theories and assumptions—the country has handled the issue of the free exercise of religion, especially for minority religious groups. Then the chapter considers how the country has dealt with the issue of state accommodation of and support for religion, with special attention being paid to public policies as they relate to issues of education and religiously based social service organizations. The final section of each chapter offers some concluding observations and evaluations of the country's church-state policies.

NOTES

1. Throughout this book we will follow conventional American usage and use the term "church" to refer generically to religion in its various manifestations. The term is a general shorthand for "religious institutions"; in some specific contexts, we use the terms "houses of worship," "faith-based nonprofits," "religious schools," or other organized expressions of religious faith.

2. Jonathan Laurence, *The Emancipation of Europe's Muslims: The State's Role in Minority Integration* (Princeton, N.J.: Princeton University Press, 2012), 2.

3. Scholars often use "pluralism" in both empirical and normative ways. See, for example, John Inazu, *Confident Pluralism: Surviving and Thriving through Deep Difference* (Chicago: University of Chicago Press, 2016). For a religious perspective on pluralism in these two senses, see Richard J. Mouw and Sander Griffioen, *Pluralism and Horizons* (Grand Rapids, Mich.: Eerdmans, 1993).

4. Clinton Rossiter, *Seedbed of the Republic* (New York: Harcourt, Brace & World, 1953), 447.

5. Will Kymlicka and Wayne Norman, "Citizenship in Culturally Diverse Societies: Issues, Contexts, Concepts," in Will Kymlicka and Wayne Norman, eds., *Citizenship in Diverse Societies* (Oxford: Oxford University Press, 2000), 1.

6. See, for example, Corwin Smidt et al., *Pews, Prayers, and Participation: Religion and Civic Responsibility in America* (Washington, D.C.: Georgetown University Press, 2008); Corwin Smidt, ed., *Religion as Social Capital: Producing the Common Good* (Waco, Tex.: Baylor

University Press, 2003); and Robert D. Putnam and David E. Campbell, *American Grace: How Religion Unites and Divides Us* (New York: Simon & Schuster, 2010).

7. See Douglas Laycock, "Formal, Substantive, and Disaggregated Neutrality toward Religion," *DePaul Law Review* 39 (1990), 1001–6; Stephen V. Monsma, *Positive Neutrality* (Westport, Conn.: Greenwood, 1993), chap. 5; and Stephen V. Monsma, *When Sacred and Secular Mix: Religious Nonprofit Organizations and Public Money* (Lanham, Md.: Rowman & Littlefield, 1996), chap. 6. It should be noted that this goal of governmental religious neutrality is itself not neutral. It makes a choice in favor of a certain type of governmental religious neutrality and thereby reflects certain assumptions and values that differ from those, for example, of Erastian or Enlightenment liberal thinking.

8. Laycock, "Formal, Substantive, and Disaggregated Neutrality toward Religion," 1001.

9. Like Laycock, we acknowledge that in other contexts alternative church-state principles might apply. See Laycock, "Substantive Neutrality Revisited," in *Religious Liberty: Vol. 1* (Grand Rapids, Mich.: Eerdmans, 2010), 240.

10. From Stewart's dissent in *Abington School District v. Schempp*, 374 US at 319–320 (1963).

11. The term is Martin Marty's. See Martin Marty, *The New Shape of American Religion* (New York: Harper & Row, 1958), 2, 31–44.

12. On this model, see Carl H. Esbeck, "A Typology of Church-State Relations in Current American Thought," in Luis Lugo, ed., *Religion, Public Life, and the American Polity* (Knoxville: University of Tennessee Press, 1994), 15–18; and Monsma, *Positive Neutrality*, 137–71.

13. John G. Francis, "The Evolving Regulatory Structure of European Church-State Relationships," *Journal of Church and State* 34 (1992), 782.

14. Esbeck, "A Typology of Church-State Relations," 15.

I

Models of Separation

Chapter Two

The United States

Strict Separation under Fire

In 1947 the U.S. Supreme Court declared in ringing words:

> No tax in any amount, large or small, can be levied to support any religious
> activities or institutions, whatever they may be called, or whatever form they
> may adopt to teach or practice religion. Neither a state nor the Federal govern-
> ment can, openly or secretly, participate in the affairs of any religious organ-
> izations or groups and *vice versa*. In the words of Jefferson, the clause against
> establishment of religion by law was intended to erect "a wall of separation
> between church and state."[1]

Later the Court insisted that the wall between church and state "must be kept
high and impregnable."[2] There is, however, more than a little irony in the
fact that the Court decided—after asserting this principle of strict, even absolute, church-state separation—that the First Amendment allows government
to subsidize the transportation of children to religious schools. As one of the
dissenting justices complained, the Court's decision reminded him "of Julia
who, according to Byron's reports, 'whispering "I will ne'er consent,"—
consented.'"[3]

   This mid-twentieth-century decision typifies the Supreme Court's modern
approach to church-state issues in many ways. The Court made "no aid to
religion" the key principle guiding its interpretations of the First Amendment's religious freedom language, but the Court also found itself unable to
hold strictly to that principle in practice. In subsequent decisions justices on
the Court could not settle on legal doctrines that clearly articulate when no
aid to religion ought to be followed and when and under what conditions
other principles should take precedence.[4] This internal debate among the

justices has resulted in a series of decisions in which the Court has been closely divided and, as one Court observer expressed it, bedeviled by "contradictory principles, vaguely defined tests, and eccentric distinctions."[5] In fact, in recent years the no-aid-to-religion principle has begun to crumble even while it continues to exert influence.

This chapter explores the American struggle to define and to practice church-state separation. First, we give context to that struggle by highlighting some relevant features of American society, political and legal structure, and history. Then we consider free exercise theories and practices with special attention to two case studies that will provide a foundation for comparative analysis throughout the book: the first on education, the second on faith-based social services. We conclude with some observations in light of the questions we asked in the introduction.

THE NATION

With a population of 320 million drawn from most of the other nations of the world, the United States is by far the most populous (four times larger than Germany, the next largest) and most diverse of the six countries considered in this book. It is also a stable democracy, despite its occasionally rancorous politics. The United States has the oldest written constitution among all states in the world, and its religious freedom protections are thereby the oldest written constitutional protections of religion.

A key characteristic of American culture is the diversity of *organized* expressions of faith.[6] Americans join religious groups at unusually high rates, and the range of these religious affiliations has grown dramatically over time. From the founding of the nation through the nineteenth century the United States was an overwhelmingly Protestant country. There was diversity within this Protestantism, but by the mid-nineteenth century the large mainline denominations—Methodists, Presbyterians, Congregationalists, Episcopalians, Baptists, and Lutherans—dominated the religious and civic life of the nation. Since then much has changed. The mainline denominations are aging and have declined in numbers since the 1960s, and both conservative, evangelical Protestants and Roman Catholics now surpass mainline Protestants as a proportion of the population and perhaps in cultural and political influence.[7] Social scientists categorize approximately 15 percent of the population as white mainline Protestants, 25 percent white evangelical Protestants, 7 percent black Protestants, and 21 percent Roman Catholics.[8] Equally important, the social and educational gap that once existed between Catholics and Protestants has closed and evangelical Protestants, constituting about one-fourth of the American electorate, have become an important political force, though their influence has faded a little in the recent decade.[9]

Adding to American religious diversity are Jews (2 percent of the population), Mormons (2 percent), Muslims (1 percent), and pockets of Hindus, Buddhists, Native American religionists, New Age spiritual seekers, and an eclectic variety of other practitioners of established sects and new religious movements.[10] Many of these smaller groups are clustered in particular regions or localities (e.g., Mormons in Utah, many Muslims in Dearborn, Michigan), which tends to amplify their voice in society disproportionately to their size.

Religion is clearly a crucial place where Americans find community. But it is important to note that other demographic characteristics cut across American religious communities in vital ways. One of the most important intersecting features of identity is race and ethnicity. Scholars almost always modify the groupings we cite in the last paragraph by the marker of race. For example, even though African American Protestants and white evangelicals share a great deal theologically—views of the authority of scriptures, beliefs about salvation through Jesus Christ, and so on—they are dramatically different in their social and political attitudes and behaviors. The intersection of race and religion is also important among some of the smallest religious traditions. While Muslims are a smaller percentage of the U.S. population than the other countries surveyed in this book, they still comprise several million residents (a larger number, if not percentage, than several other countries in this book), and they are subdivided sharply by ethnicity, with sizable populations of native-born African Americans and immigrants from Arab-speaking countries and Southeast Asia. Latino Catholics and Protestants are often further split by country of origin. Race and religion have always mixed in American culture to the point that the two characteristics are often nearly impossible to disentangle, and the combination shapes everything from worship style to voting preferences.[11]

Another important story about religious affiliation in the past two decades is the rise of the so-called nones, that is, the unaffiliated. Today, as many as a quarter of the American people claim no connection with a particular religious tradition or house of worship, and the percentage of Americans who rarely or never attend religious services is even higher.[12] To be sure, these percentages are smaller than all of the other countries we will discuss in this book; a process of secularization in western Europe is farther along than in the United States. But the growth of the unaffiliated over a short period of time within the United States is consequential. The rise of the unaffiliated has a host of potential effects, not least of which is a shift in strategies of political mobilization and movement-building in the United States. Political leaders and organizations have always relied on the resource of houses of worship.

The end result of this religious diversity, and especially the combination of declining numbers among mainline Protestants and the rise of Catholics, evangelical Protestants, and the unaffiliated, is that no one religious tradition is socially or politically dominant in the United States today. Broadly construed, Christianity remains the most prominent religion, but it is fractured into literally hundreds of separate groups.

A second important characteristic goes beyond affiliation to Americans' high rate of religious *engagement* when compared to the people of other modern industrialized countries. Attendance at religious services provides a striking snapshot. In a series of polls conducted by the Pew Research Center over the past two decades, the percentage of Americans reporting they attend religious services at least weekly has hovered around 37 to 39 percent.[13] This compares today to 10 percent in Germany, 12 percent in the Netherlands, and 15 percent in Australia[14] —numbers that are quite typical of western-style democracies. And this American religious engagement appears to extend to private devotional life as well. For example, even though regular prayer has eroded somewhat, 55 percent of Americans still report prayer is an important part of their daily lives.[15]

The engagement of religious people has always extended to all aspects of public life. We will discuss later the extensive role of religion in providing education and social services, but it is worth noting here that the political culture of the United States is unusually open to faith-based arguments and interests. Citizens are accustomed to making a faith-based case for their policy preferences or choices in elections. Most voters say they would be less likely to vote for an atheist and more likely to vote for a coreligionist, and over half worry that religion has waning influence over society in general.[16] Elected officials are generally quite open about their own religious convictions, though that varies, as we might expect, by the religious composition of their constituencies.[17] In short, the separation of church from state does not necessarily entail the separation of religion from politics.

The assumptions and structures of American politics help to foster this religious engagement. The twin principles of separation of powers (separated institutions of the executive, legislative, and judicial that nonetheless share power in important ways) and federalism (multiple layers of government—national, state, and local—with overlapping authority over the same territory) provide religious groups with countless points of contact with government, from the local municipality to the halls of Congress. The Democratic and Republican parties (and smaller parties to a much lesser extent), which act as key channels for participation throughout the political system, compete to bring blocs of religious voters under their umbrella. Religious people and groups do not merely have motive for participation; they also have ample opportunity.

For our purposes it is especially important to highlight the crucial role of the U.S. Supreme Court in shaping the legal boundaries of religious practice. While the legislative and executive branches of government have made many decisions with implications for religious freedom and church-state relations,[18] they do so on terrain that the Supreme Court largely defines. Through the power of judicial review, the nine life-appointed justices of the Supreme Court can hold any act by any branch of the national, state, or local governments to be in violation of the religious freedom language of the First Amendment and therefore null and void. Thus the story of church-state relations in the United States is to a great degree a story of the Supreme Court's interpretations of the apparently simple—yet devilishly elusive—words of the First Amendment: "Congress shall make no law respecting an establishment of religion, or prohibiting the free exercise thereof." No other country in this study vests such authority in its judicial system.

HISTORICAL BACKGROUND

The role of the Supreme Court and other branches of government in shaping church-state relations developed in multiple stages over the past three hundred years.[19] The first stage was the establishment of religion during the colonial era of the seventeenth and eighteenth centuries. When the American colonies were first settled, most followed the prevailing European pattern of creating established churches. The English Puritans in New England, the Dutch Reformed in New Amsterdam, the Anglicans in Virginia, and other colonists elsewhere assumed that "the pattern of religious uniformity would of necessity be transplanted and perpetuated in the colonies."[20] The assumption was that religious unity was essential for political unity. Thus the favored churches were granted tax supports of different types, dissenters were subjected to penalties of varying severity, and civil authorities exercised control over certain ecclesiastical affairs.

The second stage in American church-state theory and practice emerged in the second half of the eighteenth century, when a call to disestablish the churches materialized at about the same time as the colonists began to push for independence from Britain. This process of disestablishment was the result of two dissimilar movements that came together in a "strange coalition."[21] The first of these movements was the Great Awakening, a religious revival that swept through the colonies, starting in the 1740s. It is hard to exaggerate the breadth and depth of this revival. It featured itinerant preachers, mass exhibitions of religious fervor, and renewed religious commitments by the masses. It also had a strong populist undercurrent that was dismissive of the perceived formalism and dead orthodoxy of the existing, usually established churches.[22]

The second partner in the "strange coalition" consisted of the Enlightenment liberal rationalists. Led by figures such as Thomas Jefferson and James Madison, these leaders were religious, even Christian, in a broad, generic sense, but largely rejected or saw as irrelevant to government the traditional doctrines of historic Christianity. They were well read and cosmopolitan for their era, and they were revolted by the religious persecutions that had marked Europe in the recent past and that were also present in the colonies. As rationalists they argued that human reason could discern the basic precepts of religion that were necessary for a stable, moral society and political order. Doctrines peculiar to the various religious traditions were unnecessary and even dangerous for the public order, and thus they could and should be separated from the public realm and relegated to the private sphere.

These two movements came together in the last quarter of the eighteenth century to provide the impetus for the disestablishment of the churches. The Enlightenment liberals, as an intellectual and political elite, provided most of the rationale in support of disestablishment; the popular Great Awakening provided mass support for disestablishment. The events surrounding the disestablishment of the Anglican church in Virginia proved to be especially crucial for the subsequent development of church-state concepts. Events began to unfold in 1776 when the Virginia legislature repealed most of the legal privileges that had been granted Anglicans and suspended the collection of taxes for the Anglican church.[23] Then, in 1784, Patrick Henry introduced a General Assessment Bill that made clear there was to be no established church, but also provided for a tax whose proceeds were to be distributed in support of all Christian churches. It appeared to have majority support in the legislature, but Madison won a year's postponement of the vote. In the meanwhile Madison wrote his soon-to-be-famous "Memorial and Remonstrance against Religious Assessments." In it he condemned all public tax support for churches, arguing "that the same authority which can force a citizen to contribute three pence only of his property for the support of any one establishment, may force him to conform to any other establishment in all cases whatsoever."[24]

With Madison supplying the intellectual firepower, the dissenting churches with roots in the Great Awakening—largely Baptist and Presbyterian—supplied the popular opposition to the Henry bill. In 1785 the Virginia legislature turned down Henry's General Assessment Bill and enacted instead Jefferson's "Bill for Establishing Religious Freedom" that provided, in part, "no man shall be compelled to frequent or support any religious worship, place or ministry whatsoever . . . but all men shall be free to profess, and by argument to maintain, their opinions in matters of religion, and that the same shall in no wise diminish, enlarge, or affect their civil capacities."[25] Other states followed Virginia's lead. In 1833, Massachusetts was the last of the states to abandon church establishment.

Soon after these events and the writing of the First Amendment, church-state relations entered a third stage, from roughly 1800 to 1950, marked by an informal reestablishment of Protestant Christianity. At the beginning of the nineteenth century Christianity seemed to be losing its presence in society. The churches had lost their establishment status, and only about 10 percent of the population professed to be members of any church.[26] Yet in 1888 James Bryce, the respected English commentator on U.S. government and society, wrote: "The National Government and the State governments do give to Christianity a species of recognition inconsistent with the view that civil government should be absolutely neutral in religious matters. . . . The matter may be summed up by saying that Christianity is in fact understood to be, though not the legally established religion, yet the national religion."[27] One cause of this reestablishment of religion—Protestant Christianity to be precise—was the Second Great Awakening in the early years of the nineteenth century.[28] Church membership swelled, as revival again swept through the land, especially on the rapidly growing frontier. Another cause for the reestablishment of religion was the fact that the eighteenth-century disestablishment movement was clearly committed to the formal, legal disestablishment of churches, but never directly addressed the question of whether or not to allow a host of public supports for religion more generally. Clearly, the heirs of the Great Awakening assumed that government support for such measures as Sunday observance, suppression of gambling, and other such marks of a "Christian society" would continue. Even Enlightenment liberals such as Madison and Jefferson were ambiguous on this issue. Madison as president, for example, issued proclamations calling for days of national prayer and approved chaplains to be paid from public funds for the Congress, although he later wrote that on reflection he felt such actions unconstitutional.

Thus, when Christianity experienced a surge in the early nineteenth century, a vigorous, populist Protestant Christianity overwhelmed any tendencies to maintain a strict separation of church and state. Prayers and Bible readings were a regular part of state-supported common schools,[29] Christian missions to Native Americans were subsidized by government, and laws enforced Sunday observance. In 1890 most state colleges and universities had chapel services and some even required Sunday church attendance.[30]

It is especially important in understanding what happened later in church-state relations to understand the origins and rationale underlying the creation of a vast system of common schools—the precursors to today's public schools—in the nineteenth century. From the founding of the nation in 1789 Americans have worried about how to maintain national unity in the face of wide geographic distances, sharp class differences, and recurring waves of immigration. The answer Americans developed in the nineteenth century and have largely retained is the common school. In the early nineteenth century, European efforts at universal, state-run education caught the attention of Horace Mann and other New England elites. These reformers viewed the common school as the basic means by which the children of all classes—but especially the children of the lower, uneducated classes—would be taught the social and political virtues necessary for national unity and free, democratic society.

When immigration surged in the middle decades of the nineteenth century, the concept of the common school was already well developed among the elites of the young American nation and readily available for application to the new demographic realities. New arrivals from Ireland, Italy, and other predominantly Catholic countries raised fears of an American society overwhelmed and undermined by millions of hard-to-assimilate immigrants unschooled in democratic values. These fears turned the common school ideal from an elite theory into a popular ideal broadly held in American society.[31] The common school came to be seen as an increasingly crucial means for achieving national unity, assimilation, and the inculcation of habits of good citizenship.

Religion of a particular type played an important role in the vision of the common school as the seedbed of civic virtue and assimilation. Mann was a Unitarian—as were many of his fellow New England education reformers—and as such rejected both particularistic religion and nonreligious secularism. The schools were to be rational, Christian, and consensual.[32] Mann once wrote:

> Although it may not be easy theoretically, to draw the line between those views of religious truth and of Christian faith which are common to all, and may, therefore, with propriety be inculcated in school, and those which, being peculiar to individual sects, are therefore by law excluded; still it is believed that no practical difficulty occurs in the conduct of our schools in this respect.[33]

Carl Kaestle has described the resulting common school ideology as being "centered on republicanism, Protestantism, and capitalism, three sources of social belief that were intertwined and mutually supporting."[34]

There were protests to this form of liberal religion both from a few evangelical Protestants and from Roman Catholics. But Catholics in the nineteenth century were largely marginalized politically and socially, and most evangelical Protestants surprisingly came to accept the vision of the common school religion espoused by Mann and others. Many conservative Protestants—by far the numerically dominant group within nineteenth-century Protestantism—felt common schools that included Bible readings and moral lessons represented a bulwark against the threat of swelling Catholic immigration, even if the curriculum was not exactly biblical, orthodox Christianity. There was virtual unanimity among the culturally dominant Protestant elites that in the common school the ideals of democracy, liberty, and Christianity were joined together in a powerful device for uniting the nation. The elements of Christianity in the common schools meant that the then-dominant conservative evangelical Protestants saw no need for their own separate schools, and enabled them to join fully in the common school enterprise. The common school movement was supported by the same "strange coalition" that had led the disestablishment movement of the late eighteenth century. It was a crucial part of the informal, de facto establishment of a genial Protestantism in the 1800 to 1950 period.

After World War II, the United States entered a fourth stage of church-state relations that lasted until the 1980s and continues to exert great influence. It can be termed the second disestablishment of religion.[35] The legacy of Enlightenment liberal thinking reemerged and came to dominate elite thinking, including on the Supreme Court. The 1947 words of the Supreme Court decision quoted at the beginning of this chapter signaled this decisive turn of events. It established no aid to religion as a bedrock principle for interpreting the First Amendment and embraced Jefferson's wall of separation metaphor. As will be seen in more detail later, the Supreme Court banned religious elements from the public schools, declared almost all aid to religiously based schools unconstitutional, and found other forms of church-state cooperation unconstitutional. A modern liberal view of society clearly triumphed in the United States. Enlightenment liberalism in the other democracies considered in this book was generally forced into compromises with more conservative religious forces. But this did not happen in the United States. The paradox is that in the most religious of the six countries considered in this book, religion, at least for a time, had relatively little impact in carving out robust accommodations and recognition from the state.

From the early 1980s to the present day, the United States entered a fifth stage of church-state relations, one marked by a still-emerging principle of neutrality or equal treatment. In this new era the strict separation, no-aid-to-religion strand of thinking has clashed with an equal-treatment, equal-access perspective. A closely divided Supreme Court leans first one way and then the other. Heated battles are being fought among clashing advocacy groups, in the news media, in Congress and state legislatures—and among Supreme Court justices.

THE FREE EXERCISE OF RELIGION

The six countries in this study support religious freedom for all. Nevertheless, the United States—along with its fellow democracies—faces contentious issues over the exact meaning and scope of religious freedom. Most difficult is the question of whether religiously motivated behavior that is thought to be contrary to societal welfare or norms should be protected. Religious freedom is not absolute. No modern democracy would allow child sacrifice as part of a religious ritual, no matter how sincere the adherents of that religion. But many other religious practices are at the ambiguous margins of social acceptance.

The First Amendment states: "Congress shall make no law . . . prohibiting the free exercise [of religion]." Throughout the decades of constitutional development, the Supreme Court has tended to interpret this clause narrowly.[36] It has not proven to be a robust basis for protecting minorities' freedom to practice their religions as they see fit. Consider one of the first cases that called on the Court to interpret these words. It was an 1879 dispute that dealt with a federal law that prohibited polygamy, which Mormon leaders challenged as a violation of their religious beliefs at that time. The Supreme Court ruled that the federal law did not violate the constitutional rights of Mormons since it was beliefs, and not actions, that the First Amendment protected. "Laws are made for the government of actions," the Court declared, "and while [laws] cannot interfere with mere religious beliefs and opinions, they may with practices."[37] To hold otherwise "would be to make the professed doctrines of religious belief superior to the law of the land, and in effect to permit every citizen to become a law unto himself."[38]

This belief-action distinction led to what has been described as the secular regulation rule: as long as the government has a valid secular purpose and otherwise has the legal authority to engage in a certain form of regulation, the fact that it interferes with people's free exercise of their religion is not a basis for them to escape the regulation.[39] The secular regulation rule and the belief-action dichotomy on which it rests raise the question of what is left of free exercise protections. If the free exercise clause protects only beliefs and not religious practices, and if any law with secular purposes can be enforced on religious groups irrespective of sincerely and deeply held religious beliefs underlying their practices, is there any protection given by the free exercise clause?

The Court has given two primary responses to this question. The first is to presume that any governmental action that intentionally singles out a religious group for disadvantages or limitations violates its free exercise rights. In 1993, for example, the Supreme Court struck down several ordinances of the city of Hialeah, Florida, on the basis they were specifically targeted at outlawing animal sacrifices of the Santeria religion.[40] The ordinances had been narrowly drawn to outlaw the religious sacrifice of animals, but not to outlaw such practices as hunting, the slaughter of animals for food, and the kosher slaughter of animals.

A second answer to the question of what remains of free exercise protections is the so-called compelling state interest test. The compelling state interest test holds that if an apparently neutral, secular law has the effect of significantly burdening or disadvantaging people's exercise of their sincerely held religious beliefs, that law can only be enforced on those persons if the state has a "compelling" reason for doing so. Court observers generally view this principle as a modification or even an alternative to the secular regulation rule. On this basis the Supreme Court held that the Amish did not have to send their children to school beyond the eighth grade, a Seventh-Day Adventist could not be excluded from receiving unemployment benefits because she refused Saturday work, and a pacifist could not be refused unemployment compensation when he lost his job because of refusing to work on manufacturing armaments.[41] In all three of these cases the Court ruled that the government had not demonstrated a compelling societal interest that would be endangered if exceptions to existing law were made in order to accommodate religious convictions.

The Supreme Court, however, has never clearly articulated what distinguishes a "compelling" interest from other state goals. In 1961 the Court failed to extend free exercise protections to Orthodox Jewish businesspeople who had been disadvantaged by Sunday closing regulations. In 1982 it did the same in the case of an Amish employer and his Amish employees who felt their religious scruples were violated by having to pay Social Security taxes, and in 1986 it rejected the claim of an Orthodox Jewish air force officer who had insisted on wearing a yarmulke as required by his faith.[42] In all three cases, the Supreme Court essentially followed the compelling state interest standard, but set a low threshold for meeting it, holding each time that the government had successfully demonstrated a compelling interest that overruled the claimed free exercise right.

Then, in 1990, the Supreme Court considered the case of *Employment Division v. Smith*, dealing with adherents of a Native American religion who had used peyote as part of a traditional religious ceremony. As a result they had tested positive for drug use, were fired from their jobs, and were denied unemployment compensation since they were held to have been fired "for cause." The Court held that "an individual's religious beliefs [do not] excuse him from compliance with an otherwise valid law prohibiting conduct that the State is free to regulate."[43] The compelling state interest test was left in shreds: "To make an individual's obligation to obey . . . a law contingent upon the law's coincidence with his religious beliefs, except where the State's interest is 'compelling[,]' . . . contradicts both constitutional traditions and common sense."[44]

The decision was met with widespread and intense criticism. In response, a remarkable coalition of groups that traditionally had been divided on church-state questions came together and persuaded Congress to pass the Religious Freedom Restoration Act (RFRA) in 1993. The act reads in part: "Government may substantially burden a person's exercise of religion only if it demonstrates that application of the burden to the person is in furtherance of a compelling governmental interest; and is the least restrictive means of furthering that compelling governmental interest."[45] The act sought to write into law the compelling state interest standard the Supreme Court had first articulated, never fully applied, and then largely abandoned. In 1997, however, the Supreme Court declared that the RFRA could not be applied against state and local governments (it remained intact against actions of the federal government itself).[46] Congress reacted by passing in 2000 the more limited Religious Land Use and Institutionalized Persons Act (RLUIP),[47] which seeks to protect the rights of churches to build or expand in areas where zoning laws are a barrier and the freedom of prisoners to exercise their religious beliefs while incarcerated.

These efforts to respond to the Supreme Court's *Smith* decision are testimonies to the commitment of the broader society to protecting religious freedom. But that commitment always threatens to break down, especially as society grapples with religious minorities that push on the edges of widely shared norms. Nevertheless, the United States generally has not treated minorities with the level of suspicion and legal restriction we observe in other western democracies. For example, the permissibility of Muslim women wearing headscarves or other distinctive Muslim clothing at school or work has been hotly debated and often regulated in the other democracies considered in this book, but outside of a few scattered cases that were quickly resolved, it has not been an issue in the United States. No such cases have come before the Supreme Court. Most free exercise issues involving Muslims have come from prisoners who have asserted they have not been able to exercise their Muslim faith and its required practices freely while incarcerated. Even here accommodations have gradually been made.[48]

The relatively small percentage of Muslims in the United States, their comparative success at assimilating into American society, and the historically tolerant attitudes of Americans toward Muslims help to explain why free exercise issues for Muslims have not been as large an issue in the United States as in some other countries. But these factors can change quickly. In an era when a major party candidate speaks to applause against Muslims as an entire category of immigrants, and when rising concerns about Islamic extremists are emerging in surveys, there is reason to wonder whether the religious freedom of Muslim Americans might come under increasing threat.[49] Indeed, Muslim Americans have been subjected to scattered acts of social hostility and violence and to incidents of profiling by law enforcement officials.[50]

THE ESTABLISHMENT OF RELIGION AND EDUCATION

The experiences of Muslims are the latest chapter in the dynamic and complex history of free exercise of religion in the United States. That history comes into sharper focus when we consider the Supreme Court's rejection of *positive* religious rights, in contrast to other democracies considered in this book—especially in Germany. The concept here is that if people are to enjoy full religious freedom, not only must they be free from direct legal restrictions on their right to act on their religious beliefs, they may sometimes need to be aided by government in doing so, especially if nonreligious people are assisted by government to act on their secular beliefs.

Two disputes, both from the arena of education, illustrate the Supreme Court's rejection of a positive right to religious freedom. The first comes from two landmark decisions in which the Court ruled that neither a state-composed prayer nor the Lord's Prayer and a Bible reading could be a part of public school programming.[51] The lone dissenting justice in both these cases was Potter Stewart; in both cases he made a free exercise argument. He wrote, "There is involved in these cases a substantial free exercise claim on the part of those who affirmatively desire to have their children's school day open with the reading of passages from the Bible."[52] He went on to explain more fully that

> a compulsory state educational system so structures a child's life that if religious exercises are held to be an impermissible activity in schools, religion is placed at an artificial and state-created disadvantage. Viewed in this light, permission of such exercises for those who want them is necessary if the schools are truly to be neutral in the matter of religion. And a refusal to permit religious exercises thus is seen, not as the realization of state neutrality, but rather as the establishment of a religion of secularism, or at the least, as government support of the beliefs of those who think that religious exercises should be conducted only in private.[53]

Stewart contended that if public school religious exercises could be made voluntary, the free exercise rights of those who desired them would be protected without violating the rights of those who did not. As we will see later, this is the precise position the German Constitutional Court has taken. But the majority of justices on the U.S. Supreme Court decisively rejected it.

Similarly, some justices have made a free exercise argument in cases dealing with public aid to religiously based schools. Justice Byron White, for example, dissented on free exercise grounds from the conclusion of the Court majority that public aid to religious schools violates the First Amendment:

> The Establishment Clause . . . coexists in the First Amendment with the Free Exercise Clause and the latter is surely relevant in cases such as these. Where a state program seeks to ensure the proper education of its young, in private as well as public schools, free exercise considerations at least counsel against refusing support for students attending parochial schools simply because in that setting they are also being instructed in the tenets of the faith they are constitutionally free to practice.[54]

In another case he made a similar free exercise argument that denying parents who send their children to faith-based schools any financial relief "also make[s] it more difficult, if not impossible, for parents to follow the dictates of their conscience and seek a religious as well as a secular education for their children."[55]

Whatever one thinks of the wisdom of state-sponsored prayer or state funding of religious schools, the principle of positive freedom is worth serious consideration. But Justices Stewart and White have been lonely voices on the Supreme Court. The Court has consistently held that First Amendment restrictions on the establishment of religion trump a positive right to government support in freely exercising one's religion. It has not seen the free exercise clause as requiring government to take positive actions to enable religious people to practice their faith.

These arguments make a broader point: the place of religion in schools has been the key battleground where the American system has largely hammered out the meaning of the First Amendment's establishment clause. Here, more than in any other area, one can see the continuing influence of the common school ideal; the predominance of the strict separation, no-aid-to-religion principle in the post–World War II era; the challenges to strict separation since the 1980s by a principle of equal treatment; and the continuing influence of strict separation as an operating principle in church-state relations. In this section we consider the issue of religion in the public schools and then the issue of governmental funding of private, religiously based schools.

The Supreme Court crafted many of its strongest separationist arguments in response to the question of the permissible place of religion in the public schools. The thinking of the Supreme Court was clearly signaled in the early 1960s when it decided that prayer and Bible readings in the public schools violated the Constitution. In the first of these decisions the Court held that a brief, nondenominational prayer the New York authorities had composed for recitation at the start of the school day ("Almighty God, we acknowledge our dependence upon Thee, and we beg Thy blessings upon us, our parents, our teachers and our Country") violated the establishment clause of the First Amendment ("Congress shall make no law respecting an establishment of religion").[56] A year later the Court ruled that programs of Bible reading and recitation of the Lord's Prayer at the start of the school day were also unconstitutional. Here the Court argued that what was at issue were "religious exercises, required by the States in violation of the command of the First Amendment that the Government maintain strict neutrality, neither aiding nor opposing religion."[57] The Court further ruled that to pass establishment clause scrutiny "there must be a secular legislative purpose and a primary effect that neither advances nor inhibits religion."[58] Prayers and Bible readings passed neither of these tests. The fact that the religious exercises were voluntary (children who objected could be excused) made no difference, since a violation of the establishment clause does not require the presence of state coercion.

The Supreme Court also took a strict separationist position in its rulings on integrating religion into the public school curriculum. It ruled unconstitutional a released time program in which the schools and religious groups would cooperate by the schools releasing students for an hour or so a week to meet with religious groups that would come into the school to offer instruction to the adherents of their faiths. Students not desiring any religious instruction were given alternative activities. Justice Hugo Black summarized the view of the Court at that time that allowing parents to have their children instructed in their family's own faith enabled "religious groups to spread their faith" through the tax-supported mechanism of the public school.[59] A few years later the Court eased back from this strict separationist ruling when it allowed a similar program, but only when the classes of religious instruction were held on sites away from the public schools.[60]

As we will shortly see, the Supreme Court has since the 1980s moved away from strict separation in some church-state areas, but the Court has continued to take a strict separation position regarding the official sanction of religion in the public schools. It ruled against prayers at public occasions such as graduations and sporting events, moments of silence at the start of the school day for prayer or meditation, and a Louisiana law requiring that whenever evolution is taught as a theory of human origins, equal time must also be given to a literal version of creationism.[61] In all these decisions the Court has primarily relied on the principle that government may not favor, encourage, or promote religion.

The Supreme Court has always insisted its separationist positions are not hostile to religion. To forbid the state from fostering particular religious doctrines or practices still leaves open space for public schools to teach about religions in global comparative perspective, the role religion has played in history, and the sacred texts as forms of literature. In one decision, for example, the Court stated that the "study of religions and of the bible from a literary and historic viewpoint, presented objectively and as part of a secular program of education, need not collide with the First Amendment's prohibition [against supporting religion]."[62] This argument echoes the common school tradition of treating children of all faiths and of none with an even-handed and welcoming approach. To do so, the Court has worked to remove all religious observances from the schools, which can be alienating to young people in their formative years.

But these judicial efforts can also be seen as violating the common school ideal of incorporating broadly consensual religious beliefs and observances into the educational process. There have been continuing efforts to overturn some Supreme Court decisions by way of a constitutional amendment, legis-

lation, or finding loopholes in the Court's decisions, spurred no doubt by the
public's continuing support for certain religious elements in the public
schools.[63] Despite the Court's series of decisions since the early 1960s
against state-sponsored religious exercises in public schools, a sizable majority of the American public continues to support school prayer, though the
magnitude of that support has dipped slightly in the past two decades.[64] And
a 2012 survey showed that nearly two-thirds of the American public agreed
that "liberals have gone too far in trying to keep religion out of the schools
and the government."[65]

As noted earlier, the Supreme Court has since the 1980s been moving—
uncertainly, in starts and stops—in new directions of church-state interpretations. This movement toward an equal treatment approach began in 1981
when the Supreme Court ruled that a state university could not bar a religious, student-initiated club from using university facilities for its meetings, as
long as it allowed a host of other student clubs to use its facilities.[66] Then, in
1984, Congress applied the same principle to public high schools when it
passed the Equal Access Act, which provided that if a school allowed extracurricular clubs to use school facilities outside normal instructional hours, it
could not refuse a religiously based club to form and also use school facilities. The Supreme Court upheld this law when it ruled that clubs formed
under it do not violate the establishment clause, as long as "a religious club is
merely one of many different student-initiated voluntary clubs."[67] The Supreme Court reinforced the argument when it held in 2001 that an elementary
school could not exclude a parent-sponsored religious club for children held
in the school after normal class hours.[68] The Court relied on equal treatment
reasoning: since the school had allowed a variety of nonreligious groups to
use its facilities for after-school activities, it could not exclude a religious
group. The Court stated that the religious student club "seeks nothing more
than to be treated neutrally and given access to speak about the same topics
as are other groups."[69]

Nevertheless, strict separation doctrines forged a half-century ago continue to exert an influence. Even under equal treatment interpretations, the role
of religion in public schools has been limited to extracurricular clubs and
activities. The Courts have drawn a line between school accommodation of
the associations of private citizens and any official recognition or support for
religion. At the same time, the public schools have been called increasingly
to deal with morally sensitive issues such as sexuality and LGBT concerns,
teenage pregnancies, AIDS awareness, racial and ethnic respect, school violence, juvenile crime, and good citizenship. The very issues that most
Americans turn to their communities of faith to address are largely discussed
in secular terms by the schools. This results in a dilemma that the Supreme
Court and most American societal elites often fail to recognize. On the one
hand, for the public schools to integrate certain religious perspectives into the

curriculum or to conduct certain religious exercises would violate the norm of governmental neutrality on matters of religion. Even generalized, consensual religion that has the support of a majority of the community—maybe even the overwhelming majority—is rejected by some parents in the community. Those parents and their children would be potentially disadvantaged by such practices. And allowance for individual students to be excused from religious exercises or from lessons with religious dimensions may stigmatize those students in the eyes of their peers as different. Thus teacher-led prayers, the teaching of religiously based accounts of creation, and the incorporation of consensual religious exercises into the public schools would be a violation of religious neutrality. In the legacy of Enlightenment liberalism this concern has been rightly recognized and given weight by the Supreme Court and societal elites.

On the other hand—and this is what the Supreme Court and American elites have often failed to recognize—it is not simply neutral for the state to eschew any sponsorship or recognition of religion. As A. James Reichley has written, "Banishment of religion does not represent neutrality between religion and secularism; conduct of public institutions without any acknowledgment of religion *is* secularism."[70] This is not to say that the state's avoidance of religion is an explicit promotion of secularism as an antireligious ideology, but rather the implicit promotion as a latent secular ethos or force. If issues such as human sexuality, environmental ethics, AIDS, hate speech, and racism must all be discussed without reference to religion as an active moral force—not even in in-school released time programs—the implicit message is that religion is irrelevant, unimportant, or dangerous. Thus removing religion from the public schools also violates the norm of governmental neutrality, because government is indirectly and implicitly favoring secularism. Religious parents and their children are thereby alienated or otherwise disadvantaged.

There may not be a completely satisfactory answer to this dilemma. Some of the other democracies considered in the book have gone the route of released time for religious instruction or other efforts to recognize the claims of faith communities, and this has led to a greater measure of neutrality than would either incorporating certain consensual religious elements or banning all religion. Yet even in-school released time programs and moments of silence for prayer or reflection continue to be prohibited by the Supreme Court's interpretations of the First Amendment. Those decisions, as well as the reasoning the Court has used in reaching them and other decisions in regard to religion in the public schools, reveal that the Court does not recognize the dilemma outlined above. It sees only the first horn of the dilemma.

This brings us to the second key church-state question in regard to education, namely, *governmental funding of private, religiously based schools.* Nearly one in ten students in the United States attend a private school, and the vast majority of those schools have an underlying religious philosophy.[71] Here also the Supreme Court took a strict separation, no-aid-to-religion approach in the 1960s and 1970s, but here one can clearly see the shift of the Supreme Court's thinking toward equal treatment or neutrality beginning in the 1980s. The initial decision in this area yielded the quote at the beginning of this chapter: there was to be a "high and impregnable" wall between church and state and no taxes could go to support "any religious activities or institutions." It was twenty-four years later, in *Lemon v. Kurtzman* (1971), that the Court clearly and decisively ruled against public funds directly supporting private religious schools. In doing so it articulated a three-part test that has remained highly controversial today, even among many Supreme Court justices. Nevertheless, it has been used in many subsequent establishment clause decisions. To pass muster under the so-called *Lemon* test, a government program must meet all three of the following standards: "First, the statute must have a secular legislative purpose; second, its principal or primary effect must be one that neither advances nor inhibits religion; finally, the statute must not foster 'an excessive entanglement with religion.'"[72]

The Court ruled in the 1970s and early 1980s that in most cases involving state aid to nonpublic schools that there was a valid secular purpose: to help provide a general education for the children attending the nonpublic schools. But the Court held that a number of state attempts to aid religious schools failed the second part of the *Lemon* test: that they must not have the principal or primary effect of advancing or inhibiting religion. The third aspect of the *Lemon* test is that there must be no excessive government entanglement with religion. The Supreme Court used this test to invalidate a New York City program that supported remedial assistance for children from low-income families in nonpublic schools.[73] State programs often fail this test because they include mechanisms for government officials to monitor schools. In the New York program, for example, the state had established a system to make certain that religious elements were not introduced into the remedial program, which the Court decided resulted in an excessive entanglement of church and state.

But, especially in the 1990s, some Supreme Court justices relied more heavily on equal treatment reasoning, which set up conflicting interpretations. *Rosenberger v. Rector*, a key decision in 1995, illustrates the clashing no-aid-to-religion and equal-treatment principles and how close the divide on the Court had become. In the name of church-state separation, the University of Virginia had refused to fund a Christian student publication, even though it was funding print materials of fifteen other student opinion groups. In a razor-thin five-to-four vote, the Court majority held that the university's refusal to fund the publication violated the students' free speech rights, and that funding it would not violate the establishment clause. The majority opinion is clearly rooted in the equal treatment, or neutrality, principle. It states:

> A central lesson of our decisions is that a significant factor in upholding governmental programs in the face of Establishment Clause attack is their neutrality towards religion. . . . We have held that the guarantee of neutrality is respected, not offended, when the government, following neutral criteria and evenhanded policies, extends benefits to recipients whose ideologies and viewpoints, including religious ones, are broad and diverse. [74]

A program funding a religious publication was saved from establishment clause violation because religion was not singled out for favored treatment and the funding was extended to "the whole spectrum of speech, whether it manifests a religious view, an antireligious view, or neither."[75]

The neutrality line of reasoning in this decision allows limited forms of governmental accommodation and assistance—including financial assistance—to religious groups and their activities as long as that assistance is offered equally to all religious groups and to religious and nonreligious groups on the same basis. The four dissenting justices in the *Rosenberger* case saw that the decision undermined the no-aid-to-religion principle and the sacred-secular distinction under which religious groups had earlier been permitted to receive public funds. They wrote: "Even when the Court [in the past] has upheld aid to an institution performing both secular and sectarian functions, it has always made a searching enquiry to ensure that the institution kept the secular activities separate from its sectarian ones, with any direct aid flowing only to the former and never the latter."[76] They went on to advocate the continued reliance on "the no-direct-funding principle" over "the principle of evenhandedness."[77]

A series of similarly close decisions followed *Rosenberger*. A 1997 decision overruled two of its earlier decisions (mentioned above) that outlawed public school teachers coming into religiously based schools to teach remedial or enrichment courses. The Court declared an incentive in favor of religion is not present when the aid is allocated by evenhanded, neutral criteria that do not favor either religious or secular schools.[78] In 2000 the Supreme Court upheld the constitutionality of a federal program that made money available to schools—public and private alike—for computers, library books, and other teaching materials. The opinion of the Court, quoting from its 1997 decision, concluded that the challenged program "is allocated on the basis of neutral, secular criteria that neither favor nor disfavor religion, and is made available to both religious and secular beneficiaries on a nondiscriminatory basis."[79] Then in 2003, the Court upheld the constitutionality of a program in Cleveland, Ohio, that provided vouchers—that is, grants of public money—to students from failing central city schools that could be used by their parents at other public and private schools, both secular and religious in nature. The vast majority of the parents opted to send their children to religious schools. The Court majority argued that the public funds went to religious schools only by an indirect process, since the money, in effect, went to the low-income parents and they decided to which schools to direct their tuition dollars on behalf of their children. In a sense, the public money subsidized a private citizen's choice, not a school's budget. The Court tied this distinction to the neutrality, or equal treatment, principle: "In sum, the Ohio program is entirely neutral with respect to religion. . . . It permits . . . individuals to exercise genuine choice among options public and private, secular and religious."[80]

The Supreme Court has been more willing to uphold the constitutionality of some forms of governmental funding of religiously based schools than to permit religious elements into the public schools. Paradoxically, however, there is less popular support for governmental funding of religiously based schools and more support for including religious elements in the public schools. The common school ideal, as noted earlier, has deep roots in the American culture, apparently resulting in societal leaders and a majority of the public seeing religious schools as divisive or a threat to the traditional public school. One contemporary piece of evidence is support for different public policies that seek to expand educational options for parents. Overall there has been modest growth in voucher and tuition tax credit programs for educational opportunities targeted at the poor and other disadvantaged groups, and these resources often go to private religious schools. But efforts to institute statewide voucher programs by ballot initiative have generally been rejected by voters by wide margins.[81] In contrast, the popular option of charter schools—alternatives to traditional public schools that receive direct funding from the state—have grown at a rapid pace in comparison to vouchers and tax credits.[82] Charter schools, however, are prohibited from providing religious instruction.

The greater willingness of the Supreme Court to uphold government funding of religious schools than religious observances in the public schools can be seen in the history of funding for religiously based higher education. Even in the heyday of strict separation in the 1970s the Court ruled in favor of several government funding programs for religiously based colleges and universities. Three cases challenging programs sending government funds to religiously based colleges and universities came before the Supreme Court in the 1970s; in all three cases the Court held that the public funding programs did not violate the First Amendment establishment clause. The Supreme Court was able to maintain its strict separation, no-aid-to-religion line of reasoning while approving aid programs to religiously based colleges and universities, largely because of its application of two legal principles.

One of these legal principles is the sacred-secular distinction. The aid programs under challenge were approved, first, because the Supreme Court was willing to accept the separability of the secular and sacred aspects of education at religiously based colleges, and therefore it could accept the theory that public funds were supporting the secular mission, but not the religious mission of the colleges. By making a clear-cut distinction between the religious and the secular elements in a college education and then funding only the secular elements, one could have government financial aid to a religious college without giving aid to religion (at least in legal theory). In one of the cases, the Court observed that the challenged program of aid "was carefully drafted to ensure that the federally subsidized facilities would be devoted to the secular and not the religious function of the recipient institutions."[83] Another decision noted that "the secular and sectarian activities of the colleges were easily separated."[84]

But this approach in itself does not distinguish the cases dealing with higher education from those dealing with elementary and secondary education, since the Supreme Court at the same time as these decisions was largely rejecting federal funding to religiously based elementary and secondary schools. To do so the Court invoked a second legal principle, namely, the pervasively sectarian standard. The Supreme Court held that religiously based colleges and universities are not "pervasively sectarian," while religiously based elementary and secondary schools are. If an institution is "pervasively sectarian" it would be impossible to separate out the secular and religious. Thus it is only possible financially to support the secular programs of an organization without supporting the religious aspects of those programs if an organization is not "pervasively sectarian." In a case dealing with a South Carolina program assisting in the construction of college and university buildings, the Court made the point concerning the importance of a pervasively religious nature: "Aid normally may be thought to have a primary effect of advancing religion when it flows to an institution in which religion is so pervasive that a substantial portion of its functions are subsumed in the religious mission."[85]

Less clear, however, are the exact characteristics that distinguish a pervasively sectarian institution from its opposite. In recent years many justices have expressed dissatisfaction with the idea of pervasively sectarian as a legal standard, but it has never been expressly overturned. It remains "a vaguely defined work of art,"[86] as Justice Harry Blackmun once described it, and its exact legal standing is in doubt.

A coming set of challenges could either muddy or clarify the concept, or perhaps lead to its reinvention. The past decade has seen rapid acceptance of greater rights protections for LGBT persons, culminating in the landmark Supreme Court decision *Obergefell v. Hodges* in 2015 that legalized same-sex marriage across the country.[87] That decision, coupled with controversial executive orders and state-level laws and regulations on hiring discrimination and other matters, have generated growing concerns among the many religious colleges and universities in the United States that retain traditionalist views of human sexuality and marriage. Many of these institutions—not to mention other faith-based nonprofits—use their traditional positions on these matters as a basis for decisions about hiring and staff benefits.

The courts have generally held that institutions with a missional focus that is clearly embedded in a particular religious worldview are granted a "ministerial exception" from certain kinds of otherwise valid governmental decrees.[88] This exception for colleges and universities follows precisely the same logic as a house of worship discriminating in hiring clergy: just as employment discrimination law carves out a space for churches, mosques, and temples to hire exclusively Christian, Muslim, or Jewish clergy, respectively, so too a faith-based university or other nonprofit can discriminate in hiring when the acceptance of the institution's mission is relevant to a staff person's work. But of course it is often a matter of intense controversy whether a specific staff member does indeed need to accept the mission to do his or her work for the organization. Moreover, even when the relevance of a staff member accepting the organization's mission is beyond doubt, it still might disqualify an organization from public resources. Several chapters of the Christian parachurch organizations Intervarsity Christian Fellowship and the Christian Legal Society have been denied student group status at public universities because they required their leadership to subscribe to a faith statement—and the Supreme Court has held those denials constitutional.[89]

CHURCH, STATE, AND NONPROFIT SERVICE ORGANIZATIONS

These are knotty constitutional questions, and the Supreme Court has tackled a dizzying range of other issues outside the educational arena over the past fifty years. What are the constitutional limits of the government in giving symbolic recognition or honor to religion and its role in American history and society? Is it permissible for a state or local government to sponsor a Christmas display if the scene includes both religious and secular elements?[90] What about symbolic recognitions of religion by government such as the "In God We Trust" motto on coins? The display of the Ten Commandments at a state capitol building or a courthouse?[91] These questions of symbolic support continue to divide the Court, and its answers frequently perplex the Court's observers.

Another area of increasing controversy has more to do with tangible financial support from government to religious organizations outside the educational context. Under what conditions, if any, is it permissible for the government to fund private nonprofit service organizations, many of which are religiously based?[92] It is not surprising that this question would come up. On the one hand, the welfare functions of the national and state governments in the United States have grown considerably over the past century, a phenomenon even more pronounced in the other democracies in this study. Government is simply doing more today than a century ago when it comes to addressing issues in health, employment, and old age. On the other hand, faith-based nonprofits have always had a central role in providing basic services to the poor, sick, elderly, disabled, homeless, addicted, and otherwise disadvantaged in the American society. By some estimates, fully half of the activity within American civil society, those voluntary associations and organizations that function outside the state, happens under the auspices of nearly ubiquitous faith-based organizations.[93] While houses of worship are important service providers,[94] much of the faith-based service work happens apart from congregations in faith-based hospitals, community centers, drug rehabilitation facilities, adoption agencies, employment training programs, food pantries, emergency-housing organizations, and myriad other social service associations.[95] Moreover, religion channels a great deal of the philanthropic spirit in the country. Religious Americans are more likely than the religiously unaffiliated or inactive to volunteer or give money not only to faith-based organizations, but also to secular ones.[96] Taken together, faith-based nonprofits are an enormous resource for the welfare state.

To a substantial degree government has already taken advantage of this potential resource. Some of the more prominent examples of faith-based social service providers that receive extensive government grants include Catholic Charities, Lutheran Social Services, Jewish Family Services, and the Salvation Army. In some cases as much as three-quarters of these large organizations' budget have come from government sources.[97] One study found that a majority of religiously based child and family service agencies received over 40 percent of their budgets from government sources.[98] A study of welfare-to-work programs in Los Angeles, Chicago, Dallas, and Philadelphia found that about one-half of the faith-based programs received government funding, including 58 percent of the most deeply religious ones. The amount of government funds they received was significant—about 30 percent of the budgets of the most deeply religious programs came from government sources.[99]

Despite large amounts of public tax dollars going to religiously based service organizations, the Supreme Court has decided the merits in only two cases challenging this practice, and in both instances the Court found the practice constitutional. One case, from the end of the nineteenth century, dealt with aid to a District of Columbia Catholic hospital. The Supreme Court based its approval of the program of aid on the sacred-secular distinction. The Court saw the hospital as "simply the case of a secular corporation being managed by people who hold to the doctrines of the Roman Catholic Church."[100] The secular nature of the hospital's function assured the constitutionality of the aid.

The constitutional issues at stake were raised more clearly in the 1988 case of *Bowen v. Kendrick*. The Adolescent Family Life Act (AFLA) had authorized federal grants for both public and private nonprofit organizations for the purpose of providing services relating to teenage sexuality and pregnancies. By a close five-to-four vote, the Supreme Court ruled that on its face the act did not violate the First Amendment establishment clause and remanded the case to the lower courts to determine whether it did so as actually administered. The key issue with which the Court struggled concerned the second part of the *Lemon* test, namely, whether the act advanced religion. The Supreme Court majority ruled that "the programs established under the authority of the AFLA can be monitored to determine whether the funds are, in effect, being used by the grantees in such a way as to advance religion."[101] The money could only go to support the secular aspects of the agencies' programs. Further, the Court majority ruled that the agencies receiving government funds were not pervasively sectarian, but seemed to be similar to the colleges and universities for whom public funds had previously been approved: "In this case, nothing on the face of the AFLA indicates that a significant proportion of the federal funds will be disbursed to 'pervasively sectarian' institutions."[102]

The use of the no-aid-to-religion principle—in spite of the recent rise of the equal treatment principle—continues to exert a powerful force on the Supreme Court and among leaders in the media and the political arena, as we see in the controversy surrounding what has been termed "charitable choice" and President George W. Bush's faith-based initiative. In 1996 a bill made its way through Congress that enacted major welfare reforms, including a "charitable choice" amendment that changed the rules by which states work with nonprofits. The law provided that states could contract with private organizations or create voucher systems to deliver welfare services, and that any state that did so would have to allow funding of religious organizations on an equal basis with secular organizations. Most significantly, it provided that agencies receiving such funds shall maintain the right to develop and express their religious orientation, may keep religious pictures and symbols in their facilities, and may favor members of their own religious faith in hiring decisions.[103] This amendment was adopted by wide margins in Congress, President Clinton did not raise objections to it in signing the bill into law, and it was not widely criticized in the media.

Soon after President George W. Bush assumed office in 2001, he established a White House Office of Faith-Based and Community Initiatives, charged with the specific task of removing barriers for faith-based and small, community-based organizations from receiving governmental financial support for their charitable activities. Unlike the charitable choice provisions, this effort ignited a firestorm of criticism and controversy that continues today. Generally, Republican members of Congress lined up in support and

Democratic members of Congress and strict separationist advocacy groups lined up in opposition.[104] The most persistently controversial provision was that religiously based organizations receiving public funding would not lose their right to make hiring decisions based on religion. Religiously based organizations had been explicitly given this right in the 1965 Civil Rights Law that had generally outlawed discrimination in hiring, and this provision had been unanimously upheld by the Supreme Court.[105] The point of these exemptions is to protect religious autonomy of the agencies receiving government funds and thereby help maintain religious pluralism. Nevertheless, strict separationist advocates and their congressional allies denounced this provision in President Bush's initiative as a "smashing of constitutional and civil rights protection" and "discrimination based on religion."[106] But only one case reached the Supreme Court challenging the initiative in this period, and it was dismissed because the litigants did not have authority to sue.[107]

While the office was renamed the White House Office of Faith-Based and Neighborhood Partnerships under President Barack Obama, it continues to facilitate federal grantmaking to faith-based organizations. The new administration appointed a task force to consider reforms of the Office's activities,[108] but the resulting administrative regulations, as task force member Stanley Carlson-Thies tells us, "display great continuity from the Charitable Choice rules through the Bush rules and now into the Obama administration."[109] The reforms did not include restrictions on funding religious organizations that hire staff based on their religious convictions, which sparked renewed objections from some opinion leaders and legislators.

A key reason the faith-based initiatives remain controversial is the no-aid-to-religion and sacred-versus-secular assumptions that continue to shape the prevailing mind-set among much of the cultural and media elite in the United States. An equal treatment approach would argue that the basis for the constitutionality of government funding lies in the government funding religious and secular activities of a similar or parallel nature without favoring one or the other. In fact, it would say that to fund the secular activities and not religious ones would be to discriminate against religion. This is what the Supreme Court held in the *Rosenberger* case dealing with a Christian student publication at the University of Virginia. But to date that reasoning has not been applied directly to funding faith-based social service organizations. As noted earlier, in the two cases where the Supreme Court approved programs of direct funding of religious organizations, it sought to maintain the principle of no aid to religion on the theory that the government is only aiding the secular aspects of the program. It is only in cases of indirect funding—as was the case in the Cleveland voucher case—that the Court has based its decision on equal treatment reasoning.

One crucial consequence of using the sacred-secular distinction as the basis for approving public funding of religiously based organizations is that questions arise over whether religious elements may be integrated into the presumably secular activities that are being subsidized. May religious pictures or symbols be displayed in a homeless shelter receiving public funds? May a religious college receiving public funds hire only faculty members of its own faith? May a home for abused children insist on standards of behavior for its staff in keeping with the religious beliefs of the sponsoring faith? The problem is that if these religious organizations are truly providing purely secular services with no relevance to their religious beliefs, it is hard to think of reasons why they should have a right to insist that certain religious standards or elements be a part of them. But the point is that the religious identity of the organization is often intimately linked to the service the organization provides. In addition, the Supreme Court's ambiguous use of the pervasively sectarian standard—sometimes it is ignored and sometimes criticized—opens the way for program administrators or the lower courts to pressure religious agencies to give up certain religiously motivated practices. It is not surprising that questions and controversy remain over what is and is not permitted in regard to government funding of faith-based, nonprofit delivery of health and social services. Most other western democracies have avoided such uncertainty by adopting different church-state principles.

Some emerging challenges will undoubtedly push the Supreme Court to develop this area of constitutional law. In the section on religion and education we already saw how recognition of same-sex marriage and other LGBT rights has quickly become a new legal frontier for religious colleges and universities with traditionalist understandings of sexuality and family. Some of the Obama administration's directives have raised analogous issues for faith-based nonprofits and even business firms. As part of President Obama's health policy, most organizations have a responsibility to offer their employees contraceptive coverage if they are required by law to provide health insurance. After the successful challenge of that requirement in 2015 by Hobby Lobby, a for-profit company owned by conservative Christians, faith-based organizations were allowed to opt out of directly covering contraception, leaving it instead to a third-party provider.[110] But a coalition of faith-based nonprofits, led by the Catholic charitable group Little Sisters of the Poor, viewed the Hobby Lobby decision as insufficient protection of its religious freedom because it still required indirect complicity in authorizing the third party to fund contraceptive coverage. In a highly complex case, the Supreme Court handed the Little Sisters and its allies a partial victory in 2016, when a bare majority required lower courts to reconsider their decisions requiring the faith-based groups to fund the third-party coverage.[111] The final disposition of their claims was back in the hands of those lower courts when this book went to print.

CONCLUDING OBSERVATIONS

The United States is currently wavering between two conflicting church-state approaches: the strict separation, no-aid-to-religion model, with its roots in the liberal Enlightenment, and the neutrality or equal treatment model. The basic terms of the strict separation model are still in place, while the American public and the Supreme Court have been increasingly willing to make decisions based on the equal treatment model. When Congress or the Supreme Court approves government-sponsored religious displays, government funding of educational or social services, and other forms of government cooperation with religion, they seek to do so in such a way that their actions can be defended on strict separation grounds that are strained at best and disingenuous at worst. Pervasively sectarian versus nonpervasively sectarian, direct versus indirect funding, religious instruction versus secular instruction: all these have become standards that must be applied, but they are not clearly defined and therefore can be interpreted to match the desired conclusion. Most of the other countries considered in this book—and most clearly the Netherlands, which we consider in chapter 4—avoid these conflicts and uncertainties by basing their church-state thinking on equal treatment or neutrality grounds, not on a rigid no-aid-to-religion standard.

In this concluding section we return to the question of why the United States has taken this position and seek a tentative evaluation of it. The most persuasive explanation for the United States' continuing ideological commitment to a strict separation, no-aid-to-religion standard, even when it in practice is increasingly being abandoned, lies in nineteenth-century American history. At that time, Enlightenment liberals and the dominant Protestants came together to oppose Catholic influence in the United States and to impose their own generalized Protestant establishment on all of society. Throughout the nineteenth and into the twentieth century Protestants were the dominant force in this liberal-Protestant coalition. But by the mid-twentieth century, conservative Protestantism had been routed in internal church battles and replaced by a liberal Protestantism that accepted many of the basic tenets of Enlightenment liberalism. Neither evangelical Protestantism nor Catholicism was numerically or socially powerful enough to command the political and media influence to make their positions felt in the courts and among the influential elites. As a result the Enlightenment liberal view of church and state was left in a commanding position in the post–World War II world, and came largely to be incorporated into Supreme Court interpretations of the First Amendment, especially in relation to the public schools that traditionally had been seen as playing a crucial leveling and assimilating role in an otherwise divided society. It continues to assert a major influence on the American mind-set—to some degree among the American people and certainly among American social and cultural elites. Thus the American political culture is still largely imbued with the principles of strict separation, and only grudgingly makes exceptions or modifications to it.

The prevailing church-state situation as we have described it in the United States carries with it three distinct disadvantages or problems. One is the confusion, uncertainty, and even anger that the current state of church-state law and practice engenders. Scholars have used terms such as "incoherent," a "tangled body of law," and "eccentric" to describe current church-state law.[112] No one seems to be happy with the status quo. Steven Smith made a telling point when he wrote that "in a rare and remarkable way, the Supreme Court's establishment clause jurisprudence has unified critical opinion: people who disagree about nearly everything else in the law agree that establishment clause doctrine is seriously, perhaps distinctively, defective."[113] The Supreme Court justices themselves issue closely divided rulings on church-state questions, with even justices in the same majority or among the dissenters unable to reach agreement about their reasons for coming to the same conclusions. As a result of church-state confusions and hair-splitting distinctions, respect for the law suffers, uncertainty abounds, and government authorities have sometimes taken stances that appear to be at odds with similar practices that elsewhere are accepted without question.

A second problem with the American system of strict separation and neutrality living in tension is that it threatens a loss of religious freedom, or autonomy, by religious organizations and endeavors. This is due to the nature of the accommodations that the neutrality, equal treatment standard is pressured to make with the strict separation, no-aid-to-religion mind-set that still exerts influence. The perennial issue of hiring illustrates the point. If, for example, an evangelical Protestant drug treatment center must hire nonbelievers, a Jewish welfare-to-work program must hire Muslims, and a Catholic homeless shelter must hire Wiccans, those evangelical, Jewish, and Catholic programs would virtually cease to have their religious identity. Yet if the persons they are hiring are providing services with no religious elements or underpinnings, what rationale exists for hiring persons of the faith of the organization? These are the questions that emerge and are hard to answer as the United States attempts to move toward an equal treatment model without surrendering its strict separationist assumptions. Under the neutrality, equal treatment model that some other democracies have favored, a pluralism of religious traditions is honored and accommodated. Even if they receive public funding, a Muslim social service agency may hire only Muslims, a Jewish home for the elderly only Jews, and a Christian school only Christians. It is precisely by protecting this autonomy that societies both foster pluralism and use it to common benefit.

A third problem in the current American church-state scene relates directly to the vulnerable position of the basic right to the free exercise of religion. Religious minorities or adherents of nontraditional faiths face the danger of losing this right. Such faith groups as the Amish, Orthodox Jews, and Native Americans have struggled in courts to secure their free exercise of religion in the First Amendment of the Constitution. But the problem extends beyond such nonmainstream religious groups to include more traditional and much larger groups because of the absence of a concept of positive religious freedom in the American setting. Religious freedom is typically seen as a negative freedom: freedom *from* government restraints on one's religious beliefs and practice. Since government in the current American perspective is largely seen as properly occupying a neutral zone between various religious groups and between religious and secular belief systems, it is assumed there is no need for government to take affirmative steps to support or encourage religion. And the critics have a point when the state provides special support to certain religious groups or religion as a whole. To play favorites in that way would indeed be a throwback to church-state establishment and a violation of any plausible idea of neutrality. But it is also a violation of neutrality when government recognizes, favors, and aids all sorts of secular enterprises and perspectives while systematically excluding religious enterprises and perspectives. Secular perspectives and belief structures represent a point of view, a worldview, as much as various religious perspectives and beliefs do.

Although the United States has moved in the past twenty-five years toward an equal treatment, substantive, positive neutrality approach to church and state, the American mind-set to a large degree is still rooted in the liberal Enlightenment assumption that strictly separating government and religion assures governmental neutrality on matters of religion. In doing so government may violate the very neutrality that liberals are rightly eager to attain. As we compare approaches to church and state of the other countries considered in this study, we will ask whether the assumptions and ideals of Enlightenment liberalism are adequate to assure a genuine religious neutrality on the part of government in today's world.

NOTES

1. *Everson v. Board of Education*, 330 U.S. at 16 (1947).
2. *Everson v. Board of Education*, at 18.
3. From the dissent of Justice Robert Jackson, *Everson v. Board of Education*, at 19.
4. Legal scholars have identified at least a half dozen different legal tests and doctrines that individual or blocs of justices have used to give meaning to the goal of no aid to religion. For an effort to "map" those approaches, see John Witte Jr. and Joel A. Nichols, *Religion and the American Constitutional Experiment: Essential Rights and Liberties*, 4th ed. (Boulder, Colo.: Westview Press, 2016), chap. 7.
5. Phillip E. Johnson, "Concepts and Compromise in First Amendment Religious Doctrine," *California Law Review* 72 (1984), 817.
6. Diana Eck, *A New Religious America: How a "Christian Country" Has Become the World's Most Diverse Nation* (New York: HarperOne, 2002).
7. See Kenneth Wald and Allison Calhoun-Brown, *Religion and Politics in the United States,* 7th ed. (Lanham, Md.: Rowman & Littlefield, 2014), chaps. 8 and 9.

8. Scholars have given considerable attention to religious affiliation using surveys and other methods. We use numbers from a 35,000-person survey by the Pew Research Center in 2014 titled "U.S. Religious Landscape." Available at http://www.pewforum.org/religious-landscape-study.

9. Wald and Calhoun-Brown, *Religion and Politics in the United States*, chap. 8; Paul Djupe and Brian Calfano, eds., *The Evangelical Crack-Up: Will the Evangelical-Republican Coalition Last?* (Philadelphia: Temple University Press, forthcoming).

10. "U.S. Religious Landscape." For a survey of religious diversity and its political implications in the United States, see Robert Booth Fowler, Allen Hertzke, Laura Olson, and Kevin R. den Dulk, *Religion and Politics in America: Faith, Culture, and Strategic Choices* (Boulder, Colo.: Westview, 2010), chaps. 2 and 3.

11. Fowler et al., *Religion and Politics in America,* chap. 9.

12. "U.S. Religious Landscape." For deeper analysis, see Cary Funk and Greg Smith, *"Nones" on the Rise: One-in-Five Adults Have No Religious Affiliation* (Washington, D.C.: Pew Research Center, 2012), available at http://www.pewforum.org/Unaffiliated/nones-on-the-rise.aspx; and Amy Sullivan, "The Rise of the Nones," *Time* (March 12, 2012), 68.

13. Michael Lipka, "What Surveys Say about Why People Attend Worship Services—and Why Some Stay Home" (Washington, D.C.: Pew Research Center, 2013). Available at http://www.pewresearchap.org/fact-tank/2013/09/13/what-surveys-say-about-worship-attendance-and-why-some-stay-home/.

14. Ronald Inglehart et al., World Values Surveys Wave 6: 2010–14. Data available at http://www.worldvaluessurvey.org/WVSOnline.jsp.

15. Gregory A. Smith et al., "U.S. Becoming Less Religious" (Washington, D.C.: Pew Research Center, 2015), 74, 134. Available at http://www.pewforum.org/2015/11/03/u-s-public-becoming-less-religious.

16. Pew Research Center, *Religion and the Fall Campaign* (Washington, D.C.: Pew Research Center, 2016), 4, 11. Available at http://www.pewforum.org/2016/01/27/faith-and-the-2016-campaign/.

17. Fowler et al., *Religion and Politics in America,* chap. 6.

18. Allen D. Hertzke, "The U.S. Congress: Protecting and Accommodating Religion," in Derek H. Davis, ed., *The Oxford Handbook of Church and State in the United States* (New York: Oxford University Press, 2010); Louis Fisher, *Religious Liberty in America: Political Safeguards* (Lawrence: University Press of Kansas, 2002).

19. The literature on religious freedom and church-state relations is voluminous and varied. A sampling of scholarship over the past few decades: Witte and Nichols, *Religion and the American Constitutional Experiment*; Leonard Levy, *The Establishment Clause: Religion and the First Amendment*, 2nd ed. (Chapel Hill: University of North Carolina Press, 1994); David Sehat, *The Myth of American Religious Freedom* (New York: Oxford University Press, 2011); Michael I. Meyerson, *Endowed by Our Creator: The Birth of Religious Freedom in America* (New Haven, Conn.: Yale University Press, 2012); Steven K. Green, *The Bible, the School, and the Constitution: The Clash That Shaped Modern Church-State Doctrine* (New York: Oxford University Press, 2012); Steven K. Green, *The Second Disestablishment: Church and State in Nineteenth Century America* (New York: Oxford University Press, 2010); and Allen D. Hertzke, ed., *Religious Freedom in America* (Overland Park: University of Kansas Press, 2015).

20. Sidney E. Mead, *The Lively Experiment* (New York: Harper & Row, 1963), 17.

21. The term "strange coalition" is Mead's. See Mead, *The Lively Experiment*, 35. For more on the role played by these two disparate movements in the disestablishment of the churches in the eighteenth century, see Stephen V. Monsma, *Positive Neutrality* (Westport, Conn.: Greenwood, 1993), 83–113.

22. On the effects of religious populism in the United States, see Fowler et al., *Religion and Politics in America,* chap. 12.

23. For an account of these events, see Levy, *The Establishment Clause*, 58–75.

24. James Madison, "A Memorial and Remonstrance against Religious Assessments," in Daniel L. Dreisbach and Mark David Hall, *The Sacred Rights of Conscience: Selected Readings on Religious Liberty and Church-State Relations in the American Founding* (Indianapolis, Ind.: Liberty Fund, 2009), 311.

25. Thomas Jefferson, "Bill for Establishing Religious Freedom," in Dreisbach and Hall, *Sacred Rights of Conscience*, 251.

26. Rodney Stark and Roger Finke, *The Churching of America: Winners and Losers in Our Religious Economy* (New Brunswick, N.J.: Rutgers University Press, 2005).

27. James Bryce, *The American Commonwealth*, rev. ed., vol. 2 (New York: Macmillan, 1911), 769–70.

28. On the Second Great Awakening and its consequences for American Christianity, see Nathan Hatch, *The Democratization of American Christianity* (New Haven, Conn.: Yale University Press, 1989).

29. Green, *The Bible, the School, and the Constitution*.

30. See George M. Marsden, *The Soul of the American University: From Protestant Establishment to Established Nonbelief* (New York: Oxford University Press, 1996).

31. Charles Leslie Glenn Jr., *The Myth of the Common School* (Amherst: University of Massachusetts Press, 1987), 84.

32. Glenn, *The Myth of the Common School*, 154; Marsden, *The Soul of the American University*, 89.

33. Quoted in Glenn, *The Myth of the Common School*, 164.

34. Carl F. Kaestle, *Pillars of the Republic: Common Schools and American Society, 1780–1860* (New York: Hill and Wang, 1983), 76.

35. But see Steven Green's provocative argument that the seeds of the second disestablishment were planted much earlier. Green, *The Second Disestablishment*.

36. For a thorough survey of religion in constitutional development, see Witte and Nichols, *Religion and the American Constitutional Experiment,* especially chap. 6.

37. *Reynolds v. United States*, 98 U.S. at 166 (1879).

38. *Reynolds v. United States*, at 167.

39. See C. Herman Pritchett, *The American Constitution*, 3rd ed. (New York: McGraw-Hill, 1977), 392–94.

40. *Church of the Lukumi Babalu Aye v. Hialeah*, 508 U.S. at 542 (1993).

41. The cases were *Wisconsin v. Yoder*, 406 U.S. 205 (1972); *Sherbert v. Verner*, 374 U.S. 398 (1963); and *Thomas v. Review Board*, 450 U.S. 707 (1981).

42. The cases are *Braunfeld v. Brown*, 366 U.S. 599 (1961); *United States v. Lee*, 285 U.S. 252 (1982); and *Goldman v. Weinberger*, 475 U.S. 503 (1986).

43. *Employment Division v. Smith*, 494 U.S. 872, at 878–79 (1990).

44. *Employment Division v. Smith*, at 885.

45. Public Law 103–141, 103d Congress, Section 3 (b).

46. The case is *City of Boerne v. Flores*, 521 U.S. 507 (1997).

47. For information on this act and its implementation, see http://www.becketfund.org/rluipa/.

48. But see *O'Lone v. Estate of Shabazz*, 482 U.S. 342 (1987).

49. On changing public attitudes toward Muslims, see Pew Research Center, "Growing Concern about Islamic Extremism at Home and Abroad" (Washington, D.C.: Pew Research Center, 2014). Available at http://www.people-press.org/2014/09/10/growing-concern-about-rise-of-islamic-extremism-at-home-and-abroad/#views-of-islam-and-violence.

50. Asma T. Uddin, "American Muslims, American Islam, and the American Constitutional Heritage," in Hertzke, *Religious Freedom in America*, 224–47.

51. The cases are *Engel v. Vitale*, 370 U.S. 421 (1962) and *Abington v. Schempp*, 374 U.S. 203 (1963).

52. *Abington v. Schempp*, at 313.

53. *Abington v. Schempp*, at 313.

54. *Lemon v. Kurtzman*, 403 U.S. at 665 (1971).

55. *Committee for Public Education v. Nyquist*, 413 U.S. at 814 (1973).

56. *Engel v. Vitale*, 421 U.S. at 425 (1962).

57. *Abington School District v. Schempp*, 203 U.S. at 225 (1963).

58. *Abington School District v. Schempp*, at 222.

59. *McCollum v. Board of Education*, 333 U.S. at 210 (1948).

60. See *Zorach v. Clauson*, 343 U.S. 306 (1952).

61. See *Lee v. Weisman*, 505 U.S. 577 (1992); *Wallace v. Jaffree*, 472 U.S. 38 (1985); *Edwards v. Aguillard*, 107 S.Ct. 2578 (1987); *Santa Fe Independent School District v. Doe*, 530 U.S. 290 (2000).

62. *Epperson v. Arkansas*, 393 U.S. at 106 (1968). Also see a similar statement in *Abington School District v. Schempp*, at 225.

63. See Wald and Calhoun-Brown, *Religion and Politics in the United States*, 158–61.

64. Philip Schwadel, "Changes in Americans' Views of Prayer and Reading the Bible in Public Schools: Time Periods, Birth Cohorts, and Religious Traditions," *Sociological Forum* 28 (June 2013), 267; and Rebecca Riffkin, "In U.S., Support for Daily Prayer in Schools Dips Slightly," Gallup Poll, September 24, 2014. Available at http://www.gallup.com/poll/177401/support-daily-prayer-schools-dips-slightly.aspx.

65. Gregory Smith, "Little Voter Discomfort with Romney's Mormon Religion" (Washington, D.C.: Pew Research Center, 2012), 16. Available at http://www.pewforum.org/2012/07/26/2012-romney-mormonism-obamas-religion/.

66. See *Widmar v. Vincent*, 454 U.S. 263 (1981).

67. *Westside Community Schools v. Mergens*, 496 U.S. at 252 (1990).

68. *Good News Club v. Milford Central School*, 533 U.S. 98 (2001).

69. *Good News Club v. Milford Central School* at 114.

70. A. James Reichley, *Faith in Politics* (Washington, D.C.: Brookings Institution, 2002), 158. Reichley's emphasis.

71. Stephanie Ewert, "The Decline in Private School Enrollment," Working Paper, Washington, D.C.: U.S. Census Bureau, 2013, 20.

72. *Lemon v. Kurtzman*, 403 U.S. at 612–613 (1971). The internal quoted material is from *Walz v. Tax Commission*, 397 U.S. at 674 (1970).

73. See *Aguilar v. Felton*, 473 U.S. 402 (1985).

74. *Rosenberger v. Rector*, 515 U.S. 819, at 839 (1995).

75. *Rosenberger v. Rector*, at 841.

76. *Rosenberger v. Rector*, at 875.

77. *Rosenberger v. Rector*, at 882.

78. *Agostini v. Felton*, 521 U.S. 203, at 231 (1997).

79. *Mitchell v. Helms*, 530 U.S. at 829 (2000).

80. *Zelman v. Simmons-Harris*, 536 U.S. 639, at 662 (2002).

81. For example, in 2000 voucher proposals were defeated in both California and Michigan by margins of two to one in spite of well-financed campaigns in their favor.

82. Authors' analysis of data at the Friedman Foundation's and Alliance for School Choice's websites.

83. *Tilton v. Richardson*, 403 U.S. at 679 (1971).

84. *Roemer v. Maryland Public Works Board*, 426 U.S. at 764 (1976).

85. *Hunt v. McNair*, 413 U.S. at 743 (1973).

86. See *Bowen v. Kendrick*, 487 U.S. at 631 (1988).

87. *Obergefell v. Hodges*, 576 U.S. _____ (2015).

88. This legal doctrine was most recently upheld and arguably expanded to educational institutions in *Hosanna-Tabor Evangelical Lutheran Church and School, Petitioner v. Equal Employment Opportunity Commission*, 565 U.S. _____ (2012).

89. *Christian Legal Society v. Martinez*, 562 U.S. 661 (2011).

90. See *Lynch v. Donnelly*, 465 U.S. 668 (1984).

91. *VanOrden v. Perry* 545 U.S. 677 (2005) and *McCreary County v. American Civil Liberties Union of Kentucky*, 545 U.S. 844 (2005).

92. For a thorough consideration of this field, see Stephen V. Monsma, *When Sacred and Secular Mix* (Lanham, Md.: Rowman & Littlefield, 2000), 4–10 and 64–80; and Stephen V. Monsma, *Putting Faith in Partnerships: Welfare-to-Work in Four Cities* (Ann Arbor: University of Michigan Press, 2004).

93. Robert D. Putnam, *Bowling Alone: The Collapse and Revival of American Community* (New York: Simon & Schuster, 2000), 66. For a broader discussion of civil society and American religion, see Fowler et al., *Religion and Politics in America*, chap. 7.

94. Mark Chaves, "Religious Congregations," in Lester M. Salamon, ed., *The State of Nonprofit America*, 2nd ed. (Washington, D.C.: Brookings Institution, 2012), 380–84.

95. Stephen V. Monsma, *Pluralism and Freedom: Faith-Based Organizations in a Democratic Society* (Lanham, Md.: Rowman & Littlefield, 2012).

96. Corwin Smidt et al., *Pews, Prayers, and Participation: Religion and Civic Responsibility in America* (Washington, D.C.: Georgetown University Press, 2008), chaps. 3 and 4; Robert D. Putnam and David E. Campbell, *American Grace: How Religion Unites and Divides Us* (New York: Simon & Schuster, 2010), chap. 13.

97. Monsma, *When Sacred and Secular Mix,* 1.

98. Monsma, *When Sacred and Secular Mix*, 68.

99. Monsma, *Putting Faith in Partnerships*, 138, 140.

100. *Bradfield v. Roberts*, 175 U.S. at 298–299 (1899).

101. *Bowen v. Kendrick*, at 615.

102. *Bowen v. Kendrick*, at 610.

103. See Public Law 104–193, section 104. The Institutional Religious Freedom Alliance keeps track of the legacy of charitable choice at http://www.irfalliance.org/.

104. For helpful accounts and analyses of what happened, see Amy E. Black, Douglas L. Koopman, and David K. Ryden, *Of Little Faith: The Politics of George W. Bush's Faith-Based Initiative* (Washington, D.C.: Georgetown University Press, 2004); and John DiIulio Jr., *Godly Republic: A Centrist Blueprint for America's Faith-Based Future* (Berkeley: University of California Press, 2007), chaps. 3 and 4.

105. See *Corporation of Presiding Bishops v. Amos*, 483 U.S. 327 (1987).

106. *New York Times* (September 28, 2005), A26.

107. *Hein v. Freedom from Religion Foundation*, 551 U.S. 587 (2007).

108. President's Advisory Council on Faith-Based and Neighborhood Partnerships, "A New Era of Partnerships: A Report of Recommendations to the President" (Washington, D.C.: White House Office of Faith-Based and Neighborhood Partnerships, 2010).

109. E-mail correspondence with Stanley Carlson-Thies.

110. *Burwell v. Hobby Lobby*, 573 U.S. ___ (2014).

111. *Zubik v. Burwell,* 578 U.S. ___ (2016).

112. See Michael A. Paulsen, "Religion, Equality, and the Constitution: An Equal Protection Approach to Establishment Clause Adjudication," *Notre Dame Law Review* 61 (1986), 317; Reichley, *Faith in Politics*, 117; and Johnson, "Concepts and Compromise," 817.

113. Steven D. Smith, "Separation and the 'Secular': Reconstructing the Disestablishment Decision," *Texas Law Review* 67 (1989), 955–56.

Chapter Three

France

Separation from the Public Square

In July 2016, the mayor of Cannes declared that women could no longer wear full-body swimwear on the city's famous beaches. While his edict did not mention Islam, the mayor made clear that he intended to target the so-called burkini, a suit worn by a small number of French Muslim beachgoers who adhere to traditionalist views of modesty in dress. The mayor issued the ban in the name of security; he saw the public display of the burkini as a lightning rod for extremism and an affront to French secularism and unity.[1] While the ban was only temporary and limited to the city itself, and in fact was quickly suspended by France's highest administrative court, it represented yet another front in the ongoing public debate about the place of Muslims in the French Republic.

The burkini ban may appear to be largely an act of symbolic politics. After all, could a ban on swimwear really have much effect on security? But to say that bans on dress are *merely* symbolic is to misunderstand this anxious moment in French history. French citizens today are embroiled in serious soul-searching about what it means to meet the challenge of new and growing religious diversity—a challenge that has recently presented itself in violence. It is important to remember that the events in Cannes came on the heels of a Bastille Day attack in Nice, where a Tunisian man, apparently motivated by an ideology of Islamic extremism, drove a rental truck into a crowd of revelers, killing scores of people. A few days later, two Islamic militants brutally killed an elderly Catholic priest as he officiated at Mass in northern France. And those events happened against the backdrop of even greater violence. In January 2015, two terrorists opened fire at the Paris offices of *Charlie Hebdo*, apparently in retaliation for the satirical magazine's provocative depictions of Islam. By the end of the rampage, they had killed eleven staff and a police officer, and injured many others. Five other French citizens were murdered in related shootings throughout the region, including at a Jewish grocery. The reaction was tragic but predictable, with a string of revenge attacks targeted at French mosques and Muslim-owned businesses (there were no reported casualties). [2] Despite the French government's heightened alert, terror struck again—and more intensely—just ten months later when attackers killed 130 people and injured nearly four hundred in a series of suicide bombings and mass shootings at a theater and several other locations within central Paris. The terrorist group Islamic State claimed responsibility for this second round of terrorism, citing retribution for French air strikes in Syria and northern Iraq. In response to these attacks the French state imposed emergency measures; they were still in place as this book went to print.

The attacks in France and their aftermath are disturbing on their own. But they also pose an extreme test for leaders as they attempt to meet the challenge of pluralism in French society. French political culture places a high premium on a national unity rooted in Republican values inherited from the French Revolution of the late eighteenth century. [3] These values include what came to be called *laïcité*, a separation of religion from the public sphere. But the effort to implement church-state separation has taken many different forms over modern French history, from the substantive to the symbolic. Moreover, French political leaders and intellectuals often disagree about the meaning and scope of *laïcité,* and both the religious majority (Catholicism) and minorities (most recently, Muslims, but also Protestants and Jews) have sought a place in French society that does not relegate their religious practice to private spaces. The result is a complex and highly contentious history of religious freedom and church-state relations in France.

Understanding this complexity and conflict requires a sense of context. The first section of this chapter frames some basic elements of French government and society, including population statistics on contemporary religious affiliations and behaviors. The next section delves into the history of France, with special attention to the role of Catholicism in shaping French culture and to the damaging effects of the French Revolution on the public status of Catholic institutions. After a discussion about the emergence of *laïcité* as the post-Revolution church-state framework and a case study of the modern treatment of Islam, the chapter explores the status of faith-based schools and nonprofit social services. We conclude with some comparative observations.

THE NATION

The total resident population of France in 2016 was over sixty-six million, the largest in Europe after Germany and Russia.[4] France is also the largest country by area in western Europe, occupying nearly 213,000 square miles. Its strategic location between modern-day Spain and Germany, as well as close proximity to the British Isles and access to both the Atlantic and Mediterranean oceans, has made France a site of both military conflict and bustling economic activity. France also rivaled Spain, Great Britain, and other modern European powers in its drive for global expansion through colonization; from the sixteenth to nineteenth centuries it established territories on nearly every continent. The French were motivated not only by trade, resource extraction, and military advantage, but also by a mission to spread a French vision of civilization (including Christianity). The expansionist efforts of French colonizers inevitably resulted in political and cultural conflict as they encountered a remarkably diverse array of indigenous peoples. As we shall see, the legacy of those colonial conflicts persists to the present day.

France has political and cultural roots in traditional Catholicism that go back to the Roman Empire. But the relationship of faith and culture has always been uneasy. As we discuss later in the chapter, the French Revolution (1789–1799), which included a series of severe actions against the Catholic Church and other faiths, sent France down a path of considerable governmental control of religious institutions and behavior. Moreover, modern French society has become less religiously observant and more permissive than the Catholic Church on a range of issues, especially pertaining to sexuality and marriage. This cultural change poses its own challenge of pluralism for conservative religious believers.

Nevertheless, Catholicism maintains a cultural resonance in France. Over 60 percent of French citizens claim an affiliation with the Roman Catholic Church.[5] No other religious tradition comes close to that percentage of the population, and indeed the long history of Catholic predominance means that modern France had little experience with serious religious diversity until recent decades. Islam is second in size and growing in numbers and influence. In 2010, the best estimates placed the Muslim population in France at 7.5 percent, with a projected increase to nearly 11 percent within the next several decades due to higher-than-average fertility rates and expected migration.[6] While France has the third-highest Jewish population in the world (475,000 core members),[7] that ranking reflects the wide global dispersion of the Jewish Diaspora. In reality, Jews, Protestants, and other faith adherents comprise very small proportions of the French population.

At 28 percent, the second-largest religion-based grouping are those French residents who claim no affiliation at all—a group the Pew Research Center projects will become the largest religion-related demographic by

2050.[8] Some declining indicators within the Catholic Church over the past fifteen years anticipate the future growth in the nonaffiliated. In 1990, the Church reported 471,130 baptisms; by 2012, the number had slipped to 290,282. The Church has experienced similar erosion in other important aspects of life in the church, including confirmations, marriages, and admissions into the priesthood and religious orders.[9]

Even those who claim an affiliation do not always behave as if they have one. Self-identified Catholics in France have one of the lowest rates of Mass attendance in the world. Approximately 10 percent of French Catholics attend Mass at least weekly.[10] While Muslims in France have higher rates of religious participation than Catholics, their profile is not monolithic. In general, well under half of French Muslims engage in daily prayer or attend mosque regularly, and they are less active than Muslims elsewhere in Europe.[11] The French people on the whole also appear to recognize a diminishing influence of religion in their own lives; only about 13 percent say that religion is "very important" to them. These numbers reflect a long-term decline of religious practice and efficacy throughout Europe.[12]

Still, there are pockets of devotion and even religious resurgence in French public life. Some younger Muslims, for example, appear to be recommitting to their faith.[13] Jérôme Fourquet, senior demographer at France's premier opinion polling firm (*Institut français d'opinion publique,* or IFOP), tells us:

> We don't have a decline in Muslim religious practice and therefore for the time being there is no strong secularization movement. This is explained especially by an identity revival ("Muslim pride") among part of the Muslim youth who are more attached than twenty years ago to Ramadan, to prayer, and to religious prohibitions.[14]

The pattern is too focused on a subset of the population to call an intergenerational revival, but the response of Muslim youth to their experience of life in what some call a postreligion (or at least post-Christian) environment does reflect the persistent draw of religion as a source of purpose and community.

Some younger Catholics might be heading down a similar path with their own convictions and practices. *Le Figaro*, France's largest center-right newspaper, recently identified a "silent revolution" of *néocatholiques* within the contemporary church.[15] This new generation of Catholics finds itself responding to a variety of currents within French culture: the outright hostility toward religion from those who hold to long-standing secular orthodoxies; the new emergence of Islam as a competitor in the religious marketplace; and, ironically, the model of "openness" in the Catholic Church itself, which some Catholics believe has unmoored the faith from traditional doctrines on family life and education. Perhaps the most important effort of these *néo-*

catholiques is their pushback on same-sex marriage, which was legalized in France in 2013. Catholics were key leaders in La manif pour tous (The Protest for Everyone), which organized street protests and, by most accounts, won concessions from the French government on gay adoption and surrogacy.[16]

The concerns among *néocatholiques* point to broader anxieties about societal disruption and decay in French culture. Much of that anxiety has been triggered by Muslim immigration into France and a widespread perception that assimilation is failing. Michel Houellebecq's novel *Submission* (*Soumission*),[17] a 2015 bestseller published uncannily on the same day as the *Charlie Hebdo* attack, illustrates these concerns in an irreverently satirical mode. He imagines a patriarchal Muslim party, aided by the French center-left, gaining power in 2022 and enacting sweeping changes to French society. While the book uses fears of conservative Islam as a plot device, it also provoked extensive public discussion about cultural indifference and lack of solidarity among the French people.

It is not incidental that Houellebecq emphasizes the role of the state in shaping culture. Since the French Revolution, France has quite intentionally used its political system to foster its version of "Republicanism," a mode of thought and practice that emphasizes individual liberty and equality within the confines of a tightly unified political community. We will have more to say about French Republicanism later in the chapter, but it is first important to highlight a few features of the French state.

The Constitution of the Fifth Republic,[18] established in 1958 under the leadership of Charles de Gaulle, is the blueprint for the organization of the current French state. In formal terms, the French system is semipresidential. While the president, who is elected directly for a five-year term, heads the executive branch, the key executive power is shared collectively among the president, prime minister, and other leaders in the Council of Ministers. The Government of the French Republic is the bureaucratic apparatus that administers policy under the leadership of the Council. In a technical sense, French presidents appoint the prime minister and other executives, but presidents are checked by the legislature (which can dissolve the Government) and prime ministers themselves (who generally present a slate of acceptable ministers to the president). The legislative power lies in a bicameral parliament composed of the National Assembly (*Assemblée Nationale*) and the Senate. The Senate's powers are more limited than the Assembly's, in large part because the power to dismiss (and therefore, in effect, to select) the Government lies entirely with the Assembly.

France has a robust—and fractious—multiparty system that frequently requires coalition governments. In recent decades, the Socialist Party (*Parti Socialiste*) has led the center-left alliance, while the Republicans (*Les Républicains*) have brought together smaller center-right parties under its umbrella.[19] The more controversial National Front, a right-wing populist party known for its skepticism about the European Union and opposition to immigration, has recently made inroads into the French legislature. Mergers of smaller parties are quite common, as are power transitions between center-left and center-right parties. François Hollande, a Socialist, is currently the French president, succeeding Nicolas Sarkozy, a leader in the Republican party, who served from 2007 to 2015.

Unlike the Netherlands and Germany, France has struggled to establish a strong Christian democratic party. There is some irony in that struggle: Christian democratic parties sprung up around Europe partly in response to the French Revolution, which had raised great concerns about the political prospects of the Catholic Church well beyond the borders of France. The response in the Netherlands, Germany, and elsewhere was to establish parties that would give Catholics (and other Christians) a seat at the political table. But the conditions for French Catholics, who faced a greater existential threat after the Revolution than Catholics in other countries, were not as ripe for party building.[20]

France uses a civil law system, which emphasizes comprehensive compilations of statutes and other legal rules, and does not give judicial rulings authority as legal "precedent." While civil law systems trace their history to ancient Rome, the Civil Code of modern France, which was first promulgated in 1804 under Napoleon, has the unmistakable imprint of Enlightenment and Revolutionary ideas. Under civil law, the role of a judge is to determine facts in a dispute and apply the provisions of the appropriate code. The French Civil Code is distinct from the common law system of England and its colonies, where a judge's decision in one case is recorded and applied as a legitimate authority to later cases with similar legal questions. As we saw in the chapter on the United States, the result is that judicial decisions in common law systems are much more important in shaping the development of law pertaining to church-state relations and religious liberty. In France, the highest constitutional body—the Constitutional Council—generally considers the constitutionality of *proposed* legislation. But the Council is not a court; it does not hear disputes or appeals from citizens. When citizens raise concerns about how government treats religion, the dispute is generally settled through administrative review under the auspices of the Council of State.

HISTORICAL BACKGROUND

These contemporary patterns in French identity and institutions are important features of any account of church-state relations. But they are also embedded in a deep history. Indeed, many French citizens think explicitly about the implications of France's history when they discuss current events, including the role of religion in public life. Like the other countries in this book, the contemporary French landscape is a blur without a sense of how the religious people and institutions have interacted with the state over time.

In France the relevant church-state history stretches over millennia. The Roman Empire ruled "Gaul," which included the territory that constitutes modern-day France, from the first century B.C.E. until the Empire's fall to Germanic invaders five centuries later. The result of the collapse of the Empire was centuries of political fragmentation and competition among various claimants to monarchical power. The Catholic Church, however, remained a source of social stability for ordinary people. Most new ruling houses, in their struggle to consolidate power, embraced the idea of France as "the eldest daughter of the Church" and attempted to use their association with the faith to their advantage. Small populations of Jews and Muslims lived in France as early as the eighth century, but they existed on the edges of a French society.

France emerged into the early modern period as an ascendant European power with a distinctive language and identifiable territorial borders. Sometimes called the Ancien Régime (Old Regime), the political and social structure of the 1500s to 1789 was organized around distinct aristocratic orders called estates. Catholic clergy occupied the First Estate; the nobility (which included the monarch) and laboring class occupied the Second and Third Estates, respectively. While the king of France enjoyed most of the power in this arrangement, the Church's role in the estates system and its support for the aristocracy was an indispensable form of mutual church-state support. The Church was embedded in French culture in countless other ways as well. It kept registries of all births, deaths, and marriages, and baptism into the French Catholic Church was widely used as a signifier of French nationality. Catholic orders provided virtually all education and health care, with substantial monetary endowments from the nobility. Ecclesial property holdings were extensive; the Church and many of the clergy were indeed quite wealthy.

Catholicism's interweaving into French politics, economics, and culture helps explain the state's severe persecution of religious competitors. The small number of Jews, for example, endured centuries of state vacillation about their status; in some eras and regions they were tolerated or even accepted, in others shunned, expelled, or forced to convert. The Huguenots were another minority—in this case French Calvinists—who incurred a special measure of the state's wrath during the Protestant Reformation of the sixteenth century. The sporadic yet intense violence of this time period, sometimes called the French Wars of Religion, often pitted groups of Catholics and Protestants with loyalties to different leaders in the nobility. The most infamous event was St. Bartholomew's massacre (1572), a series of assassinations of Huguenot leaders that cascaded into mob violence, leaving thousands of Protestants dead. King Henry IV attempted to quell the violence by issuing the Edict of Nantes (1598), which introduced some level of tolerance for aggrieved Protestants. While the Edict's implementation was uneven, and it was weakened and eventually revoked by Louis XIV, it did introduce the possibility of accommodation of religious minorities within the French church-state system.

The French Revolution (1789–1799) was the watershed moment for modern France that uprooted the Old Regime. Revolutions, of course, seek to overturn old institutions and cultures in favor of new innovations. The revolutionaries in France, fueled by Enlightenment-era ideas about reason, equality, and the injustice of imposed authority, targeted the twin institutions of the monarchy and the Catholic Church, replacing them with what they understood as a "Republican" vision. The causes of this revolutionary movement—crushing debt, cultural polarization, failing agriculture, class distinctions, political mismanagement, even religion itself—are the subject of a great deal of debate among historians.[21] But the effects on the French societal structure were often brutally clear.

The French Republicans argued that society is not sustainable without conformity around basic values, a commitment to the same first principles among all citizens. The state, as a guardian of social cohesion and stability, has a key stake in fostering agreement on those values. The state, therefore, ought to have a direct formative relationship with citizens, and that relationship results in a deep skepticism about other types of associations that might intervene between the state and its citizens. Even before the French Revolution, this Republican perspective on the role of the state was an important strain in French political thought. It is exemplified by Jean-Jacques Rousseau (1712–1778), an Enlightenment thinker whose ideas profoundly influenced the Revolution. Rousseau advocated a radically egalitarian notion of a social contract in which citizens come to share a vision of the common good (what he called the "general will"). He also argued that the shared vision must be socialized through a "civil religion," a "purely civil profession of faith, the articles of which it is a duty of the sovereign to determine, not exactly as dogmas of [traditional] religion, but as sentiments of sociability, without which it is impossible to be a good citizen or faithful subject."[22] The civil religion might supplant or complement Christianity or other traditional faiths, but whatever its form, Rousseau thought history teaches that the state's imposition of a distinctive religion of the citizen was a necessary feature of any sustainable political system.

The French Revolution articulated a vision of equality, liberty, and community most famously in the Declaration of the Rights of Man and of the Citizen (1789), the sacred text, so to speak, of the new civil religion of Republicanism. The French Declaration is in many ways similar to Anglo-American analogues; it includes freedoms also found in the English Bill of

Rights (1689) and the U.S. Bill of Rights (written in the same year as the French Declaration). But the French Declaration frames these freedoms within a strong avowal of universal equality in its first article, which forbade all "social distinctions" unless they serve the common good (neither the British nor American bill of rights has a similar statement); and it also carefully describes an individual's liberty as subject to the "general will" of the political community.[23]

A crucial question for French Republicans is how to use the state to integrate people most effectively into the common vision. It might require, for example, state-supported education that forms citizens in certain ways—an area with enormous implications for religion, as we shall see. But integration into a new vision might also mean suppressing institutions that are too closely associated with old (and, for the revolutionaries, obstructionist) ideas. Because the Church and nobility—the first and second estates of the Old Regime—were precisely that type of institution, they were beset by the revolutionaries, even to the point of extreme violence.

One of the most notorious aspects of the Revolution was its process of "dechristianization." In its early stages, the Revolution began to dismantle many resources that gave the Catholic Church independence as well as privileges that linked the Church to the state. The revolutionary government ended the mandatory tithe, confiscated and nationalized Church property (both lands and endowments), shut down religious orders and forbade monastic vows, subjected clergy to local elections (in which non-Catholics had a right to vote), and required that clergy swear loyalty to the new order, under threat of severe persecution. In effect, clergy became state employees. As the Revolution heated up, the treatment of the Catholic clergy and institutions worsened. Revolutionaries imprisoned, deported, or simply murdered scores of priests. The Christian calendar was rewritten, Church buildings were desecrated and stripped of explicitly Christian symbols, and some houses of worship—including the famous Notre Dame de Paris—were repurposed as Enlightenment-style "temples of reason."

Many citizens recoiled at the hostile treatment of a cultural institution that had shaped French identity for centuries. Eventually the most egregious forms of anticlericalism ended with the Concordat of 1801, a conciliatory agreement between Napoleon (the French dictator who came to power in the wake of the Revolution) and Pope Pius VII. While the pope gave up his claims to confiscated Church property, the Napoleonic state recognized the special status of the Church (without declaring a state religion) and committed to pay the salaries of clergy. It is also important to remember the *relative* improvement during this period for religious minorities. Napoleon recognized the rights of Protestants and Jews, following the pattern of the Revolution. Jews, for example, had been emancipated in 1791 and given full privi-

leges of citizenship (though Jewish communities in some regions were terror-
ized at the worst moments of the Revolution).[24]

Despite the rapprochement between Napoleon and Pius and the improv-
ing status of minorities, the French Revolution had introduced a tension
between those who saw unifying potential in religious faith and others who
saw religion as an impediment to a uniquely French version of Republicanism. Many on the former side were Catholics or sympathetic to old-regime
aristocracy; many on the other were new-school Republicans, some ardently
anticlerical, and others, like the Catholic priest Henri Grégoire, religious
believers who held to both spiritual sentiments and revolutionary sympathies
with equal fervor. The nineteenth century was full of too many conflicts
between these "two Frances" to recount here, but suffice to say that the
Catholic Church was repeatedly on the losing side of the battles. Perhaps the
best example was the school reforms of the 1880s—the so-called Ferry laws,
after Minister of Public Instruction Jules Ferry—that required teachers in
public schools to be laypersons, not clergy, and to teach only secular subjects. (France still retained nonpublic Catholic schools.) Religious instruction
was relegated to one day a week.

Some prominent instances of interfaith conflict in the nineteenth century
highlight the underlying tensions over the status of the Catholic Church. The
Dreyfus Affair at the end of the nineteenth century is the most scandalous
example. Alfred Dreyfus was a Jewish officer in the French artillery, a symbol, at least on the surface, of the Revolution's detaching of public roles from
social distinctions. But after his false conviction for treason, he became an
icon of the persistent undercurrent of institutionalized anti-Semitism. That
prejudice was certainly prevalent in the French military; it was less clearly so
in the Catholic Church, at least in Dreyfus's case.[25] But whether anti-Semitic
Catholics were actually partially responsible for Dreyfus's conviction is be-
side the point; for many French Republicans with anticlerical leanings, the
complicity of Catholics in the Dreyfus Affair became the central theme of the
story they told about the injustice Dreyfus endured.

The state began developing a more comprehensive legal framework for
church-state relations in the early twentieth century. A Law on Associations
in 1901 provided a legal basis for forming voluntary associations that served
a "public utility," but the new policy had the effect of harming Catholic
institutions, especially those religious orders that had trouble obtaining per-
mission to operate with a dual function as spiritual centers and educators of
French youth. Many religious orders were expelled and thousands of Catholic schools closed. Then, in 1905, the National Assembly passed a Law on
Separation of Church and State, which breached the Concordat of 1801. The
Law on Separation (and subsequent legislation) ended public funding of
faith-based schools, expropriated existing religious buildings and shifted
their ownership to local and national governments, and banned display of

religious words and symbols on public buildings.[26] Both laws remain in force today.

In theory, the goal of these early twentieth-century laws was to reinforce the independent French Republican vision by separating the state from the church. Many architects of this new legal regime claimed their guiding principle was neutrality toward religion; all religions would be treated similarly under the new framework (even if the motivation of some advocates was decidedly antireligious). In practice, however, the laws led to a complex hodgepodge of church-state policies that are hard to square with the concept of neutrality. Because the state now owned just those church buildings that existed at the time, which were mostly Catholic, it was on the hook for subsidizing one religion out of proportion to newer arrivals. Moreover, the policy on voluntary associations effectively relegated churches and religious orders to a private sphere of worship; if some organs of the Church wished to be in the business of education or social service, they would need to reorganize as separate "cultural" voluntary associations under close control of the state. We have more to say about these arrangements in later sections.

THE FREE EXERCISE OF RELIGION

This history of state control of religious behavior and associations may appear to contradict France's stated commitment to religious freedom in its Constitution and other basic documents. Article 1 of the preamble of the French Constitution expresses fundamental law on religious freedom:

> [The French Republic] shall ensure the equality of all citizens before the law, without distinction of origin, race or religion. It shall respect all beliefs.[27]

While the preamble starts with a strong statement of equal treatment, it does not preclude treating all religions equally badly. But the second sentence, by declaring the state's respect of all beliefs, appears to prevent the outcome of equal-opportunity state oppression. Moreover, the constitutional preamble asserts that the "French people proclaim their attachments" to several fundamental principles laid out in antecedent documents, including the French Declaration of 1789 and the 1946 version of the Constitution. The French Constitutional Council, which has the power to scrutinize proposed laws for constitutional concerns, explicitly granted constitutional authority to the preambles of both of these documents.[28] Article 10 of the French Declaration is a particularly important signpost in modern church-state relations in France. It states:

No one must be disturbed because of his opinions, even in religious matters, provided their expression does not trouble the public order established by law.[29]

While this provision acknowledges that religious freedom is not an absolute—and there is indeed much room for interpretation in what it means to "trouble the public order," as we shall see—the basic idea is that the state should leave alone the orderly expression of religious belief ("opinions").

France is also signatory to various international and European covenants that support religious liberty. Article 9 of the European Convention on Human Rights, for example, asserts the following:

Everyone has the right to freedom of thought, conscience, and religion; this right includes freedom to change his religion or belief and freedom, either alone or in community with others and in public and private, to manifest his religion or belief, in worship, teaching, practice, and observance.[30]

Here the language is more explicitly oriented around a legal right to religious practice, which the Article acknowledges can include both individual and communal components (e.g., private prayers and public worship) and both private and public dimensions. These are important points of contention in the French approach to church-state relations.

So does French history belie these formal legal commitments? The answer depends on how one understands *laïcité*, the term that has come to encapsulate the French concept of church-state relations and religious freedom. It is important to note the meaning of the term is difficult to render in English, and besides, as anthropologist John Bowen suggests, the term's definition has no consensus in France itself. "In France's very recent history," he writes, "*laïcité* has become one of those 'essentially contested concepts,' such as 'freedom' and 'equality,' that provide resources for arguments, not starting points for agreement."[31] For some, *laïcité* is synonymous with a thorough "secularism,"[32] even to the point of taking on an antireligious cast. But many advocates of *laïcité* either do not reject religion per se or they do reject religion yet see a point to allowing it to flourish in a limited way. Others see *laïcité* with the narrower connotation of "separation of church and state." But that rendering is also somewhat imprecise or misleading to North American ears. France's idea of separation assumes a public-private distinction that is not as stark in the United States, where many people see no problem with public expressions of faith, even if they recoil at direct state support for religious institutions.

We define *laïcité* as separation of religion from influence over a secularized public sphere. In this sense *laïcité* introduces a distinction between public and private with profound implications for both institutions and individuals. In institutional terms, *laïcité* requires that organized religion remain, as Bowen puts it, "bounded, orderly, constrained in its buildings and defined by worship practices in those buildings."[33] Spiritual practices—the lived experience of faith—should stay in the private domain. To bring religious faith out of these private spaces into public life is an affront to the Republican vision of unity around common, not particular, values. Nicolas Sarkozy, serving as interior minister in 2003, put it this way: "freedom is the rule in the private sphere; Republican conformity is the rule in the public sphere."[34]

So to return to a revised version of our question: Does the idea of "Republican conformity . . . in the public sphere" violate France's own legal commitments in its Declaration, Constitution, and international agreements? Jean Bauberot, a prominent French historian of *laïcité,* provides some guidance. He argues that the post-Revolution history of church-state relations reflects two approaches to religion. On the one hand, the French Declaration endorses what both Anglo-American and continental European traditions have called a "freedom of conscience," a protection of personal obligations and attitudes—or, as the 1958 Constitution puts it, "beliefs"—against governmental intrusion. On the other hand, that same freedom might lead to a plurality of religious expressions, which becomes a risk to the bedrock goal of national unity in the French Republic.[35]

The solution is the Declaration's proviso that beliefs may not become actions that threaten "public order" (as the law defines "order"). And, as Article 1 of the Constitution implies, the state can regulate those beliefs as long as it treats them equally ("without distinction"). The result is that the *private* practice of belief is widely tolerated. But conspicuous practice of religion in the public sphere—in public sector jobs, in schools, even in the streets—is often subjected to curtailment and even prohibition. Hence, when the 1958 Constitution begins by asserting that France is an "indivisible, secular [*laïque*], democratic, and social Republic," the "secular" modifier refers especially to the experience of French people when they meet each other as Republican citizens in the public square. As citizens, their interactions should be secular, or nonreligious. In this sense a public secularism is embedded in the consensual values of the French Republic.

FREE EXERCISE AND ISLAM IN FRANCE: A CASE STUDY

Nowhere is this approach to religious freedom better illustrated—or more prominently challenged—than the treatment of Muslim immigrants and their descendants. French authorities resist collecting data about the ethnic or religious composition of the population, which requires making social distinctions that violate the Republican value of *égalité.*[36] The official census does keep country-of-origin statistics, however, and they tell a story of a multiethnic France, especially in comparison to other European states. Today, approximately 9 percent of residents in metropolitan France are foreign born without a French parent. Of these immigrants, 30 percent came from North Africa, 14 percent from sub-Saharan Africa, and 4 percent from Turkey.[37] France's Muslim immigrants, perhaps totaling as many as three million residents, come primarily from Algeria, Tunisia, and Morocco, three of France's former colonies in North Africa.[38]

Muslims have had a small and intermittent presence in France for centuries, but their numbers and permanency increased after France gained control of several colonies with large Muslim populations.[39] The most prominent example is Algeria, which France acquired by conquest in 1830. The flow of these colonized peoples into France was largely the result of labor needs, especially as migrant workers provided a crucial supplement to the French labor force during World Wars I and II. The French state even recognized the efforts of Muslim workers—and, in thousands of cases, soldiers—in World War I by building the Great Mosque of Paris in 1926. Immigration accelerated after World War II due to continued labor needs as France rebuilt; it increased again as France took in refugees from the brutal Algerian War of Independence (1954–1962). Most workers or displaced persons came from Turkey or North Africa.

Few expected that the demand for foreign-born labor would be permanent, not least the workers themselves. Yet, over time, many migrants began to put down roots in metropolitan France.[40] They began to transition, slowly yet inexorably, from what political scientist Jonathan Laurence calls a "majority-immigrant" group to a "majority-citizen" one.[41] But the French state, with its long history of dealing primarily with a single, culturally dominant faith tradition, did not have a playbook for this new challenge of pluralism. French leaders confronted longtime residents and emerging citizens who did not share the predominant ethnic, linguistic, or religious characteristics of the population as a whole.

The response was multipronged, though not particularly systematic. Some leaders emphasized integration; others pushed exclusion (through stricter residency requirements) and deportation.[42] Their policy efforts frequently led to vigorous pushback from affected groups, even to the point of violence in the streets. In 2005, for example, a police investigation that turned deadly ignited tensions over unemployment and French policing tactics, resulting in three weeks of intense youth rioting in suburban Paris and elsewhere in France. The North African identity of most participants suggested that a combination of race and religion contributed to their alienation and violence. French leaders took the opportunity to implement and propose stricter controls on immigration.[43] The experience was the occasion for a great deal of public soul-searching and social scientific inquiry in the disaffection of young people from ethnic and religious minorities.[44]

So how does *laïcité* frame these debates over integration and ethnorelig-ious diversity in France? Consider a case study of the ban on face coverings (later we will explore a somewhat similar issue of headscarves in schools). In 2010, at the urging of President Sarkozy, the French legislature passed legis-lation that prohibited concealment of the face in public spaces.[45] On the surface, the law was written in neutral terms because it prohibits *any* conceal-ment; in fact, it names no particular form of covering that violates the ban, which presumably also covers some visors on motorcycle helmets or the full body suits worn by street performers. But the ban is widely perceived as targeting the practice of some Muslim women who wear the *niqab*, *burqa*, or other masking clothing. Violators face a fine or, fittingly, a class in citizen-ship. When critics called out the obvious implications for the faithful practice of some Muslim women, proponents retorted that covering the face in public violates principles of both gender equality and *laïcité*.

It is a measure of the powerful cultural influence of *laïcité* that French citizens supported the ban overwhelmingly. The Pew Research Center found that 82 percent of the population approved, with strong majorities across all age, class, and ideological demographics. This finding contrasted with under a third of Americans who would support a similar ban.[46] The French parlia-ment passed the law with equally impressive majorities (though the Council of State, in reviewing possible legislation, did express hesitation). Even some Muslim leaders, including the rector of the Great Mosque of Paris, offered tepid support for the arguments behind the ban, even if they did not wish to fully endorse it.[47]

The ban faced a new twist when it was challenged in the European Court of Human Rights (ECtHR) in 2014. The ECtHR takes up disputes when residents in European countries allege that their rights have been violated under the European Convention on Human Rights (ECHR). We will see in later chapters on the Netherlands, Germany, and the United Kingdom that international covenants such as the ECHR are increasingly coming into ten-sion with domestic approaches to religious freedom. In this case, a woman, identified pseudonymously as "S.A.S.," claimed the face-covering ban vio-lated Article 9 of the Convention (the "freedom of thought, conscience, and religion" article), among other provisions. The French state responded that Article 9 allows governmental restrictions on religious exercise when they "are prescribed by law and necessary in a democratic society in the interests of public safety, for the protection of public order, health or morals, or for the protection of the rights and freedoms of others." The ECtHR's ruling rejected arguments from gender equality and human dignity, which France proffered in its defense. But the court did accept a third argument that was characteris-tically French: the ban encouraged a particular way for citizens to "live together" (*le vivre ensemble*) in "democratic society." The judges agreed this claim was a "legitimate aim" of the French state.[48]

The law on face covering affected directly just a couple of thousand Muslim women in France, but the extent of its reach was less important than its underlying principles and symbolic politics. A similar point could be made about the efforts of French authorities to regulate "cults" (*secte*) during this same period of time. But there is a key difference. While certain behaviors might be treated as simply incompatible with *laïcité*, Islam itself is widely recognized as a traditional world religion that can operate, albeit uneasily, in French culture. In fact, three-quarters of the French people generally have a favorable view of Muslims in their country, even after recent attacks.[49] "Cults" are a different category. Over the past few decades, numerous parliamentary reports and state monitoring agencies have identified groups, practices, and financing networks that have been associated with the controversial label of "cult."[50] In 2001, the French parliament passed into law a series of restrictions on religious movements that have been implicated in criminal activity, but listed broad categories of "psychological . . . subjection" and "fraudulent abuse of a state of ignorance or weakness" among punishable offenses.[51] The law prompted widespread concerns about religious freedom, and particularly about the breadth and ambiguity in the law; both the U.S. State Department and the Council of Europe weighed in with reservations.[52] But the overall point is the same as bans of face coverings: new religious movements that live on the periphery of society or refuse to conform are open to legal challenges to their very existence.

And this question of the peripheral nature of Islam in France is important. On the one hand, French Muslims are a sizable minority with at least abstract support from their compatriots. On the other hand, devout Muslims (not unlike religionists of other faiths) are often committed to particularistic beliefs and practices that put them in conflict with dominant cultural values and go well beyond veiling. What should the state do with other forms of religiously inspired dress that do *not* cover the face but are nevertheless framed as a security concern? As we saw at the beginning of the chapter, the mayor of Cannes raised precisely that question when he banned the burkini from city beaches (we will raise the question again shortly in our discussion of headscarves in schools). And the questions go beyond conspicuous religious dress. How should the state handle the traditionalist Islamic perspective on marriage, which can seem archaic in light of contemporary French norms on gender and family? How should the state address the introduction of new mosques into urban areas, especially in light of its support for Catholic and other religious institutions? And how should the state accommodate increasing calls to integrate Islamic schools into the mix of state-sanctioned educational options? These are active challenges posed by the presence of devout Muslims.

Bowen suggests the recent trends are not especially inviting to Muslims with strong religious commitments. "We are, I think, witnessing a tightening of the value-screws, a stronger rejection of pluralism in the name of national integration." He deepens the point: "But value pluralism in associational life, in religious circles, and in the family, is precisely what allowed France to 'integrate' Catholics, Protestants, and Jews into the Republic—to preserve a heritage and a set of religious beliefs (including decidedly non-gender-equal ones) in social life, and on the basis of that associational base, to embrace . . . the principles of public . . . life in the Republic."[53] The problem is that it is nearly impossible to maintain a pluralism in private when citizens cannot reconcile the pervasive requirements of their faith with the compartmentaliz-ing expectations of their political culture. Perhaps this helps explain the growing popularity of ideas that intrude even on that private space, such as the call of Marine Le Pen, the leader of the French National Front, to close "radical" mosques and to ban the building of new ones.[54]

The political scientist Jonathan Laurence sees a glimmer of hope in inte-grating French (and other European) Muslims through formal mechanisms that provide opportunities for consultation between Muslim leaders and the state.[55] He is especially optimistic about the rise of Islamic Councils through-out Europe, including the French Council of the Muslim Religion (*Conseil Français du culte musulman*, or CFCM), established in 2003 at Sarkozy's urging.[56] The point of the CFCM is to provide state officials access to key Muslim leaders for consultation over state policy that affects the Muslim religion and for communication when conflicts over religious norms and practices inevitably arise. The model is a historical fit for a French govern-ment that is accustomed to negotiating with the Catholic Church, which has clear lines of authority embedded in obvious institutional structures. Islam does not always have such lines of authority, or at least those lines can be diffuse when various ethnic groups practice Islam in their own distinctive ways. France has seen a host of Islamic federations and other groups come and go, and they have often competed with each other for public relevance.[57] These associations are often connected to transnational Muslim groups, which complicates their relationship to a state that has become suspicious about foreign culpability in the radicalization of some French Muslims. In effect, the CFCM creates a line of authority under the auspices of the French state, if only for purposes of political communication and consultation.

But this strategy of integration comes with costs. First, it is always an open question whether ordinary Muslims will accept that their appointed leaders speak with the authority of the faithful. For many rank-and-file Mus-lims, the leaders at CFCM might simply look co-opted by the government, mere tools of a sometimes oppressive French state. State and CFCM leaders have sidestepped this concern by insisting that CFCM represents the Muslim *religion*, not self-identified Muslims themselves.[58] CFCM's goal is to con-sult with the state to craft and help implement general policy that can accom-modate the unique practices and norms of Islam as a faith tradition, including prayer spaces, dietary requirements, the training of French imams and other religious leaders, and so on. CFCM does not represent the interests of individual French Muslims.

Second, the state itself might demand that its recognition of Islam's "seat at the table" comes with implicit expectations that French Muslims play by the rules of *laïcité*. In his broader discussion of European Muslims, Laurence puts it this way:

> European Muslims are experiencing . . . a dual movement of expanding religious liberty and increasing control exerted over religion. Every religious community that has joined the national fabric accepted certain restrictions on its freedoms and autonomy at the moment of recognition: from the use of local clergy who preach in the local language, to abandoning distinctive dress in the public sphere. As Muslims are transitioning from a majority-immigrant to majority-citizen group, European states have begun the effort to relieve what they consider excessive pressures of foreign political or religious influences. This dual movement is most visible in the officially encouraged "privatization" of religious practices. [59]

French Muslims will not integrate without the state's engagement and fair treatment. Hence the introduction of the CFCM and the state's pains to suggest that recent actions against veiling are religiously "neutral." But the cost of full citizenship is that French Muslims will need to cast off their "foreign" cultural legacies and embrace the Republican vision, even with its privatizing effects. Most Catholics, Protestants, and Jews did it, however grudgingly; the same demands are now on Muslims.

CHURCH, STATE, AND EDUCATION

The 2010 law on face covering was really just the latest skirmish in an ongoing series of battles about religious dress and other symbols in the public square. Not surprisingly, schools are often the battlefields. Or to switch metaphors: French schools, as French president Jacques Chirac described them in a 2003 speech, are "Republican sanctuaries."[60] The description of schools in a religious way is not quite metaphorical. It evokes the idea of French Republicanism as a civil religion, and like any religion it needs set-aside spaces to transmit itself across generations. Schools are the sanctuaries that nurture the Republican faith. The development of *laïcité* in the twentieth century requires that they remain free from competing theologies.

What happens, then, when a student wishes to express "private" religious sentiments in the public school, that sanctuary of Republicanism? Before the Ferry law of the 1880s, when education was almost entirely private (and privately funded), the question was moot. As the state developed public schools in the late nineteenth century, it embraced the opportunity for national integration, with the French language and republic citizenship as staples in the curriculum. This new mode of education set up myriad conflicts with students with deeply held religious particularities.

There is no more contentious illustration in the contemporary public school than the wearing of religious garb, which is treated with formal neutrality yet, as we saw with the face veil, clearly targets Muslim practice. The question of the status of the Muslim *hijab* (headscarf) in schools has attracted controversy since the so-called Scarf Affair (*affaire du foulard*) in 1989. A headmaster at a public middle school in a Paris suburb suspended several Muslim students for refusing to comply with his order to remove their *hijabs* on school grounds. After some effort at compromise, the situation deteriorated, with the education minister and Council of State sending conflicting messages and various French leaders and intellectuals taking sides. The result was a great deal of variation across the country in school policies on the *hijab* and an intense public debate. Pro-ban advocates argue that *hijabs* represented a fundamental violation of *laïcité,* undermined the religious choices of Muslim girls, and reinforced structures that oppress women. The opposition claimed the ban violated the principle of freedom of conscience or reflected a colonial history of oppression of darker-skinned peoples.

Head coverings became a lightning rod for debates about the intersection of religion, ethnicity, gender, and French unity. In July 2003, President Jacques Chirac appointed a study committee called the Stasi Commission, named after its presiding official, Bernard Stasi, to seek resolution by reflecting on the contemporary meaning of *laïcité.* The result was a high-profile report[61] that became the basis of a law, enacted in 2004, prohibiting religious clothing in schools. Like the 2010 ban on face coverings in public space, the legislation was primarily concerned with the Muslim *hijab* and other coverings, even though the law was written in a religiously neutral way (the ban targeted "ostentatious" religious garb of any kind). It was also the only ban of its type in Europe at the time.

The controversy swirling around the headscarf ban is not merely a challenge to the legal structures summed up in the term *laïcité*; it is, at bottom, about the conditions for living together in community and socializing the young to accept those conditions. Those Muslim girls and their parents who resisted the headmaster in 1989, or those who have fled public schools in the wake of the 2004 law, are challenging the basic conditions of French Republicanism with a competing claim to identity. The same arguments apply over everything from the national curriculum, which forbids religious instruction of any kind, to serving pork in public school cafeterias.[62] (Gilles Platret, mayor of Chalon-sur-Saone, tweeted joyously about a "victory for *laïcité*" when a court upheld a controversial ban on pork alternatives in local school cafeterias.)

And these same arguments also apply beyond Muslim concerns. Jewish students frequently face conflicts over the school calendar, which often includes examinations and other activities on Saturdays, the Jewish Sabbath. (They have faced fewer problems with wearing the kippah, or Jewish skullcap, which is generally accepted as not "ostentatious" under the meaning of the head covering ban.) On some accounts, these conflicts reflect a set of deeper concerns about anti-Semitism and other forms of marginalization among French Jews, who are often part of ethnic and class enclaves on the edge of mainstream society and face considerable impediments to integration.[63]

The headscarf and similar controversies have to do with the status of religion in public schools. But another area of conflict over education pertains to the status of private religious schools. France has over 12.8 million students in primary and secondary schools.[64] Nearly 40,000 schools are public; another 8,600 are "private."[65] When schools are "public"—i.e., operated directly by the state—the process of education is relatively easily oriented toward the Republican vision. But private schools teach nearly 20 percent of French students—twice the percentage of students in the comparatively more religious United States[66] —and more than a third of all French students will attend a private school at some point in their primary and secondary education.[67] Over 90 percent of French private schools are Catholic,[68] which is both an obvious historical inheritance and a result of barriers to entry for other religious groups.[69]

How does *laïcité* apply when the schools are private and religious? The 1905 Law on Separation was a paradigmatic response to the concern that religion competes with Republican sensibilities. By relegating the Church to the private spiritual realm, it ensured that neither the teachers nor the public coffers would advance religion in the classroom. But Catholics and other supporters of religious education demurred, and the state's need for social support in the wake of World War I and II led to greater accommodations of faith-based schools. By 1959, the French government had crafted a compromise of sorts. The Debré law permitted religious schools to deliver religious instruction, provided it is voluntary for students. In addition, the state commits substantial funding, to the point that most private schools in France today charge only marginal fees. But in exchange private schools are required to teach the national curriculum and to admit students without regard to religion.

Periodic efforts to change the terms of the law have met a third rail of French politics, with massive resistance from across the ideological and religious spectrum. This may seem unexpected in a country where religious faith is in decline. But the fact is that parents often choose private schools less for their religious identity than their reputation for quality. While aggregate, broad-based data on public- versus private-school quality is either mixed or nonexistent,[70] the government's own data suggests that many of the top-ranked schools in France are private.[71] And in any case, the regulatory hurdles for Catholic and other private schools—rules against excluding non-Catholics, the involvement of the state in selection and assessment of teachers, state curricular and testing requirements—limit faith-based instruction.[72] In many instances state intervention also arguably changes that instruction fundamentally. Scholars have often suggested that Catholic schools have been secularized.[73]

Still, many French parents choose private schools because they provide a particular kind of character formation or refuge for their children. In some cases the religious identity of the school is indeed indispensable to parents. Some Jewish schools have maintained a strict religious devotion, which generates a tension between their internal cultural integrity and national integration.[74] Some Muslim schools have struggled to adapt to broader cultural norms on science and human sexuality.[75] Yet these schools remain in demand, if the supply problems are any indication. Muslims have had a particularly difficult experience meeting demand by establishing schools, and indeed until 2003 no high school associated with Islam had been authorized by French officials.[76] This demand without supply for Islamic schools has generated unexpected interfaith fraternity. Many embattled Muslim students have found a home in Catholic schools.[77] One of the ironies of these educational trends is that for some students French public schools are far from a "sanctuary"; they seek alternatives as a refuge.

CHURCH, STATE, AND NONPROFIT COMMUNITY SERVICE ORGANIZATIONS

The school debates in France point to a broader tension between civil society and the state. As we discuss in the first chapter, civil society is a set of voluntary associations that often mediates between individuals and the state. The idea is that labor unions, churches, and other groups have a collective influence that enables them to push back against state power in ways that individuals simply lack. This role assumes that civil society maintains an independence from the state; it would be difficult for civil society to perform a mediating role if the state co-opted and controlled associations in civil society.

In France, however, the state historically sought to dominate civil society. The Revolution, for example, treated the predominant associations of the day as vestiges of an oppressive past. The new Republican order would give citizens a direct relationship with their state; intermediary institutions were a threat to that relationship. We have already seen how the revolutionary regime disposed of the Church and its network of associations, but this kind of thinking was extended to other sectors of civil society as well. The Le Chapelier law, passed by the National Assembly in 1791, dismantled the guilds and forbade the right to collection action through labor strikes, citing the Republican ideal of citizens engaging each other directly in a spirit of free exchange. The law enraged working-class citizens (the *sans-culottes*) who had partnered with revolutionary leaders, but it is evidence of the Jacobin fervor of the time that the law persisted (even at the risk of the eventual loss of working-class support). Indeed, the right to collectivize and strike, so much a staple of French society today, was not reinstated until 1884.

The pattern of statist control of associationalism runs even deeper than the Revolution. Edith Archambault, a leading French scholar of the "third sector," puts the point baldly:

> *Etatism* is no doubt the most important feature in French history. The millennial fight of the central state against local power in any form is at the root of French etatism. This was a fight against the feudal order, against urban citizens' organizations during the Middle Ages, against regional governments and religious minorities during the Old Regime, against the Church and its nonprofit appendices and against guilds during the French Revolution. During the 19th century, it was a fight against the labor movement and against political clubs.[78]

The Revolution turned this antiassociationalism into a story of egalitarianism, a gift to ordinary people who could engage the state directly as free and equal individuals without the mediating role of groups. But an unintended consequence of the Revolution's efforts at controlling and diminishing the influence of the Church was to reveal religion's social importance in the breach. Before the Revolution, the Catholic Church had been the central institution for social welfare, albeit within a complex network of support from the Second Estate. (Jewish social welfare organizations operated in parallel, but at a much smaller scale and with few resources from the nobility.) Local parishes and religious orders ran hospitals, orphanages, and schools with support from the nobility. The guilds created their own mutual aid societies that filled needs for their working-class members. The Revolution's dismantling of the Old Regime's aristocratic arrangements created a void of service that affected the poor and other vulnerable groups most acutely.[79] By the late nineteenth century, when the dehumanizing effects of the Industrial Revolution were in full view and Pope Leo XIII published *Rerum Novarum* (1891), his famous reflections on labor and poverty,[80] French leaders were turning to the Church for social support.

The 1901 Law on Associations and 1905 Law on Separation attempted simultaneously to retain and control the social service capacities of religion while compartmentalizing its spiritual components into the private sphere. Under this new legal regime, private associations could be publicly authorized, even if they had religious sensibilities, but they would be required to demonstrate their "public utility" to the central state. Archambault calls this a principle of "reverse subsidiarity,"[81] the opposite of the Catholic doctrine, first articulated publicly in *Rerum Novarum*, that social problems ought to be addressed by the lowest level of institutional competency. That doctrine has been used in Germany, the Netherlands, and the United States as a justification for decentralization and local decision making, anathema to the French *etatism* embedded in the 1905 law.

It was fortuitous for France, however, that the 1905 law left some room for religious associations to reinvent themselves, because their services were needed in response to the calamities of two world wars. During the same period of the early twentieth century, however, like many other western democracies, the French government was beginning to expand to provide a robust social safety net. The growth of the welfare state at midcentury pushed out or co-opted some of the competition from the nonprofit sector—the "laïcisation de la protection sociale."[82] Today, French residents receive "social protection" through state programs of minimum pensions, unemployment spending, and universal health provision, and many other basic services. Over 30 percent of France's GDP is spent on these programs of the welfare state, the highest of any advanced economy in the world.[83]

Despite the pressure of the growth of the welfare state, however, the relationship of the state and nonprofits over the past few decades has changed to greater partnership as the French state has experimented with decentralization of services.[84] While the trend began already in the late 1960s, a key moment came with the Decentralization Law of 1982, which shifted from the model of *etatism* to an emphasis on service provision through local agencies and voluntary associations. The new approach triggered a "renaissance of the non-profit sector,"[85] with a steady increase of annual registrations of associations beginning in 1970.[86] France may have as many as 1.3 million declared associations today, though most are sports, arts, and leisure clubs that operate without employees. Approximately 14 percent are focused on local economic development, health, residential care for the elderly, or humanitarian activities.[87] Survey data suggests about a fifth of French citizens are members of charitable or humanitarian groups, though only about half of those citizens are actively engaged.[88]

The standard explanation of what Jean-Pierre Worms calls the "co-development" of the welfare state and nonprofit organizations has been the decline in state resources, especially tax revenues, either due to economic downturns and/or conservative fiscal policy.[89] The argument is that welfare states with fewer resources will turn to the nonpublic sector to accomplish what government can no longer do on its own. Nonprofits fill the gaps left by a contracting welfare state. But there is also the counterargument that the French movement toward decentralization and greater reliance on the third sector coincided not so much with declining resources as a "crisis of state capacity," a loss of confidence in the ability of the welfare state to make good on its promises to address the increasingly complex demands of its citizens without the help of organizations that work closely with service recipients.[90] It is relevant that a Socialist, not neoconservative, government of the early 1980s gave nonprofits increasing responsibilities and the resources, both monetary and political, to match. These organizations did not fill a gap in the social welfare state; direct state expenditures on health, old-age insurance, unemployment, and the like continued to grow. Instead, nonprofit associations presided over growth in myriad other social services, from inner-city youth programs to migrant integration, that expanded the welfare state into new directions.

Faith-based organizations were poised to take the lead in this period of decentralization. The most prominent faith-based nonprofit in France is Secours Catholique, established in 1946 as the welfare state was reviving after World War II. It was state authorized (under the 1901 law) in 1962. It has adapted itself to decentralization by focusing on poverty reduction and aid to migrants with a goal of social integration. The organization serves hundreds of thousands of French residents a year through a network of sixty-two thousand volunteers distributed among dozens of local offices; it is aided by sophisticated data gathering and assessment.[91] The association appropriates the language of French Republicanism into its own mission statement, with allusions to "building a shared society," "fostering solidarity and fraternity," and "fighting against inequality."[92] The Fédération Entraide Protestante and Fonds Social Juif Unifié are networks of smaller Protestant and Jewish groups, respectively, that support social programming throughout France. Muslims have also established social service organizations, consistent with Islam's emphasis on charity, but many Muslim groups give more focus to securing religious prayer spaces, winning accommodations for dietary requirements in workplaces and schools, and other points of tension between Islam and the broader culture.[93]

This role for religious and other associations in civil society reveals an irony in the recent politics of the French welfare state. The political scientist Jonah Levy describes the increasing reliance of the French government on civil society as "Tocqueville's revenge."[94] Alexis de Tocqueville was a French social observer of the early-to-mid nineteenth century who wrote trenchantly about the French Revolution and emerging forms of democracy in the United States and elsewhere.[95] One of his theses was that the United States dealt with the many threats posed by democracy through the mediating effects of a large and rich set of associations with ties to religion and local community—and he worried about France's lack of similar networks. In his own study of France's process of welfare state devolution in the 1980s, Levy argues that the French government needed precisely those organizations of civil society that it had historically sought to diminish. It should not expect that civil society could rise up to meet the new challenges pushed its way without the government helping to build up society's capacity. For our purposes, the question is whether such active governmental capacity-building of civil society could include a serious place for religion in a state that is so deeply committed to separating religion from the public square.

CONCLUDING OBSERVATIONS

The modern French approach to church-state relations took shape with the attempt of French revolutionaries and their Republican heirs to diminish and contain the cultural influence of a previously dominant majority religion. Their efforts, enshrined in the concept of *laïcité,* have been effective in many respects, but not always in expected ways. And today the approach has been tested anew as the mechanisms of *laïcité* contend with the growing minority religion of Islam.

We argued in the previous chapter that the United States has a strong (though not exclusive) thread of separationism in its history of church-state relations. But the American version of separationism is largely institutional. The state is forbidden from supporting religion in tangible or symbolic ways that might associate government with any particular form(s) of religion or, for the strictest adherents, with religion in general. This separation of church and state, however, does not necessarily entail separation of religion and the public arena. Americans themselves say that they expect their leaders to be religious, echoing the self-reported importance of religion in their own lives. And private citizens or organizations are free to bring their own religious perspectives and behaviors into the public square. Private hospitals or social service organizations, for example, may display religious symbols or require clients to participate in worship services. As private citizens acting without the sponsorship of the state, children may generally wear religious garb or pray in public schools.

Separation in France moves beyond institutions to the cultural and ideological dimension. As political scientist Ahmet Kuru puts it, while the United States treats religion "passively," allowing religious symbols and arguments as part of public experience, France practices an "assertive secularism" (*laïcité de combat*) that actively excludes religion from the public square.[96] Compared to other countries in this study, France is, in this sense, the strongest exemplar of the model of strict church-state separation we described in the first chapter. It owes the model in large measure to the legacy of Enlightenment ideas about equality, liberty, and authority, which French revolutionaries saw opposed in the institutions of church and absolute monarchy. But the emphasis is also a result of a longer history of state control of civil society. The American state developed in a very different context in the eighteenth and nineteenth centuries, when, as nonprofits scholar Helmut An-heier suggests, the United States was "quasi-stateless and pragmatically oriented towards the maintenance of individual mobility and free choice."[97] In that developing environment, economic, cultural, and social service asso-ciations, including faith-based groups, were indispensable. For many Americans suspicious of state control, church-state separation was as much about protecting the church from the state as the state from the church.

The French model raises many questions about the proper interaction of religion and the state. For example, in the first chapter we asked a general question about the trade-offs between shared consensual values and individu-al freedom of religious expression. In France, one of those shared values is conformity to a uniform vision of public citizenship itself. But even if we accept the benefits of *laïcité* to national unity, how do we assess its costs?

Some of those costs are obvious to individuals who wish to live in French society while retaining their conspicuous religious particularities. They are often flatly forbidden from conspicuously faithful practice in the public square. Some other costs are less tangible and more abstract. Rousseau fa-mously argued that one of the virtues of his civil religion would be intoler-ance of the intolerant, that is, an unwillingness to put up with what he saw as irrational rejection of the general will. Such dissenters must be "forced to be free," as he put it. When the French system prescribes, say, citizenship train-ing for the Republican violation of wearing noticeable religious clothing, it appears to accept something like this virtue, at least when religion competes directly with the Republican vision. Critics have long retorted that the cost is self-contradiction, a violation of France's own commitment. But perhaps it is not so much self-contradictory as self-revealing. It clarifies that this kind of "intolerance" is not an end in itself, but a means to an end, which is nothing less than a preferred understanding of what it means to be human and live in community. Every society has such understandings—or multiple, sometimes competing understandings. And as we noted in the abstract in chapter 1, and observed empirically in the chapter on the United States, French Republicans are not alone in responding when those understandings are threatened.

The question, then, is not whether France ought to foster a culture per se around its understanding of consensual values. The challenge is the nature of those cultural values themselves, and how and to what effect a country ought to police the boundaries of that culture. At a microtheoretical level—the level of the individual—France has chosen to create a hard distinction between public and private that frequently leaves residents in a painful—and in some cases impossible—position of choosing from competing identities. The young French Muslim who envisions her *hijab* as a religious obligation won-ders if she must check her faith at the door to the public school. She does not accept the state's rigid distinction; for her, the lines between public and private are fluid, blurred, perhaps even nonexistent.

At a macrotheoretical level—the level of institutions and culture—France has committed itself to a conception of the good that envisions freedom itself as bifurcated.[98] The young Muslim is free to practice, just like everyone else; there is no social distinction; the posture is neutrality. But the religious practice itself is walled off in the private sphere, and therefore the young Muslim girl is free *in her particularity* only in private. The *public* square embeds a different kind of liberty, the freedom *to be* the right kind of (Republican) citizen. Religion-based associations—schools, social services— can be accommodated or even supported, but *only* to the extent they support public needs. Their value is not intrinsic, but utilitarian. They will be tolerated in public only if they are useful.

And here the French model is a normative concern. Freedom is always precarious. But it is especially precarious when it is tied to utility. When the state no longer perceives religious believers and groups as useful, they lose privileges and become marginalized—or worse. And in its most extreme form, state co-option of civil society can fuel the totalitarian impulse. Michael Burleigh, in his illuminating study of church-state relations in nineteenth- and early twentieth-century Europe, draws just this line from the French Revolution to World War I, asking whether the "civil religion" of France and other European states sowed the seeds of violent ideological conflicts of the twentieth century.[99]

None of this is to say that religious people and groups should *not* be understood as useful. Far from it. One can understand the French Revolution, in fact, as forgetting the deep foundation the Church provided for social stability. When Edmund Burke, the towering conservative thinker and British parliamentarian of the late eighteenth century, wrote his famous contemporaneous critique of the French Revolution, he showed special concern about the treatment of religion. Society is a contract, he argued, but it is not chosen as much as built and inherited over great spans of time. Religion is an inextricable part of this inheritance; indeed, religion is the "basis" of it.[100] To tear up the contract, including its most important sacred provisions, especially without a clear sense of what would replace it, was to reject human nature and invite disaster. Perhaps the French Reign of Terror proved Burke's prescience. In any case, as we discussed in chapter 1, contemporary social science has shown repeatedly that civil society—those voluntary associations that sit outside the state and market—foster the dispositions and capacities of democratic citizenship best when they maintain independence of state control. By seeking to control religion in service to citizenship, France risks the benefits to citizenship that religion can provide. The point is that the utility of religion is the *result* of religious freedom, not the basis of it.

Advocates of the two models we have explored thus far—the different approaches to church-state separation in the United States and France—envision religion as a risky social phenomenon. We now turn to a second model that has historically seen the rich diversity of religion as a potential asset: the "principled" pluralism of the Netherlands. But we also see that many of the same social trends that have challenged other countries in the west have shaken the Netherlands' commitments.

NOTES

1. Aurelien Breeden and Lilia Blaise, "The 'Burkini' Is Banned on the Beaches of Cannes," *New York Times* (August 13, 2016), A8.

2. In its own response, *Charlie Hebdo* published a front-cover cartoon of a weeping Prophet Muhammad, sparking further (and less reported) discord as far away as the African country of Niger, where spasms of mob violence shattered the uneasy peace between the Muslim majority and Christian minority.

3. Throughout this chapter, we have followed conventional practice of capitalizing "Republican" or "Republicanism" when referring to the distinctive French mode of political and cultural thinking.

4. http://data.worldbank.org/country/france. This estimate includes the overseas territories of the French Republic.

5. Conrad Hackett, Phillip Connor, Marcin Stonawski, and Vegard Skirbekk, "The Future of World Religions: Population Growth Projections, 2010–2050" (Washington, D.C.: Pew Research Center, 2015). Data available at http://www.globalreligiousfutures.org. For an extensive analysis of the geographical distribution of Catholics and other religionists in France, see Jérôme Fourquet and Hervé Le Bras, *La religion dévoilée*: *Nouvelle géographie du catholicisme* (Paris: Jean Jaurès Fondation, 2014).

6. Hackett et al., "The Future of World Religions," 50.

7. Sergio DellaPergola, "World Jewish Population 2014" (New York: Berman Jewish Databank, 2014), 26. Note that some other estimates, including the Pew Research Center's, vary slightly due to different definitions and measurements.

8. Hackett et al., "The Future of World Religions," 18.

9. Église Catholique en France, Statistiques de l'Eglise catholique en France (Guide 2014). Available at http://www.eglise.catholique.fr/conference-des-eveques-de-france/guide-de-leglise/leglise-catholique-en-france-et-en-chiffres/371402-statistiques-de-leglise-catholique-en-france-guide-2013/.

10. Pew Research Center, "During Benedict's Papacy, Religious Observance among Catholics in Europe Remained Low but Stable" (Washington, D.C.: Pew Research Center, 2013). In bordering Spain and Germany, that percentage is 24 and 16, respectively.

11. Jérôme Fourquet, "Analyse: 1989–2011: Enquête sur l'implantation et l'évolution de l'Islam de France" (Paris: IFOP, July 2011).

12. Mattei Dogan, "Religious Beliefs in Europe: Factors of Accelerated Decline," in Ralph L. Piedmont and David O. Moberg, *Research in the Social Scientific Student of Religion* 14 (2003), 161–88.

13. Fourquet, "Analyse: 1989–2011," 9.

14. Interview with Fourquet, June 20, 2016.

15. Eugenie Bastié, "La Révolution Silencieuse des Catholiques de France," *Le Figaro* (October 30, 2015).

16. Alexander Stille, "An Anti-Gay Marriage Tea Party, French Style?" *New Yorker* (March 18, 2014).

17. Michel Houellebecq, *Soumission* (Paris: Flammarion, 2015).

18. France has experienced several moments of constitutional crisis over its post-Revolution history, often resulting in full revisions of the constitution. With each new constitution the state is described as a new "republic."

19. The Republicans changed their name from the Union for a Popular Movement in 2015. "Republicans" in this chapter can refer to the fabled French public philosophy or the political party, depending on the context.

20. Stathis N. Kalyvas, *The Rise of Christian Democracy in Europe* (Ithaca, N.Y.: Cornell University Press, 1996), and Brent F. Nelson and James L. Guth, *Religion and the Struggle for European Union* (Washington, D.C.: Georgetown University Press, 2015), 170–72. Christian democratic parties in other countries have faced their own identity crisis in the post–Cold War era. See Jan-Werner Müller, "The End of Christian Democracy: What the Movement's Decline Means for Europe," *Foreign Affairs* (July 15, 2014). Available at https://www.foreignaffairs.com/articles/western-europe/2014-07-15/end-christian-democracy.

21. The literature on the French Revolution is voluminous and highly charged. A classic account comes from French social observer of the early twentieth century Alexis de Tocqueville, *The Old Regime and the French Revolution* [*L'Ancien Régime et la Révolution*], trans. Stuart Gilbert (New York: Anchor, 1983). The standard English-language history of the antecedents to the French Revolution is William Doyle, *Origins of the French Revolution,* 3rd ed. (New York: Oxford University Press, 1999); a more accessible version is William Doyle, *The French Revolution: A Very Short Introduction* (New York: Oxford University Press, 2001). On the question of the role of religion in the French Revolution, see Dale K. van Kley, *The Religious Origins of the French Revolution* (New Haven, Conn.: Yale University Press, 1996).

22. See his *Discourse on the Origins of Inequality* and *On the Social Contract* in Jean-Jacques Rousseau, *The Basic Political Writings*, trans. and ed. by Donald A. Cress (Indianapolis, Ind.: Hackett, 2011). The quote is taken from book IV, chapter 8 of *On the Social Contract.*

23. "Declaration of the Rights of Man and of the Citizen," August 26, 1789. For an excellent collection of essays on the concept of freedom in the French Declaration, see Dale K. van Kley, ed., *The French Idea of Freedom: The Old Regime and the Declaration of Rights of 1789* (Stanford, Calif.: Stanford University Press, 1994). We use a translation of the Declaration in that book; another version is available at http://avalon.law.yale.edu/18th_century/rightsof.asp.

24. For sharply contrasting views on the status of Jews in the French Revolution, see Arthur Hertzberg, *The French Enlightenment and the Jews: The Origins of Modern Anti-Semitism* (New York: Columbia University Press, 1968); Gary Kates, "Jews into Frenchmen: Nationality and Representation in Revolutionary France," in Ferenc Feher, ed., *The French Revolution and the Birth of Modernity* (Berkeley: University of California Press, 1990), 103–16; and Shanti Marie Singham, "Betwixt Cattle and Men: Jews, Blacks, and Women, and the Declaration of the Rights of Man," in van Kley, *The French Idea of Freedom.*

25. Michael Burleigh, *Earthly Powers: The Clash of Religion and Politics in Europe, from the French Revolution to the Great War* (New York: Harper, 2005), 352–56.

26. The law does not apply in several French territories, including Alsace-Lorraine, which was part of the German Empire at the time of the law's enactment.

27. This and following quotations from the French Constitution are taken from the English translation available from the National Assembly. A version of that translation is available at https://www.constituteproject.org/constitution/France_2008.

28. Conseil Constitutionnel, "Décision no. 71-44 DC," July 1, 1971. Available at http://www.conseil-constitutionnel.fr/conseil-constitutionnel/francais/les-decisions/acces-par-date/decisions-depuis-1959/1971/71-44-dc/decision-n-71-44-dc-du-16-juillet-1971.7217.html.

29. Article 10, "Declaration of the Rights of Man and of the Citizens, 1789," in van Kley, ed., *The French Idea of Freedom.*

30. European Convention on Human Rights (1950), Article 9. Available at http://www.echr.coe.int/Documents/Convention_ENG.pdf.

31. John Bowen, *Why the French Don't Like Headscarves: Islam, State, and Public Space* (Princeton, N.J.: Princeton University Press, 2007), 2.

32. "Secular" or "secularism" are themselves vexed concepts among social scientists, historians, and philosophers. Charles Taylor, in his monumental *A Secular Age* (Cambridge, Mass.: Belknap, 2007), identifies several secular narratives over the course of the modern history of

the west. For an accessible guide to Taylor's thinking, see James K. A. Smith, *How (Not) to Be Secular: Reading Charles Taylor* (Grand Rapids, Mich.: Eerdmans, 2014).

33. Bowen, *Why the French Don't Like Headscarves*, 18.

34. Quoted in Bowen, *Why the French Don't Like Headscarves*, 157.

35. Jean Baubérot, *Histoire de la laïcité en France,* 4th ed. (Paris: Presses Universitaires de France, 2007). Bowen discusses this history in *Why the French Don't Like Headscarves*, 22–28.

36. Alexander Still, "Can the French Talk about Race?" *New Yorker* (July 11, 2014); *Guardian*, "To Count or Not to Count" (March 28, 2009). For a discussion of the problems of measurement of Islam in France, see Jonathan Laurence and Justin Vaisse, *Integrating Islam: Political and Religious Challenges in Contemporary France* (Washington, D.C.: Brookings Institution, 2006), 17–22.

37. Institut National de la statistique et des études économiques, "Les immigrés par sexe, âge et pays de naissance," 2012. Available at http://www.insee.fr/fr/themes/tableau_local.asp?ref_id=IMG1B&millesime=2012&niveau=1&typgeo=METRODOM&codgeo=1.

38. Phillip Connor, "Faith on the Move: The Religious Affiliation of International Migrants" (Washington, D.C.: Pew Research Center, 2012), 32. Other estimates put the number of Muslims in France at 1.8 million. See Fourquet and Le Bras, *La religion dévoilée*, 64.

39. Joel Fetzer and Christopher Soper provide a concise account of this immigration history in *Muslims and the State in Britain, France, and Germany* (Cambridge: Cambridge University Press, 2005), 63–69.

40. "Metropolitan" France is a common—though not uncontroversial—term used to name the territory of France on the European continent, in contrast to its territories overseas.

41. Jonathan Laurence, *The Emancipation of Europe's Muslims: The State's Role in Minority Integration* (Princeton, N.J.: Princeton University Press, 2012), 6.

42. Laurence and Vaisse provide an overview of recent policy and a deeper look at French attitudes toward inclusion and exclusion in *Integrating Islam*, chaps. 7 and 2, respectively.

43. Rüdiger Falksohn, Thomas Hüetlin, Romain Leick, Alexander Smoltczyk, and Gerald Traufetter, "Rioting in France: What's Wrong with Europe?" *Der Spiegel* (November 7, 2009).

44. See, e.g., Yvonne Yazbeck Haddad and Michael J. Balz, "The October Riots in France: A Failed Immigration Policy or the Empire Strikes Back?" *International Migration* 44 (2006), 23–34.

45. Texte adopté n° 524: Project de loi interdisant la dissimulation du visage dans l'espace public. Available at http://www.assemblee-nationale.fr/13/ta/ta0524.asp.

46. Pew Global Attitudes Project, "Widespread Support for Banning Full Islamic Veil in Western Europe" (Washington, D.C.: Pew Research Center, 2010). Available at http://www.pewglobal.org/2010/07/08/widespread-support-for-banning-full-islamic-veil-in-western-europe.

47. Steve Erlanger, "Parliament Moves France Closer to a Ban on Facial Veils," *New York Times* (July 14, 2010), A6.

48. European Court of Justice, Case of *S.A.S v. France* (No. 43835/11), July 1, 2014.

49. Bruce Stokes, "Faith in the European Project Reviving" (Washington, D.C.: Pew Research Center, 2015), 21.

50. The most discussed example was a controversial 1995 report that identified Scientology and Jehovah's Witnesses as potential threats. Alain Gest and Jacques Guyard, "Au nom de la commission d'enquête sur les sectes," Assemblée Nationale, December 22, 1995. Available at http://www.assemblee-nationale.fr/rap-enq/r2468.asp.

51. "Loi No. 2001-504 . . . tendant à renforcer la prévention et la répression des mouvements sectaires portant atteinte aux droits de l'homme et aux libertés fondamentales," June 12, 2001. Available at https://www.legifrance.gouv.fr/affichTexte.do?cidTexte=JORFTEXT000000589924&dateTexte=&categorieLien=id.

52. Bureau of Democracy, Human Rights, and Labor, "International Religious Freedom Report: France" (Washington, D.C.: Department of State, 2001). Available at http://www.state.gov/j/drl/rls/irf/2001/5646.htm; and Committee on Legal Affairs and Human Rights, "Report 9612: Freedom of Religious and Religious Minorities in France" (Strasbourg, France: Council of Europe, 2002).

53. John R. Bowen, *Can Islam Be French? Pluralism and Pragmatism in a Secularist State* (Princeton, N.J.: Princeton University Press, 2010), 196.

54. Nick Robins-Early, "A Field Guide to Europe's Radical Right Political Parties," *Huffington Post* (February 2, 2015). Available at http://www.huffingtonpost.com/2015/02/12/europe-far-right_n_6511022.html.

55. Laurence, *The Emancipation of Europe's Muslims.*

56. Laurence and Vaisse, *Integrating Islam*, chap. 5.

57. Laurence and Vaisse, *Integrating Islam*, chap. 4.

58. Laurence and Vaisse, *Integrating Islam*, 153.

59. Laurence, *The Emancipation of Europe's Muslims*, 6.

60. Quoted in Bowen, *Why the French Don't Like Headscarves*, 157.

61. Bernard Stasi et al., "Rapport au President de la Republique," Commission de reflexion sur l'application due principe de *laïcité dans la Republique*, December 11, 2003. Available at http://www.ladocumentationfrancaise.fr/var/storage/rapports-publics/034000725.pdf.

62. Angelique Chrisafis, "Pork or Nothing: How School Dinners Are Dividing France," *Guardian* (October 13, 2015). Available at http://www.theguardian.com/world/2015/oct/13/pork-school-dinners-france-secularism-children-religious-intolerance.

63. Kimberly A. Arkin, "The Vanishing State: Religious Education and Intolerance in French Jewish Schools," in Adam B. Seligman, ed., *Religious Education and the Challenge of Pluralism* (New York: Oxford University Press, 2014), 96–118.

64. Paul Esquieu et al., "L'état de l'école 2015" (Paris: Ministére de L'Education Nationale, 2015), 11. This excludes students in the preprimary years.

65. Esquieu, "L'état de l'école 2015," 12.

66. Esquieu, "L'état de l'école 2015," 12; National Center for Education Statistics, "The Condition of Education 2016" (Washington, D.C.: Department of Education, 2016), 82–87.

67. Gabriel Languouet and Alaine Leger, "Public and Private Schooling in France: An Investigation into Family Choice," *Journal of Educational Policy* 15 (2000), 41–49.

68. Denis Meuret, "School Choice and Its Regulation in France," in Patrick J. Wolf and Stephen Macedo, *Educating Citizens: International Perspectives on Civic Values and School Choice* (Washington, D.C.: Brookings Institution, 2003), 249; Ahmet T. Kuru, *Secularism and State Policies toward Religion: The United States, France, and Turkey* (New York: Cambridge University Press, 2009), 109.

69. Meuret lays out the considerable regulatory hurdles in "School Choice and Its Regulation in France," 246–48.

70. Meuret, "School Choice and Its Regulation in France," 251.

71. *Le Parisien*, "Découvrez le palmarès 2013 des lycées," March 27, 2013. Available at http://www.leparisien.fr/societe/decouvrez-le-palmares-2013-des-lycees-26-03-2013-2672843.php.

72. Meuret, "School Choice and Its Regulation in France," 247–48.

73. See, e.g., Edith Archambault, "Historical Roots of the Nonprofit Sector in France," *Nonprofit and Voluntary Sector Quarterly* 30 (June 2001), 219.

74. Arkin, "The Vanishing State."

75. Bowen, *Can Islam Be French?*, chap. 4.

76. France opened its first publicly subsidized Muslim school, Averroés Lycée, in 2003. Elaine Sciolino, "Muslim Lycée Opens in Secular France, Raising Eyebrows," *New York Times* (September 9, 2003). For the history of public funding of Islamic schools prior to 2003, see Fetzer and Soper, *Muslims and the State*, 85–87. Bowen conducts an illuminating ethnography of an Islamic school in chapter 6 of *Can Islam Be French?*

77. Katrin Bennhold, "Spurring Secularism, Many French Muslims Find Haven in Catholic Schools," *New York Times* (September 26, 2008), A6.

78. Archambault, "Historical Roots," 205.

79. Archambault, "Historical Roots," 208.

80. Pope Leo XIII, *Rerum Novarum*, May 1891. Available at http://w2.vatican.va/content/leo-xiii/en/encyclicals/documents/hf_l-xiii_enc_15051891_rerum-novarum.html.

81. Archambault, "Historical Roots," 206.

82. Bruno Palier and Philip Manow, "A Conservative Welfare State Regime without Christian Democracy?" in K. van Kersbergen and Philip Manow, eds., *Religion, Class Coalitions, and the Welfare State* (New York: Cambridge University Press, 2009), 150–51.

83. https://data.oecd.org/socialexp/social-spending.htm.

84. Archambault, "Historical Roots." On broader political trends in France, see Pepper D. Culpepper, Peter A. Hall, and Bruno Palier, eds., *Changing France: The Politics That Markets Make* (New York: Palgrave, 2006).

85. Thomas Bahle, "The Changing Institutionalization of Social Services in England and Wales, France and Germany: Is the Welfare State on the Retreat?" *Journal of European Social Policy* 13 (2003), 12.

86. Jean-Pierre Worms, "France: Old and New Civic and Social Ties," in Robert Putnam, ed., *Democracies in Flux: The Evolution of Social Capital in Contemporary Society* (New York: Oxford University Press, 2004), 144.

87. Lise Reynaert, "Neuf assocations sur dix fonctionnent sans salarié," *INSEE Première* 1587 (March 2016), 1.

88. World Values Survey Wave 6: 2010–14. Data available at http://www.worldvaluessurvey.org/WVSOnline.jsp.

89. Worms, "France," 146.

90. Claire Frances Ullman, *The Welfare State's Other Crisis: Explaining the New Partnership between Nonprofit Organizations and the State in France* (Indianapolis: Indiana University Press, 1998).

91. Secours Catholique, "Statistiques d'accueil 2014" (Paris: Secours Catholique, 2014). For an assessment of its innovative experiments in microlending, see Georges Gloukoviezoff and Jeanne Lazarus, "Evaluation d'impact des Crédits: Projet personnel du Secours Catholique," 2007. Available at https://hal-sciencespo.archives-ouvertes.fr/hal-01074245/document.

92. http://www.secours-catholique.org/agir-avec-les-plus-fragiles. In French: "Construire ensemble une société de partage"; "éveiller à la solidarité et à la fraternité"; and "lutter contre les inégalités."

93. Laurence and Vaisse, *Integrating Islam*, chap. 4.

94. Jonah Levy, *Tocqueville's Revenge: State, Society, and Economy in Contemporary France* (Cambridge, Mass: Harvard University Press, 1999).

95. Tocqueville, *The Old Regime and the French Revolution*; and Alexis de Toqueville, *Democracy in America*, trans. Gerard Bevan (New York: Penguin, 2003).

96. Kuru, *Secularism and State Policies toward Religion*, chap. 1.

97. Helmut K. Anheier, *Nonprofit Organizations: Theory, Management, Policy* (New York: Routledge, 2014), 42.

98. The prominent French scholar Pierre Manent argues that France has struggled to include Muslim perspectives precisely because citizens have forgotten that the French conception of the "good" is partly rooted in the heritages of religion (i.e., Christianity and Judaism). See *Beyond Radical Secularism: How France and the Christian West Should Respond to the Islamic Challenge*, trans. Ralph C. Hancock (South Bend, Ind.: St. Augustine's Press, 2016).

99. Burleigh, *Earthly Powers.*

100. Edmund Burke, *Reflections on the Revolution in France* (Indianapolis, Ind.: Hackett, 1987), 79. See also Ian Harris, "Burke and Religion," in David Dwan and Christopher J. Insole, eds., *The Cambridge Companion to Edmund Burke* (New York: Cambridge University Press, 2012), 92–103.

II

Models of Pluralism

Chapter Four

The Netherlands

Principled Pluralism

The Netherlands has a justified reputation as a stable, prosperous democracy with a long tradition of religious liberty. It is also a comparatively tolerant—some would say a permissive—society. Many of the hot-button cultural issues that continue to roil other countries have been largely settled in the Netherlands with a combination of broad-mindedness and a few legal boundaries. Prostitution and the use of marijuana are permitted in some quarters; same-sex marriage has been legal since 2001; state-supervised euthanasia has been available since 2002. This emphasis on freedom and tolerance is part of a long historical legacy. Since the seventeenth century the Netherlands has often served as a refuge for persecuted religious groups and, along with Denmark, is often cited as doing much to protect its Jewish citizens during the Nazi occupation.

But the famous Dutch tolerance has been pushed to the limit in recent years. The chief challenge has been the integration of Muslim immigrants, an issue familiar from our discussion of France in the previous chapter. But that challenge reflects a broader set of questions about whether Dutch norms and legal structures themselves are well adapted to the twenty-first century. Nowhere is this strain felt more keenly than in the Netherlands' approach to church-state relations. On the one hand, the Netherlands' approach is perhaps the most philosophically coherent and pragmatically tested of any of the western democracies we survey in this book. On the other hand, Dutch culture has changed profoundly since its church-state framework was forged a century ago, including the influx of new religious minorities with attitudes that do not always fit neatly into the traditional mold. This tension makes the study of the Netherlands especially illuminating.

This chapter opens with a brief survey of the Netherlands' religious demography and its political system and culture. This discussion provides context for understanding the church-state framework. Like previous chapters, we explore the church-state framework through both a broad look at the Netherlands' vital history and formal legal statements and a deeper dive into case studies of education and nonprofit social services. We conclude with some comparative observations between Dutch pluralism and the church-state separationism of France and the United States.

THE NATION

The Netherlands, with nearly seventeen million people crowded onto sixteen thousand square miles of land, is one of the most densely populated countries in the world.[1] It is often said that Dutch history and geography have molded people who are, paradoxically, both fiercely independent and strongly committed to cooperation. The independence of the Dutch has resulted in a surprisingly large degree of societal pluralism for so small a country. It was historically fostered by the low-lying, marshy ground of the deltas of the Rhine, Meuse, and Scheldt rivers that resulted in areas developing in relative isolation from each other.[2] This geography kept even the Romans from uniting under their rule the area that is today the Netherlands. During the Middle Ages this area consisted of several autonomous duchies. It was only in the late sixteenth century that a loose confederation of provinces came together to form a single republic. Even today the Frisian language is spoken by 650,000 persons living in the province of Friesland in the northern part of the country.[3]

The Protestant Reformation resulted in further division between a Catholic south and a Protestant north. The Protestants themselves were divided among the dominant Reformed, or Calvinist, group and other Protestant groups such as Lutherans and Mennonites. Meanwhile, the "golden age" of Dutch commercial prosperity developed as a colonial power in the seventeenth century, when truly the business of the Dutch was business. The commercial elites of Amsterdam and elsewhere concentrated more on making money and managing overseas colonies than pursuing theological truth, with the result that the Dutch tolerated a variety of religious traditions (at least domestically) when much of the rest of Europe was still at war in the name of religion. Even today the Dutch are a mosaic of religious, ethnic, and regional groupings, each protective of its distinct identity and independence.

But the independence of the Dutch is only one part of the picture. Another is a strong commitment to cooperation. Many observers of the Dutch experience trace this characteristic to the relentless battle against the sea. Sixty percent of the population inhabits the 25 percent of the land area that is below sea level. This way of life is made possible only by a complex, integrated series of canals, pumps, and seawalls. Dutch survival down through the centuries has necessitated collaborative efforts to hold back the sea. As recently as 1953 spring runoff and a series of heavy storms resulted in the drowning deaths of over 1,800 persons. As the population of the Netherlands swelled in the twentieth century, that same cooperative spirit was put to use in urban planning, housing development, and public transportation. In these cooperative efforts to fight the sea and build a prosperous economy, the Dutch learned to accept existing differences and work together in spite of them.

The combination of independence and cooperation helps explain how many religious groups found a place in the Netherlands. Today, a quarter of adults identify as Roman Catholic and 16 percent as Protestant.[4] Historically, most Dutch Protestants were Reformed, but in 2004 the two largest Reformed denominations and the Lutherans merged to form the Protestant Church in the Netherlands. There are also 850,000 to 1,000,000 Muslims (about 5 percent of the population), most of whom trace their lineage to Turkey or Morocco. Many Muslims are clustered in large population centers such as Amsterdam (24 percent) and Rotterdam (13 percent).[5] The Dutch religious makeup is rounded out by between 100,000 and 250,000 Hindus, 17,000 Buddhists, and 30,000 Jews.

An equally important part of the religion story is that the Netherlands has experienced a secularization trend along with much of the rest of Europe. The Catholic Church has lost 30 percent and the two largest Reformed churches nearly 60 percent of their membership since 1959.[6] In that same year only 21 percent reported no religious affiliation, compared to perhaps half the population today.[7] Some 71 percent of the population report hardly ever or never attending worship services, a percentage that is higher than in any other country examined in this book except France.[8]

Despite this secularization trend, however, strong religious affinities remain among a minority of the population. In 2012, 16 percent reported regularly attending a religious service,[9] higher than in France, Germany, and many other western European countries. A great deal of this religious participation is concentrated regionally in the Netherlands' "Bible belt," an area with relatively high numbers of orthodox Reformed believers that runs from the southwest to eastern part of the country.[10] Second-generation Muslims in the Netherlands have also bucked expectations of declining religious practice.[11] Moreover, there is some evidence that the Netherlands' population is increasingly interested in spirituality, even as residents eschew organized religion.[12]

The Netherlands' political system provides many points of contact for religious groups. The Netherlands is a constitutional monarchy, with King Willem-Alexander serving as the head of state, a largely symbolic position.[13]

It has a parliamentary form of government with a bicameral legislature called the States-General. The upper house has seventy-five members elected indirectly by the members of provincial councils and the lower house has 150 members elected directly by the populace by a strict system of proportional representation. Most legislation originates with the cabinet and must be passed by both houses of the States-General, but only the lower house may amend or introduce bills. There are several major political parties: the Christian Democratic Appeal (CDA), the Labour Party (PvdA), the Socialist Party (SP), and the People's Party for Freedom and Democracy (VVD)—a center-right, business-oriented party. The Party for Freedom (PVV), a right-wing party with a reputation for skepticism of European integration and a hard line on immigration, has been gaining seats in the legislature as the challenges of a multicultural society have increased. The current government, formed after the 2012 elections, is a coalition led by the VVD. The prime minister, Mark Rutte, is a member of the VVD and has occupied that office since 2010. The CDA had been a part of every government from 1918 to 1994, but in recent years it has declining electoral support and has found itself in the governing coalition less frequently.

The Dutch political system has been described as corporatist and consociational.[14] The former term emphasizes the tendency for institutionalized representatives of key societal groups to make public policy through a process of negotiation and compromise among themselves and with governmental officials. The Netherlands gives those groups formal access to government through an extensive range of advisory councils, among other mechanisms. Consociational democracy emphasizes the tendency for elites in a segmented, or sharply divided, society to replace the incompatible demands of their constituent groups with pragmatic compromises that maintain the unity of society.

The Dutch political system has been undergoing significant change in the past twenty years, leading some commentators to wonder if corporatism and consociationalism are eroding.[15] Still, the Dutch political system continues to be marked by relatively high levels of negotiation, discussion, and compromise rather than by adversarial confrontations with outright winners and losers. Rudy Andeweg and Galen Irwin have written that "obituaries of neo-corporatism seem premature. . . . [T]he incorporation of interest groups into the decision-making process . . . is still characteristic of Dutch policy-making in many fields."[16] Recently the Dutch concluded that the number of advisory bodies was too large and unwieldly and in the late 1990s through the mid-2000s their number was sharply reduced. Most executive departments, however, continue to have several permanent advisory councils and additional ad hoc ones.

We will return to these aspects of political culture later in the chapter as we seek to understand Dutch church-state principles and practices. But first it is important to gain insight into the historical forces that have shaped distinctive Dutch church-state practices and the assumptions that underlie them.

THE HISTORICAL BACKGROUND

The United States, France, and the Netherlands confronted similar ideas from the liberal Enlightenment during the nineteenth century. But each country responded in different ways, and as a result their approaches to church-state issues have sharply diverged. The story of these ideas, how the Dutch responded to them, and the consequences for church-state relations largely revolve around the issue of education.

The Dutch liberals in the nineteenth century reacted against the old conservative order that had featured a semiestablished Reformed Church (*Hervormde Kerk*) and a host of privileges for the aristocratic classes. In reaction against the old order, the liberals worked for more popular participation in government, a more limited role for the state, and no state favoritism toward religious groups. Underlying these liberal reforms was a particular view of the ideal society. They believed there could be more popular participation in the political system without societal divisions and greed destroying social stability, as the conservatives feared. Dutch scholar Siep Stuurman has described the basic liberal view of that time: "Through education and propagation of (Liberal) 'culture' among all classes the circle of citizens could be broadened and the basis of the state as well. On this course a homogeneous Dutch nation would come into being, and would naturally take on a liberal coloration."[17] The public schools were to play an especially important role in the teaching of a common, nonsectarian, and liberal culture of national unity, tolerance, and virtue.

Armed with these ideas, liberals at the beginning of the nineteenth century started a strong movement in the Netherlands to create publicly funded common schools that all children would be required to attend. Stuurman writes that the homogenization of the nation was "the political core of the liberal school policies. The school as a nation-forming institution must not be divided among competing 'sectarian schools' or left in the hands of an exclusive political or church party."[18] In the liberal view religion and morals were not to be ignored; instead, children ought to be taught a "Christianity above doctrinal differences."[19] While this perspective differs from the active anticlericalism of France during the same period, it was very similar to the view of education advocated in the United States by Horace Mann and his supporters, as we saw in chapter 2. Education ought to be universal and carefully regulated by the government to make sure that divisive, parochial Christian doctrines were eliminated in favor of broad moral themes that would produce national unity and responsible citizens.

But where did that leave the diverse religious communities of the Netherlands? The answer is that in the liberal scheme of things particularistic, divisive religious beliefs were to be relegated to the private sphere. As a result schools outside the common framework were at best viewed with suspicion, and at worst simply banned.

As the nineteenth century wore on, increasing opposition to this concept of education grew among Catholics and especially among a number of orthodox Reformed groups, including the large, semiestablished *Hervormde Kerk* and an assortment of Reformed churches that had seceded from it.[20] From out of this opposition both the orthodox Reformed and the Catholics started to develop their own political movements in the 1860s.

Meanwhile liberalism was also changing, leading to a hardening of the lines. In strong echoes of the French Revolution, it was becoming more anticlerical and more committed to a secular philosophy. Political scientist Stanley Carlson-Thies summarizes the changes in Dutch liberalism in the 1870s: "Progress, advance through science, . . . liberation from outmoded dogmas—these were the watchwords of the younger generation. Simple dismissal of the benighted, who clung tenaciously to outmoded Christian beliefs, was no longer enough; those beliefs, and the schools and political initiatives embodying them, had to be confronted and defeated."[21]

The tensions that had been building for some time between the Enlightenment-inspired liberals, who were dominant in parliament, and Reformed and Catholic forces came to a head in reaction to the passage of a new school law in 1878. Led by Kappeyne van de Coppello, the liberals pushed through parliament higher standards for all schools—public schools run by municipalities, as well as alternative schools run by Catholic and orthodox Reformed groups. It then provided generous financial subsidies from the central government to pay for these mandated improvements for the public schools, but not for the religious alternative schools. The alternative schools would have to come up with the additional funds, and if they could not, they could be closed by the education authorities. In the context of the times, the Catholics and orthodox Reformed viewed this law as an all-out attack on the religiously based schools and as reneging on the freedom of education liberals had earlier supported in the 1848 constitution and an 1857 school law.

The 1878 law ignited a mass political movement and drove the orthodox Reformed and Catholics—two groups with long histories of antagonism and distrust—into a formidable political alliance. In only five days the orthodox Reformed groups collected over 300,000 signatures in opposition to the new education law. Catholics soon after added another 160,000. As Carlson-Thies has written, "Compared to the total population of only some four million and an electorate of 122,000, this was an outpouring of popular sentiment of startling size."[22] Within a year the Reformed groups had established the Anti-Revolutionary Party (ARP), a name that used the symbolism of opposition to the French Revolution as a way to show the party's rejection of Enlightenment liberal principles. The ARP was sophisticated and highly successful in the strategies of mass mobilization. As political scientist Hans Daalder reported, the ARP "pioneered modern mass-party organization techniques in the Netherlands."[23] By 1883 Catholics had also written and circulated a program for their own party, although it was several decades before the formal establishment of a Catholic party.

The 1878 school law led to a "monstrous alliance," as one Dutch observer termed it,[24] between the orthodox Reformed groups and the Catholics. The ARP-Catholic alliance quickly became a major political force, winning an absolute majority of the lower house in 1888. Over a period of forty years and in a series of stages it won total approval of its vision of education: religiously based schools of various types and public schools espousing a "neutral," consensual philosophy all sharing fully and equally in public funding. This concept was enshrined in the Constitution of the Netherlands in 1917, where it remains today.[25] This constitutional victory was made possible by a pragmatic coalition among the ARP-Catholic forces, which wanted equal funding for their schools; the social democrats, who wanted universal male suffrage; and the Liberal Party, which wanted proportional representation in the electoral system. All three received what they wanted in what has been termed "the pacification of 1917."

The powerful Catholic-Reformed alliance was undoubtedly motivated by political pragmatism: both were minority groups that were unlikely to be able to impose their beliefs on the nation as a whole. Equally important, however, is the fact that this alliance prevailed on the intellectual front. Several Reformed thinkers, with support of the Catholic leadership, developed key theories to uphold the alliance's position of government support for all education, public and private alike. Their ideas were also applied to areas of society other than the schools, and gained broad acceptance in Dutch society. While today these ideas are fraying with new challenges to pluralism, they are in many ways still a part of the Dutch mind-set on issues of church and state. They form the heart of the principled pluralism we have noted in the title of this chapter.

Two persons—a Calvinist and a Catholic—were especially important standard-bearers for this nascent pluralism. The central Dutch Calvinist was Abraham Kuyper (1837–1920), theologian, journalist, university founder, and, from 1901 to 1905, prime minister. Michael Fogarty has written that Kuyper was "the greatest leader whom Dutch Protestantism in modern times has produced."[26] Kuyper explicitly rejected the creation of a theocracy where the state would promote Christian beliefs and values to the exclusion of all others. He repeatedly spoke in favor of, and when in political power worked for, a political order that recognized and accommodated the religious pluralism of society. In the words of his biographer James Bratt, his goal was "to devise a system whereby those loyal to each of the Netherlands' salient belief-blocs—Reformed or Anabaptist, Roman Catholic or Jewish, liberal Protestant or labor-socialist—could assert their claims in public affairs without apology, but also without aiming to take over the whole and subordinate the rest."[27] When in 1898 Kuyper was invited to give the prestigious Stone Foundation lectures at Princeton University, he stated that government should allow "to each and every citizen liberty of conscience, as the primordial and inalienable right of all men."[28] He also praised the concept of "a free Church, in a free State" and criticized czarist Russia and the Lutheran concept of secular rulers determining the religion of their kingdoms as violating this ideal. But—and this is highly significant—he also criticized "the irreligious neutral standpoint of the French revolution" as violating the ideal of a free church in a free state.[29] Kuyper often spoke in support of "parallelism," that is, the right and freedom of differing religious and philosophical perspectives and movements to develop freely on separate, parallel tracks, neither hindered nor helped by the government.

The Canadian political scientist Herman Bakvis has concluded: "It was the example of the Calvinists under the leadership of . . . Abraham Kuyper that gave the Catholics impetus towards developing some sort of party organization."[30] The person who emerged to lead this drive was a Catholic priest, journalist, and member of parliament, Herman Schaepman (1844–1903). His thinking paralleled Kuyper's in many ways. The Catholic party he desired, according to Carlson-Thies, "would seek only equality for the Catholic church, not predominance, and would promote freedom of religion, independence of the churches from the state, and equal rights for all citizens and all religious bodies. . . . No special rights were needed, but there must be acceptance of the special character of Catholic desires and demands."[31] He also argued there was "a common cause to be made between Catholics and Anti-Revolutionaries on the schools issue; both groups wanted control of their own educational system."[32]

These pluralistic principles—tolerant, yet insisting that a variety of religious views and perspectives had as much right to sit at the public policy table as their secularly based counterparts—triumphed over liberal thinking in the early twentieth century. When this victory was ensconced in the Constitution in 1917 by the guarantee of full funding for schools of all faiths on par with the public schools, the principles of pluralism came to dominate public thinking and to be copied in many other areas of public life. From the 1920s to the 1960s—and some would say down to today—a system of pluralism referred to as pillarization (*verzuiling*) structured Dutch society.

Under pillarization most areas of group human activity—political parties, labor unions, education, television broadcasting, retirement homes, social service agencies, and recreation clubs—were marked by separate organizations representing the different religious and secular points of view.[33] There were several main pillars: Reformed, Catholic, socialist, and liberal. This segmentation meant, for example, that there was a Catholic political party, a Catholic labor union, Catholic schools from primary to university, a Catholic radio network, Catholic newspapers, various Catholic recreation clubs, and more. These organizations would constitute the Catholic pillar. A person growing up in a Catholic household would live his or her life largely in the context of Catholic organizations (the Catholic pillar). A person growing up in a Reformed home or in a home without particular religious commitments but of a socialist (for the working class) or liberal (for the business and small entrepreneur) bent would have similar pillars. This social structure fit well with the principles articulated by Kuyper and adopted by Catholics. If all of life is touched by religion, one's religious beliefs (or their secular counterparts) would be relevant to what one reads, how one votes, how one seeks an education, and even how one recreates. As foreign as such a system seems to the American observer, this unique version of multiculturalism worked well in the Netherlands in the 1920–1960 period.[34] In contrast to nearby continental European nations such as Germany, France, Spain, and Italy, the Dutch lived and prospered in social and political stability through this system of multiple subcultures in balance.

In recent decades, however, pillarization has faced two very basic challenges that have fundamentally altered it, even while the Netherlands has retained its legacy. One challenge is the strong secularization trend noted earlier; the other is the influx of large numbers of Muslims from abroad, including a small number of radicals who have no wish to assimilate into Dutch society. We discuss each of these in turn.

The strong secularization trend from the 1960s onward has undercut much of the cultural resonance of the religious pillars. In fact, pillarization in the Netherlands today is often treated with either indifference or outright rejection—something that is in the past, a vestige of an era of religious exclusiveness and division. Voting by religion has fallen precipitously. Although a sizable majority of Dutch children still attend Catholic or Protestant schools today, parents now select schools for reasons other than their religious character. Many Protestants attend Catholic schools, Catholics attend Protestant schools, and nonbelievers attend both. Support for other forms of pillarized organizations has dissipated. As a result, many of the formerly pillarized organizations are combining: Protestant with Catholic, and both with secular. The Dutch no longer live most of their lives within a single pillar, but pick and choose. Members of a family may belong to the newly formed Protestant Church in the Netherlands, yet send their children to a Catholic school. Meanwhile, the wife may work at a secular drug treatment center, the husband may belong to the CNV (a Christian—Catholic and Protestant—labor union), they may largely listen to the new commercial television channels, and in the last election they may have voted for the nonreligious, right-of-center VVD.

Is then pillarization dead? Many would say yes. But others say pillarization has simply evolved from forty or fifty years ago. When in 2006 we asked Sophie van Bijsterveld, then a member of the upper house of the States-General and probably the foremost church-state scholar in the Netherlands, whether or not pillarization was dead she responded:

> Many of the [pillarized] organizations still continue to exist, but of course society has changed and we have become a post-modern, secularized, individ-ualized society, as a lot of societies in Europe have. But these organizations to a large extent continue to exist; the legal framework is still the same. . . . Pillarization was a very closed sort of society with everybody living in his or her own pillar. . . . That sort of a closed society of course is long gone. But that doesn't mean those institutions have disappeared. [35]

She went on to make the point that recently many organizations, rather than ignoring or relegating to the dustbin their religious or philosophical roots, have been self-consciously reexamining those roots in an effort to establish a religious or philosophical identity adapted to the present-day setting. In many fields, organizations rooted in religious or secular principles still exist and are recognized and allowed for by official government policy as organizations reflecting a particular religious or secular point of view. And in corporatist fashion the leaders of these groups are often called upon to advise the government on issues of concern to them. It is not assumed that a neutral, secular organization representing a segment of the population can speak for all. This aspect of the old pillarization system is still alive, even as the subcultures with long historical roots appear to wane.

A second major factor affecting the pillarization model is the presence of a large Muslim minority. A small number of Muslims are not assimilating into Dutch society and a very small number are radical theocrats who resist assimilation and reject democratic norms. A 2005 government report estimates that among the Muslims only several hundred persons are in the radical category, but it also notes there are several thousand who sympathize with the hard-core radicals, a number that "is currently growing in size."[36] Moreover, although the Netherlands has been spared the sort of mass-level terrorist attacks of 9/11 and those later experienced in Madrid, London, and Paris, the limits of the Netherlands' vaunted tolerance was tested by violence toward key political and cultural leaders in the early 2000s. In 2002 Pim Fortuyn, a leading anti-immigration politician, was assassinated, and in 2004 the filmmaker Theo van Gogh was killed by a Muslim extremist who, in an especially horrendous act, shot van Gogh, slit his throat, and left a note with verses from the Qur'an pinned to his body with a knife.

In the years since the assassinations of Pim Fortuyn and Theo van Gogh and terrorist attacks elsewhere in the West, the Dutch political scene has been shaken by sharp debates over immigration, religious freedom, and assimilation.[37] Shifting support for parties provides a snapshot of underlying conflicts. Under the leadership of Geert Wilders, the strongly anti-immigration—many would say anti-Muslim—PVV has increased its share of seats in parliament over the past decade, though it lost some ground in 2012 and now has 15 seats with 10 percent of the total vote. The conservative, more moderately anti-immigration party, VVD, gained 10 seats in the lower house in 2012 (it currently has 41 total seats, the highest in the House of Representatives) and garnered 27 percent of the vote.[38] Meanwhile, the Labour Party (PvdA), with a more open attitude toward immigrants, gained eight seats.

The Dutch model of pillarization as it still exists today reflects a choice between two approaches: integration into a shared "Dutch" identity or the accommodation of multiple cultural identities within the same state. There is a renewed emphasis in the Netherlands on integration, that is, on ways to assimilate immigrant communities into the common values of a tolerant, democratic polity. And there is a parallel de-emphasis on maintaining and making allowances for distinctive religious and ethnic communities.

Just as with the recent secularization process, however, this focus on integration does not necessarily mean pillarization has become irrelevant. As we will shortly see, many Muslim schools are fully funded by the government, television time has been allotted for Muslim programming, and there have even been two state-sponsored training programs for imams (at the University of Amsterdam and Leiden University; the latter is now defunct). Two scholars describe the current situation in these words:

> Minority groups are provided instruction in their own language and culture; separate radio and television programs; government funding to import religious leaders; and subsidies for a wide range of social and religious organizations; "consultation prerogatives" for community leaders; and publicly financed housing set aside for and specifically designed to meet Muslim requirements for strict separation of "public" and "private" spaces.[39]

The religious-belief-ethnic pluralism of society—including the Muslim segment, if not "pillar"—is still being recognized and accommodated.

All this is not without controversy. To some, the traditional emphasis on separate organizations representing religious and philosophical traditions, including now the Muslim tradition, is divisive and is being used by radical Muslims to resist assimilation and to spread their radical doctrines. Veit Bader has argued, however, that in the case of separate schools such fears "are theoretically implausible and empirically untenable."[40] He goes on to suggest that under what he terms "associational democracy" ethnic-religious minorities "are more likely to create fair and stable forms of cohesion and political unity, to create toleration and the appropriate civic virtues and bonds, and at least help to reduce the chances of violent conflicts and terrorism."[41] The underlying assumption is that as Muslims form their own schools and other organizations, as they receive public subsidies, and as they are drawn into negotiations over public policies and their implementation, they will feel more accepted as a part of Dutch society and will come to accept more fully the norms of individual freedom and democratic governance.

This argument has gained currency in some unexpected places. Scholar George Harinck told us that Christian Democratic Appeal

> would have said [two decades ago], "Well, we are against an Islamic pillar because it means you lock these people in their own tradition and don't make them Dutch." Nowadays [party members] have changed their opinion and they say, "Well, we support Islamic organizations because we have learned in the last ten years that these people don't integrate into society just by living here. So, you want to tell them . . . [to] found an Islamic political party, and your leaders will learn to deal with the other Dutch in parliament and they will learn that they need to negotiate." The Netherlands is a country with all kinds of minorities and no majority, so if you want to form a majority you have to make coalitions. . . . Well, the best way to support it [Muslim integration into Dutch society] we think now is by supporting them in founding their own organizations.[42]

In summary, while pillarization has changed since the 1960s, it is still a part of the Dutch way of governing society. But the term itself is no longer very descriptive or widely used. What still exist are societal-political organizations segmented by religious-philosophical orientations, and a society and a government that accept the legitimacy of and seek to accommodate such organizations in a wide variety of fields. They are seen as reflecting points of view of significance in the populace and as serving segments of the taxpaying populace, and for both reasons deserve recognition and support. In the following sections we explore this pluralistic view of society for church-state.

THE FREE EXERCISE OF RELIGION

The basic right to the free exercise of one's religion is laid down in Articles 1 and 6 of the Dutch Constitution, as revised in 1983. Article 1 states:

> All persons in the Netherlands shall be treated equally in equal circumstances. Discrimination on the grounds of religion, belief, political opinion, race or sex or on any other grounds whatsoever shall not be permitted.[43]

And Article 6 reads:

> 1. Everyone shall have the right to profess freely his religion or belief, either individually or in community with others, without prejudice to his responsibility under the law.
> 2. Rules concerning the exercise of this right other than in buildings and enclosed places may be laid down by Act of Parliament for the protection of health, in the interest of traffic and to combat or prevent disorders.

In addition to the language of the Constitution of the Netherlands, the Dutch implementation of religious freedom includes a key statute called the Equal Treatment Act (passed in 1994), along with the quasijudicial decisions of the Equal Treatment Commission, which was created by the Equal Treatment Act and operated until 2011.[44] The act provides "protection against discrimination on the grounds of religion, belief, political opinion, race, sex, nationality, heterosexual or homosexual orientation or civil status."[45] It forbids both direct and indirect discrimination, the latter being actions which, while not intending to discriminate, have the effect of discriminating.

It is important to note that the Dutch judiciary does not have the power of judicial review over acts passed by parliament that might undermine religious freedom. Article 120 clearly states: "The constitutionality of Acts of Parliament and treaties shall not be reviewed by the courts." The courts, however, can find and sometimes have found acts of municipal and provincial councils and executive branch agencies to be unconstitutional. In addition, Article 94 provides that acts of parliament and other statutes that conflict with treaties—such as the European Convention on Human Rights—are not applicable, a point we discuss in greater detail below. The Dutch courts have historically been hesitant to hold acts of local councils and executive agencies unconstitutional or to enforce Article 94 against acts of parliament, although they have become somewhat more activist in doing so in recent years. Dutch citizens and groups, when compared to Americans, are also slower to assert their perceived constitutional rights in the courts. The Dutch culture is more committed to negotiation than to legal confrontation. As a result of these legal structures and cultural norms, like we saw in France, judicial interpretations have not been a dominant influence on the development of free exercise rights, as they have in the United States. Nevertheless, the constitutional provisions are important, both as a reflection of Dutch thinking and as legally enforceable provisions.

Articles 1 and 6 express four distinctive ideas compared to the United States and (in some instances) France. First, Article 6 provides for the free exercise of both religion and "belief." The 1983 revision to the Constitution includes protection of both "belief" and religion in order to make clear that secular beliefs should have the same legal protection as religious views. This is consistent with the Dutch aspiration that all religions, as well as their secular equivalents, deserve respect and protection. The Dutch word translated as "belief" is *levensovertuiging* and more literally could be translated as "life conviction." It is not just any belief that has constitutional protection, but deep-seated convictions that guide one's life, even if they are not rooted in religion in the traditional sense.

Second, Article 6 makes clear that one's freedom to profess religion or belief is protected whether one exercises it as an individual or "in community with others." Individual rights are protected, but so are the rights of people to act as part of a larger community or group. This communitarian emphasis can also be traced back to Dutch pluralism, with its emphasis on a plurality of religious and "life conviction" groups and associations and the important, legitimate role they play in society. It contrasts with the approach of Enlightenment liberalism that tends to focus on the protection of individual, private religious belief with less attention to the communal practice of religion.

Third, the second section of Article 6 embeds an explicit constitutional exception similar to the American Supreme Court's "compelling state interest" test. The exercise of the right to religious freedom may be regulated in the interest of public health, the free flow of traffic, or the prevention of civil disorder. While these are broad concepts that leave open room for a great deal of interpretation, they reflect the idea that constitutional liberties are not absolute.

A fourth point is especially important. Article 1, by stating that all people are to be "treated equally in equal circumstances," lays the groundwork for the free exercise right of religious organizations to receive the same sort of governmental assistance that their secular counterparts receive. Legal scholar van Bijsterveld has written:

> [Article 1] guarantees equal treatment in equal circumstances to all persons. . . . It is clear that under the Constitution public-authorities in the Netherlands shall be neutral with respect to the various religious and non-religious denominations. . . . [I]t is clear that once authorities subsidize or support certain activities, religious counterparts cannot be excluded for that reason. Article 1 forbids this.[46]

Elsewhere she has written, "No *general* state support to churches exists." But then she goes on to note that "financial support to churches and religion is allowed under special circumstances in order to prevent the free exercise of religion from becoming illusory."[47] In an interview van Bijsterveld gave an example of what she had in mind when she explained that government should enable the free exercise of religion, not make it impossible. "So [it means] the positive protection of religion, so to say. In the case of ancient church monuments, we say the government supports old castles and other old buildings, so it should also protect ancient church monuments. They should not be excluded. That is what equal treatment means."[48] To the Dutch pluralist mind, nondiscrimination and equal treatment in similar circumstances means that general programs of aid or support may not exclude religiously based beliefs and organizations. A variety of religious and secular beliefs and their organizations and programs are to be treated equally by government. This principle is basic to the Dutch approach to church-state issues.

But applying the principle is not always straightforward in practice. Two categories of church-state challenges help to illustrate how the Netherlands has dealt with the free exercise rights in an increasingly pluralistic society. The first category focuses on external pressures from the Netherlands' European peers; the second category focuses on internal tensions between broader consensual norms and the beliefs and practices of minority religions.

The external pressures on the Netherlands largely flow from its consent to a set of complex political and economic agreements with most other European countries. These arrangements are commonly associated with the European Union, a powerful postwar alliance of nearly all European states. The Netherlands and many other European countries have also committed to uphold international human rights agreements such as the European Convention on Human Rights, often under the monitoring eye of the Council of Europe and its legal enforcement arm, the European Court of Human Rights. The challenge is that a member state's understanding of a right to religious practice or speech might not be consistent with international interpretations of human rights. For example, the Netherlands was criticized by international observers when in 2011 a Dutch court acquitted Geert Wilders, the anti-immigration leader of the PVV, of charges that his explosive language about Islam violated hate speech prohibitions.[49]

In general, while the Netherlands has always been a leader in advancing human rights as part of its foreign policy, the idea of human rights has not been a part of domestic discussions about religion and speech until very recently.[50] Part of the reason appears to be the assumption that the Netherlands already had relatively strong protections for its residents and therefore did not need the added imposition of international conventions. Another reason is undoubtedly the Dutch hesitancy to settle disputes by claiming rights in court rather than through processes of mediation and negotiation.

But this hesitancy might be changing. Consider that the Netherlands, in response to a Council of Europe directive, replaced the Equal Treatment Commission in 2011 with a new Netherlands Institute for Human Rights, which "monitors and protects human rights, promotes respect for human rights (including equal treatment) in practice, policy and legislation, and increases the awareness of human rights in the Netherlands."[51] The head of the Institute has publicly argued that the goal of human rights promotion and enforcement is not always in line with the Dutch tradition of negotiation and consensus-building. In her explanation of the Institute's most recent recommendations, President Laurien Koster acknowledges that "political consensus achieves many good results" and prevents the need in many cases to invoke human rights. But she goes on to say that "what is referred to as 'the polder model' [a consensus-based process of decision making] is simply unsuitable" when human rights are violated; such cases warrant a more forceful response from the state. [52]

Recent conflicts over gay rights or gender roles reflect this tension between domestic and international norms. The Dutch criminal code makes it a felony to incite hatred or discrimination against others by way of written or oral expression. [53] Prosecutors have brought some charges against Muslims as well as theologically conservative Reformed Christians who oppose homosexuality or a liberated role for women, and some private citizens have filed hiring discrimination and other complaints against these groups. The religious groups' claims of protection under the free exercise of religion or speech have usually prevailed in Dutch courts. But increasingly these kinds of disputes are making their way into international discussion and, in some cases, international tribunals, pitting European norms on discrimination and hate speech against the Netherlands' traditional emphasis on freedom of belief and practice. [54]

Another challenge to the Netherlands' approach to freedom of religion is its internal debate about how to accommodate the religious practices of the growing Muslim population. A familiar conflict from the discussion about France in chapter 3 is illustrative: the wearing of religious clothing and especially headscarves and *burqas* (the latter cover the entire body, including the face). But in contrast to France, in almost all cases the Equal Treatment Commission ruled Muslim women may not be denied employment or schooling due to wearing headscarves or *niqabs* and *burqas*. Van Bijsterveld has summarized the position the Commission has developed: "When an applicant is refused a job because she wears a headscarf *as an expression of religion*, this constitutes a *direct* distinction on the basis of religion and contravenes the Equal Treatment Act." [55] On this basis the Commission held in separate cases that a Muslim court registrar, a Muslim cashier at a private bank, and Muslim children *and* teachers in public schools must be allowed to wear a headscarf. [56] That such cases are pushing the limits of Dutch tolerance, however, is revealed by the fact that in the case of the court registrar, the Commission's decision was publicly condemned by the minister of justice, who announced he would seek a change in the law in order to ban the wearing of any religious symbols during court hearings. [57]

The wearing of the traditional face-covering *burqa* in public has also proven to be controversial in recent years. A French-style ban on wearing them in public came close to passage several times in the Dutch parliament over the past decade and a half. In 2015, Rutte's centrist coalition authorized a less expansive ban than France's by prohibiting face coverings only in those public contexts where visible facial features serve a public good (e.g., safety in public streets, teaching in schools). The government insisted that the decision was "religion-blind" and applied to other face coverings as well (e.g., motorcycle helmets). But it was nevertheless a somewhat ambiguous step for traditional Dutch tolerance and equal treatment.

The conspicuous presence of Muslims manifests in other ways as well. Periodically, questions have arisen over such issues as the frequency and allowable volume of Muslim calls to prayer and the building of large mosques that in the view of many do not fit in with prevailing architectural styles. Especially controversial was the Essalam mosque in Rotterdam, a large building that holds 1,200 worshippers and has minarets soaring forty-four meters into the air. It was initially approved by the Rotterdam municipal council in 1999, but after a change in the political composition of the council there were attempts to block its construction or, at the least, lower the height of the minarets so they would no longer tower over the surrounding area. There have been similar controversies elsewhere. Some mosques have been attacked and set afire by right-wing malcontents. These controversies and conflicts, however, are a sign of shifting attitudes among the Dutch populace, which polls suggest are increasingly worried about and unfavorable toward Muslims.[58] These events do not necessarily signal dramatic changes in the legal status of Muslims or other religious minorities. The Essalam mosque was built and opened its doors in 2010. Large mosques in other cities have also been built, even though protests have sometimes attended them.

In summary, the Netherlands has a more expansive understanding of the free exercise of religion than does the United States or France. This free exercise is interpreted to include the equal treatment of religious and nonreligious organizations and programs, and protects most practices of minority religious groups. Nevertheless, the Netherlands continues to struggle with free exercise questions in the face of increasing international emphases on human rights and the growth of domestic religious pluralism resulting from the increasing numbers of non-Christians—and especially of Muslims. In dealing with minority religions and their practices, accommodation is the norm, but Dutch leaders and citizens are asking hard questions about when freedom of religious expression needs to yield to a perceived need for greater integration into the values and norms of Dutch society. The Dutch proclivity for toleration and flexibility is being stretched to the limit, but with a few exceptions it is still the dominant model in Dutch law and politics.

CHURCH, STATE, AND EDUCATION

The Dutch concept of pluralism translates, when applied to education, to a deep and lasting commitment to freedom of choice. There is strong support for the proposition that parents should be able to choose the sort of education their children receive, whether that be Catholic; Protestant in a genial, broad sense; Reformed in a strict, orthodox sense; Jewish; Muslim; Hindu; secular; or secular with certain special teaching techniques or philosophies such as Montessori. A study by the Organization for Economic Cooperation and Development (OECD) concluded that the Netherlands' constitutional principle of freedom of choice in education made it one of the "most devolved" of all advanced industrial economies, which means much of the work of educating young people is pushed to local school boards that exercise comparatively high levels of autonomy and to parents who have unusual freedom of school choice.[59] While the Netherlands continues to debate whether separate schools may stifle the integration of Muslim immigrants into Dutch society, freedom of education has persisted as a defining national norm.

The result is enrollment at nonpublic schools at rates that are unique among western democracies. About two-thirds of primary and secondary school students attend nonpublic schools, by far the highest level of the six countries considered in this study (for example, nonpublic schools in France and the United States serve 20 and 10 percent of schoolchildren, respectively). The Netherlands is also distinctive in the range of schools that receive support. Unlike other European states with a legacy of a predominant religion (e.g., Catholicism in France), the Netherlands has never had a single faith that thoroughly dominated the religious landscape. Out of 7,300 primary schools in 2013, for example, 31 percent of students attended public schools, 34 percent in Catholic schools, 28 percent in various kinds of Protestant schools (from generically mainline to intensely orthodox Reformed), and the remainder attended a range of private school types.[60] There are about forty-six Muslim primary schools (two Muslim secondary schools were shut down for lack of quality), as well as six Hindu schools.[61] All of these schools are fully funded by the central government.

This pattern of multiple types of schools, all funded by the government, is enshrined in Article 23 of the Constitution, which states: "All persons shall be free to provide education" and "Private primary schools . . . shall be financed from public funds according to the same standards as public-authority schools." The Constitution also states that private secondary schools shall receive public funding, as determined by the States-General. L. S. J. M. Henkens, who served as the director of secondary schooling in the Ministry of Education and Science, has written that Article 23 protects three distinct freedoms: the freedom of private associations to found schools, the freedom to determine the principles on which schools are to be based, and the freedom to organize the instruction. The second of these freedoms "entitles the competent authority of a school to choose the ideological or philosophical principles on which teaching at the school is to be based. The third . . . [entitles] the competent authority to decide on the content of teaching and the teaching methods to be used in the school."[62] This means that whenever there are sufficient numbers of parents who want a new school that incorporates a certain distinctive religious or secular philosophy (*richting*, or direction), the government is committed to fund it as fully as it does the public schools. This includes the construction of facilities.

While these principles might seem straightforward, in practice the Netherlands' basic policy of fully funding all schools still leaves many unresolved issues. One issue is how many parents and pupils asking for a new school are sufficient for the government to accede to their request. The numbers of students needed to found a new, publicly funded school are set by national standards that vary based on pupil density in the area. In rural areas as few as eighty pupils may be enough, while two to three hundred are generally required in urban areas. Education officials also consider whether a school of the same or similar orientation is nearby. If there already is a school of the same religious or secular orientation in the area, authorities may require a higher threshold of students before they approve a new school, even though attending the existing school may require a lengthy trip. Moreover, in recent years the government has been seeking economies of scale by merging or closing very small schools. There are seven hundred fewer primary schools today than just a decade ago, a nearly 10 percent decline. [63]

A second issue is determining exactly what constitutes a new or distinctive religious or secular direction. If there already is a Protestant school in a community, but some parents believe it is too modern or contemporary in its theology, is that a sufficient basis for the government to fund a new school? Some Muslims have thought that the government has been insensitive to the variety *within* Islam and should allow for more variety of Islamic expressions. Even the basic idea that nonpublic schools must have a distinctive faith-oriented or philosophical direction is facing increasing questions, including most recently from Sander Dekker, an official at the Ministry of Education, Culture, and Science, who has publicly advocated for allowing a greater range of ideas as bases for nonpublic schools. [64]

Several factors seem to make a system with potential for conflict and abuse in fact work with a manageable number of tensions and conflict. One is that Dutch society as a whole—including the public authorities—is genuinely committed to a pluralistic education system. Thus groups of parents wishing to maintain or start a school—while not automatically granted their request—are received with respect and given serious consideration. Second, the famous Dutch system of governing by discussion, negotiation, and consensus-building comes into play. There are umbrella organizations representing the various religious and secular groups active in education, and thus active discussions and negotiations ensue when an issue arises over the founding or closing of a school of a particular group. Third, partly because of the equal funding from the state, the Netherlands has avoided social stratification and wide disparities of quality in its schools and the "skimming" of top students from public to nonpublic schools. [65]

Although this system works well for most of Dutch society, it poses some problems for Muslims. First, the attacks of 9/11, the murder of Theo van Gogh in 2004, and subsequent terrorist attacks by Muslim extremists throughout Europe have all worked to create a spirit of suspicion and distrust that was previously unknown in Dutch society, or at least limited to the fringes of society. Second, Muslims themselves are sharply divided among different national origins—largely Moroccan, Turkish, Indonesian, and Surinamese, with some recent growth from Syrian refugees—and between more radical and more moderate elements. With the exception of Contactorgaan Moslims en Overheid (Contact Committee between Muslims and Government), established in 2004, there are few Muslim umbrella organizations that can discuss and negotiate with public authorities on behalf of large segments of the Muslim community. As a result, although the pluralism of the Dutch—including the old pillarization model—would seem ready-made for dealing with the needs of a minority religious community such as the Muslims, all has not gone smoothly. Some social observers are looking to the traditional Dutch system of full government funding for a variety of religiously and philosophically based schools as a means not to divide Dutch society and to alienate its Muslim minority, but as a seedbed for integration.

In both principle and practice, funding of this sort fits with a Dutch vision of pluralism. The vast majority of the private schools receiving full public funding are religious in nature. When pressed as to the nature of the Catholic schools, Dominique Majoor of a Catholic umbrella education organization acknowledged that some Catholic schools are Catholic only in name, but then went on to state: "But I think still a lot of schools are Catholic not only in name but also by what they are doing and how they are doing it. The ideal within my organization is that we should work on it and improve it. . . . But I look at my own schools—the schools I've seen—and you can really recognize them as being Catholic." [66]

Even more telling, a small proportion of the Dutch population belongs to several strictly Reformed, or orthodox, Protestant denominations with their own schools. [67] These schools are free to hire only teachers in agreement with their religious commitments and to accept students based on the religion of their families. In the term used by the U.S. Supreme Court, they are "pervasively sectarian" schools. They are also fully funded by the government. Even though they clearly are based in a minority religious community that runs counter to the strong forces of secularization dominant in Dutch society, they have experienced minimal problems in obtaining governmental approval for opening new schools, obtaining full government funding, and maintaining the freedom to teach their beliefs in the classroom.

In short, although most of the religious schools receiving full public funding are religious in a very general sense—as one would expect in a very secularized society—some are also very specifically, distinctively religious in nature. They too receive full funding from the government.

The Dutch typically characterize their system as one of church-state separation.[68] When we asked the legal scholar van Bijsterveld how church-state separation can be squared with financial support for religious organizations, including deeply religious schools, she replied that the Netherlands has no established church and that the state does not directly finance the churches, but if the state subsidizes education and social work, it must not discriminate against religion. If it funds neutral organizations, funding religious ones does not violate church-state separation.

> There have also been court decisions that government doesn't have to subsidize social work, charitable work, or youth work, but when it subsidizes this type of work it should make no discrimination on the basis of religion or belief. So if a "neutral" organization applies for this work it may receive it, but if a church or religious organization wants to carry out this work, it should not be excluded because that would not be equal treatment.[69]

It is on the basis of equal treatment—of making funds available neutrally for all types of religious schools and for religious and secular schools alike—that funding of religious schools and church-state separation are seen as being compatible.

This leads to the question of how much freedom or autonomy is granted religious schools. Are they fully free to be as religious as they wish? Or are there overt or subtle pressures to conform and to water down their religious message? First, it is clear that all schools—public and private, religious and secular—are under numerous limitations and constraints. The Netherlands is a highly regulated society, with government regulations affecting almost all areas of life. Education is no exception. Much of the curriculum is set on the national level, as are the certification standards and the working conditions for teachers. All students from all schools take the same comprehensive exams. Schools clearly are not free to have whomever they want, teaching whatever they want them to teach.

Nevertheless, schools are, in a formal sense, completely free to be as religious as they wish to be. Article 23 of the Constitution seeks to protect this religious freedom when it states that government standards shall give "due regard, in the case of private schools, to the freedom to provide education according to religious or other belief." It later goes on to state that the funding "provisions shall respect in particular the freedom of private schools to choose their teaching aids and to appoint teachers as they see fit." In this context "teaching aids" refer to such learning supports as textbooks, maps, and films. The director of an umbrella Catholic school association has written that "educational institutions at all levels are permitted to teach in the manner they please. They can choose their own texts and their own teachers, including the possibility of using religion and lifestyle as a criterion for hiring."[70] Chris Janse, who is from one of the small, strictly orthodox Protestant groups, discussed some tensions they had experienced with government officials over the teaching of evolution and some other curriculum matters, but then he concluded: "In general, you can't say that the government makes it very difficult for us."[71]

This is not, however, the entire story. There are two sources of pressures or constraints on the religious character of the schools. First, in reaction to fears that some of the Muslim schools might be teaching violence or hatred, a system of school inspections now looks more closely than it did earlier on what is being taught in the schools. It is still the case that "confessional schools are subject to state inspections, but the teaching of religion itself is not."[72] An attempt to include the content of religion courses being taught in the schools in the inspections was rejected by parliament. Nevertheless, school inspections can reach conclusions concerning the general atmosphere or teachings of a school. Veit Bader of the University of Amsterdam reported to us that a 2005 official report on fifty-two Muslim schools found only two where serious concerns over the teaching of hatred and violence existed.[73] Some schools in the strict, orthodox Reformed tradition have felt under some new pressures over what they are teaching, since they feel that in the public mind they are being lumped in with the Muslim schools.[74] But these concerns and pressures must be viewed in the context of Dutch pluralism, which has traditionally given religiously based schools a great deal of freedom.

A second way in which government pressures can be brought to bear on religious schools relates to their hiring practices. When there is a vacancy, schools are legally free to hire any qualified applicant, but there are certain financial advantages in hiring a currently unemployed teacher, whether or not he or she agrees with the religious character of the school. As the principal of one Protestant school has written: "At the moment we are forced to give precedence to teachers from other schools who have, for some reason or other, lost their jobs, unless there are very clear and relevant reasons for not doing so."[75] These pressures can be resisted, but they are there. Also, the right to make hiring decisions based on religion is not automatically accorded all religiously based schools. Rather, they need to demonstrate that doing so is necessary in order to preserve the school's religious identity.[76] As a result, ironically, it is easier for the more pervasively religious schools to justify hiring decisions based on religion than it is for the more nominally religious schools.

What about the role of religion in the public schools? Article 23 stipulates: "Education provided by public authorities shall . . . [pay] due respect to everyone's religion or belief." This has been "interpreted as a neutrality clause which requires a positive attitude towards religion. . . . Provision is made for [voluntary] religious education in public-authority schools. . . . A whole series of court rulings established that instruction in non-religious (humanist) belief should be offered and subsidized on the same basis as religious instruction."[77] Exactly how these requirements are met varies from one locality to another. Usually they are met by some form of objective teaching about religions and the role they play in society. Sometimes released time programs have been adopted, where students are taught by representatives of the various faiths after normal school hours. Prayer and other devotional activities are very rare in public schools, but have never been explicitly outlawed by either court decision or parliament. There is no attempt to encourage or promote consensual religious beliefs and traditions in the public schools. Such efforts would run counter to the principle of religious pluralism embraced by the Dutch.

There is, however, little educational choice on the university level. While there are one Reformed and two Catholic universities, most students attend public universities. And this is only a part of the story. The Protestant and Catholic universities are almost indistinguishable from their public counterparts. In fact, the universities are so similar that students are centrally assigned to the various universities, with a lottery system used in cases of excess demand. All universities, including those with a religious tie, are funded by the central government. Theological schools are also funded by the government, and here distinctive religious differences, of course, still exist. Since 1962 the education of humanist counselors has also been included in the system of government support. And currently there is also a government-funded program for Islamic spiritual leaders at the Free University of Amsterdam (a similar program at Leiden University is defunct). Again, one sees the Dutch understanding of governmental religious neutrality, a neutrality gained not by rejecting funding for theological education, as is the case in the United States, but by funding theological training for all religions and for secular, humanist counselors as well.

Educational choice, as we said at the beginning of this consideration of education, is the cornerstone of the Dutch approach to education. Religious schools are fully funded, and this is seen not as a violation of church-state separation and religious neutrality, but as a necessity if government is to be truly neutral among competing religious and nonreligious belief systems. To do otherwise would be to pick sides and thereby violate the free exercise rights of those left out.

CHURCH, STATE, AND NONPROFIT SERVICE ORGANIZATIONS

The struggle over the financing of private religious schools and the settlement reached on that issue historically did much to shape the Dutch approach
to the role nonprofit service organizations play in society and their funding
by the government. The field of education established the pattern of relying
upon private organizations to provide a vital public service. It became "an
important foundation for publicly funded private action as a dominant modus
in other fields and as a growth model in [the] post-war Dutch welfare
state."[78]

Some fifty-five thousand private—sometimes religiously based—agencies provide services related to health, poverty, media, and other areas.[79]
This work is complementary to the goals of the Netherlands' large welfare
state. Public spending on social programs accounts for nearly a quarter of the
Netherlands' GDP, well above the average for advanced industrial economies.[80] Approximately 60 percent of nonprofit budgets flows from this state
largesse; support is even higher for nonprofits that are heavily involved in
public services.[81] Remaining revenue comes from fees-for-service and private donations. Contrary to conventional wisdom, the high rate of government spending in the nonprofit sector is associated with *higher* rates of
philanthropic giving to nonprofit groups.[82] The pattern of government support for nonprofits shows no sign of reversing itself. In a move similar to the
American, British, and French devolution of some social service activity to
local departments and private associations in the 1980s, the Dutch government has "privatized some of its agencies and transformed them into private
nonprofits," which remains a "vital factor in [the] functioning" of both nonprofits and the welfare state.[83]

But this coevolution of the welfare state and nonprofit sector has raised
some questions about the continued autonomy of religious associations in
civil society. From the Middle Ages, religious groups in the Netherlands
were the primary sources of aid to the poor, sick, and elderly, and their work
was largely independent of the fragmented state. In the heyday of pillarization, the same system that nurtured schools within distinct subcultures also
existed in the areas of social services.[84] The pillars were separate, to be sure,
but they did take care of their own by building hospitals, economic associations, charities for the poor, and cultural groups focused on everything from
music to sports. This work was buttressed by sophisticated theological ratio-
nales. Dutch Catholics adapted the doctrine of subsidiarity to the context of
the Netherlands.[85] Subsidiarity is the principle that social problems should be
addressed at the lowest level of institutional competency; advocates often use
the principle to argue that we should always start with local or community
solutions to public problems. Pope Leo XIII articulated the doctrine in his
famous 1891 encyclical, *Rerum Novarum*, at the same time that Kuyper and

other Dutch Reformed leaders were developing a complementary doctrine. The Reformed idea of "sphere sovereignty" envisioned a society of distinctive types of human association—family, business, education, church, government, and so on—that God had created with inviolable purposes. This comprehensive Reformed vision provided a rationale for Christians to engage in all spheres of human life—and also to respond vigorously through the state when a sphere faltered in fulfilling its God-given purposes.

The upshot, historically, is that "religion was a major factor in the creation and development of the Dutch nonprofit sector."[86] One area that illustrates this influence is international aid. The Netherlands has been a longtime leader in providing financial and other resources for social and economic development abroad. Until recently, the state has budgeted more than 0.7 percent of the country's GDP to support programs for these purposes, exceeding United Nations' targets for advanced economies. But consistent with the Dutch model in education, organizations in civil society have been indispensable to the development of foreign aid programs. The state developed this "cofinancing" approach in the waning years of pillarization, resulting in the distribution of funds to nongovernmental organizations associated with different segments of society: Catholic (Cebemo, today called Cordaid); Protestant (ICCO); and social-democratic and nonreligious (Oxfam Novib and, later, Hivos). These organizations, among others, continue to draw heavily from the Dutch government. State officials are slowly rethinking development strategies as the Dutch public turns inward and wary of international entanglements; the prospects for private-public partnerships are not as strong as a few decades ago.[87] But the church-state relationships do continue at a high level in comparison to other countries.

It is also important to note that the area of international aid, like most other areas of the nonprofit service sector, has been affected by the "depillarization" and secularization trends that have swept through the Netherlands— more so than education. The secularization trend means that many faith-based social service agencies have lost the constituency or base that in the past had supported them and provided a rationale for their existence. With their constituencies melting away, the religious agencies possess weak means with which to resist pressures from the state to adapt. When this occurs, nonprofit service organizations lose the same protections that schools have by way of Article 23 of the Constitution.

Relying on the state for resources presents its own threats to the integrity of religious groups. Government cost-saving pressures have forced many agencies to change practices or to merge with other agencies, including Protestant or Catholic agencies with secular agencies. Stavros Zouridis, an official in the Ministry of Justice, explained to us that if one agency is spending more money for a certain item or service than others, it is called upon by government officials to explain why. They are thereby forced to adopt the lower-cost practices of other agencies—and in the process lose more of their autonomy. He concluded that private social service agencies "are now controlled by the state. The welfare agencies have lost their autonomy."[88] This same conclusion is echoed by many others working in the nonprofit sector.[89]

Other organizations face persistent concerns about quality and endurance. There are Muslim social service agencies that also receive government funding, such as several Islamic homes for the elderly that are government funded. According to one team of scholars, Muslim agencies have "achieved a strong position in civil society, thanks to the existing legislation and the protection of freedom of religion."[90] There is government-subsidized Muslim television programming. Nevertheless, problems remain, and Muslim organizations do not take part in the nonprofit sector as fully as do Christian, Jewish, and secular agencies. The key problem is that even when Muslims develop social service programs, questions of stability, openness, and organizational strength that the Dutch system expects are often not there.

In short, the Dutch make extensive use of nonprofit organizations to deliver a wide variety of public services, and many of these organizations possess—to greater and lesser degrees—religious orientations. The system has been battered by the secularization of Dutch society, not-always-successful moves to incorporate Muslims and other religious minorities into the system, and governmental moves to enforce cost savings and regulations. But the system still exists.

To many Americans such practices would raise concerns about religious freedom. After all, tax money from nonbelievers funds Jewish homes for the elderly, money collected from Jews supports Christian family counseling programs, and taxes paid by Christians fund Muslim television broadcasts. But the Dutch response is to insist that to withhold funding from religious organizations would be a denial of religious freedom. This came out in our interviews time and again. Frans Koopmans, of De Hoop (The Hope) drug treatment center, made a point that is fundamental to the Dutch mind-set in regard to state funding of religious service organizations: "Every hospital, every helping facility has its principles, its priorities, its fundamentals. Even though they are perhaps not Christian. Everyone is working out of a philosophy. We are working out of a Christian philosophy because we are wholeheartedly convinced it is the truth."[91] As a result of this perspective, equal treatment demands that religious and nonreligious organizations be funded in the same manner. As Koopmans also said, "We have Christians in the Netherlands and we should have facilities to help that specific part of our population. If people are humanistic, you should have a humanistic hospital."[92]

Similarly, when asked concerning possible negative reactions of nonbelievers, Jews, or Muslims over their taxes going to fund his explicitly Christian organization, Martin de Jong, of a distinctively Christian agency serving disabled children and their families, responded:

We [Dutch] almost never have that kind of discussion, because they can get money for the same kind of activities in their interpretation of life. It's a right for everyone to get money for such kind of activities. . . . They have a right to get money for such kind of activities; we have the right to get money for such kind of activities. So when they say that to me I can say that is a common right, it is not only my right. . . . It's not a right especially for Christians, or for the Jewish; it's a common right. [93]

Maria Martens of VKMO (an umbrella organization of Catholic social service organizations) defended her agencies' receiving public funds with these words: "When the government gives money for housing for the elderly, why not to Catholics? . . . When we are all paying our taxes, for these kinds of initiatives, and we have our [initiatives], why should we be left out?"[94]

Koopmans, de Jong, and Martens appeal to a basic sense of governmental neutrality or evenhandedness based on the concept of a pluralistic society, whose various elements have distinctive philosophies or approaches and are deserving of the same support. In the dominant Dutch view public funding of social service organizations does not violate church-state separation or governmental religious neutrality, as long as such funding goes to the organizations of all religious traditions and to those of nonreligious secular groups as well. In fact, to do otherwise is seen as discriminating against religion. Undergirding this perspective is the rejection of an assumption often made in the United States, namely, that religious organizations have a bias or a distinctive ax to grind, while nonreligious secular organizations are neutral. In the Netherlands secular and religious organizations alike are seen as inevitably operating out of certain distinctive philosophies or beliefs.

But this assumption about neutrality does raise the question of the limits to the religious freedom possessed by religious nonprofit service organizations that receive public funds. On the one hand, as we have already seen, there are strong and convincing claims that government funding has led to considerable government control over nonprofit organizations. On the other hand, there is persuasive evidence that the control exercised by government officials usually does not extend to the religious activities and identity of nonprofit organizations. Koopmans of the evangelical drug rehabilitation program De Hoop suggests a balance between government power and nonprofit autonomy: "What we do have, of course, are regulations for every psychiatric hospital—Christian or non-Christian, humanistic, anthroposophic—which we have to subscribe to. But they are not anti-Christian regulations. . . . The Netherlands always has been known as a very tolerant country in which everyone could believe whatever you wanted as long as you did not hurt anyone else. Well, it's still so."[95]

In fact, more than one observer told us that those agencies that are more distinctively religious are in a better position to resist governmental pressures to merge with other agencies or to alter their practices than those with a more nominal religious or a fully secular character.[96] Van Bijsterveld stated that "it is easier for organizations to resist pressure to merge with other organizations if they are very distinctively Christian, and harder if they are more generally Christian. Then it is harder for them to document a distinct identification or direction—we say *richting*—that is lost if they would merge with another."[97] From a pluralist perspective, an agency's distinct religious or philosophical orientation is something to be respected and accommodated, not something looked down upon or ignored.

In summary, Dutch policies regarding religiously based schools and social service organizations are similar. In both cases the government—supported by attitudes prevalent in Dutch society—provides generous levels of funding to a wide variety of service organizations, religiously and secularly based alike. This public policy is rooted in a pluralistic concept of society that recognizes a variety of religious and secular belief systems present in society, all of which are held to be legitimate, contributing forces and therefore possessing an equal right to expect an appropriate share of public support. This system has, however, had some difficulties accommodating itself to the various immigrant Muslim communities, and therefore Muslims, while taking part in this system, do not do so to the same extent as other religious and secular groups. As is the case throughout Dutch society, there are many government regulations affecting the service organizations receiving public funds, a regulatory environment reinforced by recent government efforts to achieve economies of scale in the delivery of social services. The general secularization of Dutch society—and therefore of many of its previously religiously based nonprofit organizations—has made it harder for many agencies to resist the homogenizing influence of government regulations. Nevertheless, the religious missions of religiously based agencies appear largely to be respected, at least when those religious missions are clearly in evidence and articulated.

CONCLUDING OBSERVATIONS

The Netherlands is a clear example of the second model of church-state relations presented in chapter 1, the pluralist model. The Dutch seek to attain governmental neutrality on matters of religion, not by a strict church-state separation that sees all aid to religion as a violation of the norm of neutrality, but by a pluralism that welcomes and supports all religious and secular structures of belief on an equal, evenhanded basis. This is a system of principled pluralism—as we put it in the title of this chapter—in that the Netherlands' pluralist approach to church and state is rooted in certain self-consciously held beliefs.

The principled nature of the Dutch church-state pluralist system is rooted in two basic assumptions. One is a pluralistic view of society that sees a variety of religious and philosophical movements—even when they are full participants in the public life of the nation—as normal and no threat to the unity and prosperity of society. Unlike France, such movements are not relegated to the private realm, with only consensual civil religious beliefs and values allowed into the public realm.

But this perspective has been seriously tested in recent years due to debates over the role of immigrant Muslim groups in Dutch society. Many have questioned whether or not Muslims fit into a Dutch system of religious pluralism that developed out of a cultural milieu rooted in largely western ideas of religion and society. Although those ideas were diverse—Catholic, Reformed, secular—they nevertheless combined to provide shared traditions and values that bind the Dutch into a single people. The challenge is whether the distinctive traditions and values of Muslim immigrants into the Netherlands overlap enough with the rest of Dutch society to make the system of pluralism work. Some skeptics have simply rejected the underlying multiculturalist assumptions in arguments for continuing immigration, frequently arguing that multicultural aspirations are damaging to both immigrants and native residents alike.[98]

For our purposes the important point is that the traditional pluralistic legal forms and—even more important—cultural assumptions continue to be dominant. To be sure, pluralism has been battered in the past fifteen years in a way it had not since the "pacification" of 1917. In response to growing concerns about the Muslim minority, some of the political parties on the right, such as the VVD and the PVV, are raising new questions about how far the state should go in recognizing and funding the schools and social service agencies of religious groups. Nevertheless, a commitment to religious pluralism persists in the legal structure and in the dominant mind-set. And perhaps in this pluralism the Netherlands will find a way to address the challenge of integrating a new subculture. As Veit Bader of the University of Amsterdam related to us:

> The system for financing religious schools in the Netherlands is entrenched. . . . And in a comparative perspective, this opened more opportunities for Muslims to have their own schools in the Netherlands compared to all other European countries. In the UK there is now after a long battle two publicly financed schools—directly recognized Muslim schools—France has none, and in the Netherlands we have some 50 Muslim schools, in a much smaller country, with many fewer practicing Muslims.[99]

While the situation in France and the United Kingdom has changed in the ten years since this interview took place, the underlying point about the *comparatively* greater number of Muslim schools in the Netherlands is still accurate.

It remains to be seen whether the Netherlands' efforts at accommodation yield comparatively better results as its Muslim minority moves from the status of immigrants to citizens.

A second underlying assumption is that nonreligious organizations and movements are not truly neutral—as is often assumed within the liberal Enlightenment view of society—but are yet another *richting*, or direction, equally legitimate but no more legitimate than a host of other religious and nonreligious philosophies or directions. The United States Supreme Court often assumes that separating church and state means that the state is neutral with respect to religion, that by withholding support for all religious groups the state avoids playing favorites. But the Dutch would view that approach as simply introducing a specific *richting*—a set of assumptions about religion and the state—that is value laden and not really neutral at all. In a sense the French own up to this lack of neutrality by embedding a Republican philosophy and tolerating public expressions of religiosity only to the extent that they have public utility. But the Dutch would view that approach as a violation of the freedom in principle, because the French state envisions its own *richting* as superior and primary to all others.

Public policies that respect, accommodate, and support public roles for a plurality of religious and secular belief structures emerge out of the Dutch assumptions about neutrality. The comments of Bob Goudzwaard, a retired professor of economics at the Free University of Amsterdam, made to us two decades ago still hold true in understanding Dutch policies in regard to church-state issues: "Nondiscrimination, when it comes to religion, always also means in the Dutch mindset that if you have an organization that thinks it good to have a Christian approach, that cannot be a reason in itself to withhold subsidies because that would be discrimination. That is still very often present in the mindset."[100] This is a basic point that has emerged at various points throughout this chapter. What is often viewed in the United States as discriminating in favor of religion, and thereby a form of establishing religion, is viewed in the Netherlands as necessary in order not to discriminate *against* religion. On this basis the government funds a wide variety of private religiously based schools, universities, theological schools, and social service and health agencies. To do otherwise would violate the free exercise rights of those not recognized or accommodated on a basis equal to other religious or secular movements. As van Bijsterveld said, "Freedom of religion is not only a negative freedom in the sense that the government not infringe upon it, but also the structure of the law must create an atmosphere so that religion can really be exercised."[101] If religion is to be fully free, government must take certain positive steps to accommodate it so that religion, along with secular beliefs, can in practice be freely exercised.

There is a paradox here. In the name of opposing the liberal vision of society based on privatizing particularistic religious beliefs and favoring a generic moral consensus, the Dutch have forged an approach to church and state that achieves the liberal goal of religious freedom for all. It does so by allowing the recognition and support for the full range of particularistic religious beliefs, a practice that liberalism traditionally had assumed inevitably would lead to divisiveness and religious repression of one group by another. Once one accepts the fact that consensual moral-religious beliefs that are accepted by most but not all of the population and that public institutions and programs purged of all religious elements are not truly neutral, but reflect certain philosophical or moral perspectives, it is hard to disagree with the basic Dutch contention that true governmental neutrality can only be attained by treating people and organizations of all religious and nonreligious perspectives and beliefs equally—not by favoring one over the other.

In seeking to understand how the Netherlands successfully arrived at its commitment to a principled pluralism, the role played by Catholic-Protestant cooperation must be recalled. It was the "monster alliance," forged in the 1870s between Catholics and the more orthodox among the Reformed Protestants, that was able to overcome the previously dominant liberal forces and carry the day politically. In the United States, as we saw in chapter 2, Protestants largely made common cause with liberals in opposition to the Catholic Church. In France, as we saw in chapter 3, the predominant Catholicism has experience over two centuries of conflict with the post-Revolution state. Yet it is important to note that the theories of religious pluralism that were developed by the Dutch alliance were much more than a rationalization for the advancement of its members' own causes. It was an ideology to which they were in reality committed. Jews, socialists, and secular humanists were early included within it, and today Muslims and Hindus—with considerable difficulties and uncertainty, to be sure—are as well. It was a genuine, not a sham, commitment to pluralism.

Finally, it is important to note that in part this system may work as well as it does in the Netherlands because of certain unique Dutch conditions. Even the small, compact size of the country enters in, served as it is by excellent public transportation and an ubiquitous system of bicycle paths. This means schoolchildren can safely ride to schools some distance from their homes, thereby making it easier to sort out the children by religious or philosophical conviction. The public transportation system makes it possible for citizens to reach the social or health service agency they wish to use. The sense of cooperation and national unity forged by a common history and language (except for a small minority of Frisian speakers) may also play a role. Countries without the same long tradition of working together may have a harder time maintaining a sense of national unity and purpose than has the Netherlands. Nevertheless, the Netherlands stands as a testimony to the possibility of combining genuine governmental religious neutrality, a broad system of recognition and support for religious and secular private schools and social service organizations, and national purpose and unity. There is much to learn from the Dutch experience.

NOTES

1. Current population estimates are available at http://data.worldbank.org/country/ netherlands.
2. For a brief, readable account of the historical background of Dutch pluralism, see Robert C. Tash, *Dutch Pluralism* (New York: Lang, 1991), chap. 2.
3. Centraal Bureau voor de Stratistiek, "Bevolkinsontwikkeling; region per maand," *Statline* (May 24, 2016). Available at http://statline.cbs.nl/Statweb/.
4. For these and following statistics, see Hans Schmeets and Carly van Mensvoort, "Religieuze betrokkenheid van bevolkingsgroepen, 2010–14" (Den Hague: Centraal Bureau voor de Statistiek, 2015), 4; and Pew Research Center's Religion and Public Life Project (available at http://www.globalreligiousfutures.org/countries/netherlands/religious_demography#/? affiliations_religion_id=0&affiliations_year=2010).
5. Jonathan Laurence, *The Emancipation of Europe's Muslims: The State's Role in Minority Integration* (Princeton, N.J.: Princeton University Press, 2012), 4.
6. See G. A. Irwin and J. J. M. van Holsteyn, "Decline of the Structured Model of Electoral Competition," in Hans Daalder and Galen Irwin, eds., *Politics in the Netherlands: How Much Change?* (Totowa, N.J.: Cass, 1989), 34. On the recent secularization trend also see Hans Knippenberg, "Secularization and Transformation of Religion in Post-War Europe," in Stanley D. Brunn, ed., *The Changing World Religion Map* (Dordrecht: Springer, 2015), 2106; and James Carleton Kennedy, *Building the New Babylon: Cultural Change in the Netherlands during the 1960s* (Ph.D. dissertation, University of Iowa, 1995).
7. Pew's estimate of the unaffiliated is 42.1 percent, but the European Values Survey reports over half. See Knippenberg, "Secularization and Transformation of Religion in Post-War Europe," 2106. See also Schmeets and van Mensvoort, "Religieuze betrokkenheid," 4, which reports 49.2 percent. But while the data vary a little, the story of secularization is the same.
8. European World Values Survey, Wave Five, 2005–09, 2006. The European Values Study Foundation and World Values Survey Association. Data are available at http://www. worldvaluessurvey.org/wvs.jsp.
9. *Statistical Yearbook of the Netherlands, 2014,* 96.
10. Central Bureau voor de Stastistiek, "Fewer Churchgoers, Especially among Catholics." Available at https://www.cbs.nl/en-gb/news/2014/40/fewer-churchgoers-especially-among-catholics. The World Values Survey finds a slightly lower percentage. See European World Values Survey, Wave Five, 2005–09, 2006. The European Values Study Foundation and World Values Survey Association.
11. Mieke Maliepaard, *Religious Trends and Social Integration: Muslim Minorities in the Netherlands* (Ph.D. dissertation, University of Utrecht, 2012).
12. Steff Aupers, "'We Are All Gods': New Age in the Netherlands 1960–2000," in E. Sengers, ed., *The Dutch and Their Gods: Secularization and the Transformation of Religion in the Netherlands since 1950* (Hilversum: Verloren, 2005), 181–201.
13. For an excellent introduction to Dutch government, see Rudy B. Andeweg and Galen A. Irwin, *Dutch Government and Politics* (New York: St. Martin's Press, 1993).
14. See Andeweg and Irwin, *Dutch Government and Politics*, chaps. 2 and 7. On consociational theory see Arend Lijphart's classic discussion in "Consociational Democracy," *Comparative Political Studies* 1 (1968), 3–44.
15. See the discussion in Andeweg and Irwin, *Dutch Government and Politics*, 33–44. Also see Arend Lijphart, "From the Politics of Accommodation to Adversarial Politics in the Netherlands: A Reassessment," in Daalder and Irwin, eds., *Politics in the Netherlands*, 140–53.
16. Andeweg and Irwin, *Dutch Government and Politics*, 175.

17. Quoted by Charles L. Glenn Jr., *The Myth of the Common School* (Amherst: University of Massachusetts Press, 1987), 46.

18. Quoted by Glenn, *The Myth of the Common School*, 46. Emphasis removed.

19. Quoted by Glenn, *The Myth of the Common School*, 47.

20. Some factions had left the church out of concern that it had deserted traditional, orthodox Calvinist theology and practice. For English-language accounts of this struggle, see Glenn, *The Myth of the Common School*, 244–49; and Stanley Carlson-Thies, *Democracy in the Netherlands: Consociational or Pluriform?* (Ph.D. dissertation, University of Toronto, 1993), 44–231. Much of what follows is based on these accounts.

21. Carlson-Thies, *Democracy in the Netherlands*, 138.

22. Carlson-Thies, *Democracy in the Netherlands*, 144.

23. Hans Daalder, "The Netherlands: Opposition in a Segmented Society," in Robert A. Dahl, ed., *Political Opposition* (New Haven, Conn.: Yale University Press, 1966), 201.

24. The term is from G. J. Rooymans, used in a publication put out by the Catholic party in 1948. See Carlson-Thies, *Democracy in the Netherlands*, 175.

25. It is a testament to the deep-seated nature of this funding approach that the education provisions of the 1917 Constitution survived a massive overhaul of the Constitution of the Netherlands in 1983.

26. Michael P. Fogarty, *Christian Democracy in Western Europe, 1820–1953* (London: Routledge & Kegan Paul, 1957), 172. The best English-language history of Kuyper is James D. Bratt, *Abraham Kuyper: Modern Calvinist, Christian Democrat* (Grand Rapids, Mich.: Eerdmans, 2013). On Kuyper and his theological influence also see John Bolt, *A Free Church, a Holy Nation: Abraham Kuyper's American Public Theology* (Grand Rapids, Mich.: Eerdmans, 2001), and Vincent Bacote, *The Spirit in Public Theology: Appropriating the Legacy of Abraham Kuyper* (Grand Rapids, Mich.: Baker, 2005).

27. Bratt, *Abraham Kuyper*, xvi.

28. Abraham Kuyper, *Calvinism: Six Stone Foundation Lectures* (Grand Rapids, Mich.: Eerdmans, 1931), 108.

29. Kuyper, *Calvinism*, 106.

30. Herman Bakvis, *Catholic Power in the Netherlands* (Kingston, Ont.: McGill-Queen's University Press, 1981), 61.

31. Carlson-Thies, *Democracy in the Netherlands*, 168–69.

32. Bakvis, *Catholic Power in the Netherlands*, 62.

33. On pillarization, see Erik H. Bax, *Modernization and Cleavage in Dutch Society* (Aldershot, U.K.: Avebury, 1990), chaps. 5 and 6; and Harry Post, *Pillarization: An Analysis of Dutch and Belgian Society* (Aldershot, U.K.: Avebury, 1989).

34. Justus Uitermark, "Conclusion: The Dynamics of Power," in Justus Uitermark, *Dynamics of Power in Dutch Integration Politics: From Accommodation to Confrontation* (Amsterdam: Amsterdam University Press, 2012), 247–64.

35. Interview with Sophie C. van Bijsterveld (September 25, 2006).

36. "Radicalism and Radicalisation" (Report of the Directorate of General Judicial Strategy to the Speaker of the Lower House of the States General, 19 August 2005, Ref no. 5358374/05/AJS), 33.

37. "Policy Document on Fundamental Rights in a Pluralistic Society" (Ministerie van Binnenlandse Zaken en Koninkrijksrelaties, May 2004), 3–4.

38. The exact 2012 election results can be found at http://www.nlverkiezingen.com/TK2012.html.

39. Paul M. Sniderman and Louk Hagendoorn, *When Ways of Life Collide: Multiculturalism and Its Discontents in the Netherlands* (Princeton, N.J.: Princeton University Press, 2007), 15.

40. Veit Bader, *Secularism or Democracy? Associational Governance of Religious Diversity* (Amsterdam: Amsterdam University Press, 2007), 297.

41. Ibid.

42. Interview with George Harinck, director of the Historical Document Center for Dutch Protestantism, Free University, Amsterdam (September 20, 2006).

43.   The Netherlands Constitution was last amended in 2008. This and following quotations are available from the Constitutional Affairs and Legislative Division of the Ministry of the Interior and Kingdom Relations at https://www.government.nl/documents/regulations/2012/10/18/the-constitution-of-the-kingdom-of-the-netherlands-2008.

44.   For a helpful report on the activities and decisions of this Commission in 2002 see Sophie C. van Bijsterveld, "Church and State in the Netherlands, 2002," *European Journal for Church and State Research* 10 (2003), 80–91.

45.   Equal Treatment Act (Commissie Gelijke Behandeling). Available at http://www.mensenrechten.nl/publicaties/detail/35931.

46.   Sophie C. van Bijsterveld, "The Constitutional Status of Religion in the Kingdom of the Netherlands," *The Constitutional Status of Churches in the European Union Countries* (European Consortium for Church-State Research, proceedings of the 1994 meeting, University of Paris), 207 and 211.

47.   Sophie C. van Bijsterveld, "State and Church in the Netherlands," in Gerhard Robbers, ed., *State and Church in the European Union,* 2nd ed. (Baden-Baden, Germany: Nomos Verlagsgesellschaft, 2005), 384. Italics added.

48.   Interview with Sophie C. van Bijsterveld (February 9, 1996).

49.   Barbara Oomen, "The Rights for Others: The Contested Homecoming of Human Rights in the Netherlands," *Netherlands Quarterly of Human Rights* 31 (2013), 50. Wilders went on trial again in 2016, but in that case prosecutors defined the issue as speech against a *racial*, rather than religious, group, which has a different status under the Dutch legal code.

50.   Barbara Oomen, *Rights for Others: The Slow Home-Coming of Human Rights in the Netherlands* (New York: Cambridge University Press, 2013).

51.   http://www.mensenrechten.nl/mission-and-ambition.

52.   Laurien Koster, *Human Rights in the Netherlands 2014: Summary and Recommendations of the Annual Status Report* (Utrecht: National Institute for Human Rights, 2015), 1.

53.   Articles 136 and 137, available at http://wetten.overheid.nl/BWBR0001854/2016-04-20#BoekTweede_TiteldeelV_Artikel136. See van Bijsterveld, "State and Church in the Netherlands," 387.

54.   Oomen, *Rights for Others,* chap. 8; Barbara M. Oomen, Joost Guijt, and Matthias Ploeg, "CEDAW, the Bible and the State of the Netherlands: The Struggle over Orthodox Women's Political Participation and Their Responses," *Utrecht Law Review* 6 (2010), 158–74; Barbara Oomen and Rijke Niels, "The Right to be Different: Homosexuality, Orthodoxy and the Politics of Global Legal Pluralism in Orthodox-Protestant Schools in the Netherlands," *Journal of Law and Religion* 28 (2012), 361–99.

55.   van Bijsterveld, "Church and State in the Netherlands, 2002," 81. Italics present.

56.   Ibid., 83–84; "Advisory Opinion of the Dutch Equal Treatment Commission on Niqaabs and Headscarves in Schools" (CGB Advisory Opinion/2003/01, April 16, 2003).

57.   See the speech by A. Nicolai, the Dutch state secretary of foreign affairs, in *Report of the International Conference on Fundamental Rights in a Pluralistic Society* (The Hague: Ministry of the Interior and Kingdom Relations, 2004), 60.

58.   Pew Global Attitudes Project, "Islamic Extremism: Common Concern for Muslim and Western Publics" (Washington, D.C.: Pew Research Center, 2015), 3–4.

59.   Deborah Nusche, Henry Braun, Gábor Halász, and Paulo Santiago, *OECD Reviews of Evaluation and Assessment in Education: Netherlands 2014* (Paris: OECD, 2015), 20–21. See also Organization for Economic Cooperation and Development, *School: A Matter of Choice* (Paris: OECD, 1994), 68. The quotation is from an earlier OECD study.

60.   "Key Figures 2009–2013" (The Hague: Ministry of Education, Culture, and Science, 2014). Available at https://www.government.nl/documents/reports/2014/08/12/key-figures-2009-2013-ministry-of-education-culture-and-science.

61.   Jaap Dronkers, "Islamic Primary Schools in the Netherlands," *Journal of School Choice* 10 (2016), 7.

62.   L. S. J. M. Henkens, "The Development of the Dutch Education System," in Tymen J. van der Ploeg and John W. Sap, eds., *Rethinking the Balance: Government and Non-Governmental Organizations in the Netherlands* (Amsterdam: VU University Press, 1995), 52. Sophie van Bijsterveld has more recently reiterated these three freedoms. See van Bijsterveld, "The

Permissible Scope of Legal Limitations on the Freedom of Religion or Belief in the Netherlands," 941.

63. "Key Figures 2009–13," 17.

64. Sander Dekker, "Het is maar wat je vrijheid van onderwijs noemt," *NRC,* July 2, 2015. Available at http://www.nrc.nl/nieuws/2015/07/02/het-is-maar-wat-je-vrijheid-van-onderwijs-noemt.

65. Anne Bert Dijkstra, Jaap Dronkers, and Sjoerd Karsten, "Private Schools as Public Provision for Education: Market Forces in the Netherlands," in Patrick J. Wolf and Stephen Macedo, eds., *Educating Citizens: International Perspectives on Civic Values and School Choice* (Washington, D.C.: Brookings Institution, 2003), 79–80.

66. Interview with Dominique Majoor of the General Bureau for Dutch Catholic Education (January 26, 1996).

67. See Oomen and Niels, "The Right to Be Different."

68. Van Bijsterveld, "Church and State in the Netherlands," 373. Although we cite here the second, 2005 edition of this work, the same quotation can be found in the first edition, published in 1996.

69. Interview with Sophie C. van Bijsterveld (February 9, 1996).

70. Bartho M. Janssen, "The Position of Umbrella Organizations, Advocacy and Commitment to the Central Policy," in van der Ploeg and Sap, eds., *Rethinking the Balance,* 68.

71. Interview with Chris Janse (September 21, 2006).

72. Van Bijsterveld, "State and Church in the Netherlands in 2002," 91.

73. Interview with Veit Bader, University of Amsterdam (September 22, 2006).

74. Interview with Chris Janse (September 21, 2006).

75. M. L. Kreuzen, "Freedom within Bounds—or the Regulated Autonomy," in van der Ploeg and Sap, eds., *Rethinking the Balance,* 73.

76. A recent example is an orthodox Reformed school that was pressed to defend its hiring practices when it terminated employment of a teacher who came out as gay. See Oomen and Niels, "The Right to Be Different."

77. Van Bijsterveld, "State and Church in the Netherlands," 379.

78. Paul Dekker, "Shifting Ideas of Subsidiarity in the Netherlands: Old and New Private Initiatives in the Social Domain," in Pierrepaulo Donati and Luca Martignani, eds., *Towards a New Local Welfare: Best Practices and Networks of Social Inclusion* (Bologna: Bolonia University Press, 2015), 113–40.

79. Pamala Wiepking and René Bekkers, "Giving in the Netherlands: A Strong Welfare State with a Vibrant Nonprofit Sector," in Pamala Wiepking et al., eds., *The Palgrave Handbook of Global Philanthropy* (New York: Palgrave, 2015), 211–29.

80. https://data.oecd.org/socialexp/social-spending.htm.

81. Phuong Ahn Nyugen, "The Influence of Government Support for the Nonprofit Sector on Philanthropy across Nations," in Wiepking et al., eds., *The Palgrave Handbook of Global Philanthropy*, 531; Lester M. Salamon, S. Wojciech Sokolowski et al., *Global Civil Society: Dimensions of the Nonprofit Sector*, vol. 2 (Bloomfield, Conn.: Kumarian Press, 2004), 301.

82. Nyugen, "The Influence of Government Support," 531.

83. Vic Veldheer and Ary Burger, "History of the Nonprofit Sector in the Netherlands," *Working Paper of the Johns Hopkins Comparative Nonprofit Sector Project*, no. 35, Lester M. Salamon and Helmut K. Anheier, eds. (Baltimore, Md.: Johns Hopkins Institute for Policy Studies, 1999), 23, 26.

84. Tymen J. van der Ploeg, "Changing Relationships between Private Organizations and Government in the Netherlands," in Kathleen D. McCarthy, Virginia A. Hodgkinson, and Russy D. Sumariwalla, eds., *The Nonprofit Sector in the Global Community* (San Francisco: Jossey-Bass, 1992), 194.

85. Pope Leo XIII, *Rerum Novarum,* May 1891. Available at http://w2.vatican.va/content/leo-xiii/en/encyclicals/documents/hf_l-xiii_enc_15051891_rerum-novarum.html. See Bekker, "Shifting Ideas of Subsidiarity."

86. Veldheer and Burger, "History of the Nonprofit Sector in the Netherlands," 24. Also see Ralph M. Kramer, "Governmental-Voluntary Agency Relationships in the Netherlands," *Netherlands' Journal of Sociology* 25 (1979), 155.

87. Gabi Spitz, Roeland Muskens, and Edith van Ewijk, *The Dutch and Development Cooperation: Ahead of the Crowd or Trailing Behind?* (Amsterdam: NCDO, 2013).

88. Interview with Stavros Zouridis, Ministry of Justice, Strategy Development Department (September 19, 2006).

89. Jaap E. Doek, "Relations in Child Protection: An Overview," in van der Ploeg and Sap, eds., *Rethinking the Balance*, 86.

90. Froukje Demant, Marcel Maussen, and Jan Rath, *Muslims in the EU: Cities Report, the Netherlands* (Open Society Institute, EU Monitoring and Advocacy Program, 2007), 35.

91. Interview with Frans Koopmans of De Hoop (February 5, 1996).

92. Interview with Frans Koopmans (February 5, 1996).

93. Interview with Martin J. de Jong (January 30, 1996).

94. Interview with Maria Martens of VKMO (February 5, 1996).

95. Interview with Frans Koopmans (February 5, 1996).

96. For example, George Harinck of the Free University of Amsterdam told us of a Protestant agency working with the blind that has requested one of his graduate students or him to do a study of the agency and its Protestant roots and rationale and their relevance for today. It hopes that with a more clearly articulated, religiously based vision it will be in a better position to resist governmental pressures. Interview with George Harinck (September 20, 2006).

97. Interview with Sophie C. van Bijsterveld (February 9, 1996).

98. The most powerful statement in this vein is Paul Scheffer, who prompted public debate with his essay, "The Multicultural Tragedy," in 2000. He elaborated on his position in *Immigrant Nation* (Hoboken, N.J.: Wiley, 2011).

99. Interview with Veit Bader (September 22, 2006).

100. Interview with Bob Goudzwaard of the Free University (February 7, 1996). Professor Goudzwaard is now retired.

101. Interview with Sophie C. van Bijsterveld (February 9, 1996).

Chapter Five

Australia

Pragmatic Pluralism

The most important principles in church-state relations in Australia are pragmatism and tolerance. Pragmatic considerations have structured the state's resolution of church-state issues at every point in Australian history, and because the "practical" solution to church-state problems has changed over time, Australia has vacillated among four different church-state models in its two-hundred-year history: establishment, plural establishment, liberal separationism, and pragmatic pluralism. As with the Netherlands, Australian policy is consistent with governmental neutrality and religious pluralism, but it is rooted in pragmatic concerns, not in basic, theoretical principles as in the Netherlands. At the same time, there has been very little support in Australia for an American-style separationist model that would challenge public finance of religious schools, religious activities in public schools, and state financial support for religious service organizations. Underlying this policy pragmatism is a socially tolerant political culture—a live and let live attitude—that has led to a respect for and protection of the rights of religious minorities.

THE NATION

Australia has a population of more than twenty-three million people spread over a continent roughly the size of the United States. Australia has doubled in population over the past fifty years and is currently growing faster than any other country in our study. Because of harsh environmental conditions—much of Australia is virtually uninhabitable—nearly 90 percent of the popu-

121

lation live in urban areas, and most of them reside along a thousand-mile stretch of the southeastern seaboard between the cities of Adelaide and Brisbane. Immigration has been a key factor throughout Australian history, and the country has a higher percentage of foreign-born population than any in our study. According to the 2011 census, just over one-quarter of the resident population of Australia was born overseas. By comparison, the 2010 Census of the United States noted that 13 percent of the American population was foreign born.[1]

As with every other country in our study, over the past several decades Australia has become more religiously pluralistic, less Christian, and more secular. Christian traditions still predominate in Australia, though the percentage of those identifying as Christian decreased from 68 percent of the total population in 2001 to 61 percent in 2011. The proportion of Australians who identify as Christian still dwarfs the second-largest religious group in the country, Buddhism (2.5 percent). The two largest Christian denominations are Catholic (25 percent of the total population) and Anglican (17 percent), followed by the Uniting Church, Presbyterian, Eastern Orthodox, and Baptist. Declines in the larger denominations have been somewhat offset by increases in some of the smaller evangelical (Baptist) and Pentecostal (Assemblies of God, Christian City Church) churches. The number of people who reported a non-Christian faith nearly doubled during the same ten-year period, growing from 4.9 percent of the population in 2001 to 7.2 percent in 2011. The largest non-Christian religions after Buddhism were Islam (2.2 percent) and Hinduism (1.3 percent). Much of that growth has come by way of immigrants, who have higher rates of religious identification than native-born Australians. A very large proportion of Australian Buddhists (69 percent), Muslims (61 percent), Hindus (84 percent), and Eastern Orthodox (44 percent) were foreign born. [2]

The other significant trend in recent decades has been an increase in those who report having no religion, rising from 6.7 percent in 1991, to 15 percent in 2001, and to just under 22 percent in 2011. Those who report that they do not have a religion are disproportionately young, suggesting that this secularizing trend might continue in the decades ahead.[3] There has been a corresponding decline among those Australians who believe in God or some higher power (78 percent in 1993 to 69 percent in 2009), and attendance at religious services has similarly gone down. Monthly church attendance has dropped from an estimated 24 percent in 1989, 20 percent by 2001, and 15 percent in 2009. In comparative terms, the rate of monthly church attendance in Australia is higher than that of the European countries in our survey but well below the rate in the United States.[4]

In terms of its political structures, Australia combines England's parliamentary form of government with America's institutional federalism.[5] The titular head of the Australian state is the British monarch, represented by a governor-general, who has very little real power. The prime minister is responsible to the House of Representatives and has effective executive power. The 150-member House of Representatives parallels the British House of Commons in that it forms a government, it is where the prime minister sits, and it has evolved into the more important of Australia's two legislative chambers. Like its American counterpart, states have equal representation in the seventy-six-member Senate, although it has fewer institutional powers than the House and has become a house of review. By American standards, Australia's electoral system is distinctive and complex. Voting is compulsory in federal elections, and turnout rates in those elections are consistently over 90 percent. House elections use a preferential voting system where voters rank candidates in order of the voter's preference. The candidate with the lowest vote total has his or her vote reallocated to the remaining candidates until a single candidate has a majority of the vote. The Senate, by contrast, utilizes a modified version of proportional representation. There are two major and several minor political parties in Australia. The largest parties are the center-right Liberal Party and the center-left Australian Labor Party (ALP). The National Party, which represents rural interests, is a coalition partner with the Liberal Party and, with nine House and five Senate seats, is Australia's most significant third party.

While there was a denominational character in the development of the Australian party system, religion was not as decisive a point of political cleavage between the Australian political parties as it was in many European countries. Catholics supported the Labor Party and Protestants generally voted for the Coalition, but for the most part religion was a secondary concern for voters and politicians rarely mobilized on the basis of religion.[6] Ironically, as Australia became less religious at the turn of the twenty-first century, religion became more important in party politics. A large part of the reason for this was John Howard's tenure as leader of the Liberal Party government from 1996 to 2007. Howard used religious discourse to cultivate conservative Christian voters on such issues as same-sex marriage, abortion, school choice, family values, and state support for faith-based social services.[7] In particular, Howard appealed to members of the newer and fast-growing evangelical and Pentecostal churches, but he also expanded support for the Liberal Party among Roman Catholics, particularly those who were religiously active. His public advocacy for conservative Christian causes coincided with the founding in 1995 of the Australian Christian Coalition (later renamed the Australian Christian Lobby). The ACL became an influential lobbying group on both sides of the political aisle.[8]

Howard's Liberal Party lost the 2007 parliamentary elections, but the political profile of religion remained high. His successor, Labor Party prime minister Kevin Rudd (2007–2010; 2013), was a frequent church attendee who spoke openly of his admiration for the German theologian Dietrich

Bonhoeffer. Shortly after his installation as prime minister, Rudd offered a formal apology to indigenous Australians for their mistreatment at the hands of the government, a decision that he connected to his theological convictions. Even the self-described atheist, Labor Party prime minister Julia Gillard (2010–2013), talked openly about her Baptist upbringing and the importance of Christian values in Australian culture.[9] The current prime minister, Malcolm Turnbull of the Liberal Party, converted to Roman Catholicism in 2002, but he has parted ways with the church on issues such as abortion, stem cell research, and same-sex marriage, an issue that has seen much political debate in recent years. Australia and Germany are the only countries in our study that have not legalized same-sex marriages, although same-sex couples can enter a civil partnership in both places. Most, but not all, of the largest religious groups oppose same-sex marriage, although a majority of Australians support legalization. In the lead-up to the 2016 federal election, Turnbull has called for a national plebiscite on the issue, while the Labor Party has pledged to hold a vote in parliament on marriage equality within one hundred days of forming a government. Regardless of the election outcome, religious groups are certain to play a prominent role in this issue going forward. The reemergence of religion onto the Australian political stage in many ways mirrors the situation in Britain. Both countries have become more secular, but the tidy assumption that this would inevitably lead to the demise of religion as a political variable has been disproved. Both countries have experienced political leaders who spoke openly about their faith (Howard and Rudd in Australia, Blair and Cameron in Britain), cross-denominational voting has upset the sectarian party split of the past, and religious groups are more willing than ever to press politicians for their positions on various issues.

As with most federal polities, Australia's federalism is a complex and dynamic relationship among the federal and six state governments and two self-governing territories. At the time of federation, the federal government's power was limited to its enumerated constitutional powers in interstate commerce, defense, foreign affairs, mass media, and immigration. States enjoyed "residual powers," which meant they could legislate in areas not specifically assigned to the federal government.[10] The balance of power, however, has shifted dramatically in the past fifty years toward the federal government as a consequence of pragmatic responses to pressing social needs, High Court interpretations of the Constitution that have encouraged greater concentration of power, and, perhaps most important, changing political values about what voters wanted in terms of Australia's federal system.[11] The national government has sole access to personal and corporate income taxes, sales tax, and excise duties, and the commonwealth raises more than 80 percent of all tax revenue.[12] State and local governments, however, continue to have jurisdiction over important policy areas such as education, health, welfare, criminal law, urban affairs, and the administration of justice. What this has meant is that the commonwealth government increasingly finances programs administered at the state and local levels. The commonwealth spends roughly one-third of its total budget on outlays to state and local governments.[13] Australia's religious composition and political structures have had an important impact on the resolution of church-state practices. In order to appreciate how these factors have helped shape church-state policy, we turn now to an analysis of Australia's political history that has provided the framework for its model of pragmatic pluralism.

THE HISTORICAL BACKGROUND

Religion did not give birth to the first Australian settlements as it did in America, and church-state issues assumed a very different form in the emerging Australian state. The original purpose of the British settlement in New South Wales in 1788 was to imprison criminals from English cities. The British needed to find an alternative location for their prisoners after the American Revolution stopped them from being shipped to Georgia; convicted criminals made up half of the fifteen hundred people in the first fleet of ships to settle Australia. The church in Australia originated as a part of the British penal system. British authorities sent The Reverend Richard Johnson as the colony's first chaplain; he was joined shortly thereafter by Samuel Marsden, "the flogging pastor," so named because of his use of severe disciplinary measures on a population he believed to be morally and spiritually corrupt. As with many other early religious leaders, Marsden served both as chaplain and as a magistrate and superintendent of public affairs. Colonial elites assumed there would be an established Church of England in the Australian colonies, as there was in England, and for the first several decades the Anglican Church alone received state aid for education, clergy, and church buildings.[14]

While the institutions were closely united, an activist and powerful state dominated the church and other institutions of civil society. The Anglican Church was at the mercy of colonial authorities for financial aid and there were persistent disputes between chaplains and governors about the appropriate levels of state support. The state provided aid, but often on utilitarian and pragmatic grounds. Many assumed that religion served the state's interests by providing moral order and social control among a penal population considered dangerous and morally corrupt. In return, colonial authorities expected the church to help foster political legitimacy in the new state.[15] Some Anglicans challenged the relationship on the grounds that it compromised the church's evangelistic message and independence, but many others saw moral reform as an essential part of their Christian witness. Given the traditional dependence of the Church of England on the British crown, it is not surprising that religious and political authorities worked together toward a common end. The church had grown accustomed to looking to the state for support and providing political legitimacy in return. As one analyst has noted, "the Anglican church existed before 1820 as the arm of the government that provided financial backing and practical support."[16]

The degree of state regulation of religion varied among the Australian colonies. In the earliest days of colonial settlement in New South Wales, the state appointed Anglican clergymen and did not allow clergy from other faiths to minister to the convict population. Despite the fact that Irish Roman Catholics made up fully one-third of the convict population by the early 1800s, for example, prison authorities initially barred Catholic priests from celebrating the Mass and required attendance at Anglican chapel services. Not surprisingly, the convict population largely rejected the established Church of England, although the Church had greater success attracting the growing number of free and freed colonists. For the most part, however, the colonies did not regulate religious practices or place severe social and political disabilities on those who practiced other faiths. As a result, a more liberal policy of religious free exercise rights gradually developed in each of the colonies. The absence of a state-imposed religious monopoly allowed Australia to become a religiously diverse mix of Anglicans, Catholics, Presbyterians, and other religious nonconformists.

This diversity made it increasingly difficult for the colonies to maintain the English church-state model, however, as state support for the Anglican Church aroused hostility from the competing denominations. Because state elites did not have a strong theological attachment to an established church model, they could more easily contemplate a different political arrangement than their English counterparts, and they began to look for a more palatable church-state arrangement. The New South Wales Church Act of 1836 seemed to offer the ideal solution. The act revised the established church model by allocating colonial funds on a more equal basis to the largest denominations in the colony without discrimination. It was the brainchild of Richard Bourke, a deeply religious Anglican, who believed that a more equitable arrangement would be a more effective way to expand Christianity in the colony.[17] Under that act, the state provided funds to recruit and deploy clergy, to defray the cost for the building of churches, and later to help finance schools run by the churches. Even the small Jewish community eventually received grants for religious personnel.[18] This plural or multiple establishment was a bold and innovative policy at the time, and the other Australian colonies followed with similar acts within a few decades.[19]

The Church Act was driven by political pragmatism and a conviction that government evenhandedness served a moral purpose. This outlook led Australian colonial leaders to "invent their own solution to the problems of church-state relations," as Michael Hogan has noted, that borrowed from but also differed from England with its established church and the United States with its principle of church-state separation.[20] Colonial governors turned to religious neutrality to take religion out of the political arena and to enable the churches more effectively to promote a Christian moral order and political legitimacy in the Australian state. Since the initial impetus for Anglican ascendancy in New South Wales had been the promotion of moral order among the convict population, how much more effective could that process be if money flowed to all of the churches? If the "problem" with Britain's established church model was that it pitted religionists against each other, why not fund all of the churches and thereby depoliticize religious disputes? Contrary to the Dutch experience, however, Australian elites provided little philosophical justification for this kind of state neutrality. It was not a principled commitment to pluralism that drove the policy; few people argued that the Church Act could be defended on the ground that the policy was a nondiscriminatory way to protect and promote Australia's religious diversity. The intent of the policy was to make life easier for colonial authorities who had grown weary of denominational conflict and to empower churches to provide moral guidance to their members.

At the same time, the Church Act established two important precedents that continue to shape public policy in contemporary Australia. First, when the government provides funds to a religious denomination, they are generally available to all denominations on some basis of equality.[21] There was and is a basic commitment to a nondiscrimination principle among the churches when the state provides aid. This will become even more apparent when we look at the current policy on state aid to religious schools and nonprofit organizations. Second, pragmatism has been the norm when political leaders deal with church-state issues. Policy makers viewed religious issues as a problem to be solved in the most expedient manner possible, which in the mid-nineteenth century led them to support what was, for the time, a remarkable policy of plural establishment. The policy exhibited a respect for the rights of religious minorities that was distinctive by the standards of the day. In England, by comparison, the state barred Catholics from admission to universities and had only just granted them political emancipation when New South Wales passed the Church Act.

Despite the intent of the Church Act, it did not dissipate sectarian rivalry among the denominations. Initially, many Anglican Church leaders opposed the system on the ground that aid should only go to the one true church; most of the other churches, by contrast, contended that the policy advantaged the Church of England because of its size, organization, and the lingering prejudice of the Anglican governing class against Roman Catholics and nonconformists. While the act reduced the disparity in state aid among the denominations, because it was the denomination with the largest number of members the Anglican Church was the principal beneficiary of a system.[22] Roman Catholics pressed for a reformation of the act, some nonconformists pushed for the voluntary principle of no state aid as a way to escape Anglican domination, and secularists—who were indifferent to Christianity—had gained a foothold in Australia by the end of the nineteenth century. Given the political controversy among the churches, political leaders had fewer grounds on which to defend the policy. Because there had never been an overriding commitment by the state to promote religious pluralism, governing officials quickly abandoned the act when it proved costly, difficult to administer, and politically contentious. By the turn of the century each of the Australian states adopted a new policy of church-state separation rooted in the principles of Enlightenment liberalism. This meant an end to direct state funding for clergy, church buildings, and church schools.

The major political challenge to the model of plural establishment occurred in the field of education. Religious schools, particularly Anglican schools, had a virtual monopoly on education in the Australian colonies in the early nineteenth century. Colonial governments, under the Church Act, funded denominational schools on a largely equal basis. Religious schools could not keep up with the demand for public education in the mid-nineteenth century, however, and pressure grew in all the Australian colonies for a free, compulsory, and "secular" education system.[23] Until the 1860s, Anglicans and Catholics formed a powerful political coalition that preserved the denominational system from religious dissenters and secular liberals who wanted to make education a state function and believed that religious control of education threatened to undermine the assimilationist purposes of a universal system of education.

Anglican church leaders were not, however, as committed to the principle that education should be a religious function as were their Catholic counterparts, and their opposition to state control of education gradually dissipated. Many of the church's leaders joined forces with secular rationalists to end state aid to denominational schools. As in the United States, the Protestant objection to public finance of religious schools had much to do with Protestant hostility to Catholicism.[24] Protestants did not generally believe that a secular educational system threatened their religious values because it allowed for instruction and worship of the general principles of Christianity. In contrast to the Netherlands and similar to the United States, there was no Protestant movement in Australia that saw public schools as a threat to their religious values. The New South Wales Public Instruction Act of 1880 typified this "secular" approach to teaching religion: "In all schools under this Act the teaching shall be strictly non-sectarian, but the words 'secular instruction' shall be held to include general religious teaching as distinguished from dogmatical or polemical theology."[25] To make clear that a secular education did not preclude religious instruction, the author of the act, Sir

Henry Parker, noted: "it was never the intention of the framers of this Bill to exclude such knowledge of the Bible as all divisions of the Christian Church must possess, or a knowledge of the great truths of Revelation."[26]

Australia's secular educational system shared several of the liberal presuppositions of the American common school movement. First was the belief that a primary function of the public school was to assimilate persons of different religious, class, and ethnic backgrounds by introducing them to the key values of Australian society. In Australia, this primarily meant Roman Catholics, who had "alien" religious views and suspect political sympathies. It is not surprising, for example, that all schoolchildren were required to pledge their loyalty to God as well as to the king or queen and the British Empire. Patriotism was among the key political virtues that the public schools would inculcate children with, particularly Irish Catholic immigrants who had a history of opposition to the British crown and who needed to be socialized with "proper" social and political values.

Second, the Enlightenment liberals leading the public school movement believed that a nonsectarian, moralistic religion had a place in the schools. While reformers viewed the particularistic elements of the various churches as divisive and dangerous, they thought that the core consensual features of the Christian faith could provide the basis for a common morality. They shared Horace Mann's optimism that common religious beliefs were discoverable by human reason. What this ignored was the incommensurability of religious and moral viewpoints and the political power structures that lay behind the claim that the established Protestant viewpoint was rational or consensual. Protestant church leaders did not challenge this liberal vision because they saw it as consistent with their understanding of the social role of Christianity. Nor did they appreciate that the rationalistic assumptions of the liberal educational model undermined a distinctively religious point of view in the schools.

The education acts passed by the various states allowed independent religious schools to operate, but they rescinded public finance of them. State officials expected that Catholic schools would collapse without state funding and that the public schools would become a vehicle for Irish Catholic assimilation. This did not happen. The Catholic hierarchy rejected the public schools as dangerously liberal and antireligious, defended their educational principles, and committed additional resources to the preservation of a Catholic school system. Catholic parents similarly viewed the public schools as unsympathetic to their cultural and religious sensibilities. Fueled in part by Protestant antipathy, the Catholic school system incorporated most Catholic children and the religious rivalry between Protestants and Catholics intensified in Australia for the next half-century.

Religion played only a small role as Australia moved toward federation at the end of the century. The six colonies that united to form the Australian commonwealth in 1901 asked for the "blessings of Almighty God" in the preamble to the new national Constitution, and the drafters self-consciously modeled Section 116 on the First Amendment of the U.S. Constitution. Section 116 states:

> The Commonwealth shall not make any law for establishing any religion, or for imposing any religious observance, or for prohibiting the free exercise of any religion, and no religious test shall be required as a qualification for any office or public trust under the Constitution.

The purpose of Section 116 was to depoliticize religion as much as possible in order to keep the commonwealth out of the religious field. As we have seen, sectarian strife was a political reality in each of the Australian colonies, and political leaders did not want religious rivalries spilling over into federation politics. Australia's religious diversity made it difficult to defend an established church. At the time of federation, Anglicans represented a plurality of the nation's population at 40 percent, but Catholics were 23 percent, and Methodists and Presbyterians each had 12 percent. [27]

In addition, there were no practical reasons for the drafters of the new constitution to press for an established Anglican Church in the Australian commonwealth. The Anglican Church lacked the political power to force this model on a recalcitrant public. Political elites in Australia did not assume, as they likely would have in England at the time, that the state had a positive obligation to defend an established church. Without this philosophical commitment to an establishment model, political leaders did all that they could to maximize support for the federation. This meant giving individual states effective power over religious matters. The Constitution was not, however, a secular attempt to keep religion out of politics. [28] While the Constitution forbade the commonwealth from formally establishing a church or restricting religious free exercise rights, states could do both. The importance of state governments in the resolution of church-state issues became particularly apparent in subsequent rulings of the Australian High Court dealing with free exercise rights.

THE FREE EXERCISE OF RELIGION

As with the other countries in our study, Australia struggles with the question of how far to go to permit religious beliefs and practices that conflict with social welfare and societal norms. In balancing individual rights and state power, however, Australia has more closely followed the British model that trusts the democratic political process rather than America or Germany, where the courts play a key role in defining and applying rights against state and federal actions. There are two important reasons for this. First, the Australian Constitution lacks a comprehensive bill of rights. As a consequence, the High Court has had few opportunities to play an aggressive role in defining and protecting rights. One of the few expressed constitutional rights is that of freedom of religion, found in Section 116, which was explicitly modeled on the First Amendment to the American Constitution. Even here, however, the Court has played a limited role. In three key free exercise clause cases, the Court has established the precedent that the Constitution provides very little protection for the religious beliefs and practices of Australian citizens. The Court has interpreted Section 116 narrowly, which has meant that religious liberty rights are at the mercy of the political process. As one analyst has noted, there has never been a successful claim against the government on religious free exercise grounds.[29]

A second reason for the court's limited role in rights protection is that there is no Australian equivalent to the due process clause of the U.S. Constitution's Fourteenth Amendment and its provision that "no state shall make or enforce any law which shall abridge the privileges or immunities of the citizens of the United States." Absent such language, the Australian Supreme Court has been unable to incorporate the religious provision of Section 116 of the Constitution and apply it to the states. In theory, state and territory governments could establish a state church or religion, oppress religious beliefs, or require a religious test as a qualification for public office. A proposal to amend Section 116 to include coverage to the states failed in referendums in 1944 and 1988.[30]

The first major Australian case that tested free exercise rights was *Adelaide Company of Jehovah's Witnesses Inc. v. Commonwealth* (1943). This case involved opposition by the Jehovah's Witnesses to Australian involvement in World War II. A number of Australian churches opposed the war on religious grounds, including the Quakers, but they were able to convince the government that they did not pose a security risk to the state. The Jehovah's Witnesses were not so fortunate and the commonwealth government seized church property and declared the Adelaide branch of the church a proscribed organization. Since the proscription came from the Australian commonwealth, rather than a state government, the church appealed on the ground that the law violated their free exercise rights guaranteed in Section 116 of the federal constitution. In his decision, Chief Justice John Latham recognized that the purpose of Section 116 was to "protect the religion (or absence of religion) of minorities, and, in particular, of unpopular minorities." Nevertheless, he ruled that the state may infringe upon religious liberty when it is necessary to protect civil government or the continued existence of the community: "Section 116 of the Constitution does not prevent the Commonwealth from making laws prohibiting the advocacy of doctrines which, though advocated in pursuance of religious convictions, are prejudicial to the prosecution of a war in which the Commonwealth is engaged."[31]

Latham emphasized an important point in his decision: it is appropriate for the state to restrict religious freedom when the exercise of that right has the effect of endangering the entire political community. Australia faced the very real danger of being invaded by Japan during World War II, which had earlier bombed the city of Darwin. The state had legitimate concerns about groups that actively opposed the Australian state. The problem with the decision, however, is that Latham did not examine in any detail the words and actions of the Witnesses to determine if they posed a genuine threat to the government or the community. Instead, he inferred that the church's teaching that the commonwealth was an organ of Satan was necessarily prejudicial to the defense of the commonwealth and that the government could legitimately proscribe the organization. The Court did not use the decision, therefore, to articulate a standard by which to judge when it was appropriate for the state to limit free exercise rights. The contrast with the Netherlands, France, and the United States is instructive. Article 6 of the Dutch Constitution and, to a lesser extent, Article 10 of the French Declaration of Rights specifically articulate the conditions under which the state can limit religious liberty. The U.S. Supreme Court similarly wrestled with balancing state interests against the free exercise rights of members of the Jehovah's Witnesses during the Second World War, but came down on the side of protecting religious freedom. In its 1943 decision, *West Virginia State Board of Education v. Barnette*, the Court ruled that schoolchildren (who in this case were also Witnesses), could not be forced to pledge allegiance to or salute the U.S. flag, even during wartime.

The 1984 case of *Grace Bible Church Inc. v. Reedman* reinforced the limited nature of free exercise protections under the Australian Constitution. The case involved the conviction of a Grace Bible Church for running an unregistered private school contrary to South Australia's Education Acts between 1972 and 1981. Under that act, the state could fine the governing authority of an unregistered school that enrolled students for instruction. The church claimed that registration would place the church school under the state's authority, which violated their religious belief that God controlled the school. South Australian authorities convicted Grace Bible Church and fined the school's governing authority $365. The school appealed the conviction to the High Court and argued that South Australia's Education Act interfered with the freedom of religious worship and expression that is an inalienable right under the Australian Constitution. The Court rejected this argument with the terse statement that the rights guaranteed in Section 116 "cannot be of any relevance because it only imposes a prohibition upon the law-making powers of the Commonwealth Parliament."[32] The issue of whether a state's action limits a person's free exercise right was moot, therefore, because the Court did not have the power to overturn such a state law.

The 1997 case of *Kruger v. Commonwealth*, also known as the Stolen Generation case, confirmed the limits of free exercise protections under the Australian Constitution. The case was brought by indigenous Australians from the Northern Territory, where the 1918 Aboriginals Ordinance authorized the forced removal of children from reserves. The policy had been repealed in 1953, although in some states children were still being removed in the 1970s. A 1997 report by the government's Human Rights Commission condemned virtually every aspect of the removals policy, and Prime Minister Kevin Rudd would later submit a formal government apology for what amounted to state-enforced kidnapping of indigenous children. The plaintiffs sought to establish the illegality of the Ordinance at the time it was passed, and one of the grounds they used to challenge the policy was that it prohibited the free exercise of aboriginal religious rights, by separating children from their aboriginal culture. The court rejected the free exercise claim. The court drew a distinction between the *purpose* and the *effect* of laws. Only laws whose purpose was to restrict religious freedom are protected under Section 116, and since the justices could not establish that this had been a purpose of the 1918 Ordinance they rejected the free exercise claim. [33]

In practice, therefore, the courts have played a marginal role in protecting religious freedom in Australia. The defense of religious rights has come, instead, from a combination of laws, the work of the Human Rights Commission, an independent statutory agency that reports to the commonwealth government, and public opinion. There is no national legislation that specifically bars discrimination on the basis of religion. Tasmania has a religious free exercise provision in its Constitution, and Victoria and the Australian Capital Territory have passed Human Rights acts that include religious freedom. Each state and territory, with the exception of New South Wales and South Australia, contains a prohibition in its antidiscrimination laws against discrimination on the grounds of religious belief. [34]

A 1998 report by the Human Rights Commission on religious freedom concluded that current law does not adequately protect religious rights; new religious movements, indigenous beliefs, and minority faiths are the most susceptible to discriminatory treatment. Borrowing language from the International Covenant on Civil and Political Rights, the Commission recommended that the Commonwealth Parliament should enact a Religious Freedom Act that would protect persons against religious discrimination and provide for the "freedom to hold a particular religion or belief" and to "manifest religious or belief in worship, observance, practice and teaching." [35] The recommendations were never implemented by the federal government.

The current status of religious rights in Australia is not ideal; there is no enshrined, constitutional protection of religious liberty and no commonwealth law that specifically bars religious discrimination. Still, Australia has made progress in the area of religious rights. A growing number of private businesses and government agencies make provisions for religious free exercise in such areas as dress codes, dietary restrictions, and recognition of religious holidays. Public opinion and cultural values have been the most significant determinants of this change. As Gary Bouma writes, Australia has developed "a notion of fair play, (the) equal worth of human dignity and live and let live."[36] The introduction to the Commission's report on religious freedom similarly noted that "we Australians pride ourselves on tolerance and easy-going acceptance of other cultures and beliefs."[37] These social values have contributed to an atmosphere that supports religious free exercise rights and has generally allowed new religious groups to negotiate their way into Australian society.

THE CHALLENGE OF MUSLIM INCORPORATION

Public opinion and cultural values can be a nebulous way to protect religious freedom, particularly for politically vulnerable minorities. As we noted above, the percentage of Australians from non-Christian religions nearly tripled from 1991 to 2011, rising from 2.6 to 7.2 percent of the total population. The primary reason for this was a liberalization of the government's immigration policy. An open preference for white, western immigrants characterized Australia's immigration policy for much of the past century. From 1900 until 1945 the so-called White Australia policy used racial characteristics to exclude nonwhites and thus most non-Christians from entering Australia. From 1947 to 1972, the state used public moneys to induce immigration among preferred migrant groups, which were the British and northern and southern Europeans. In 1957, for example, the state launched a "Bring out a Briton" campaign and worked closely with churches to implement the policy. The purpose of the policy was to facilitate the migration of whites and of Roman Catholics and Protestants, groups that fit comfortably into the established cultural and religious molds. The few non-Christian Australians were expected to assimilate to those values.[38]

The dissolution of the White Australia Policy in the early 1970s led to a dramatic increase in Australia's racial and religious diversity. The immigration of new religious groups has helped to make Australia among the most ethnically and religiously diverse countries in the world. Sixty percent of the Australian Muslim community, as an example, is foreign born, and they come from a staggering 183 countries of the world.[39] This new diversity, however, has brought some policy challenges, the most notable of which surround the Australian Islamic community. Australian Muslims share some of the concerns of their European counterparts. While the level of educational attainment for Muslims compares favorably with the entire Australian population, they are more likely to be unemployed, living in poverty, or in prison. There was also an increase in the number of reported occurrences of discrimination and abuse directed toward Muslims after the September 2001 terrorist attacks on the United States and the Bali bombings in October 2002 that killed eighty-eight Australian tourists. A similar spike in targeted attacks against Australian Muslims occurred after the 2015 Paris attacks. Public fears of an attack by Islamic extremists has also increased in recent years among the general public.[40]

For the most part, however, Australia has not responded defensively to the immigration of Muslims and other non-Christian groups. Ikebal Patel, president of the Australian Federation of Islamic Councils, the national umbrella organization representing Australian Muslims, commented to us that there is some Islamophobia in Australian society and it is particularly pronounced "around election times because some politicians believe it helps to win races."[41] There is, however, no Australian equivalent to the Dutch Party for Freedom, the Alternative for Germany, or the French National Front, right-wing populist parties that are explicitly anti-Islamic and that mobilize large numbers of voters. Public opinion polls confirm the limited popular appeal for anti-Islamic rhetoric. A 2015 national survey found that 70 percent of Australians had very low levels of Islamophobia and only 10 percent were highly Islamophobic, percentages that compare very favorably to European countries.[42]

There is also little empirical evidence of widespread alienation among Australian Muslims. Three-quarters of Muslim respondents in a 2015 nationwide survey identified themselves as Australian (despite the fact that a large percentage are recent immigrants) and more than 90 percent affirmed the statement that they can be a good Muslim and a good Australian. Ninety percent of respondents in a 2015 survey of Muslims living in Sydney agreed that "it is important to me that my children are/would be fully accepted as Australians" and 84 percent indicated that they "felt like they were an Australian," while only 15 percent disagreed with the statement that "relations between Muslims and non-Muslims in Australia are friendly."[43]

By virtually every measure, Australia has had less political conflict around the rights of Muslims than have the European countries in our study. As a country of immigration, it is possible that Australia is more accustomed to dealing with a heterogeneous population than its European counterparts. Australia seems fully committed to a process of negotiation and compromise with Muslims and other religious minorities. Patel himself noted that state and federal government officials are "by and large very fair and equitable in their treatment of Muslims."[44] While not without its difficulties, Australia has clearly made strides toward the pluralistic goal of equal treatment of all religious groups. Nowhere is this commitment more evident than on the establishment issues of public finance to religious schools and nonprofit organizations.

CHURCH, STATE, AND EDUCATION

The Australian educational system mixes features of the American and British systems. As in the United States, individual states and territories have the primary responsibility for funding government schools in Australia. Unlike the United States, however, the federal government has become the primary source of funding for private schools. Like England, as we will see in the next chapter, religious schools receive considerable funding from the state, but in contrast with England those schools are considered nongovernment schools that are not part of the state sector. Australia's history and politics help to explain its unique educational policy.

Catholics retained their independent school system at the end of the nineteenth century despite the fact that the state rescinded state aid to denominational schools. A smaller number of high-fee independent schools more loosely associated with Protestant denominations also continued to exist. With limited financial resources and rising school costs, however, Catholic schools increasingly found it difficult to compete with government schools. By the late 1950s the disparity between state-run and Catholic schools became apparent and the church concluded that the Catholic school system would cease to exist without state support. The bishops committed themselves to preserving Catholic schools and they intensified their political pressure for state aid.

The federal election of 1963 brought the issue of state aid back onto the political agenda for the first time since the previous century. The push for state aid coincided with a growing split between the Catholic right and the secular left within the Labor Party. Working-class Catholics, who traditionally voted Labor, pressed the party to abandon its long-standing opposition to state aid for religious schools. Hoping to capitalize on Catholic disaffection with the Labor Party, Liberal prime minister Robert Menzies committed his party to a policy that would have provided commonwealth grants to public and private schools for the purpose of science education. Protestants had originally joined forces with secular liberals to oppose public finance of religious schools because of their hostility to Roman Catholics. By the early 1960s, however, Protestant opposition to Catholics had waned considerably, making it easier for the largely Protestant Liberal Party to support state aid to private religious schools. Support grew among Protestants for the right of parents to exercise a choice in schooling and for the government to fund students exercising that right. In response, Gough Whitlam, the Labor Party candidate for prime minister, successfully pressed his party to abandon its opposition to school funding.[45] Menzies's initiative was the first formal entry of the commonwealth government into direct school funding, but it proved to be the tip of the iceberg. Both the Liberal and Labor Parties had a political imperative to press for state aid, and in the 1972 federal election both parties pledged major increases in grants to all private schools in need of support. The Labor Party, led by Whitlam, won the election and created the Schools Commission to formalize commonwealth educational policy. Under the policy instituted by the commission in 1974 the commonwealth provided direct grants to nongovernment schools.

Opponents of state aid challenged the policy on the grounds that the payment of government grants to denominational schools violated Section 116 of the Australian Constitution, which does not allow the commonwealth to make any law "for establishing any religion." The vast majority of private schools had some religious affiliation, and opponents contended that aid to religious schools constituted a de facto establishment of religion. In *Attorney General for the State of Victoria v. The Commonwealth of Australia* (1981), the High Court in a 6–1 vote affirmed the validity of the legislative action. Relying upon what he called the "plain" or "usual" meaning of the words "for establishing any religion" in Section 116, Justice Garfield Barwick, writing for the majority, argued that establishing a religion involves "the identification of the religion with the civil authority so as to involve the citizens in a duty to maintain it and the obligation of, in this case, the Commonwealth to patronize, protect and promote the established religion."[46] According to this reading of Section 116, Barwick could not rationally see how "the law for providing the funds for the forwarding of the education of Australians by non-government schools is a law for establishing Christian religion."[47] The Court rejected the plaintiffs' attempts to use the U.S. Supreme Court's rendering of the First Amendment no establishment clause cases as a guide for this decision. Barwick contended that the American cases that barred aid to religious schools were irrelevant because of the "radically different language in our Constitution."[48] Barwick asserted that the wording of the Australian Constitution, "for establishing any religion," was narrower in meaning than the "respecting an establishment of religion" phrase of the American First Amendment. The Australian Constitution, Barwick argued, prohibits only those parliamentary laws that formally establish *a* religion (our emphasis); it does not involve "the prohibition of any law which may assist the practice of religion."[49] The decision removed the last serious obstacle to state aid for religious schools.

There are two main categories of nongovernment schools in Australia: Catholic schools and independent schools (85 percent of which are religious). Both are eligible for capital and recurrent funding from the commonwealth government. Under the Capital Grants Programme, the Australian government spent over $3 billion in 2010 for capital improvements at private schools, which represented two-thirds of capital expenditures in the nongovernment sector.[50] Recipients of a capital grant in 2013 included the Langford Islamic College (Muslim) in Western Australia, the Maharishi School of the Age of Enlightenment (Transcendental Meditation) in Victoria, the Kesser Torah College (Jewish) in New South Wales, Xavier Catholic College in the Northern Territory, and Coomera Anglican College (Anglican) in Queensland, to name just a few.[51]

General recurrent funding is provided by the government on a per student basis and is the largest source of commonwealth funding for private schools. In 2012–2013, the government distributed just over $8 billion to private schools in per capita grants. The government uses a needs-based model to determine the socioeconomic status of the school's community. The poorest schools receive the largest grants, but even the wealthiest independent schools receive some state aid. Funding for nongovernment schools varies from 13.7 to 70 percent of the Average Government School Recurrent Costs (AGSRC), which in 2014 translated into per student grants ranging from $1,854 to $8,344 for primary schools and from $2,439 to $10,974 for secondary schools. This funding is indexed each year according to increases in AGSRC. Commonwealth and state funding accounted for roughly three-quarters of the recurrent cost of students in Catholic schools and 40 percent of the cost for students in independent schools. The primary reason for the difference is the fee structure in the two types of schools; the average annual fee in a Catholic school in 2010 was $2,383, compared to $8,468 in independent schools.[52]

State aid to private schools has had a profound impact on education in Australia. Enrollment in those schools had been gradually falling throughout the 1960s, reaching a historic low of 22 percent of all students in 1971, but with government funding the percentage of students in private schools rose to 28 percent in 1990 and 30 percent in 2000. During the Howard years, the government eased the process for approving new schools and established a more favorable funding scheme for the nongovernment sector. The result was a further expansion in the number of nongovernment schools, particularly those in the independent sector. By 2014, 35 percent of all students were enrolled in nongovernment schools. Between 1999 and 2011, government schools grew by 2 percent, compared to an enrollment increase of 25 percent in nongovernment schools. The original purpose of state aid was to save the Catholic school system; an unintended consequence of the policy has been the proliferation of non-Catholic, but religiously based private schools. In 1971, Catholic schools enrolled over 80 percent of nongovernment school students; this proportion fell to 70 percent in 1990 and to 59 percent in 2010. The growth in the nongovernmental school sector has been particularly strong among evangelical Protestant and Islamic schools.[53]

For the most part, state and federal administrators have consistently pursued a neutral policy in which aid is available equally to religious and nonreligious schools alike. This is a stark contrast with England where, as we will see in the following chapter, funding for Islamic schools took decades to achieve. In 2010, government funds went to a plethora of religious schools, including Roman Catholic (1,643 schools), Anglican (156), nondenominational Christian (188), Lutheran (85), Seventh-Day Adventist (56), Baptist (47), Uniting Church of Australia (43), Islamic (32), Jewish (20), Pentecostal (16), Assemblies of God (10), Greek Orthodox (8), Ananda Marga (3), and Hare Krishna (1), to name some. In addition, the state provides aid to nonreligious private schools with a distinctive pedagogical focus such as Rudolph Steiner (42) and Montessori (39). No country in our study has as diverse a population of nongovernment schools as does Australia. In England, which similarly finances religious schools, 98 percent of such schools are Anglican or Roman Catholic. The Catholic and Anglican share of the Australian private school market, by comparison, is less than 70 percent.[54]

There are various reasons why state aid has fueled the rise of private schools. For one, such schools are now more affordable; lowering their cost has made them more attractive to middle-income parents. For some, those schools reflect a parental preference for an education infused with religious values. Rates of attendance at Jewish schools in Australia, as an example, are among the highest in the world. According to one study, 70 and 62 percent of Jewish children in Melbourne and Sydney, respectively, attend Jewish schools.[55] A report by the Immigration Bureau of the Jewish community concluded: "there is a growing and widely shared belief that young people are more likely to develop a solid and lasting sense of Jewish ethnic identity if they spend at least some of their school years in a pedagogical and social environment that is strongly supportive of Jewish ideas and values."[56] The same parental interest in a religiously grounded education likely explains the fourfold increase in the number of students attending Islamic schools, rising from 2,500 to 28,068 students from 1994 to 2010.[57] The Islamic Schools Association of Australia estimates that one-quarter of Muslim children attend an Islamic school, though the demand for those schools is much higher.[58] Nonetheless, the expansion of religious schools has coincided with Australians becoming less religious. It is not surprising, therefore, that parental surveys indicate that religion is not generally the most important factor in school choice, a pattern we saw in France and the Netherlands as well. More important to parents are discipline, the quality of the education, and the school's ability to develop a child's potential.[59]

Schools are free to develop their own educational mission. The mission for the Islamic College of South Australia is to "provide our children an environment which will enable them to achieve their highest potential, founded on Islamic morals, scholastic excellence and good citizenship."[60] Schools that are members of Christian Schools Australia promote the idea that "spiritual formation is an essential component of a Christian school education."[61] According to the guidelines of the National Catholic Education Commission, the curriculum in Roman Catholic schools "must give a central place to education in faith and acknowledge the relevance to all areas of teaching of a Christian view of life as interpreted in the Catholic tradition."[62] Religious schools are also allowed to give preference in faculty hiring and student admission to people who share the school's governing philosophy and who are members of the founding church. Catholic schools usually hire Catholic teachers, and 70 percent of the students in those schools are coreligionists. A similar percentage prevails in Jewish, Islamic, and evangelical Protestant schools, though a smaller percentage of coreligionists would be found in Anglican and other mainline Protestant schools.[63] Religious schools are generally exempt from antidiscrimination legislation if they can demonstrate that the proposed policy violates a religious principle.[64] While they have to teach the mandated curriculum, religious schools have latitude in what they teach beyond that. There are, for example, evangelical Protestant schools that teach creation science, which they are allowed to do so long as they do not omit the required elements dealing with evolutionary biology.

It is important to note that independent schools that receive grants have to be accredited by the state and commonwealth governments and they must be nonprofit organizations. There are accountability requirements for schools in such areas as student assessment and proper accounting for all monies spent. Religious schools are required to follow the state curriculum, submit to the same testing requirements as all other schools, and hire teachers with the same minimum qualifications as government schools.[65] Some private school advocates have suggested that the tests can function as a de facto national curriculum. Bob Johnson, executive director for the Australian Association of Christian Schools, commented to us that the tests have led some state education officials to "become more prescriptive in making schools accountable for the content of their courses."[66]

Oftentimes the pressure religious schools face is less from government officials and more from parents who want students to do well on examinations at the end of secondary education. There are numerous difficulties in drawing comparisons between government and nongovernment schools, but by virtually all measures private schools fare very well. Private school students, in both Catholic and independent schools, have higher test scores and retention rates than their state-run counterparts, and a greater percentage of private school graduates enter a university. Government schools, however, are required by law to take all students, and they have a higher percentage of students with a socioeconomic disadvantage. Independent schools can be exclusive in their admissions policy, though Catholic schools are committed to educating children regardless of socioeconomic circumstances, and the percentage of children with a socioeconomic disadvantage is increasing in the nongovernment sector.[67]

Questions have been raised in parliament and the media about the curriculum in some religious schools. The most frequent claim is that such schools undermine social cohesion by segregating students on the basis of religion and that they fail to teach the values necessary for living in a pluralistic democracy. Shortly after the London train bombings in 2005, Prime Minister Howard held a counterterrorism summit to discuss a coordinated Australian effort against terrorist attacks; one of the summit's recommendations was that Islamic schools should be encouraged to denounce terrorism and teach about Australian values and culture. His education minister, Brendan Nelson, suggested that those Islamic schools that failed to do so should "clear off."[68] Similar concerns were raised after the 2014 terror attacks by Muslim extremists in Sydney and Melbourne, and when it was discovered that more than one hundred Australian Muslims were fighting for groups in Syria and Iraq.[69] Fundamentalist Christian schools have similarly been questioned for the values that they promote. While he was in the opposition, Kevin Rudd described the Exclusive Brethren (whose schools receive state funding) as an "extremist cult" that breaks up families.[70]

There is, however, no evidence to support the claim that religious schools are promoting illiberal or dangerous values. An analysis of Australian jihadists found that almost all of the teenagers who had traveled overseas to fight in Iraq or Syria attended government-run schools.[71] The leaders of religious schools consistently affirm the importance of promoting positive values. The Muslim Schools' Charter in New South Wales, as an example, proclaims that Islamic schools will "teach children to be proud Australians and model citizens, to respect the rights of others and to understand the different backgrounds and religions of Australia's multicultural society, and to stand against those who preach violence and hatred in the name of any religion, including Islam."[72] An exhaustive survey of religious schools concluded that there is "little support for the idea that government schools have a stronger claim to delivering civic and democratic virtues and values. Indeed, if any pattern can be discerned, it is the opposite."[73] From the standpoint of promoting shared values, having religious schools within the larger state system has some potential advantages. Ikebal Patel, president of the Australian Federation of Islamic Councils, noted to us: "I would much rather have Islamic schools operating under the auspices of a government that makes them go through a rigorous regulation process, instead of having independent Islamic schools that are under virtually no government control and oversight."[74] Patel's point seems to be that private Islamic schools are going to exist and that it is far better to have them within the state system—where they are accountable for their actions—than out of it—where they are not.

What is even more instructive, however, is the degree to which other school organizations and leaders have come to the defense of their Muslim colleagues. The executive officers of the National Catholic Education Commission and the Australian Association of Christian Schools indicated to us, for example, that they have supported expanding government funding to Muslim schools. As Bob Johnson, executive director for the Australian Association of Christian Schools, pointed out to us: "an even playing field [in education] means that what is allowed for one religious group must be allowed for others."[75] The formation of dozens of independent school organizations, both denominational and peak bodies, has eased the application process for new schools and provided valuable political support for the sector as a whole. Organizations give advice to prospective new school applicants and represent their political interests before the various government agencies. Because state aid had foundered on the sectarian divide in the past, the major churches joined forces in the 1960s to present a united front for state aid, and these school organizations advocate for government funding for all eligible schools. There are some groups in Australia that are implacably opposed to the current system of aid to private religious schools, but as Johnson pointed out to us, "when 33 percent of the student population is in nongovernment schools, and when 90 percent of those students are in religious schools, there is a critical mass that will protect the current policy."[76]

In our view, Australian policy is neutral in that it neither advantages nor disadvantages any particular religion, nor does it advantage or disadvantage religion or secularism generally. State aid to religious schools makes it possible for parents who want a religious education for their children to exercise that option, while parents who want a nonreligious secular education can opt for a state school or a nonreligious private school. Government officials justify the policy in precisely these terms. One educational official noted to us that

> These [educational] priorities are aimed at ensuring that all students are allowed to realize their full potential and they include support for the principle of access, choice, equity and excellence in schooling by encouraging the provision of a strong, viable and diverse selection of schools from which parents may choose.[77]

Australia also seems to have discovered a healthy balance between allowing religious schools to maintain a clear sense of their mission, on the one hand, with appropriate regulation of their practices, on the other.

Finally, there is the question of the role of religion in state-run schools.[78] Each state provides for General Religious Education (GRE), which offers education about diverse religions, and Special Religious Instruction (SRI), which allows for instruction in a particular religion.

As we noted, liberal reformers opposed "sectarian" religious instruction in public schools, but they believed that secular instruction should include the consensual features of the Christian faith that would provide the basis for a common morality. When states began to provide public education at the end of the nineteenth century, therefore, the legislation typically allowed for nondogmatic religious instruction. In practice, GRE focused almost exclusively on Christianity, even Protestant Christianity when antipathy to Roman Catholics remained high. The New South Wales State Supreme Court ruled in 1976 that prayers, Bible readings, hymns, and grace before school meals were consistent with the provisions of GRE. The opinion of the court stated that religious instruction, even Christian instruction, was appropriate, so long as the state did not promote the teachings of a particular church: "It is natural that where a common form of teaching Christian beliefs had been adopted for use in State schools, and was acceptable to the various Christian churches, the State, in promoting secular education, should be at pains to prevent the beliefs of anyone church from being advanced over others, and to ensure a lowest common denominator for general religious teaching."[79] Most states continue to permit prayers, though they generally require that those prayers be "interdenominational Christian or multi-faith to reflect the diversity of the school community."[80]

As Australia became more religiously pluralistic, the problems with this approach have become more apparent. The presence of Christian, non-Christian, and nonreligious traditions that are uncomfortable with a lowest common denominator Christianity in the public schools challenges the optimistic assumption of the nineteenth-century legislation that it is possible to discern consensual religious beliefs, incorporate them into the public schools, and make them the basis for a common religious education and social morality. While there is a need for some common values and beliefs to bind society together, attempts to root them in a religious tradition violates governmental religious neutrality. In recent years, most states have included the study of diverse religious traditions in their GRE. Western Australia's Department of Education describes the focus of its general religious education to be "the study of major forms of religious thought and expression that are characteristic of Australian and other societies in the world." In keeping with the value of neutrality, New South Wales notes that its program "does not seek to establish [knowledge of] one religious tradition to the exclusion of all others."[81]

What have been more controversial are the various state Special Religious Instruction (SRI) programs. Under SRI, or what Americans term released time programs, accredited representatives of a faith group can provide religious teaching in the school for those children whose parents want them to receive it. The amount of time varies by state, but is generally thirty minutes per week. Parents have the right to withdraw their children from SRI in all states and territories. This is a type of program that the American Supreme Court has rejected under strict separation reasoning and, as we will see later, is widespread in Germany. At their best, SRI programs reflect Australia's religious diversity. The inner city West End School in Queensland, for example, offers faith classes in Bahá'í, Buddhism, Orthodox/Greek Orthodox, Protestant, Roman Catholic, Hinduism, and Islam. Those offerings reflect the religious background of the student population.[82] However, not all schools display this kind of diversity, and only one state, New South Wales, offers secular ethics as an alternative to religious instruction. SRI programs, in our view, are consistent with the value of neutrality, but only if a secular ethics option is available to those parents wishing to exercise this choice for their children.[83]

Even more unique is Australia's school chaplaincy program. Initiated in 2006 by the Howard government, the three-year, $90 million National School Chaplaincy Programme provided federal money to supplement the cost of hiring a chaplain in the schools. The program's aim was to assist in the support of the emotional well-being of students. The teacher unions universally rejected the proposal while church leaders generally supported it. What is more surprising, at least by American standards, is that the opposition Labor Party did not universally oppose the program. The next Labor prime minister, Kevin Rudd (2007–2010), expanded commonwealth funding for chaplains by an additional $42 million and all subsequent prime ministers, Labor or Liberal, have preserved the program. Despite a good deal of controversy surrounding the chaplaincy initiative, it has not been abandoned.[84]

In theory, the program meets the challenge of diversity and evenhandedness. Schools do not have to apply for funding under the program, participation by students is entirely voluntary, chaplains are not allowed to proselytize, and they must "respect, accept and be sensitive to other people's views, values and beliefs."[85] An educational official pointed out to us what she considered to be a crucial point about the program: "It is important to note that the National School Chaplaincy Programme is voluntary and school communities decide if they want to apply for funding. School communities will also determine the role and the faith and/or denomination of the chaplain."[86] What this official assumes, and what is so different from American practices and legal precedents, is that so long as a program is voluntary and the government is evenhanded among religious traditions, there is nothing wrong with funding a religious program.

In practice, however, the program fails the neutrality test. The evidence suggests that Christian chaplains dominate the field. According to a 2012 Commonwealth Senate report, 99.5 percent of all chaplains in the program were Christian.[87] In contrast with state funding for religious schools, therefore, the playing field is uneven among the different religious traditions. The program also rather naively presumes that a chaplain from a particular religious tradition (Protestant, Catholic, Jewish, Muslim) can provide generic moral instruction for an increasingly diverse student population. However, persons occupying the position reflect a specific tradition, and those traditions often have distinctive moral worldviews. Neutrality requires that the state not tip the scales toward a particular perspective in state-run schools, and so chaplains may not proselytize and they have to respect the values and beliefs of all students. While those are reasonable requirements, the state essentially asks that chaplains forgo their religiousness and provide secular welfare services. While those services are highly valued, providing them by a person with the title, education, and skills of a chaplain threatens to undermine governmental evenhandedness among religious perspectives and between a secular and religious viewpoint.

CHURCH, STATE, AND NONPROFIT COMMUNITY SERVICE ORGANIZATIONS

Australia's nonprofit sector is complex, expanding, and diverse. It includes churches, hospitals, universities, sports and recreation clubs, ethnic associations, professional associations, and political advocacy groups, to name a few. According to the Bureau of Statistics, there are some sixty thousand nonprofit organizations in Australia. Collectively those groups had an income of $107 billion in 2012–2013, they employed more than one million persons, and they utilized the help of 3.9 million volunteers. Religious groups are by far the largest group within the nonprofit sector.[88]

Christian groups have dominated the community service field throughout Australia's history. Churches or church-based organizations took the lead in providing social welfare in colonial Australia. Evangelical Protestants gave a religious impetus for the formation of charitable organizations that addressed the problems of poverty, child neglect, and homelessness. For these groups and the individuals who founded them, evangelism and the relief of poverty were twin religious duties. The same was true for various Catholic organizations formed later in the nineteenth century that linked the teachings of the Church to their social work in the community. Most of the finance for these charities came initially from the churches and wealthy philanthropists. Reformist ideas emerged at the turn of the century that questioned the value of church-based charitable organizations by promoting the notion of a universal right to services and support based on need, and not the selective idea of moral worth. At the same time, church agencies could not meet the growing demand for services brought on by the economic depressions of the 1890s and 1930s. Gradually, the state began to take over more of the functions it previously had subsidized and adopted some reforming ideas with policies of basic income support, child care, and old age pensions.[89]

The Constitutional Amendment of 1946 overcame doubts about the commonwealth government's power with regard to social welfare by establishing its sovereignty to legislate in eleven key areas of social welfare, including maternity and family allowances, widow pensions, child endowment, and unemployment and sickness benefits. The government expanded its welfare role in the 1960s and 1970s as public support grew for health insurance, income redistribution, and aboriginal rights. A large number of secular non-profits also emerged in the postwar years that utilized a professional social work model in service provision. The conservative critique of welfare systems in Britain and the United States in the 1970s and 1980s also affected Australian policy. Nonprofit organizations benefited, at least in the short run, from new right attacks on the welfare state because they were seen to be more flexible, efficient, and cost-effective than services provided directly by the government. Policy makers began to favor the devolution of services to nonprofit groups, and in the decade between 1976–1977 and 1986–1987 direct support for nonprofit organizations by all levels of government in Australia more than doubled in real terms.[90]

Australian welfare policy demonstrates the same kind of pragmatism that has been evident in the field of education. The federal government collects most of the tax revenues and establishes national welfare priorities, but nonprofit agencies provide most of the human services. According to one recent estimate, church-related nonprofit organizations delivered half of all social services in Australia.[91] Many of the largest nonprofits in terms of total annual income have a religious affiliation, including the Salvation Army ($375 million), World Vision ($380 million), Mission Australia ($337 million), the St. Vincent de Paul Society ($318 million), and Anglicare ($435 million). There are thousands of smaller Christian, Jewish, Buddhist, Hindu, and Muslim agencies as well. The cooperation between the government and religious nonprofits is most evident in various governmental funding programs. The most common arrangement is a fee for service. Organizations contract with the government to provide specified services, such as residential aged care, emergency relief, or child welfare services, for a fixed fee. In 2014, three of the country's largest community service agencies, the Salvation Army, Mission Australia, and Anglicare Australia received, respectively, 50, 70, and 41 percent of their total budgets from commonwealth and state grants.[92]

At the federal level, money flows to a wide array of Christian agencies. In 2015, the commonwealth government had formal funding arrangements with mainline Protestant church agencies (Anglicare, Australian Lutheran World Service, UnitingCare), evangelical Protestant organizations (the Salvation Army, Mission Australia, Adventist Development and Relief Agency, Teen Challenge), and Roman Catholic service agencies (St. Vincent de Paul, CatholicCare).[93] Grants at the state level demonstrate even greater evenhandedness on the part of the government. In 2012–2013, for example, the State of New South Wales provided grants to Jewish (JewishCare), Islamic (Muslim Women's Association), and Buddhist (Karuna Hospice Care) nonprofit organizations.[94]

Religious agencies have taken the lead in questioning the appropriateness of applying free market economic principles and evaluations to social welfare provision. In response to a 2009 government report on the Australian not-for-profit sector, Catholic Social Services of Australia succinctly noted that "the contributions of the not for profit sector to society is not analogous to the contribution of business to the economy. Much of the contribution of the community of faith-based agencies cannot be expressed in economic terms."[95] The government's focus on efficient and cost-effective services will not settle the difficult question of how to assess the quality of services an organization provides, but the larger question for religious agencies is whether or not government funding makes it more difficult for them to maintain their distinctive identity. There is little doubt that many religious nonprofits have lost or minimized their religious identity over the past several decades. The reasons for this shift are complex, but they likely have something to do with agency dependence on state finances, their adoption of the norms of the social welfare profession, the regulatory burdens associated with the receipt of government funds, and the fact that a religious identity seems somewhat anachronistic in an increasingly secular Australia.[96]

This process seems not to be driven, however, by overt efforts by the government to secularize religious organizations. In practice, the degree to which a religious ethos permeates the activities of these religious agencies varies a great deal. Nonetheless, the mission statements for many of these organizations retain a strong link to their religious heritage. JewishCare affirms that "Our values, *chessed, mishpacha, derech eretz* and *tzedakah*, define who we are and underpin everything we do. They are also particular to the Jewish approach of creating a meaningful life and a strong, cohesive community."[97] BaptistCare describes its vision as "a dream—A transformed society based on Christ's values."[98] Anglicare Sydney avows that "Christian care is at the heart of what we do at Anglicare. It flows from our faith in Jesus Christ which compels us to serve others, help the vulnerable, and be a voice for the disadvantaged. We want to follow Christ's example, reaching out to others with the same compassion he has shown us."[99]

Religious agencies are generally exempt from equal opportunities legislation, and until recently this led to very little political controversy. For example, under existing law religious agencies and schools may discriminate in hiring to "avoid injury to the religious susceptibilities of adherents of that religion."[100] This has enabled religious organizations and schools to hire on the basis of religion for key positions within an organization. While not all agencies give preference to coreligionists in hiring, a majority of the ones we interviewed do, either explicitly or implicitly. Marilyn Webster of the Catholic Social Welfare Commission noted that "service agreements do not specify staff qualifications and the standard practice in most Catholic agencies is, whenever possible, to hire within the Catholic social welfare network."[101] World Vision, the Salvation Army, and Mission Australia also give a preference in hiring to coreligionists. An "essential criteria" for an employment opportunity with the Adventist Development and Relief Agency (ADRA) is that the candidate have a "personal commitment to the Seventh-day Adventist church and ADRA's mission, vision, values and beliefs."[102]

These exemptions have recently come under some assault. In 2013, the Labor-led Gillard government passed the Sex Discrimination Amendment (Sexual Orientation, Gender Identity and Intersex Status) Act, which barred discrimination against lesbian, gay, bisexual, transgender, and intersex people. Despite some heated debate, however, the bill preserved existing exemptions in antidiscrimination legislation, thus allowing religious organizations to refuse to employ LGBT individuals. In the lead-up to the 2016 federal election, the Green Party called for an end to religious exemptions to this antidiscrimination law, a position rejected by the leaders of all the major religious groups and the two largest political parties.[103] In striking a balance between the rights of religious organizations to conduct their affairs in accordance with their own beliefs and values and general nondiscrimination principles, Australian policy has thus far erred on the side of religious freedom.

Faith-based organizations have a similar autonomy to offer religious services as a part of their program. Ed Dawkins, the community services secretary for the Salvation Army Eastern Command, noted that "we have drug and rehabilitation programs that have a strong spiritual dimension, including chapel services. We believe that the spiritual dimension is crucial to rehabilitation."[104] The Salvation Army makes clients aware of the religious elements of their various programs, but it does not discriminate against non-Christians who choose to sign up for one of them. The Teen Challenge drug and alcohol rehabilitation program similarly requires participants to participate in daily religious devotionals and church services.[105] Overseas aid and development agencies are not allowed to use government money for religious purposes in their projects, but religious values and practices are still an important part of the work of many of these organizations. The initial point of contact for most church-based development agencies is a local church, and a number of these agencies, including the largest, World Vision, emphasize the connection between development and evangelism in their literature.[106] In short, faith-based agencies have a good deal of autonomy to maintain their religious identity if they choose to do so.

By law and conviction, religious agencies do not discriminate among clients on the basis of religion. There is often a self-selection bias, however, on the part of clients who want a religiously oriented social service. Paul Tyrell, executive director of Centacare, the national body of Catholic welfare agencies, indicated to us that Centacare agencies do not discriminate among clients on the basis of religion, but that the government understands that "as a Catholic agency a majority of our clients are going to be Catholic."[107] According to Tyrell, half of all Centacare clients are Roman Catholics, many of them having been referred to the agency by a local priest. Given the fact that they run support centers for Muslim women and offer various settlement services for Muslim immigrants, it is not surprising that virtually all of the clients of the United Muslim Women's Association are Islamic.[108] There is, in fact, a long tradition in Australia of immigrants preferring services provided by their own community organizations rather than the government. While they are hardly new to the Australian scene, a survey of the Australian Jewish population found that 82 percent of the elderly would prefer accommodation in a specifically Jewish hostel or nursing home.[109] The same is often true for Muslims and Buddhists, and the government has responded by turning to religious and ethnic organizations as the primary service providers for those communities.[110] This fact reflects once again the pragmatism that is the norm with aid to nonprofit organizations that has allowed for a diversity of religious organizations to receive public aid.

CONCLUDING OBSERVATIONS

In slightly more than two hundred years, Australia's church-state policy has vacillated among four distinct models: religious establishment, plural establishment, liberal separationism, and pragmatic pluralism. Because Australian policy makers have never committed themselves to a single church-state model, they have had the freedom to adopt the most politically favorable policy at a given time. Political and pragmatic considerations, in other words, have been far more important in Australian church-state issues than theoretical considerations. This is in stark contrast to France with its deep ideological commitment to *laïcité*, or even the United States with its less aggressive form of church-state separation. Australia's church-state practices, though they are pragmatically based, come closest to those of the Dutch. Both countries seek to accommodate and support a wide diversity of religious and secular systems of belief. Australian policy, therefore, fits most closely with the second of our church-state models: pluralism. The state recognizes that religious life is not limited to the private sphere, but has an important public component, and accommodates a wide variety of religious groups with funding for such diverse societal activities as education, mental health, and welfare services, to name a few. This is most evident in state funding for private religious schools. In addition, the government generally does not favor any one religious group over another, nor does it advantage religious over secular perspectives.

Australia's pragmatic pluralism has gradually increased the free exercise rights of religious groups. Australian practice in this area is not much different from that of the other countries in our study. Like these countries, Australia struggles with how far to extend religious rights, but there is a cultural commitment to the values of accommodation, tolerance, compromise, and neutrality that makes possible the free expression of religious ideas. A problem with the Australian approach, however, is that the state has not solidified its guarantee of religious liberty through judicial decisions or legislation. The Australian High Court has narrowly interpreted the free exercise right of Section 116 of the Constitution, and there is no federal law that specifically bars religious discrimination. This is a significant deficiency, in our view, not because there is widespread religious discrimination in Australia, because there is not, but because there are no established guidelines as to how far groups can go to exercise their religious liberty. This seems to be a particular issue for Muslims, who have been the targets of abuse in the aftermath of 9/11 and the Bali bombings.

Pragmatism has also driven the state's commitment to providing aid to religious schools and nonprofit organizations, and to the state's policy of religion in the public schools. The impetus for state aid to schools in the 1960s and 1970s was political and pragmatic; both major political parties hoped to secure Catholic support with schemes of direct aid to parochial schools. Similarly, a pragmatic concern about cost-effectiveness drove the government's decision to devolve service delivery to nongovernment organizations in the 1970s and 1980s. As the state became multicultural and the desire for religiously grounded education and services intensified, Australia successfully integrated new religious groups, such as Muslims, and allowed them to express their differences in publicly financed organizations. This demonstrates a practical commitment by the state both to encourage religious pluralism and to diversity. To its credit, Australia has adopted these policies without the level of political conflict that has occurred around identical issues in many of the other countries in our study. There is agreement between Australia's two largest parties—the left-leaning Labor Party and the right-leaning Liberal Party—on these policies. That is an impressive achievement.

Australian policy makers have rarely given much thought to the normative implications of Australia's church-state policy. There is little explicit reference to religious freedom as a positive right that the state has an obligation to accommodate. Nevertheless, Australia's pragmatic pluralism implicitly reaches the goal of governmental neutrality that we established as the basic ideal for church-state relations on this question. In practice, if not always in theory, Australian policy discriminates neither among religious groups nor between religious and nonreligious belief systems.

NOTES

1. Population data is available from the Australian Bureau of Statistics at http://www.abs.gov.au.

2. Desmond Cahill, Gary Bouma, Hass Dellal, and Michael Leahy, "Religion, Cultural Diversity, and Safeguarding Australia" (Canberra: Department of Immigration and Multicultural and Indigenous Affairs and the Australian Multicultural Foundation, 2004); "Cultural Di-

versity: Reflecting a Nation, Stories from the 2011 Census, 2012–2013." Available at http://www.abs.gov.au/ausstats/abs@.nsf/Lookup/2071.0main+features902012-2013.

3. "Losing My Religion?" *Australian Social Trends*, November 2013. Available at http://www.abs.gov.au/ausstats/abs@.nsf/Lookup/4102.0Main+Features30Nov+2013.

4. Gary D. Bouma and Michael Mason, "Baby Boomers Downunder: The Case of Australia," in Wade Clark Roof, Jackson W. Carroll, and David A. Roozen, eds., *The Post-War Generation and Establishment Religion* (Boulder, Colo.: Westview Press, 1995), 27–58; "2011 National Church Life Survey," available at www.ncls.org.au; and "How Religious Are Australians?," available at http://www.christianitytoday.com/edstetzer/2013/december/how-religious-are-australians.html.

5. Jeremy Moon and Campbell Sharman, eds., *Australian Politics and Government: The Commonwealth, the States, and the Territories* (New York: Cambridge University Press, 2003); David Solomon, *Australia's Government and Parliament* (Melbourne: Longman Cheshire, 1988).

6. Anna Crabb, "Invoking Religion in Australian Politics," *Australian Journal of Political Science* 44, 2 (2009), 259–79.

7. Marion Maddox, *God under Howard: The Rise of the Religious Right in Australian Politics* (Sydney: Allen and Unwin, 2005).

8. John Warhurst, "Religion and Politics in the Howard Decade," *Australian Journal of Political Science* 42, 1 (2007), 19–32.

9. Gregory Melleuish, "Religion and Politics in Australia," *Political Theology* 11, 6 (2010), 909–27; Todd Donovan, "The Irrelevance and (New) Relevance of Religion in Australian Elections," *Australian Journal of Political Science* 49, 4 (2014), 626–46; and Stuart Piggin, "Power and Religion in a Modern State: Desecularization in Australian History," *Journal of Religious History* 38, 3 (2014), 320–40.

10. Graham Maddox, *Australia's Democracy: In Theory and Practice* (Melbourne: Longman Cheshire, 1985), chap. 5.

11. Alan Fenna, "Centralising Dynamics in Australian Federalism," *Australian Journal of Politics and History* 58, 4 (2012), 580–90.

12. Richard Allsop, "Four Points on Federalism," *Institute of Public Affairs Review* (January 2008).

13. Solomon, *Australia's Government and Parliament*, chap. 2.

14. Ian Breward, *A History of the Australian Churches* (Sydney: Allen and Unwin, 1993), chap. 2; Bruce Kay, ed., *Anglicanism in Australia: A History* (Melbourne: Melbourne University Press, 2002).

15. Michael Hogan, *The Sectarian Strand* (New York: Penguin Books, 1987), chap. 1; Bryan S. Turner, "Religion, State, and Civil Society: Nation Building in Australia," in Thomas Robbins and Roland Robertson, eds., *Church-State Relations: Tensions and Transitions* (New Brunswick, N.J.: Transaction Books, 1987), 233–51.

16. Brian Fletcher, "The Anglican Ascendancy," in Bruce Kay, ed., *Anglicanism in Australia: A History* (Melbourne: Melbourne University Press, 2002), 9.

17. David Stoneman, "Richard Bourke: For the Honour of God and the Good of Man," *Journal of Religious History* 38, 3 (2014), 341–55.

18. Suzanne Rutland, "Early Jewish Settlement, 1788–1800," in James Jupp, ed., *The Australian People: An Encyclopedia of the Australian Nation, Its People and Their Origins* (Cambridge: Cambridge University Press, 2002), 525–28.

19. Gary D. Bouma, "The Emergence of Religious Plurality in Australia: A Multicultural Society," *Sociology of Religion* 56 (1995), 285–302; Hans Mol, *The Faith of Australians* (Sydney: Allen and Unwin, 1985), chap. 9.

20. Michael Hogan, "Worrying about Religion," *Australian Review of Public Affairs* 7, 1 (2006), 102–5.

21. Hogan, *The Sectarian Strand*, chap. 2.

22. Breward, *A History of the Australian Churches*, chap. 4; Patricia Curthoys, "State Support for Churches: 1836–1860," in Kay, ed., *Anglicanism in Australia*, 50.

23. Peter Meadmore, "Free, Compulsory and Secular? The Re-Invention of Australian Public Education," *Journal of Educational Policy* 16, 2 (2001), 113–25.

24. Hogan, *The Sectarian Strand*, chap. 4.

25. Quoted in *Discrimination and Religious Conviction* (Sydney: New South Wales Anti-Discrimination Board, 1984), 319.

26. Quoted in *Discrimination and Religious Conviction*, 321.

27. Mol, *The Faith of Australians*, chap. 1.

28. Stuart Piggen, "Power and Religion in a Modern State: Desecularisation in Australian History," *Journal of Religious History* 38, 3 (2014), 332.

29. Carolyn Evans, "Religion as Politics not Law: The Religion Clauses in the Australian Constitution," *Religion, State, and Society* 36, 3 (2008), 283–302.

30. Pervaiz Ahmad Buttar and Lynette Joy Mattingley, *Religious Conviction and the 'New Magna Carta'* (Brisbane: James Cook University, Centre for Southeast Asia Studies, 1986); Jeffrey Goldsworthy, "Introduction," in Tom Campbell, Jeffrey Goldsworthy, and Adrienne Stone, eds., *Protecting Rights without a Bill of Rights: Institutional Performance and Reform in Australia* (Aldershot, U.K.: Ashgate, 2006), 1–13.

31. Quoted in Hogan, *The Sectarian Strand*, 228.

32. *Grace Bible Church Inc. v. Reedman*, 54 ALR 571 (1984).

33. *Kruger v. Commonwealth*, ALR 126 (1997); Sarah Joseph, "Kruger v. Commonwealth: Constitutional Rights and the Stolen Generations," *Monash University Law Review* 24, 2 (1998), 486–98.

34. *Religious Freedom Roundtable—Issues Paper* (Sydney: Australian Human Rights Commission, 2015).

35. *Article 18: Freedom of Religion and Belief* (Sydney: Human Rights and Equal Opportunity Commission, 1998), 3–4.

36. Gary D. Bouma, *Mosques and Muslim Settlements in Australia* (Canberra: Australian Government Publishing Service, 1994), 90.

37. *Article 18: Freedom of Religion and Belief*, 7.

38. John Chesterman, "Natural Born Subjects? Race and British Subjecthood in Australia," *Australian Journal of Politics and History* 51, 1 (2005), 30–39; Lois Foster and David Stockley, *Australian Multiculturalism: A Documentary History and Critique* (Philadelphia: Multilingual Matters, 1988); and Anthony Moran, "White Australia, Settler Nationalism and Aboriginal Assimilation," *Australian Journal of Politics and History* 51, 2 (2005), 168–93.

39. "Islamophobia, Social Distance and Fear of Terrorism in Australia: A Preliminary Report," International Centre for Muslim and Non-Muslim Understanding (Adelaide, South Africa: University of South Australia, 2015), 5.

40. Scott Poynting, "Living with Racism: The Experience and Reporting by Arab and Muslim Australians of Discrimination, Abuse and Violence Since 11 September 2001," A Report to the Human Rights and Equal Opportunity Commission (April 2004); "Extremism Concerns Growing in West and Predominantly Muslim Countries," Pew Research Center (July 16, 2015); Zia Ahmed, "Dramatic Increase in Islamophobia after Paris Attacks," *Australian Muslim Times* (December 2, 2015); "Australian Muslims: A Demographic, Social and Economic Profile of Muslims in Australia 2015," International Centre for Muslim and Non-Muslim Understanding (Adelaide, South Africa: University of South Australia, 2015), 15.

41. Telephone interview with Ikebal Patel, president, Australian Federation of Islamic Councils (June 5, 2007).

42. "Islamophobia, Social Distance and Fear of Terrorism in Australia: A Preliminary Report."

43. "Australian Muslims: A Demographic, Social and Economic Profile of Muslims in Australia 2015," International Centre for Muslim and Non-Muslim Understanding (Adelaide, South Africa: University of South Australia, 2015); "The Resilience and Ordinariness of Australian Muslims: Attitudes and Experiences of Muslims Report, 2015," available at https://www.uws.edu.au/_data/assets/pdf_file/0008/988793/12441_text_challenging_racism_WEB.pdf.

44. Telephone interview with Ikebal Patel, president, Australian Federation of Islamic Councils (June 5, 2007).

45. Hogan, *The Sectarian Strand*, chap. 9.

46. *Attorney General for the State of Victoria (at the relation of Black) v. The Commonwealth of Australia*, 146 CLR 559 at 328 (1981).

47. *Attorney General for the State of Victoria (at the relation of Black) v. The Commonwealth of Australia*, at 330.

48. *Attorney General for the State of Victoria (at the relation of Black) v. The Commonwealth of Australia*, at 326.

49. *Attorney General for the State of Victoria (at the relation of Black) v. The Commonwealth of Australia*, at 330.

50. Marilyn Harrington, "Australian Government Funding for Schools Explained: 2013 Update," Parliamentary Library, Canberra.

51. "Summary of Capital Grants and Project Descriptions for Non-Governmental Schools, 2013." Available at https://docs.education.gov.au/documents/part-d-capital-grants-funding-2013.

52. For data on school funding see Harrington, "Australian Government Funding for Schools Explained: 2013 Update"; "Report on Government Service Provision: Education 2015," available at http://www.pc.gov.au/research/ongoing/report-on-government-services/2015/childcare-education-and-training/school-education; and "Independent Schools in Australia: Snapshot 2015," Independent Schools Council of Australia, available at http://isca.edu.au/publications/independent-schooling-in-australia-snapshot/.

53. For data on enrollment trends, see David Gonski et al., "Review of Funding for Schooling: Final Report," Department of Education, Employment and Workplace Relations, Commonwealth of Australia, 2011.

54. Gonski et al., "Review of Funding for Schooling," 8.

55. Zehavit Gross and Suzanne D. Rutland, "Intergenerational Challenges in Australian Jewish Education," *Religious Education* 109, 2 (2014), 143–61.

56. John Goldlust, *The Melbourne Jewish Community: A Needs Assessment* (Canberra: Australian Government Publishing Service, 1993), 15.

57. *Discussion Paper: Review of the New Schools Policy* (Canberra: Australian Government Publishing Service, 1995), 15; "Independent Schools in Australia: Snapshot 2015," Independent Schools Council of Australia, available at http://isca.edu.au/publications/independent-schooling-in-australia-snapshot/.

58. Natasha Bita, "Parents Turn to Muslim Schools to Enforce Values," *Australian* (May 25, 2015).

59. Jennifer Buckingham, "The Rise of Religious Schools" (St. Leonards, NSW: Centre for Independent Studies, 2010).

60. Islamic College of South Australia. Available at http://www.icosa.sa.edu.au/.

61. Christian Schools Australia. Available at http://www.csa.edu.au/about/about-csa/vision-and-purpose.

62. *National Catholic Education Commission: School Funding Policy*, http://www.ncec.catholic.edu.au/resources/publications/388-funding-principles-for-catholic-schools-2016/file, 3.

63. For data on Catholic schools, see http://www.ncec.catholic.edu.au/images/stories/documents/NCEC_Brochure_Web.pdf; and Buckingham, "The Rise of Religious Schools," 26.

64. Carolyn Evans and Beth Gaze, "Discrimination by Religious Schools: Views from the Coal Face," *Melbourne University Law Review* 34, 2 (2010), 392–424.

65. Buckingham, "The Rise of Religious Schools," 12.

66. Telephone interview with Bob Johnson, executive officer, Australian Association of Christian Schools (June 4, 2007).

67. Gonski et al., "Review of Funding for Schooling," 9–11 and 19–34; and Marion Maddox, "Are Religious Schools Socially Inclusive or Exclusive? An Australian Conundrum," *International Journal of Cultural Policy* 17, 2 (2011), 170–86.

68. "Minister Tells Muslims: Accept Aussie Values or 'Clear Off,'" *ABA Online*. Available at http://www.abc.net.au/news/newsitems/200508/s1445181.htm.

69. "Gen Y Jihadists: Preventing Radicalisation in Australia," Australian Strategic Policy Institute, 2015. Available at https://www.aspi.org.au/publications/gen-y-jihadists-preventing-radicalisation-in-australia.

70. "Brethren Schools to Get $70m in Funding," *Australian* (January 11, 2010).

71. Natalie O'Brien, "Most Radicalised Australian Teenagers Attended Public Schools," *Sydney Morning Herald* (October 11, 2015).

72. "Islamic Schools in New South Wales," Association of Independent Schools of New South Wales. Available at https://www.aisnsw.edu.au/Publications/Other/Documents/Islamic%20Schools%20in%20NSW.pdf.

73. Buckingham, "The Rise of Religious Schools," 20.

74. Telephone interview with Ikebal Patel, president, Australian Federation of Islamic Councils (June 5, 2007).

75. Telephone interview with Bob Johnson, executive officer, Australian Association of Christian Schools (June 4, 2007).

76. Telephone interview with Bob Johnson, executive officer, Australian Association of Christian Schools (June 4, 2007).

77. Personal correspondence from Suzanne Northcutt, branch manager for schools funding and coordination and the Schools Resource Group, Department of Education, Science and Training (July 2, 2007).

78. For an excellent overview of religion in state-run schools, see *Discrimination and Religious Conviction,* chap. 6.

79. Quoted in *Discrimination and Religious Conviction*, 325.

80. "Religious Education Implementation Procedures, Department of Education," New South Wales. Available at https://www.det.nsw.edu.au/policies/curriculum/schools/spec_religious/REimplementproced.pdf.

81. "Guidelines for Religious Education," Department of Education, Western Australia, available at http://www.det.wa.edu.au/curriculumsupport/religiouseducation/detcms/portal/; "Studies in Religion, Department of Education," New South Wales, available at http://www.schools.nsw.edu.au/learning/yr11_12/hsie/religion/index.php.

82. "West End State School Parent Handbook," available at https://westendss.eq.edu.au/Supportandresources/Formsanddocuments/Documents/WESS%20Parent%20Handbook.pdf.

83. For criticisms of the program see Cathy Jane Byrne, "Jesus Is Alive! He Is King of Australia: Segregated Religious Instruction, Child Identity and Exclusion.," *British Journal of Religious Education* 34, 3 (2012), 317–31; Catherine Byrne, "Free, Compulsory, and (Not) Secular: The Failed Idea in Australian Education," *Journal of Religious History* 37, 1 (2013), 20–38.

84. Jeremy Patrick, "Religion, Secularism, and the National School Chaplaincy and Student Welfare Program," *University of Queensland Law Review* 33, 1 (2014), 187–219.

85. "National School Chaplaincy Programme." Available at https://www.education.gov.au/national-school-chaplaincy-programme.

86. Personal correspondence from Suzanne Northcutt, branch manager for schools funding and coordination and the Schools Resource Group, Department of Education, Science and Training (July 2, 2007).

87. Patrick, "Religion, Secularism, and the National School Chaplaincy and Student Welfare Program," 205.

88. "Non-Profit Institutions, 2012–2013," Australian Bureau of Statistics, available at http://www.abs.gov.au/AUSSTATS/abs@.nsf/Lookup/5256.0Main+Features12012-13?OpenDocument; Penny Knight and David Gilchrist, "Australia's Faith-Based Charities: A Summary of Data from the Australian Charities and Not-for-Profits Commission," Melbourne.

89. Brian Dickey, *No Charity There* (Sydney: Allen and Unwin, 1989); *Charitable Organizations in Australia* (Melbourne: Australian Government Publishing Service, 1995); Beth R. Crisp, "Catholic Agencies: Making a Distinct Contribution to Australian Social Welfare Provision?" *Australian Catholic Record* 87, 4 (2010), 440–51; and Piggin, "Power and Religion in a Modern State," 326–28.

90. *Australia's Welfare 1993: Services and Assistance* (Canberra: Australian Government Publishing Service, 1993), chap. 1; Adam Graycar and Adam Jamrozik, *How Australians Live: Social Policy in Theory and Practice* (Melbourne: Macmillan, 1989).

91. Paul Oslington, "Sacred and Secular in Australian Social Services," *Pacifica* 28, 1 (2014), 79–93.

92. Financial data available at https://salvos.org.au/scribe/sites/auesalvos/files/TSA-annual-report-2015.pdf; https://www.missionaustralia.com.au/publications/annual-reports/annual-report-2015; and http://www.anglicare.asn.au/docs/default-source/default-document-library/annual-report-2014-15.pdf?sfvrsn=2.

93. "Organisations Currently Allocated Funding," Department of Health, available at http://www.health.gov.au/internet/main/publishing.nsf/Content/drugtreat-fund-org; "List of Australian Accredited Non-Government Organisations (NGOs)," Department of Foreign Affairs and Trade, available at http://dfat.gov.au/aid/who-we-work-with/ngos/Pages/list-of-australian-accredited-non-government-organisations.aspx.

94. "Grant and Subsidies Payments Including Funding to Nongovernment Organisations 2012–13," New South Wales Family and Community Services. Available at http://www.community.nsw.gov.au/home.

95. "Valuing Social Service: Submission to the Productivity Commission Study into the Contribution of Australia's Not for Profit Sector," Catholic Social Services Australia. Available at http://www.pc.gov.au/inquiries/completed/not-for-profit/submissions/sub117.pdf.

96. Oslington, "Sacred and Secular in Australian Social Services," 86–90.

97. http://www.jewishcare.org.au/about/mission-and-values/.

98. http://www.baptistcareaustralia.org.au/about/vision-mission-values.

99. https://www.anglicare.org.au/christian-care.

100. "List of Exemptions in Commonwealth Anti-Discrimination Legislation." Available at https://www.ag.gov.au/RightsAndProtections/FOI/Documents/Commonwealth%20Anti-Discrimination%20Legislation.pdf.

101. Personal interview with Marilyn Webster, Catholic Social Welfare Commission (July 18, 1995).

102. https://www.adra.org.au/jobs.

103. David Crowe, "Federal Election 2016: Greens under Pressure on Religion Reforms," *Australian* (May 24, 2016).

104. Personal interview with Ed Dawkins, community service secretary for the Salvation Army Eastern Command (July 31, 1995).

105. "About Our Rehabilitation Program," Teen Challenge. Available at http://teenchallengeqld.org.au/what-we-do/rehabilitation/rehabilitation-program/.

106. "World Vision Australia: About Us." Available at https://www.worldvision.com.au/about-us.

107. Personal interview with Paul Tyrell, executive director of Centacare (July 26, 1995).

108. http://www.mwa.org.au/.

109. Goldlust, *The Melbourne Jewish Community*, xv–xvii.

110. Patricia Sherwood, "Buddhist Contribution to Social Welfare in Australia," *Journal of Buddhist Ethics* 8 (2001), 61–74.

III

Models of Establishment

Chapter Six

England

Restrained Establishment

England is the only country in our study with a formally established church, the Church of England, which has been the recognized church since the middle of the sixteenth century. The church's political powers and privileges have diminished over time, and recent decades have seen a dramatic decline in the percentage of the Christian population and equally sharp increases in those with no religion or that identify with non-Christian traditions. Yet the religious establishment prevails, a majority believes that it should be retained, and it remains an important factor in the resolution of church-state issues in contemporary politics. This church-state model, what we term a restrained establishment, does much to frame church-state debates between the state and religion. It is restrained in the sense that virtually all of the disabilities associated with membership outside of the Church of England have been eliminated, while most (but not all) of the privileges given to the established church now apply to other faiths as well. Yet England retains its religious establishment and that model in turn helps to sustain a cultural assumption that religion has a public function to perform, that it is appropriate for the state and religious groups to cooperate in achieving common goals, and that political and religious authorities can and should negotiate on key policy issues of interest to both of them. The model has also led to formalized institutional arrangements between religious groups and the state, arrangements that have proven resistant to radical change.

THE NATION

Great Britain comprises the three countries of England, Scotland, and Wales. The United Kingdom includes these three countries plus Northern Ireland. In 2010, the United Kingdom had a total population of just over sixty-three million, making it the third most populous country in the European Union behind France and Germany. With more than 80 percent of the total population, England is by far the largest of the countries in the United Kingdom. Pragmatism characterizes English political culture, with a greater orientation toward what works than abstract theorizing. In this way, England is much like Australia. As a result of this practical orientation, change in English history has been incremental, not revolutionary. Politically, England has gradually evolved from a limited representative democracy in the thirteenth century, with the signing of the Magna Charta, to a full and participatory democracy by the end of the nineteenth century. Today, Britain has a parliamentary form of government with a bicameral legislative branch. The 650 members in the House of Commons are popularly elected and politically powerful. The Commons makes primary legislation—other than for matters devolved to the Scottish Parliament and the Northern Ireland Assembly—and selects the prime minister, who serves as the head of the government and is the highest political authority in the land. The nearly 760 members in the House of Lords are not elected, but serve by virtue of birth, appointment by the Crown, or position. Although the prime minister and both houses of Parliament must formally pass legislation, by convention and law the Lords does not overturn a government bill and limits its role to discussion and debate. [1]

Unlike the other countries in our study, England does not have a written constitution, which has some effect on church-state issues. There is an uncodified British constitution that embodies the principle of a higher law, the most significant provisions of which are the rule of law, parliamentary government under a limited monarch, a unitary political system, and parliamentary sovereignty. The 1998 Human Rights Act incorporated the European Convention on Human Rights (ECHR) into British law, and it includes various civil liberties. Fundamental freedoms, including religious rights, however, lie as much in the capacity of the democratic society and Parliament to preserve shared values, which for the most part has been done, as they do in any legislative mandate.

The most significant trends in religious identification over the past several decades have been the decline in the Christian population, an increase in the nonreligious population, and growth among those who identify with non-Christian traditions. According to the 2011 Census, Christianity remained the largest religion in the country, representing 59 percent of the population, but that was a marked decline from the 71 percent who claimed a Christian affiliation a decade earlier. By contrast, the percentage of those who reported that they had no religion grew from 15 to 25 of the population, the Muslim share rose from 3 to 4.8 percent, and other religions (Jewish, Buddhist, Hindu, Sikh) increased from 2.8 to 3.6 percent of the total. Christians have the oldest age profile for any of the religious groups, suggesting that their share of the overall population will continue to decline.[2]

England vies with France as the least churched country in our study. According to one exhaustive study, in 2010 only 11.2 percent of the population in the United Kingdom was a member of a church, and an even smaller percentage was religiously active.[3] While the data is difficult to confirm, the media frequently reports that the number of religiously active Muslims, and even Hindus, has or will soon surpass that of regular worshippers in the Church of England or the Roman Catholic Church.[4] The largest Christian denominations are Anglicans and Roman Catholics, each representing roughly one-quarter of all church members, followed by the smaller Presbyterian, Methodist, Baptist, Pentecostal, and Orthodox communities. The only Christian churches that are experiencing sustained growth are those that serve the burgeoning migrant African and eastern European communities.[5] Based on the current trends, the demographer David Voas contends that the future of religion in England is to be "found in Islam and the black [overwhelmingly Christian] majority churches."[6] For larger percentages of the population the situation is one that has been described by Grace Davie as one of "believing without belonging."[7] Belief in God or some higher being remains relatively high (62 percent), nearly half (47 percent) affirm that religion is extremely, very, or somewhat important in their daily life, and 43 percent say that they pray several times a year or more.[8] However, there has been a decline even on these soft indicators of religiosity in recent decades, particularly among younger cohorts, signifying perhaps that increasing percentages of the British public neither believe nor belong. While formal membership in the Church of England is low, it is concentrated in the middle and upper classes. In addition, many of the nation's elite private schools, called "public" schools in Britain, are affiliated with the Anglican Church. Both of these facts help to explain how the Anglican Church has come to have significant representation in the upper echelons of the nation's political, legal, and cultural institutions.[9]

The Church of England was once famously described as the Conservative Party at prayer, indicating the close political alliance between the two powerful institutions. Historically, the Conservatives represented the political interests of the established church, while dissenting Protestants and Catholics identified with the Liberal Party, and later the Labour Party. At least at the elite level, those historical connections have clearly weakened. Beginning in the 1980s, support among Anglican clergy for the Conservative Party dwindled, while support for both the Labour and Liberal Democratic parties increased. Only one-quarter of Anglican clergy described themselves as Conservative in 1985, and in 1997 a mere 9 percent of Anglican clergy indicated that they intended to vote Conservative in what turned out to be a landslide victory for the Labour Party.[10] Support in the pews for the Tory Party has, however, remained much stronger. In a 2015 survey, Anglicans were more likely than any other religious group to identify with the Conservative Party, and by a two-to-one margin they indicated they would vote Conservative in the upcoming election.[11]

With the exception of Northern Ireland, the political salience of religion fell throughout the twentieth century as social class, rather than religion, became the most important point of political cleavage. In contrast with the United States, there is no informal disability associated with persons running for political office who have no religious faith. A 2013 poll found that 43 percent of Americans would not vote for an atheist for president, even if that person were nominated by their party and were well qualified for the position.[12] By contrast, in the 2015 British general election two of the three leading candidates for prime minister, Nick Clegg of the Liberal Democratic Party and Ed Miliband of the Labour Party, said that they did not believe in God. For much of the past fifty years, politicians saw little gain in making religious appeals to voters, and by American standards candidates were not demonstrative about their faith. Before he could answer a question about his faith in an interview, Tony Blair, Labour Party prime minister from 1997 to 2007, was interrupted by his communications director, who told the interviewer that "we don't do God." This comment was reflective of the times, but also somewhat ironic as Blair was quite sympathetic to religious groups in public policy, he was deeply religious, and over time he became more expressive about his faith.[13] Interestingly, it is a pattern that was repeated by Conservative Party prime minister David Cameron (2010–2016), who similarly expressed his Christian convictions and called on religious groups to play a "leading role" in public life.[14]

The tidy assumptions about church membership and party support in England are not as relevant as they once were, but in many respects the role of religion in public life is returning to British politics, brought on in large measure by the country's growing religious diversity and the political debates inherent in that demographic change.

THE HISTORICAL BACKGROUND

When Pope Clement VII famously refused to grant Henry VIII an annulment from Catherine of Aragon in 1527, Henry broke from the Roman Catholic Church, married Anne Boleyn, and took political control of the English church. While Henry's divorce was the occasion for the religious split, the causes of the rift lay much deeper and they led eventually to the establishment of the broadly Protestant Church of England during Elizabeth I's reign. From the earliest days of the establishment, the Church of England enjoyed an unusual degree of autonomy in the power of appointments and in managing its own funds, but a close relationship nevertheless developed between the state and the Anglican Church in which the institutions worked in concert for shared political and religious goals. The ideal envisioned by Richard Hooker, the sixteenth-century apologist for the Anglican establishment, was to unify church membership with membership in the political community so that there would be no division between the secular goals of the state and the sacred purposes of the church. Hooker provided a theological justification for this political arrangement; he believed that the church had a positive obligation to be involved in civil society and in the value of the state to the church. In terms of the law, this came to mean a state-supported and state-enforced religion with the imposition of various restrictions on religious dissenters. The Corporation Act of 1661 and the Test Act of 1673, for example, effectively excluded Roman Catholics and Protestant nonconformists from participation in political affairs. [15]

Religious pluralism and intense conflict among Anglicans, Roman Catholics, and Protestant nonconformists made it difficult to sustain Hooker's organic vision. The Treaty of Union with Scotland in 1707, for example, allowed for the establishment of the Presbyterian Church of Scotland and the Church of Wales was similarly disestablished in 1920. Driven by this division in the rest of Great Britain, the state grudgingly conceded freedom of worship to Protestant religious dissenters with the passage of the Toleration Act of 1689. It was not until the nineteenth century that the state lifted the remaining disabilities attached to religious nonconformity. Protestant nonconformists and Roman Catholics won political emancipation in 1824 and 1829, respectively, in 1858 Jews were able to become members of Parliament, and in 1871 Parliament abolished religious tests for admission to universities. [16]

The relaxation of restrictions on religious dissenters in the nineteenth century, coupled with the growing secularity of British society, helped to depoliticize religious disputes in the early twentieth century. The emerging Labour Party had roots in the nonconformist chapels, but it gradually became more closely associated with a socialist ideology as the twentieth century progressed. When the Labour Party displaced the Liberal Party as one of the two main parties in the 1920s, social class, rather than religious issues, became politically salient. [17] Unlike many of its European counterparts, British politics never experienced a strong anticlerical movement, or a direct threat from sectarian liberalism. [18] However, it was not so much the power of the churches that explains the absence of this political challenge, but the fact that religion had become politically less important. Even the socialist Labour

Party was more indifferent than hostile to religion. As a consequence, the churches did not feel compelled to defend and preserve their role in society; it is noteworthy that a Christian Democratic movement and political party never emerged in England as it did in Germany and the Netherlands.

In practice, if not always in law, the Anglican Church that emerged from the sectarian rivalries of the late nineteenth and early twentieth centuries was far different from the one envisioned by Hooker two centuries earlier. The Church of England retained its establishment status, in contrast to the religious establishments in two former British colonies, America and Australia, but the nature of that establishment had radically shifted. The formal ties between church and state loosened as Parliament ceded greater control over the church's spiritual direction to ecclesiastical bodies, and the church's social and political role became more diffuse and ceremonial. In contrast to Hooker's model, the Church of England came to see itself as a comprehensive national institution that would guard and preserve the nation's shared cultural norms and serve as a religious counterpart to civil society. As religion became less socially significant, the Anglican Church became more ecumenical and accepting of pluralism. As a result, both church and state supported other denominations seeking the state's public recognition, and politicized religious disputes largely disappeared from British politics in the twentieth century. The Church continued to press for a political role, but it began to advocate an ecumenical Christian view of the nation's affairs, rather than a denominational one.

The debate around the Education Act of 1944 demonstrates the changing role of religion in England. The established Church of England and other Christian denominations fought one another on the education issue in the late nineteenth century, but religious animosities had been reduced by 1944 and the churches formed a powerful political coalition to protect the privileged position of their schools. Anglicans and Catholics, who had the largest stake in private religious schools, argued together that denominational schools deserved public funding because church schools provided a public good and gave parents the opportunity to exercise their right to direct the education of their children. Policy makers, who recognized the political power of these religious bodies and generally shared their view that religious education provided a public good, financed almost all the costs of existing church schools. The Education Act created a dual system with state-run and religious schools sharing the responsibility for the education of English children.[19]

Policy makers self-consciously designed religious education as a way to further the goals of the state, and not simply as a way to placate church leaders. There was great optimism in the early years after the act passed that religious education could provide some unity of purpose for English schoolchildren. The hope was that it would nurture children in the dominant values and beliefs of English society, which were broadly Christian. Religious education became a part of the civic culture and national heritage. Religious education in state-supported schools was consistent with a cultural consensus about the role of the established Church of England. In both instances, political elites viewed religion, the Christian religion specifically, as a significant influence on English culture, society, and history that could continue to play a useful role in shaping citizens' moral values.

Of the six countries in our study, England's establishment model lent itself most easily to a state promotion of "consensual" religious values. The established Church had historically seen its role as working in concert with the state to promote common values, which it increasingly viewed in ecumenical and pluralistic terms. Religious education seemed ideally suited to this task as it could provide the moral framework necessary to inculcate English schoolchildren with norms that would bind society together. There was little appreciation, at this point, that religious diversity and secularization might introduce conflict and thereby challenge this civil religious model, or that religionists might oppose so utilitarian an understanding of the place of faith in public life. Developments in the latter half of the twentieth century challenged these assumptions and led, as we will show in our review of current educational policy, to questions about the place of religion in state-supported schools. For now, however, we want to turn to a review of the Church of England's legal status that continues to influence the resolution of church-state issues in England.

ENGLAND'S RESTRAINED ESTABLISHMENT

While the Church of England lost most of its political privileges by the end of the nineteenth century, the ties between the Church and the state remain remarkably strong and the power of the establishment model still runs deep. In no other country in our study are church and state as intertwined as they are in England. As an established church, the canon law of the Church of England is a part of English law, and until the early twentieth century Parliament passed much legislation affecting the Church. Under the Enabling Act of 1919, the Church's General Synod gained the authority to make changes in church liturgy and doctrine, although Parliament remains technically responsible for some matters of church law and can (but seldom does) reject a measure passed by the General Synod. For example, when the General Synod voted to allow women bishops in the Church of England in 2012, that choice had to be confirmed by a vote in both houses of Parliament. By law, the monarch is the head of the Church and may not be nor marry a Roman Catholic. If and when Prince Charles ascends the throne to become the king of England, the service will be held in Westminster Abbey and will be conducted by the Archbishop of Canterbury (head of the Church of England), who will lead the new monarch in the coronation oath. In that oath, Prince Charles will vow to be a Defender of the Faith, the title held by each monarch since it was given by Pope Leo X to Henry VIII in 1521.[20]

In addition, the monarch, advised by the prime minister, has the power to appoint the archbishops and the diocesan bishops of the Church of England. Until quite recently, the Church, through its Crown Nominations Commission, presented two names to the prime minister, who in turn recommended one of the two candidates to the king or queen. While it was rare, occasionally a prime minister vetoed both recommended candidates, as both Margaret Thatcher and Tony Blair did. In 2007, Prime Minister Gordon Brown, the son of a Church of Scotland minister, suggested that the prime minister should have no role in the selection of bishops. In what might be seen as a case of classic British compromise, however, it was agreed that in the future the prime minister would continue to forward the name of the candidate to the Crown, but that the prime minister would simply choose the first of the two names presented to him or her by the Church.

Given the occasional rancor between prime ministers and bishops of the Church of England, it is perhaps not surprising that political leaders have wanted to wash their hands of any role in clerical appointments. In 1982, the Church's Board for Social Responsibility released a report, *The Church and the Bomb*, which advocated unilateral nuclear disarmament, a position directly at odds with the policy of the Thatcher government. Three years later, the Archbishop of Canterbury's Commission on Urban Priority Areas released *Faith in the City*, which repudiated much of Prime Minister Thatcher's social welfare and economic policies.[21] Labour Party prime ministers have not fared much better. The bishops openly opposed Britain's involvement in the 2003 invasion of Iraq under Tony Blair's leadership, and the bishops called for the nation's Christian leaders to make a public act of repentance for Britain's involvement in the war and its aftermath.[22] A 2015 letter signed by twenty-seven of the fifty-nine Church of England bishops declared that Conservative prime minister David Cameron's welfare cuts were "a disgrace."[23]

The Church of England continues to have a formal political role by virtue of the automatic membership in the House of Lords for the archbishops of Canterbury and York and the twenty-four senior diocesan bishops of the Church. Collectively, these twenty-six bishops are known as the Lords Spiritual. The Church of England is the only religious body with reserved seats, although there is an implicit understanding that other faith communities shall have representation. There are, at present, Jewish, Sikh, Hindi, and Muslim members of the Upper House. There have been numerous proposals to alter the composition of the religious seats in the Lords. In 1999, the Blair government appointed a royal commission to make recommendations about the future of the House of Lords. The resulting report, *A House for the Future*, proposed that twenty-six places be reserved for members of the British faith community, but in contrast with historical precedent those places would not automatically go to bishops of the Church of England, but would be selected to "be broadly representative of the different non-Christian faith communities."[24] Under that proposed scheme, twenty seats would have been apportioned to the Church of England and six to the other faith communities. Those recommendations were never enacted by the Blair government. In 2012, Deputy Prime Minister Nick Clegg introduced the House of Lords Reform Bill which, among other features, would have reduced the number of seats allocated to clerics from the Church of England from twenty-six to twelve. That bill was eventually abandoned by the government following stiff opposition from within the Conservative Party.[25]

From the standpoint of democratic norms, the House of Lords is anachronistic in various ways. Its members are not popularly elected but are instead appointed by an independent commission, the members serve life terms, and there is no fixed number of seats in the House. The political powers of the Lords diminished throughout the twentieth century, however, and its role is now subordinate to that of the House of Commons. Nonetheless, the Lords can offer advice to the government, delay legislative action, and, most important, debate government bills and other important public issues. A debate on the government's 2013 Marriage Act, which extended marriage to same-sex couples, highlights the role played by the bishops in the House of Lords. Justin Welby, archbishop of Canterbury, contended that "the majority of faith groups remain very strongly against the Bill, and have expressed that view in a large number of public statements." He went on to argue that "traditional marriage is a cornerstone of society, and rather than adding a new and valued institution alongside it for same-gender relationships . . . the Bill weakens what exists and replaces it with a less good option that is neither equal nor effective."[26] In a similar vein, the bishop of Leicester asked, "Do the gains of meeting the need of many LGBT people for the dignity and equality that identifying their partnerships as marriage gives outweigh the loss entailed as society moves away from a clear understanding of marriage as a desirable setting within which children are conceived and raised?"[27] He concluded that they did not. Nine of the fourteen Anglican bishops attending the debate voted against the bill and five abstained. Despite this fairly unified opposition to the bill among the Lords Spiritual, it nonetheless comfortably passed by a vote of 390–148.

This debate underscores both the opportunities and limitations afforded to the Church of England through its formal membership in the House of Lords. On the one hand, the presence of Anglican clergy in the Upper House supports the idea that the Church of England and its bishops, along with other religious leaders, will have a voice in major pieces of moral legislation and when legislation touches on the work of the churches. In describing their role, the Church of England notes that the bishops "provide an important independent voice and spiritual insight to the work of the Upper House and . . . they seek to be a voice for all people of faith, not just Christians."[28] Membership in the Lords clearly gives bishops the opportunity to voice their moral concerns with legislation. On the other hand, the 2013 Marriage Act easily passed despite religious opposition, which simply reinforces the secularizing trend within England. Religious leaders had the opportunity formally to voice their concerns, but it hardly assured them that they would be able to dictate the outcome of the legislation. It is also instructive of the larger point that while religious voices and perspectives are not politically irrelevant in England, there is no British equivalent of the politically influential American Christian right.[29]

The Church of England also has what Paul Weller describes as a "structurally privileged position" on such policy issues as education, state provision of hospital and military chaplaincies, and religious broadcasting on the publicly supported British Broadcasting Corporation (BBC) and the Independent Television Authority (ITA).[30] To the extent that the Church does enjoy such a position, however, it has largely used it to make it easier for other religious groups to gain access to state benefits. An exhaustive study of prison chaplaincies demonstrated the creative efforts of Anglican clergy to make chaplain positions available to religious leaders outside the Christian tradition.[31] A survey of Muslim chaplains found that they expressed few concerns about being excluded or marginalized where they work.[32] A similar dynamic has occurred in the hundreds of hours of required religious broadcasting on the BBC and ITA. Historically, virtually all of those programs would have been Christian, and most of them would have been Anglican. In recent years, however, the content of the religious programs more accurately reflects the country's religious diversity.[33] Perhaps because of England's establishment model, the print media also gives considerable coverage to religion generally, and the Church of England specifically. It seems as if the media treats the established church as a formal political institution that warrants press coverage.

More important than the Church's legal status is the cultural assumption that sustains a public, political role for the Church of England, specifically, and for religious groups more generally. This model affirms the idea that religious groups have an important cultural and social function to play, which the state should both recognize and support. The state pursues policies that accommodate organized religion as a whole because of a conviction shared by most political elites and the public that religion is morally and socially beneficial. It is an archetype Queen Elizabeth II affirmed when she suggested in a 2012 speech that the role of the established Church is "not to defend Anglicanism to the exclusion of other faiths" but to "protect the free practice of all faiths in this country."[34] Religious minorities have not so much opposed the current system as they have argued that it should be expanded to include more religious groups. Muslim leaders consistently argue that a virtue of the religious establishment is that it preserves the idea that religion has a public political role to play. Dr. Fatma Amer, director of education and interfaith relations at the London Central Mosque, put it succinctly when she noted to us: "There is much good in keeping the religious establishment intact. It makes possible a recognition of a person's right to put into action what he most sincerely believes in."[35] Tariq Modood, director of the University of Bristol's Research Centre for the Study of Ethnicity and Citizenship, similarly contends that Britain's "reformed establishment" is a positive way to "institutionalize religious pluralism."[36]

For many religious minorities, English secularization poses a much more serious challenge to religion than does the established Church. Based on research conducted for the Policy Studies Institute, Modood contends that "the real division of opinion is not between a conservative element of the Church of England versus the rest of the country, but between those who think that religion has a place in secular public culture, that religious communities are part of the state, and those that do not."[37] In a 2012 speech delivered at the Vatican, Baroness Warsi, the Tory Party chairman and British Muslim, contended that a "militant secularisation is taking hold of our societies" and, as a consequence, "religion is sidelined and downgraded in the public sphere."[38] In contrast to state secularism, the religious establishment preserves the idea that religion should be actively involved in social and political affairs, and facilitates a space for religious groups who believe that the public sphere should take their values seriously. The point of contention for many religious minorities is not the religious establishment per se; what they argue instead is that the system should officially expand to include them in the benefits that come with state recognition.

There is little formal political opposition to the religious establishment. The Liberal Democratic Party periodically advocates against it, as do politically marginal interest groups such as the National Secular Society and the British Humanist Association, but these efforts have gone nowhere.[39] A survey of public opinion found that more than half of those polled (54 percent) agreed or strongly agreed that the Church of England should keep its status as the official established church in England, while only 16 percent disagreed or strongly disagreed with the status quo.[40] Nor is there much opposition from religious groups that are not formally part of the establishment. A survey of religious leaders outside the Church of England found that one-third opposed the current system, one-third supported it, and one-third had reservations about the system, but mostly they wished to expand the system to include additional faith traditions. One way of interpreting the results, in short, is that two-thirds of religious leaders *outside* of the Church of England support the current system or advocate an enhancement of that arrangement.[41] In large measure, religious elites and the British public perceive the religious establishments as, at best, a source of social cohesion and consensus and, at worst, as harmless.

THE CHALLENGE OF MUSLIM INCORPORATION

A recurring theme in this chapter is how the British state has accommodated the religious needs of its burgeoning non-Christian population. Most of this growth has come as a consequence of the immigration of Muslims, Hindus, and Sikhs from India and Pakistan after the Second World War. In the midst of postwar labor shortages, England actively recruited low-wage labor from its former colonies to help rebuild cities devastated by the war. For various reasons, a good percentage of those economic migrants eventually settled in England, the result of which has been a dramatic growth in the number of religious minorities, particularly Muslims.[42] Between 1971 and 2011, the Muslim population in the United Kingdom grew from 226,000 to 2.7 million, and increased their share of the overall population from 0.46 percent to 4.8 percent. Because they are younger and have larger families, the British Islamic population will likely continue to grow over the next several decades.[43]

One of the first political controversies affecting the British Muslim population had to do with a very old law. Historically, Christian, or more specifically Anglican, doctrines were protected against blasphemy. Non-Christian religions received no specific legal protections.[44] To the extent that people even knew that the law existed, however, they had largely concluded that it was an ancient relic. The law was, in fact, abolished by the government in 2008. What brought the blasphemy law to the forefront, however, was the publication of Salman Rushdie's 1988 novel, *The Satanic Verses*. Rushdie's portrayal of the prophet Muhammad deeply offended many British Muslims. The book was burned in public demonstrations in two British cities; protestors demanded that the book be banned in the United Kingdom; and many Muslim leaders argued that the blasphemy law should be expanded to protect Islamic doctrines.[45] The controversy brought the issue of state accommodation of British Muslims to the political forefront. With the encouragement of both of the major political parties, it led eventually to the formation of the Muslim Council of Britain to act as lobbying group on behalf of British Muslims.[46]

Reflecting its establishment model and official state-religion connections, England has largely supported multicultural policies that recognize the religious beliefs and practices of its Muslim population. One example is how England handled Muslim schoolgirls and teachers who wear the *hijab*. This issue has caused considerable controversy in both France and Germany but, with little fanfare or debate, British policy makers reached a compromise that allows Muslim girls to wear the *hijab* so long as it conforms with the color requirements of the school uniform.[47] Not one Muslim interviewed for this project suggested that there is any problem associated with the right of Muslim schoolgirls or teachers to wear the *hijab*. England has demonstrated a similar willingness to expand religious instruction in state-run schools to include a treatment of Islam in its required education classes, and after some initial resistance the government now finances Islamic schools under the same conditions that apply to Christian ones. In all of these efforts, the Christian churches, and in particular the established Anglican Church, have been institutional allies to British Muslims.

Persistent questions remain, however, on the effectiveness of Britain's policy—concerns that intensified in the aftermath of high-profile attacks by Islamic extremists. In particular, the 2005 London train transit bombings that killed fifty-two civilians and injured seven hundred more, a 2013 "lone wolf" attack on a soldier by self-radicalized British Muslims, and the realization that some seven hundred British Muslims, including three teenage girls, had joined the fight in the Middle East for ISIS and the Nusra Front has raised alarms about the degree to which Muslims were successfully integrating into mainstream British culture.[48] Sensing that the schools were failing to promote British values, in 2002 citizenship education was introduced as a required subject in the National Curriculum for all students aged eleven to sixteen years old. The program is based on the key concepts of participatory democracy, civic engagement, human rights, and cultural diversity. A succession of prime ministers has expressed concern about the degree to which some British Muslims lead separate lives. During a 2007 debate on a proposed regulation that would allow school authorities to ban the wearing of the *niqab,* a veil that covers all of the face except the eyes, Tony Blair argued that the *niqab* was a "mark of separation" that made "other people from outside the community feel uncomfortable."[49] A minuscule percentage of British Muslims wear the *niqab*, but for some it represented a step too far. In a 2015 speech on extremism, David Cameron acknowledged the "profound contribution Muslims from all backgrounds and denominations are making in every sphere of our society." Nonetheless, he argued that "under the doctrine of state multiculturalism, we have encouraged different cultures to live separate lives, apart from each other and the mainstream" and that as a result "we have even tolerated these segregated communities behaving in ways that run counter to our values."[50]

There is hardly much debate that in many respects British Muslims *do* lead different lives in England, though the cause of that segregation is much in dispute. According to an exhaustive study of the 2011 Census by the Muslim Council of Britain, British Muslims are twice as likely as the general population to be unemployed, they are more likely to be in poor health, homeless, or in prison, and while they have nearly attained educational parity with the country as a whole, almost half of the British Muslim population resides in the bottom 10 percent local authority districts for deprivation. For the authors of this report Islamophobia, economic deprivation, and racial and cultural discrimination are the primary causes of these indicators rather than the self-segregation of British Muslims.[51]

A recent controversy about the acceptance of Islamic law in Britain highlights some of the unique challenges facing England, and the novel features of the British establishment model. In 2008, Rowan Williams, who was at the time the archbishop of Canterbury, suggested that it was "unavoidable" that certain elements of Islamic law or Sharia will have to be accepted in Britain.[52] Williams was in part making a philosophical argument about why the secular British state should preserve space for orthodox religious believers who wish to live in accordance with their religious norms. He was also making the empirical point that many British Muslims do in fact turn to unofficial Sharia councils for religious legal advice on matters of marriage, divorce, and inheritance; official recognition of this reality, he contended, would benefit the Muslim community and the state.[53] His suggestion set off a wave of criticism that was covered extensively in the elite and popular press. Williams later clarified his stance by saying that he believed that Sharia should only apply in limited areas such as family law, as it does for Orthodox Jews in certain cases, and only when all parties agreed to submit to the alternative legal forum.

The debate, however, is instructive of several points. First, as we have noted before, the established church came to the defense of British Muslims, and in this instance British Muslims largely returned the favor. In the midst of the debate, the Islamic Human Rights Commission strongly defended Williams, saying that it was "shocked by what seems to be a systematic and malicious misunderstanding of what the Archbishop of Canterbury said in his speech about accommodating religious minorities in Britain."[54] The controversy underscores that challenges remain as policy makers seek to identify the root causes for the extremism of a small number of British Muslims while protecting the religious rights of the community as a whole. Second, there is a growing public anxiety in England about the degree to which British Muslims are adopting liberal political values and cultural norms. One indication of this is that support for the right-wing populist UK Independence Party (UKIP) has risen in recent years, from less than 1 percent in 1997 to 12.6 percent in 2015. While the party is not as virulently anti-Islamic as some of its continental counterparts, or even its nativist predecessor the British National Party, growing support for it is almost certainly tied to unease about the immigration and settlement of Muslims in England. On a more hopeful note, Sadiq Khan, who grew up in public housing and is the son of a bus driver, became London's first Muslim mayor in 2016, despite attempts by his opponent to tie him to Islamic extremism.

THE FREE EXERCISE OF RELIGION

Unlike the other countries in our study, England does not have a written constitution or a bill of rights, and so there are no constitutional guarantees for religious freedom. There is no equivalent in England to the First Amendment to the United States Constitution. The absence of constitutional protections for religious rights has meant that the English courts have not historically been a forum where religious groups have been able to protest their treatment. England also lacks the theoretical commitment to religious freedom as a positive right that is so strong in both Germany and the Netherlands. Instead, religious rights in England are ensured by domestic legal provisions and international law, both of which have at times been wanting. However, in the past decade there have been significant legal changes in both arenas that have moved England more in the direction of its continental counterparts.

Historically, the most important legal assurances for religious liberty were the acts passed at the end of the nineteenth century that gave religious dissenters various rights. These laws, however, were never interpreted as guaranteeing people a fundamental right of religious free exercise or protecting them against religious discrimination. The Race Relations Act of 1976 provided a legal framework for fighting racial discrimination, and the courts deemed Sikhs and Jews to be racial groups that deserved legal protection under that legislation. Christians and Muslims, however, were considered to be religious groups and were not covered under the provisions of the act.[55] It was not until the turn of the century that British legislation began systematically to address the rights of religious persons under the law. In clear violation of basic religious free exercise rights, British law had historically disqualified clergy of the Churches of England, Scotland, and Ireland, and the Roman Catholic Church from sitting in the House of Commons. The House of Commons (Removal of Clergy Disqualifications) Act of 2001 removed those restrictions. Even more significantly, the 2003 Employment Equality (Religion or Belief) Regulations banned direct and indirect discrimination in all aspects of employment on the basis of a person's religion or lack of a religion. The 2006 Equality Act expanded these protections by outlawing discrimination in the provision of goods and services on the grounds of religion and belief.[56]

In the years leading up to the 2016 referendum vote that led the United Kingdom to leave the European Union, the most significant development in the area of religious freedom was the growing body of international legal rulings that affected religious rights in England. As we will note below, the perception that British law was being internationalized and that Parliament was losing its political sovereignty was one of the core arguments for those who supported a British exit from the European Union. England was at the forefront in helping to draft the European Convention on Human Rights (ECHR) after the Second World War. Article 9 of the ECHR provides that "everyone has a right to freedom of thought, conscience and religion . . . and . . . to manifest his religion or belief in worship, teaching, practice, and observance." This freedom is qualified, however, by limitations that are "prescribed by law and are necessary in a democratic society in the interests of public safety, for the protection of public order, health or morals, or for the protection of the rights and freedoms of others." The Convention established the European Court of Human Rights (ECtHR) to apply the provisions of the treaty to the member states. The ECtHR became a full-time institution in 1998, the same year that the Labour-controlled House of Commons passed its own Human Rights Act (HRA) that legally incorporated all the rights contained in the Convention. Both the ECHR and the HRA make it possible that Britain will become more like the United States and the Netherlands in how it recognizes and protects religious free exercise.

A 2013 landmark decision by the ECtHR in *Eweida and others v. United Kingdom* suggests that the verdict is out in terms of how far international norms might shape British practice. The judgment dealt with two pairs of cases concerning religious freedom brought against the United Kingdom under Article 9 of the Convention. In the first set of cases, an employee at British Airways and a nurse in a state hospital were not allowed to wear a visible cross at their place of employment. The latter two cases dealt with a registrar of marriages and a relationship counselor who had lost their respective jobs because they had refused to offer their services to same-sex couples because of their religious objections to homosexuality. They too argued that British policy restricted their religious freedom rights under Article 9.[57]

As we observed in our discussion of French face veiling, the ECtHR is sensitive to the national traditions and societal values of the different member states; the court generally gives states some latitude in terms of how they balance the interests and rights under Article 9. Given that precedent, it was not particularly surprising that in three of the four cases, the ECtHR sided with the British government. In the cases dealing with the employees who had religious objections to providing services to same-sex couples, the court acknowledged that the litigants were motivated by their religion and that their choice was a "manifestation of religion" under Article 9. However, the court argued that the nondiscrimination policies of both the employer and the local government were legitimate and could override the religious freedom claims of the employees.

In the fourth case, however, the court overturned the ruling of the British government, it offered a more expansive definition for what constituted a "manifestation of religion" under Article 9, and it concluded that the British tribunal had not struck the appropriate balance between protecting the religious freedom of employees and the right of employers to establish uniform dress codes. The decision reflected a move, albeit a gradual one, toward the universalization of human rights, including religious liberty rights. Over time this could lead to an expansion of the range of Article 9 protections going forward and move England closer to its continental counterparts in having strong legal protection for religious rights.[58]

The case garnered a significant amount of public attention and political controversy. For the Conservative Party government, the issue was not so much the court's actual decision in *Eweida*, as much as it was the fact that the court felt empowered to make it. In response to a question during Prime Minister's Question Time prior to the court's decision, David Cameron said that he would support a change in the law to allow persons to wear religious items at work.[59] What concerned Cameron and many of his Conservative Party colleagues was the so-called imposition of a legal ruling from the Strasbourg-based European court. Partly in response to the *Eweida* decision, the 2014 Conservative Party manifesto pledged to rescind the 1998 Human Rights Act and to withdraw from the Convention if Parliament failed to secure the right to veto judgments from the ECtHR. Cameron also vowed to hold a national referendum on the question of the United Kingdom's membership in the European Union.[60]

The 2016 Brexit vote reflected the strength of the Eurosceptic tradition in England, the country's history of challenging supranational European organizations, and a knee-jerk reaction against anything that is perceived as a loss of parliamentary sovereignty on political and legal issues.[61] In terms of religious freedom, the Brexit vote changes nothing and changes everything. As an act of Parliament, the HRA could have been removed at any time by a new act of Parliament. Brexit did not change that fact. On the other hand, the HRA was a particular target for the leave campaign, and the Brexit vote gives greater political weight to those who want to rescind that act. If that act is overturned, the protection of religious liberty rights will once again be a function of British law.

This is not to suggest that religious discrimination is widespread in England, or that without the European Convention the country would systematically fail to protect religious liberty. It says more about different ways in which states do and do not protect those rights. In the case of England, the protection of religious freedom has historically been a function of parliamentary laws, domestic court rulings, and a strong tradition of political pragmatism. In that context, however, the groups that have the most to fear from the absence of legal or constitutional protections are new religious movements whose practices are not as socially accepted as the older, more traditional religions. As Eileen Barker notes, "the longer a religious movement has been around, the greater the chance it has of being protected by the law."[62] Formerly excluded religious groups, such as Roman Catholics and Jews, have become integrated and respected members of the English community, and

, not face religious discrimination. The public has come to accept and ,ciate both of these religious traditions, and the increasingly generic, ,rained religious establishment has been able to incorporate their views. ,hat is less certain is the protection of religious liberty rights for religious newcomers, particularly immigrants, who were often the target of the sometimes hyperbolic rhetoric of the leave campaign.

CHURCH, STATE, AND EDUCATION

England's educational system differs from those of every other country in our study, both in terms of actual policy and even in the use of terms to describe that policy. As an example, the term "public schools" in England usually refers to what Americans would call "private" or independent schools, while the vast majority of "religious" schools in England are considered to be a part of the state system. The distinguishing mark of the English educational system is that religious schools (schools that are owned by a religious body and that have religious exercises and teachings) are public (in the sense of being financed by the government). The vast majority of religious schools get state funding under virtually the same conditions that apply to community schools, i.e., schools that are publicly funded but have no religious character. When applied to education, the English model promotes equality between religious and nonreligious educational perspectives, although it raises controversial issues about which schools should receive state funding and under what conditions.

The genesis for this dual educational system dates back to the middle of the nineteenth century, when churches began offering basic education to poor children at a time that the state did not. State provision of universal elementary education came with the passage of the Education Act of 1870. The act led to the creation of thousands of state schools, but they supplemented rather than replaced the existing Church schools. Gradually the state developed a pattern of working with the churches in providing education. The 1944 Education Act solidified this partnership and is more or less in effect today.[63]

The act created county (later renamed "community") schools that are wholly owned and maintained by the Local Education Authorities (LEAs) and two broad categories of Church schools that are also part of the state or maintained system, voluntary aided and voluntary controlled. In voluntary-aided schools, the Church appoints a majority of the school governors and the governors determine the school admission policy and hire the teaching and support staff. In voluntary-controlled schools, by contrast, the Church appoints a minority of the school governors, and the governors share with their LEA the responsibility for the school admission policy and employment decisions. The state covers all capital costs for voluntary-controlled schools and 90 percent of those costs in voluntary-aided schools. A majority of Church schools are voluntary aided. All maintained schools (community, aided, controlled) receive a tuition grant from their LEA for each pupil who attends, they must follow the national curriculum, and they are all subject to state inspection. Faith schools make up nearly one-third of all publicly financed English schools, and they educate about one-quarter of all English schoolchildren.[64]

Church schools are popular in England, both because they generally outperform state schools on standardized tests and because there is a strong desire on the part of parents, who may or may not be religiously active, for their children to have a religious education. Church schools have greater control over admissions procedures than do community schools, and in many cases preference is given to coreligionists, particularly when the school is oversubscribed. A recent survey conducted by the Church of England's Board of Education found that more than three-quarters of voluntary-aided schools had a religious affiliation in their admissions criteria.[65] While this might on paper seem to promote a sectarian viewpoint, Church school advocates understand their role as offering a valuable public service. David Lankshear, former executive director of the Board of Education for the Church of England, articulated this perspective to us in an interview: "In Church of England schools there is a clear understanding that the churches are in partnership with the state. Very many of our schools operate on the basis of a commitment to Christian service to the public."[66] Anglicans and Roman Catholics had the largest stake in education in 1944, and they quickly became partners with the state in terms of policy formation and planning for education. Both churches have powerful education boards that negotiate with government officials on issues of funding, curriculum, and school governance.[67] At present, they represent nearly 95 percent of pupils in religious schools. Because the state determines which new church schools to finance, however, there has been considerable controversy in recent decades on whether to expand the existing system to include other religious groups, particularly Muslims.

For many years, Muslims pressed for their own publicly funded religious schools, but they were consistently turned down by the government. A 1985 government report concluded that "separate schools would not be in the long term interest of ethnic minority communities."[68] The report recognized the need for a multicultural education that would expose students to the religious pluralism in Britain, but implied that state schools would better serve ethnic and religious minorities because they would more effectively integrate minorities into mainstream British culture. These concerns intensified in the aftermath of racial riots in the cities of Oldham and Bradford in the summer of 2001. A Home Office–commissioned study of the riots highlighted the problem of racial and religious segregation and recommended that all religious schools offer 25 percent of all places to students of other faiths or no faith. Such a practice would be "more inclusive and create better representation of all cultures and ethnicities."[69] The government briefly considered making this recommendation on admission policy mandatory, but quickly backed down in the face of united opposition from faith school providers. On three separate occasions, the government turned down applications from Muslim schools. In each case, the secretary of state for education claimed that the refusal had nothing to do with the school being Islamic. Muslims, however, were understandably frustrated with a system where Christian and Jewish schools were fully financed by the government but their own schools were not. As one British Muslim leader noted to us, "the fact that there were no government-funded Muslim schools was a ridiculous anomaly that had to go."[70]

In 1997 the Blair Labour government approved the first Muslim state primary schools. He reinforced this decision with a Green Paper on education that proposed expanding both the number of religious schools and their diversity: "We welcome more schools provided by the churches and other major faith groups."[71] Since 1997, Muslim, Sikh, Seventh-Day Adventist, Greek Orthodox, and Hindu schools have joined the maintained sector. There are now forty-eight Jewish schools, eighteen Islamic schools, eight Sikh schools, and a handful from other religious traditions, but more than 98 percent of all faith schools are Anglican or Roman Catholic.[72] Nonetheless, the Blair government moved the system in a more pluralistic direction and subsequent prime ministers, including David Cameron, have continued this trajectory by approving the creation of additional faith schools representing diverse traditions.[73] Like their Christian school counterparts, Islamic schools incorporate religious elements into the curriculum and they give preference to Muslim applicants in the admission process. Demand for spots in these schools is very high, and there is a growing body of evidence that students in those schools score above the national average on standardized tests.[74]

Public funding for Islamic schools has occasioned some political controversy. A poll conducted shortly after the 2005 train bombings found that nearly two-thirds of the British public opposed the government's plan to increase the number of religious schools, a finding that was almost certainly more a function of the publicity surrounding the attacks than any deeply grounded public opposition to faith schools.[75] Concern has also been raised about the possibility that separate schools will reinforce the social and cultural segregation of British Muslims. Muslim leaders perceive attacks on faith schools as an implicit criticism of their schools. Ibrahim Hewitt, deputy chairperson of the Association of British Schools, wryly noted that "recent criticism of faith schools is not a new phenomenon, but neither is it historically based. Education for centuries had a religious foundation. Until Muslim schools came on the scene, though, faith schools weren't described as 'separate' schools nor were they criticized as they are today."[76]

In addition to the publicly financed Islamic schools within the state sector, there are many more independent Islamic schools that are not financed by the government and are not part of the state system. These schools are not required to follow the national curriculum and they face far less governmental oversight than do religious schools that are in the maintained sector. There are good reasons to believe that bringing more of those independent schools into the state system is a better way to ensure the successful integration of Muslims and other religious minorities into the liberal values of British culture than leaving them outside of the current dual system. This point was reinforced in the statement signed by the government and faith school providers: "[faith schools] have a particular role to play in helping to meet the needs of those people in their faith communities who would otherwise be hard to reach, thus enabling them to integrate into society."[77]

The British educational policy demonstrates healthy neutrality on the part of the state between a religious and nonreligious perspective, and stands in stark contrast to policy in the United States that disadvantages parents who desire an education for their children in the context of their religious beliefs. State aid to religious schools in Britain, as is the case in the Netherlands, makes possible a more robust form of pluralism and allows religious groups to teach their children their distinctive religious and cultural beliefs and practices in the schools. The Church of England affirms that "the justification for Church schools lies in offering children and young people an opportunity to experience the meaning of the Christian faith,"[78] while the website for the Islamia Primary School, the first publicly financed Islamic school in Britain, proclaims that the school "strives to provide the best education, in a secure Islamic environment, through the knowledge and application of the Qur'an & Sunnah."[79] The current system is balanced between secular and religious viewpoints and is increasingly equitable among religious groups.

Religious education and worship have also been a part of the formal curriculum in all maintained schools since the 1944 Education Act. Under the law, the LEA works with the Standing Advisory Council for Religious Education (SACRE) to draft a syllabus for religious education and a policy on religious worship. The Education Reform Act of 1988 reaffirmed those requirements and strengthened the specifically Christian aspects of the policy. The law now requires that religious instruction "reflect the fact that the religious traditions in Great Britain are in the main Christian whilst taking account of the teaching and practice of the other principal religions represented in Great Britain," and mandates that the daily act of worship be of a "broadly Christian character." Parents have the right to withdraw their children from religious instruction and worship, and schools may petition their SACRE to allow the daily act of worship to reflect the predominant faith found in the school, or the range of faiths in the school.[80] Because of its establishment model, however, Britain has not chosen the route of released time programs either for religious instruction or collective worship, as is the case with other countries in our study.

While on its surface the law clearly preferences Christianity, in practice most religious education curricula take a multicultural and multifaith approach to the topic. The Durham agreed syllabus on religious education, as an example, includes a consideration of Christianity, Judaism, Buddhism, Hinduism, Sikhism, and Islam.[81] For the most part, religious minorities have not opposed the religious requirements of the act, but have instead sought to work with the government to ensure that their tradition is adequately presented. Dr. Fatma Amer, former head of education and interfaith relations at the London Central Mosque, noted to us that "we [Muslims] have a good relationship with the government's Department for Children, Schools and Families . . . and we have good relations with SACREs in most boroughs."[82] The data is mixed on the effectiveness of these policies. A government evaluation on this issue discovered that many schools fail to comply with the requirements for collective worship and that SACREs are not particularly successful at making compliance a high priority.[83]

The fact that there is religious education and worship reflects the continued significance of England's established church-state model. However minimal its formal powers might be, the established church sustains a view that religion has a role to play in public institutions. Public support for religious education is high and no government, Labour or Conservative, has argued that the existing arrangements should be fundamentally changed. As we have seen, the religious establishment is not aggressively Christian. The rationale for the policy is that religious education and worship can be the basis for moral development, cultural awareness, and civic mindedness. Religious education, one government document asserts, can "develop a respect for and sensitivity to others, in particular those whose faith and beliefs are different from their own . . . [and] enable pupils to combat prejudice and contribute to community cohesion."[84]

There are, of course, a number of philosophical and practical difficulties inherent in the English arrangement. The policy implies that religious education and worship, of a very general character and guided by an establishment, nonsectarian perspective, can provide moral absolutes for schoolchildren. But that begs the question if religion can be the basis for the definition of consensual values in a society increasingly divided by religion and one with a growing population of people with no religion. The difficulty that many local education authorities have had in following the policy's guidelines on collective worship suggests that religion, by itself, cannot perform this cultural function. On the other hand, there is probably a greater need than ever for an effective religious education program in England. As the country becomes more religiously diverse and more secular, religious education can promote greater awareness of the myriad groups that are part of British society, a greater respect for differences of others, and the teaching of values and ideals necessary for living together.

CHURCH, STATE, AND NONPROFIT SERVICE ORGANIZATIONS

As with education, British churches led the way in forming social service agencies in the late nineteenth century.[85] Religious values motivated the work of these early reform efforts in child care, poor relief, prison reform, and public health. Religious charities could not generate adequate resources to meet the growing demand for human services in the twentieth century, nor did they provide their services evenly. They practiced what Lester Salamon calls philanthropic particularism.[86] Religious philanthropy focused on specific subgroups of the population but often ignored others. Evangelical groups, who led the way in welfare reform in Britain, frequently made a distinction between the "deserving" and "undeserving" poor. As popular support for public welfare grew, government involvement increased to correct for inherent shortcomings of the voluntary sector.

Following World War II, legislation on health, housing, and income support formed the basis for a comprehensive British welfare state. Social welfare provision in England differed from that of Germany and the Netherlands in that it was never structured on the basis of religion; there was no social welfare equivalent to the 1944 Education Act that would formalize the relationship between religious groups and the state. Religious philanthropy survived in the postwar period, but in the new statutory system the role of religious nonprofit agencies gradually diminished as the state assumed primary responsibility for the delivery, regulation, and funding of public welfare.[87] Religious agencies also faced increasing secularizing pressures from the emerging social work and health care professions that dominated public welfare. Social work professionals stressed "objective" and "scientific" criteria that they often believed excluded or made irrelevant a religiously informed point of view. Christian agencies often fueled the secularization process by redefining their work in nonreligious terms. As one expert on the history of voluntary organizations has noted, the state expanded its social welfare provision often at the expense of efforts by Christian agencies.[88]

Conservative Party prime minister Margaret Thatcher introduced considerable change to the voluntary sector, particularly in her third term of office at the end of the 1980s. These changes would have a considerable impact on faith-based organizations (FBOs). In keeping with her commitment to privatization, public choice, and reducing the government's role, Thatcher stressed the benefits of using voluntary organizations and for-profit companies rather than the state to provide public services. She argued that voluntary agencies could expand consumer choice, reduce costs, and promote efficiency by introducing competition to public services. Thatcher's policies shifted the responsibility for social services from the national government to local communities' social welfare departments, and those agencies increasingly turned to the voluntary and for-profit sectors to deliver social services. In 1990–1991, government grants and contracts for services to voluntary organizations stood at £2.6 billion—a rise of more than 100 percent in real terms since 1980–1981. That amount increased to £9.7 billion in 2001 and £13.3 in 2013.[89]

The push to change how the state was involved in social welfare policy continued with the election of Tony Blair, who institutionalized the devolution of social welfare provision to voluntary agencies.[90] In a 2006 speech, Blair outlined an arrangement where the state would finance most social services, but it would turn to the voluntary sector to deliver them: "government as a whole is necessary in terms of funding, it is necessary in terms of setting clear objectives, it is not always necessary in terms of delivering the actual service. . . . Those organisations that are doing the most ground-breaking work, most innovative work are to be found in the voluntary sector today."[91] He also created a cabinet-level Office of the Third Sector (later renamed Office for Civil Society) to coordinate and strengthen the bonds between government and the voluntary sector. David Cameron's "Big Society" initiative of 2010 followed a similar path.

The transformation of social welfare policy that began in the 1980s has reduced the role of the government in providing services and increased the responsibility of nonprofit groups, including FBOs. The state has become dependent on nonstate actors to assist in the delivery of services. Because many of them already existed, FBOs have thus become an even more important part of the voluntary sector.[92] With an annual budget of more than £270 million, the Salvation Army is the United Kingdom's fourth-largest charity, and it is the largest service provider outside of the government itself. According to its mission statement, the Salvation Army is "called to be disciples of Jesus Christ," and "exists to save souls, grow saints and serve suffering humanity." In 2013, the organization served three million meals, ran sixty-two residential houses for homeless persons, and provided addiction services to one thousand people at any one time. In 2011, the government chose the Salvation Army to be the central contractor for managing support services for adult victims of human trafficking, and in 2013 the organization provided services to 782 adult victims. A majority of its budget comes in the form of government grants and contracts for services.[93] One of England's oldest voluntary organizations, Livability, was founded in 1844 by the Christian philanthropist Lord Shaftesbury; it receives more than 90 percent of its £40 million budget for working with disabled people from the government.[94]

Christian agencies have historically dominated the social welfare scene, although the Church of England never had a monopoly in charity provision. Of the nearly one hundred social welfare and children's care and adoption agencies listed in the most comprehensive guide to Christian agencies in the United Kingdom, 60 percent are nondenominational, 20 percent are Roman Catholic, 10 percent are Anglican, and the rest are from various Christian churches.[95] Jewish organizations have a similarly long history in England. The largest, Jewish Care, provides health and social welfare support services for members of the Jewish community, particularly the elderly. More than half of its £54 million budget comes from government grants.[96] Muslim and Sikh agencies are in their infancy; of the more than 180,000 registered charities in England, only 2,000 are Islamic. The government has funded some of them, however. According to Sadiq Khan, who was at the time the government's communities minister and would later become the mayor of London, in 2007–2008 the government provided funds to the Muslim Youth Development Partnership, the Sufi Muslim Council, FATIMA Women's Network, and British Muslims for Secular Democracy, to name a few.[97]

Public funding of faith-based groups has not been without controversy. Government funding increases the regulatory burdens for FBOs and threatens their independence. A national survey of charities indicated that only a quarter of the agencies that receive government money agreed with the statement that they are free to make decisions without pressure to conform to the wishes of the funders.[98] Government funding can also pose a unique challenge for religious agencies where, as Peter Dobkin Hall notes, "quality of service has tended to be defined in less than calculable ways."[99] Finally, some questions have been raised about the ideological and political views of the recipients of some grants. A recent example of this was the Faith Minorities in Action project, funded in part by the Department for Communities and Local Government. The program was designed to encourage integration through interfaith work and other projects. In 2014, however, the government withdrew almost £140,000 in project funding to the Muslim Charities Forum over concerns about extremism and the charity's poor performance against project objectives, claims the group bitterly rejected.[100]

There is also some uncertainty on whether or not religious agencies that wish to retain a distinctive set of values on questions related to hiring and offering services consistent with their religious mission may do so. The 2010 Equality Act requires equal treatment in private and public services and access to employment irrespective of a citizen's social character. Age, gender, disability, secular orientation, and religion are among the protected characteristics under the act. Under certain conditions, however, religious organizations are exempt from some of those provisions, and the definition of religious organization in the act is relatively broad.[101] The recent experience of the Yeldall Christian Centres is instructive of this tension. Yeldall is a nonprofit agency that runs residential drug and alcohol rehabilitation homes in Britain. For Yeldall, there is a very close link between its religious and social work. The organization describes its mission in this way: "Yeldall is a Christian centre. This means that all of the members of the staff are Christian and that we use the bible as the basis for much of the teaching and groups in the programme."[102] Because it receives government funding, Yeldall may not discriminate in whom it serves. It was this provision that led to the closure of the Catholic adoption agencies because of their refusal to place children with same-sex couples. However, Yeldall may hire on the basis of religion and they can require clients to respect the Christian aspects of the program. In their most recent application for government funds, however, Ken Wiltshire, the director of one of Yeldall's residential centers, noted that "they [government officials] kept asking questions about why our staff were exclusively Christian and why there had to be a Christian component to our regime."[103]

In many respects, English policy is bifurcated. On the one hand, Labour and Conservative governments are equally committed to giving faith-based organizations greater responsibility and flexibility in delivering social services. Somewhat in tension with this principle, however, has been a push by the government to ensure that any organization that receives government funds comply with equal opportunities legislation. As England becomes ever more secular, and possibly less sympathetic to deeply religious viewpoints, it is possible that FBOs will increasingly face pressures by the government to secularize their programs, or will at least be asked to justify a link between their provision of social services and their religious mission. Like the other countries in our study, England is having to balance the sometimes competing values of religious freedom and nondiscrimination.

Our interviews with agency heads suggest that agencies can, and in many cases do, retain a distinctive religious orientation if they are clear and consistent with government officials about why those values are important to them. David Tribble, divisional director for social services of the Yorkshire Division of the Salvation Army, noted to us both the challenges of the current policy, but also the freedom that the Salvation Army has to pursue its distinct mission:

> We have a commitment to Equal Opportunities Employment, i.e., we do not discriminate on the basis of race, faith, or sexual orientation. However, if in the job description there is a specific need for a faith element then we can employ a person with that qualification. So, as part of a social project we need the managers to lead (as a part of their work) Christian worship. As this is an explicit part of their work it is not considered, legally, an issue to recruit for this. This is not always appreciated by some funders . . . who are not always happy about us employing only Christian managers.[104]

It is common for Salvation Army service centers to have religious symbols on the walls, spoken prayers at meals, voluntary religious services, and Bible studies. In short, while the policies of religious agencies receiving government funds have been an issue, they have not risen to the level of contentiousness that we saw they have in the United States.

Nor does the religious establishment serve as a deterrent for voluntary groups outside of the Church of England. As another person from the Salvation Army said to us, "it [the religious establishment] helps the Salvation Army because it creates a certain viewpoint that is accepting of state support for the religious activities of social service agencies."[105] We believe that there is much to this argument; the fact that there is an established church in Britain makes it easier for religious groups and the state to work in a cooperative relationship. The state accommodates religious social service organizations because the state perceives them to be for the public good. Church-based agencies have worked in partnership with the state, and, because virtually all religious agencies are eligible for public funds, there has not been the conflict that has occurred with state funding of religious schools.

CONCLUDING OBSERVATIONS

England is the only country in our study that has retained a formal religious establishment, the second of our three church-state models. At first glance, this religious establishment might seem little more than a cultural relic of a bygone era that has little or no practical meaning today. It is certainly true that the partnership between church and state is not as strong as it once was, when the relationship between these two powerful institutions was seen as crucial for the nation's political stability and religious prosperity. We contend, however, that England's religious establishment continues to provide an alternative church-state model for pluralistic democracies, particularly in terms of the cultural assumptions and values it represents. The most important of these assumptions is that religion and religious organizations have an important public role to perform and that it therefore is appropriate for the state to take positive measures to recognize, accommodate, and support religion. The religious establishment serves as an acknowledgment by the state that faith has a public character to it, and that public policy can accommodate faith in a way that is equitable among religious groups and between religious and nonreligious perspectives.

To some degree the English church-state model does undermine, however, the basic goal of governmental neutrality on matters of religion. The key limitations of the current system are that it does not provide religious freedom for all or equal treatment among religions, specifically on the issue of religious instruction and worship in state-run schools. The rights of religious minorities have gradually expanded since the formal establishment of the Church of England in the sixteenth century. There are, however, no constitutional provisions protecting religious rights and not the same kind of theoretical commitment by the state to religious free exercise that is so robust in the Netherlands and in Germany. The passage of the Human Rights Act indicated a statutory movement in that direction, as did the European Court of Human Rights *Eweida* decision that expanded religious liberty protections. The legal and political implications of the 2016 Brexit vote, however, will challenge anything that looks like an internationalization of rights protections in England.

Equally problematic, from the standpoint of equal treatment, is the place of religion in state-run schools. Under the current policy, religious instruction and acts of collective worship are intended to be primarily Christian. The current practice is oftentimes justified as a natural and necessary by-product of England's establishment model, but the policy raises any number of concerns. Historically, the religion provided in the schools was generically Christian, a recognition on the part of policy makers that it would be unacceptable for the schools to teach the particularistic doctrines of the Church of England. This accommodation worked particularly well in a culture where most people shared similar values and few took religion seriously. However, in a more religiously diverse and a more secular England, there are an increasing number of people who reject the "consensual" religion taught in the schools. Seen in this light, the current policy disadvantages secularists, Sikhs, Pentecostals, Muslims, and any others who do not consider themselves "generically" Christian. To be sure, many local education authorities have drafted curricula and instituted worship practices that introduce students to diverse religious traditions, and students can excuse themselves from the collective worship if they wish, but the law clearly preferences one religious viewpoint over others.

The paradox of England's partial religious establishment is that while it hinders the realization of governmental neutrality that we established as the basic standard by which to evaluate church-state practices in some cases, the system helps the state to achieve neutrality in even more respects. In terms of public funding for religious schools, the current system expands choice for Jewish, Christian, and Islamic parents who want a school permeated by religious ideas. In this way, the system is more neutral between a religious and nonreligious educational perspective than in the United States. This is also true for nonprofit social service organizations where the state provides funds for a wide variety of religious agencies to serve particular groups in the population. These nonprofit agencies achieve a diversity of service that would simply not be possible if the state provided the services by itself.

In some respects, religious pluralism in England has made it difficult to sustain this establishment model. One way to meet the goal of pluralism might be to stop funding religious schools and remove religious instruction and worship from state-run schools. Justice is best served, it could be argued, when state neutrality among the various religious traditions is gained by a strict separationist, no-aid-to-religion approach. This is the argument American and French strict separationists have made. Neutrality, in this view, means no state financial support or involvement with religious schools. In this way the state avoids favoring any particular faith, as it currently does with its partial support for church schools. The problem with this separationist approach, however, is that it is not truly neutral, but favors a nonreligious ethos over religious ones.

An alternative option that we believe is more genuinely neutral, and that has been increasingly practiced in England, has been the expansion of the current system to recognize more religious traditions, along the lines of the Dutch or Australian models. Religious minorities have looked to the state to recognize their rights, finance their schools, and make possible the public manifestation of their faith. In many respects, the religious establishment does make this possible. Not one of the Muslims that we interviewed for this project expressed opposition to the religious establishment; instead most of them see it as an ally in their quest for public recognition. Much as the state pragmatically accommodated Roman Catholics, Jews, and Protestant nonconformists in the past, England is increasingly accommodating Muslims, Sikhs, Buddhists, and other religious minorities in the present. In our view, this policy is consistent with the goal of neutrality among religious groups and between religious and nonreligious perspectives.

The limits to this expansion will come from secular voices that want to get rid of the religious establishment and from those who wish to defend a specifically Christian establishment. Neither group is particularly large in number and they obviously have divergent political goals, but they can and have joined forces on some matters, particularly on the issue of public funding for Islamic schools. In the aftermath of the terrorist attacks in Britain, secular and some conservative Christian voices questioned the wisdom of aiding "separate" Islamic schools. However, the government, the politically powerful churches, and the general public support both the establishment and an expansion of the current system. There is every reason to believe that England's religious establishment will continue to move toward the goal of recognizing and accommodating the diversity of religious voices in England.

NOTES

1. For a good account of the British political system, see Philip Norton, *The British Polity*, 5th ed. (New York: Routledge, 2010).

2. Census data on religion in England and Wales are available from the Office for National Statistics at http://www.ons.gov.uk/ons/index.html.

3. Peter Brierley, ed., *UK Church Statistics, Number 2, 2010 to 2020* (Tonbridge, England: ADBC Publishers, 2014).

4. Nicholas Hellen and Christopher Morgan, "Muslims Outpace Anglicans in UK," *Times Online* (January 25, 2004); Jonathan Petre, "Facing the Axe: Diocese That Has Twice as Many Muslim Worshippers as Anglicans," *Daily Mail* (October 23, 2010).

5. Ruth Gledhill, "Church Attendance Has Been Propped Up by Immigrants," *Guardian* (June 3, 2014). Available at http://www.theguardian.com/.

6. Ruth Gledhill, "Future of Religion in Britain Is Islam and Black Majority Churches," *Christian Today* (February 9, 2015).

7. Grace Davie, *Religion in Modern Europe: A Memory Mutates* (Oxford: Oxford University Press, 2000).

8. Data on religious views available from National Centre for Social Research, British Social Attitudes Survey, 2008 [computer file]. Colchester, Essex: UK Data Archive. Available at http://www.bsa.natcen.ac.uk/.

9. George Moyser, ed., *Church and Politics Today* (Edinburgh: T&T Clark, 1985).

10. Clive D. Field, "Rendering unto Caesar? The Politics of Church of England Clergy since 1980," *Journal of Anglican Studies* 5, 1 (2007), 89–108.

11. Paul Whiteley, Patrick Seyd, and Jeremy Richardson, *True Blues: The Politics of the Conservative Party* (Oxford: Clarendon Press, 1994); John Bingham, "Anglicans Almost Twice as Likely to Vote Conservative," *Telegraph* (April 10, 2015). Available at http://www.telegraph.co.uk/news/general-election-2015/11525188/Anglicans-almost-twice-as-likely-to-vote-Conservative.html.

12. Jeffrey M. Jones, "Atheists, Muslims See Most Bias as Presidential Candidates." Available at http://www.gallup.com/poll/155285/atheists-muslims-bias-presidential-candidates.aspx.

13. Philip Stephens, *Tony Blair: The Price of Leadership* (London: Politico's Publishing, 2004); Anthony Seldon, *Blair* (London: Free Press, 2005).

14. Stuart McAnulla, "Cameron's Conservatism: Why God, Why Now," *Political Quarterly* 85, 4 (2014), 462–70.

15. Peter Cornwell, *Church and Nation* (Oxford: Basil Blackwell, 1983); W. L. Sachs, *The Transformation of Anglicanism from State Church to Global Communion* (Cambridge: Cambridge University Press, 1993); and Mark Chapman, *Anglicanism: A Very Short Introduction* (Oxford: Oxford University Press, 2006), 13–37.

16. For a good review of this period, see John Marshall, "Some Intellectual Consequences of the English Revolution," *European Legacy* 5, 4 (2000), 515–30; and John Madeley, "Politics and the Pulpit: The Case of Protestant Europe," *West European Politics* (April 1982), 149–71.

17. Samuel Beer, *Modern British Politics* (London: Faber and Faber, 1969), chap. 2.

18. Michael Fogerty, "The Churches and Public Policy in Britain," *Political Quarterly* 63 (July–September 1992), 300–317.

19. Bernadette O'Keeffe, *Faith, Culture and the Dual System* (London: Falmer Press, 1986).

20. David McClean, "State and Church in the United Kingdom," in Gerhard Robbers, ed., *State and Church in the European Union*, 2nd ed. (Baden-Baden, Germany: Nomos Verlagsgesellschaft, 2005), 553–75; Kenneth Medhurst and George Moyser, *Church and Politics in a Secular Age* (Oxford: Clarendon Press, 1988).

21. Hugo Young, *One of Us: A Biography of Margaret Thatcher* (London: Macmillan, 1989), 416–17.

22. Ruth Gledhill, "Bishops Want to Apologize for Iraq War," *Times* (September 19, 2005).

23. Jason Beattie, "27 Bishops Slam David Cameron's Welfare Reforms as Creating a National Crisis in Unprecedented Attack." Available at http://www.mirror.co.uk/news/uk-news/27-bishops-slam-david-camerons-3164033.

24. *A House for the Future* (London: Stationery Office, 2000).

25. Robert Winnett, "David Cameron Retreats on House of Lords Reform," *Telegraph* (August 2, 2012).

26. HL Deb 3 Jun 2013, vol. 737, col. 954.

27. HL Deb 3 June 2013, vol. 737, col. 963.

28. "A Christian Presence in Every Community (Lords Spiritual in the House of Lords)." Available at https://www.churchofengland.org/our-views/the-church-in-parliament/bishops-in-the-house-of-lords.aspx#Who%20do%20they%20represent%20in%20Parliament.

29. Stephen Hunt, "Negotiating Equality in the Equality Act 2010 (United Kingdom): Church-State Relations in a Post-Christian Society," *Journal of Church and State* 55, 4 (2012), 690–711.

30. Paul Weller, "Equity, Inclusivity and Participation in a Plural Society: Challenging the Establishment of the Church of England," in Peter W. Edge and Graham Harvey, eds., *Law and Religion in Contemporary Society: Communities, Individualism, and the State* (Aldershot: Ashgate, 2000), 53–67.

31. James A. Beckford and Sophie Gilliat, *Religion in Prison: Equal Rites in a Multi-Faith Society* (Cambridge: Cambridge University Press, 1998).

32. James A. Beckford and Ilona C. M. Cairns, "Muslim Prison Chaplains in Canada and Britain," *Sociological Review* 63 (2015), 36–56.

33. Paul Donovan, "Faithful Service: Radio Waves," *Times* (December 30, 2007).

34. "The Queens Speech at Lambeth Palace, February 15, 2012." Available at http://www.royal.gov.uk/.

35. Personal interview with Dr. Fatma Amer, director of education and interfaith relations at the London Central Mosque (April 11, 2001).

36. Tariq Modood, "Moderate Secularism, Religion as Identity and Respect for Religion," *Political Quarterly* 81, 1 (2010), 7.

37. Tariq Modood, "Establishment, Multiculturalism and British Citizenship," *Political Quarterly* 65 (January–March 1994), 59.

38. Patrick Wintour, "'Militant Secularisation' Taking Hold of British Society, Says Lady Warsi," *Guardian* (February 13, 2012). Available at http://www.theguardian.com/world/2012/feb/13/militant-secularisation-christianity-lady-warsi.

39. Matthew Grimley, "The Dog That Didn't Bark: The Failure of Disestablishment since 1927," in Mark Chapman, Judith Maltby, and William Whyte, eds., *The Established Church: Past, Present and Future* (London: T&T Clark International, 2011), 39–55.

40. Ben Clements and Nick Spencer, "Public Opinion in Britain towards the Disestablishment of the Church of England," *Journal of Anglican Studies* 13, 1 (2015), 30–49.

41. Iain McLean and Benjamin Linsley, *The Church of England and the State: Reforming Establishment for a Multi-Faith Britain* (London: New Politics Network, 2004).

42. For a broad overview of this process, see Joel S. Fetzer and J. Christopher Soper, *Muslims and the State in Britain, France, and Germany* (Cambridge: Cambridge University Press, 2005).

43. "Hindu, Muslim and Sikh Populations," http://www.brin.ac.uk/figures; "How Many Muslims? British Religion in Numbers," http://www.brin.ac.uk/, September 21, 2010.

44. Eileen Barker, "The British Right to Discriminate," in Thomas Robbins and Roland Robertson, eds., *Church-State Relations: Tensions and Transitions* (New Brunswick, N.J.: Transaction Books, 1987), 270–84.

45. Philip Lewis, *Islamic Britain: Religion, Politics and Identity among British Muslims* (London: I.B. Taurus, 1994), 158–64.

46. Jonathan Laurence, *The Emancipation of Europe's Muslims: The State's Role in Minority Integration* (Princeton, N.J.: Princeton University Press, 2012), 144–45.

47. Lina Molokotus-Liederman, "Pluralism in Education: The Display of Islamic Affiliation in French and British Schools," *Islam and Christian Muslim Relations* 11, 1 (2000), 105–17.

48. Mary Anne Weaver, "Her Majesty's Jihadists," *New York Times Magazine* (April 14, 2015).

49. Alan Cowell, "Britain Proposes Allowing Schools to Forbid Full-Face Muslim Veils," *New York Times* (March 21, 2007), 5.

50. David Cameron, "Extremism: PM Speech," July 20, 2015. Available at https://www.gov.uk/government/speeches/extremism-pm-speech.

51. The Muslim Council of Britain, "British Muslims in Numbers," http://www.mcb.org.uk/wp-content/uploads/2015/02/MCBCensusReport_2015.

52. Joel C. Daniels, "Rowan Williams on Sharia, Secularism, and Surprise," *Journal of Ecumenical Studies* 49, 3 (2014), 405–19.

53. Lisa Pilgram, "British-Muslim Family Law and Citizenship," *Citizenship Studies* 16, 506 (2012), 769–82.

54. "Islamic Human Rights Commission Press Release: UK—Shock at Backlash against Archbishop of Canterbury" (February 8, 2008). Available at http://www.ihrc.org/.

55. Muhammad Anwar, *Race Relations Policies in Britain* (Warwick: Centre for Research in Ethnic Relations, 1991).

56. Grace Davie, *Religion in Britain: A Persistent Paradox* (Hoboken, N.J.: John Wiley and Sons, 2015), 197–202.

57. Mark Hill, "Religious Symbolism and Conscientious Objection in the Workplace: An Evaluation of Strasbourg's Judgment in *Eweida and others v. United Kingdom*," *Ecclesiastical Law Journal* 15, 2 (2013), 191–200.

58. Sir Terence Etherton, "Religion, the Rule of Law and Discrimination," *Ecclesiastical Law Journal* 16, 3 (2014), 265–82.

59. Rosa Prince, "David Cameron: I Will Change the Law to Allow Crosses at Work," *Telegraph* (July 11, 2012), 3.

60. Kylie MacLellan, "Cameron—I Won't Rule Out Leaving European Convention on Human Rights," UK Reuters (June 3, 2015). Available at http://uk.reuters.com/article/2015/06/03/uk-britain-politics-rights-idUKKBN0OJ1HK20150603.

61. Brent F. Nelson and James L. Guth, *Religion and the Struggle for European Union* (Washington, D.C.: Georgetown University Press, 2015), 226–32.

62. Barker, "The British Right to Discriminate," 279.

63. For good reviews of the history of British educational policy, see O'Keeffe, *Faith, Culture and the Dual System*; Skinner, "Religious Pluralism and School Provision in Britain"; and *Faith in the System: The Role of Schools with a Religious Character in English Education and Society* (London: Department for Children, Schools and Families, 2007).

64. Robert Burgess, "Five Items for the Policy Agenda in Church Schools," in Bernadette O'Keeffe, ed., *Schools for Tomorrow: Building Walls or Building Bridges* (London: Falmer Press, 1988), 162–81; David W. Lankshear, *A Shared Vision: Education in Church Schools* (London: Church House, 1992); and "Schools, Pupils and Their Characteristics." Department of Education, January 2014. Available at https://www.gov.uk/government/statistics/schools-pupils-and-their-characteristics-january-2015; https://www.tes.co.uk/article.aspx?storycode=6006501.

65. *The Way Ahead: Church of England Schools in the New Millennium* (London: Church House Publishing, 2001), 27.

66. Personal interview with David Lankshear, executive director of the Board of Education for the Church of England (May 13, 1994).

67. Robert Waddington, "The Church and Educational Policy," in Moyser, ed., *Church and Politics Today*, 221–55.

68. O'Keeffe, *Schools for Tomorrow*, chap. 1.

69. *Community Cohesion: A Report of the Independent Review Team Chaired by Ted Cantle* (London: Home Office, 2001).

70. Personal interview with Dr. Hesham El-Essawy, executive director of the Islamic Society for the Promotion of Religious Tolerance (April 10, 2001).

71. *Schools: Building on Success* (London: Crown Copyright, 2001).

72. "Schools, Pupils and Their Characteristics." Department of Education, January 2014; David Marley, "Muslim Schools Prove Stars of the Higher-Performing Faith Family," *Times Educational Supplement* (January 17, 2014). Available at https://www.tes.co.uk/article.aspx?storycode=6006501.

73. Sally Weale, "David Cameron Announces 49 New Free Schools," *Guardian* (March 9, 2015). Available at http://www.theguardian.com/education/2015/mar/09/david-cameron-faith-schools-academies.

74. Fran Abrams, "Islamic Schools Flourish to Meet Demand," *Guardian* (November 28, 2011). Available at http://www.theguardian.com/education/2011/nov/28/muslim-schools-growth.

75. Matthew Taylor, "Two-Thirds Oppose State Aided Faith Schools," *Guardian* (August 23, 2005), 4.

76. Ibrahim Hewitt, "Schools of Good Faith," *Q News* 339–400 (January–February 2002), 14.

77. *Faith in the System*, 1.

78. *The Way Ahead*, 11.

79. http://islamiaprimary.org.uk/content/view/127.

80. Richard Gold, *The Education Act Explained* (London: Stationery Office, 1999).

81. See http://www.coxhoe.durham.schap.uk/curriculum-links/religious-educationchap.

82. Personal interview with Dr. Fatma Amer, head of education and interfaith relations, London Central Mosque (April 11, 2001).

83. "An Evaluation of the Work of Standing Advisory Councils for Religious Education" (London: Crown Copyright, 2004).

84. *Faith in the System*, 10.

85. For a review of this activism, see D. W. Bebbington, *Evangelicalism in Modern Britain* (London: Unwin Hyman, 1989), and June Rose, *For the Sake of the Children: Inside Dr. Barnardo's* (London: Hodder and Stoughton, 1987).

86. Lester Salamon, "Partners in Public Service: The Scope and Theory of Government-Nonprofit Relations," in Walter M. Powell, ed., *The Nonprofit Sector: A Research Handbook* (New Haven, Conn.: Yale University Press, 1987), 99–117.

87. Nicholas Deakin, "Religion, State, and Third Sector in England," *Journal of Political Ideologies* 15, 3 (2010), 303–15.

88. Frank Prochaska, *Christianity and Social Service in Modern Britain: The Disinherited Spirit* (New York, Oxford: Oxford University Press, 2006).

89. Perri 6 and Penny Fieldgrass, *Britain's Voluntary Organizations: Snapshots of the Voluntary Sector* (London: NCVO Publications, 1992); "UK Civil Society Almanac 2015," NCVO. Available at http://data.ncvo.org.uk/.

90. Margaret Harris and Colin Rochester, eds., *Voluntary Organizations and Social Policy in Britain: Perspectives on Change and Choice* (New York: Palgrave, 2001); Thomas Bahle, "The Changing Institutionalization of Social Services in England and Wales, France and Germany: Is the Welfare State on the Retreat?" *Journal of European Social Policy* 13, 1 (2003), 1–20.

91. Full text of the speech is available at http://www.number10.gov.uk.

92. Amos Zehavi, "Religious Supply, Welfare State Restructuring and Faith-Based Social Activities," *Political Studies* 61 (2012), 561–79; İpek Göçmen, "The Role of Faith-Based Organizations in Social Welfare Systems: A Comparison of France, Germany, Sweden, and the United Kingdom," *Nonprofit and Voluntary Sector Quarterly* 42, 3 (2013), 495–516.

93. *Salvation Army Annual Review 2013.* Available at http://www.salvationarmy.org.uk/about-us.

94. *Livability Annual Review 2013–2014.* Available at http://www.livability.org.uk/.

95. Heather Wraight, Peter Brierley, and David Longley, eds., *United Kingdom Christian Handbook: 2007/2008* (London: Christian Research, 2006).

96. *Jewish Care Annual Review, 2013–2014.* Available at https://www.jewishcare.org/.

97. For a complete list, see http://www.theyworkforyou.com/wrans/?id=2009-02-26f.259139.h.

98. *Stand and Deliver.* Charity Commission, 2007. Available at https://www.gov.uk/government/publications/stand-and-deliver-rs15.

99. Peter Dobkin Hall, "The History of Religious Philanthropy in America," in Robert Wuthnow and Virginia A. Hodgkinson, eds., *Faith and Philanthropy in America* (San Francisco: Jossey-Bass, 1990), 56.

100. Shafaq Hasan, "UK Cuts Funding to Muslim Charities Accused of Extremist Ties," *Nonprofit Quarterly* (January 13, 2015).

101. "Equality Act (2010) Explained." Available at http://www.equalityhumanrights.com/legal-and-policy/legislation/equality-act-2010/what-equality-act.

102. "Information Packet for Applicants" (Undated Publication of Yeldall Christian Centre). Available at http://www.yeldall.org.uk.

103. Quoted from Jonathan Oliver, "One Third of All Christians Say We've Suffered Discrimination," *Daily Mail* (March 17, 2007).

104. Personal correspondence with Major David J. Tribble, divisional director for social services of the Salvation Army, Yorkshire Division (February 14, 2008).

105. Personal interview with Christine McMillan, associate director, London Homeless Shelters for the Salvation Army (May 13, 1994).

Chapter Seven

Germany

Church-State Partnership

In a 2016 interview, Bishop Heinrich Bedford-Strohm, the head of the German Protestant Church, called for Islam to be taught in all state schools. Seven of Germany's sixteen federal states currently offer some form of Islamic religion classes in their schools, while all of the states provide Catholic and Protestant religious instruction. Bishop Bedford-Strohm proposed that Islamic associations should organize themselves to be a "clear partner" with the German state in offering Islamic religious instruction that was fully compatible with the country's democratic political values. He further contended that this religious education could help prevent young Muslims from being drawn into radicalization.[1]

At first glance, it might seem unusual to include Germany in our model of religious establishment. After all, the German Constitution clearly states that "There shall be no state church," and Germany lacks the formal religious establishment that we saw in England. The anecdote about Bishop Bedford-Strohm, however, demonstrates that on many issues a close partnership exists between the German churches and the state. In the case of education, this partnership means that Protestant and Catholic Church officials work closely with the public universities to train teachers for religious education, and they cooperate with state educational authorities to develop a religious education curriculum for the schools.

Two additional values supplement this idea of church-state partnership: neutrality and freedom of religion as a positive freedom. Neutrality, as one German authority on church-state relations has noted, means "the State [is] not to be identified with a Church; there is to be no Established Church. The State is not allowed to have any special inclination to a particular religious congregation. . . . On the other hand, religious institutions must not be placed in a more disadvantageous position than societal groups."[2] Among all religious groups and between the religious and the nonreligious the state is to be neutral, not favoring one over another. Freedom of religion as a positive freedom insists that freedom of religion is more than a negative freedom; it extends beyond freedom *from* government restrictions on one's religious beliefs or practices to include positive efforts *by* the government to ensure that religious persons are in a position actually to exercise the freedoms assured them. Donald Kommers has put it well: "Freedom of religion in the positive sense implies an obligation on the part of the state to create a social order in which it is possible for the religious personality to develop and flourish conveniently and easily."[3]

These three principles work together to create an approach to church-state relations that to most Americans appears puzzling. There is no official state church in Germany, yet the emphasis on church-state partnership, neutrality, and religious freedom as a positive freedom has led to practices many Americans would find in violation of church-state separation and neutrality. As we will see in the pages below, there are numerous ways that church and state work together to contribute to a prosperous, stable German society. Germany's church-state thinking and practices have many parallels with the partial establishment of England.

THE NATION

Germany is a country of a little more than eighty-one million people and 137,000 square miles, making it second to Russia as the most populous country of Europe. It has risen from the ashes of World War II to become a European and even a world economic and political powerhouse. Some have argued that the "economic miracle" of the 1950s, as it was often called, has been exceeded by the political miracle that has transformed a nation that had been marked by authoritarian government and political instability into a model of stability and liberal democracy for almost seventy years.[4]

The German population is nearly evenly divided among Protestants (29 percent), Catholics (30 percent), and those with no religion (38 percent). The Evangelical Church in Germany (EKD) is by far the largest Protestant church with twenty-three million members. The EKD is a federation of twenty regional Protestant churches, which are mostly Lutheran in background, while some come out of the Reformed (that is, Calvinist) tradition and some are products of a union between Lutheran and Reformed churches.[5] There are also 1.6 million members of the Orthodox Church, and a scattering of free Protestant churches that are not a part of the EKD. With somewhere between four and five million adherents, Islam is the largest non-Christian religion in

Germany, representing nearly 5 percent of the country's total population. While there are only 200,000 Jews currently living in the country, Germany is now home to the fastest-growing Jewish community in all of Europe.[6] By many measures, Germany is an increasingly secular society. The percentage of Germans attending religious services at least once a month has declined from 37 percent in 1981 to 19 percent in 2014; two-thirds of Germans assert that religion is not very important in their lives, more than half (51 percent) say that they never or almost never pray, a majority (61 percent) claim that they have little or no confidence in the churches, and the percentage of Germans who are members of the historically dominant EKD and Roman Catholic churches has declined from 72 percent in 1991 to 59 percent in 2013. In marked contrast with the United States, personal faith plays little to no role in German public political discourse.[7]

But this low level of religious involvement can be misleading. The churches were one of the few German social structures that offered any significant opposition to the Nazi regime, and provided a certain moral strength in the immediate post–World War II period. The churches and the closely related Christian Democratic movement played major roles in the rise of Germany from the devastation of the war during the 1945–1960 period. The Christian Democratic Union (CDU) political party has dominated the postwar era. According to the party manifesto, the "Christian concept of mankind forms our ethical basis for responsible politics."[8] While she rarely talks about her faith, Angela Merkel, the party leader since 2000 and Germany's chancellor since 2005, is a member of the Evangelical Church and the daughter of a Lutheran pastor from the former East Germany. There has also been renewed politicization around religion in recent decades. A 1995 Constitutional Court decision ruling that crucifixes may not be displayed in public school classrooms if any student objects on religious grounds was greeted by a storm of denunciation and protest throughout Germany. More recently, Catholic and Protestant church leaders embraced Merkel's original open-door policy toward Syrian and other refugees in the fall of 2015. And, as we will note later in the chapter, there has been increasing controversy surrounding the integration of the growing German Islamic population.

Politically, Germany has a federal system with sixteen states (Länder). More power is centralized in the national government than is the case in the United States, but significant powers are assigned to the states. Germany has a parliamentary system of government, with a lower house, the Bundestag, directly elected by the people and an upper house, the Bundesrat, composed of representatives of the states. The Bundesrat's approval is generally needed for legislation affecting the states, but on other legislation the Bundestag can override a negative vote by the Bundesrat by a simple majority. The chancellor is elected by the Bundestag.

Germany has two major parties, the Christian Democratic Union (the Christian Social Union in Bavaria) and the Social Democratic Party. Following the 2013 elections the Christian Democrats had 310 of the 630 seats in the Bundestag and the Social Democrats had 193 seats. The two most important smaller parties at present are the Alliance 90/Greens with 63 seats (a reform-minded environmental party), and the Left Party with 64 seats (a union of the recast Communist Party and several other left-wing parties).

It is also important to note the role of the Federal Constitutional Court, since it has the power of judicial review. This is a court created by the 1949 Constitution to decide questions of constitutional interpretation.[9] It is divided into two Senates, as they are called, each composed of eight justices, and cases considered by the Constitutional Court are considered by one Senate or the other (referred to simply as the First Senate or the Second Senate). Half the justices are elected by the Bundestag and half by the Bundesrat. All serve twelve-year terms and are not allowed to serve more than one term. As we shall shortly see, the Constitutional Court has dealt with a number of crucial church-state issues.

HISTORICAL BACKGROUND

There are five historical periods that are important in giving insight into German church-state practices. The first period is that of the Middle Ages and the Protestant Reformation. Throughout this era what is Germany today was a host of kingdoms and principalities very loosely tied together in the Holy Roman Empire; Germany as a nation-state did not exist. During the Middle Ages the concept of the "two swords" or two authorities—church and civil rulers—took deep root in the German territories, as it did through most of Christendom. Under this concept the people were under two rulers, the prince and the church, and both worked for the stability and prosperity of society. This concept left undefined exactly which authority was responsible for what and led to many conflicts between the papacy and the Holy Roman Emperors, such as that between Pope Gregory VII and King Henry IV in the eleventh century.

The Reformation shattered the unity of European Christendom. Most of the German territories followed the practice of *cuius regio, eius religio* (the religion of the ruler is the religion of the state). The 1648 Peace of Westphalia, which ended the devastating Thirty Years' War, reaffirmed the right of rulers to determine the religion to be followed in their territories, but also provided for the rights of dissenters. In each region, the prince determined whether his people were to be Catholic, Lutheran, or Calvinist. Given the relatively small size of many of the German principalities, this practice created areas almost totally committed to one of these religious traditions within

Christianity. Until the post–World War II era with its increasing prosperity and greater mobility many areas of Germany remained overwhelmingly Catholic or Protestant. Even today this is still the case to a significant degree in some areas. The practice of *cuius regio, eius religio* also perpetuated the "two swords" concept, although in practice the secular authority came to dominate the spiritual authority. With the church (Protestant or Catholic) usually dependent on the civil rulers for its existence, this is not surprising.

It was from out of this time period that the tradition of a church-state partnership emerged. The well-being of society rested on the two pillars of church and state, or throne and altar, as it is often put. They were seen as united in a common cause. Thus cooperation and mutual support came to be the norm. The religious uniformity within the separate principalities made church-state cooperation and mutual support possible, for the most part, without raising charges of religious discrimination and favoritism. Paradoxically, the German tradition of church autonomy can also be traced to this same time period. The "two swords" doctrine held in theory—even if it was often not followed in practice—that the church and the state, the two swords, were coequal institutions, each with rights and responsibilities. In theory at least, the church was not an arm of or subservient to the state.

The second time period of importance for understanding the development of church-state relations in Germany is the era stretching from the Congress of Vienna in 1815 through World War I. At the close of the Napoleonic era the degree of unity that Napoleon had imposed dissipated. Germany was composed of nearly fifty principalities united into a very loose confederation and with conservative, nondemocratic forces dominant. From 1815 to 1871 weak liberal movements were usually outmaneuvered and failed to gain ascendancy. Prussia gradually arose as a dominant force, and by 1871—with the help of military victories over Denmark, Austria, and France—had united Germany in a modern nation-state. Prussia thereby established the second German empire, which lasted until the end of World War I. It was a conservative regime, with a monarch (first William I, then Frederick III for a few months, followed by William I's grandson William II in 1888) and a parliament that was often overshadowed by a powerful chancellor responsible to the monarch. Otto von Bismarck engineered the unification of Germany and served as its chancellor until 1890.[10]

Three marks of this period are important to note for understanding subsequent church-state developments and patterns. One is the nature and relative weakness of the liberal movement. Enlightenment liberalism never became the powerful, independent force it did in the other countries considered in this book. Instead, while present and influential, it cooperated with and in many ways came to be integrated with the still-powerful conservative landowning and titled classes. It never developed the same antireligious character it did in other European countries. This meant that the Catholics and Protestants did not face an independent, anticlerical liberal movement that might have forced them into cooperative efforts, as had occurred in the neighboring Netherlands; instead the Catholics were overshadowed by the Protestant leadership of the empire, who made common cause with the conservative forces.

The second point to be noted is that the second empire was marked by a very strong alliance between the Protestant church and the newly formed German state. The various regional governments provided direct financial subsidies to the church, and "the church and its liturgical ceremonies became an important unifying force, binding the nation to the ruling dynasty and securing it through a providential interpretation of German history."[11] The close alliance between church and state that had existed from the Medieval and Reformation eras was maintained during the second empire.

A third important point is that it was during this era that the Catholics developed a significant political movement. At the time of German unification the new nation was clearly a Protestant nation. Its moving force was Prussia, which was strongly Protestant. For a period of time in the 1870s Bismarck launched what came to be called *Kulturkampf* (culture war), a series of oppressive and discriminatory measures against the Catholics. Doing so had the opposite effect of what was intended, as Catholics rallied behind their leaders and the Catholic Center Party developed into a political force that had to be reckoned with. Most of the discriminatory measures were repealed in the early 1880s, but the Center Party retained its political influence.

Following the defeat of Germany in World War I the second empire came to an end and was replaced by the Weimar Republic, named after the city of Weimar where the new constitution was written. This is the third historical period to be noted here. Given the crisis created by the German defeat, the spirit of revolution that was in the air, and the generally liberal nature of the new constitution, one might suppose that the Weimar Constitution would break with past church-state practices. While a variety of subsidies and privileges were kept by the Catholic and Evangelical churches, the Weimar Constitution for the first time formally adopted the principle of church-state separation, declared there was to be no state church, and provided that "civil and political rights and duties shall be neither dependent on nor restricted by the exercise of religious freedom."[12] It thereby recognized the basic principle of governmental neutrality on matters of religion, as well as the earlier principle of autonomy. The significance of the Weimar Constitution for religious freedom can be seen in the fact that the current Constitution, adopted after World War II, incorporated by reference the basic articles establishing religious freedom found in the Weimar Constitution.

The Nazi era is the fourth era of significance for present-day German church-state relations. Most of the Evangelical and Catholic church leadership had remained largely negative toward the Weimar Constitution, attitudes that seemed to be vindicated when Germany experienced a series of severe economic reversals and political difficulties. Thus when Adolf Hitler and his National Socialists promised stability, prosperity, freedom to the churches, and greatness for the Fatherland, the churches, for the most part, initially rallied in support. The Catholic Center Party unanimously supported the Enabling Act in 1933 that gave Hitler dictatorial powers. In the same year the Vatican signed the famous Reichskonkordat with the Nazi regime, which assured the Catholic Church certain rights but also helped the Nazis consolidate their power. Within the Evangelical Church, a "German Christian" movement emerged that enthusiastically supported Hitler's rise to power and thoroughly wedded German discipline and greatness with Christianity.

On the other hand, the Catholic Church never fully supported the Nazi regime. It was more concerned with protecting its own institutional autonomy and maintaining a semblance of normal church life in the midst of political upheaval and war than either supporting or opposing Nazism. Also, many individual Catholic leaders, such as Cardinal Graf Galen of Munich, courageously opposed the Nazi regime. Within the more culturally powerful Evangelical Church—after an initial enthusiasm for Hitler—opposition to him quickly arose as the true nature of Nazism became evident. Frederic Spotts reports that already by May 1934 "anti-Nazi resistance had sufficiently crystallized for a Reich Synod of the opponents to be held in the Rhineland town of Barmen. Here, largely under the influence of Karl Barth, a 'Confessing Church' . . . was organized, based upon a confession of faith in the supremacy of Scripture which might not be changed to suit prevailing ideological or political convictions."[13] This Confessing Church gained wide support and successfully opposed the pro-Nazi "German Evangelical Church." During the Hitler regime, 3,000 pastors were arrested, at least 125 were sent to concentration camps, and 22 were executed, including the famous pastor and theologian Dietrich Bonhoeffer.[14] After the war the newly constituted Evangelical Church—under the leadership, among others, of Martin Niemoller, who had recently been released from seven years in a concentration camp—adopted the Stuttgart Declaration, which acknowledged the churches' and the nation's guilt:

> We know ourselves to be with our nation not only in a great community of suffering but also in a solidarity of guilt. With great pain we say: because of us, infinite suffering has been brought to many peoples and countries. . . . We condemn ourselves because we did not believe more courageously, did not pray more devotedly, did not believe more joyously, and did not love more deeply. Now a fresh start is to be made in our churches.[15]

As a result of this highly traumatic era two lessons with lasting implications for church-state relations have been burned into German thinking. One is that the church flirts with enormous danger when it is too subservient to the state. The church to that point in German history was suddenly seen as too subservient to the state, too ready to make common cause with the state, and too quick to advance whatever policies the state was supporting. The principle of church autonomy, already present in the German tradition, received a new and urgent emphasis. A second lesson was that the church must play a role in the political and social life of the nation. The big error of the church was not seen as being its active support of Hitler—which had been brief and limited—but its silence and acquiescence. Both the Catholic and Evangelical churches emerged from the era of National Socialism with a greatly strengthened resolve to be active, positive forces in society. The concept of strict church-state separation even today is seen as a dangerous doctrine, one that implies the political realm is to be secularized, with religion's influence muted or nonexistent.

The postwar era is the fifth of the historical time periods. It saw the rise of the Christian Democratic movement in West Germany, the most powerful political force in the postwar era. This new party was interconfessional—including both Catholics and Protestants—and was firmly committed to liberal democracy and to learning from the bitter experiences under the Weimar Republic and the Third Reich. The party also actively supported the movement toward European integration after the war. By firmly linking Christianity—both Protestant and Catholic—to the powerful democratic impulses sweeping postwar Germany, it made possible the continued cooperation or partnership of the state with religion. Religion and Christianity came to be seen as positive, democratizing forces and as bulwarks against the reemergence of Nazism. Church-state cooperation was thereby seen not as a danger to be avoided, but as an asset to be used in the search for democracy.[16]

In 1948 the Western allies decided it was time to move ahead with a constitution for the three zones of Germany under their jurisdiction. The parliaments of the eleven German states that had been previously set up elected a Parliamentary Council to write the constitution. Working from a draft that a conference of experts had put together, the council wrote a new constitution.[17] It was approved by the Allies and the state parliaments, and went into effect in May 1949. Its preamble begins with a recognition of God: "Conscious of their responsibility before God and Humankind."[18] The first nineteen articles constitute a bill of rights, with Article 4 assuring that "(1) Freedom of faith and conscience as well as freedom of creed, religious or ideological, are inviolable," and "(2) The undisturbed practice of religion shall be guaranteed." Its third section provides for conscientious objectors to be relieved from military service. It is helpful to note that ideological as well as religious freedom and the practice of religion as well as the freedom of conscience are safeguarded. Article 3 is also relevant to church-state issues. It provides that "All people are equal before the law" and "Nobody shall be prejudiced or favoured because of their sex, birth, race, language, national or social origin, faith, religion or political opinions." The basic principle of neutrality is seen in these provisions. The provisions of Articles 3 and 4 are supplemented by Article 140, which incorporates the basic religious freedom provisions of the old Weimar Constitution into the current Basic Law. Among the provisions thereby included in the Basic Law are a ban on the existence of a state church and, as we will see later, several provisions with implications for religious establishment issues.

The situation in the communist-controlled German Democratic Republic (GDR) after the Second World War was quite different. Although the outright opposition of the communist authorities waxed and waned during the forty years of their rule, even in the best of times East German parents were pressured not to baptize their children, church-going young people were often unable to obtain a college education, and active Christians were often denied government and business promotions. At the same time, an uneasy détente between the state and the churches emerged that was marked by pragmatism and accommodation by both sides. The state tolerated churches so long as they were not too political, while the churches acquiesced to the state so long as it gave them some measure of control over their internal affairs. Nevertheless, both the Protestant and the Catholic churches played a significant role in the demise of the East German state.[19] As one of the few institutions that was at all autonomous from the state, the churches provided the space and the opportunity to mobilize opposition to the regime. Numerically, the churches suffered during this time period. From 1961 to 1989 the West German Evangelical Church lost 15 percent of its membership, but the East German Evangelical Church lost over 50 percent. When East and West Germany reunited in 1989, nearly two-thirds of the East German population was without any church affiliation.[20] Thus the unification of Germany in 1990 meant that German society as a whole became more secular than it had been when West Germany existed as a separate state. Also, the church leadership from the old GDR had a more cautious, suspicious outlook toward the government than was the case for the West German church leadership. For the East Germans, over forty years under communist rule reinforced the lessons learned from Hitler's subversion and persecution of the churches.

FREE EXERCISE ISSUES

In Germany, the free exercise of religion is seen as a basic, fundamental right that has been interpreted broadly by the courts. The free exercise of religion trumps, so to speak, concerns over the establishment of religion. The fact that Germany's Constitutional Court has interpreted free exercise rights more broadly than has the U.S. Supreme Court can be seen in the Constitutional

Court's unambiguous holding that the free exercise of religion includes not only the right to believe, but also the right to act on one's beliefs. In a case dealing with a pastor who refused to take an oath when called to testify as a witness in a criminal trial, the Constitutional Court stated: "Religious freedom under Article 4(1) of the Basic Law . . . encompasses not only the (internal) freedom to believe or not to believe but also the individual's right to align his behavior with the precepts of his faith and to act in accordance with his internal convictions."[21] The court upheld the right of the clergyman to refuse to take the oath.

The strong emphasis on the free exercise of religion can also be seen in the tendency of the German courts to decide cases on free exercise grounds that in the United States would be seen as establishment of religion cases. This is due to the German courts' seeing religious freedom as having a positive as well as a negative aspect to it. In a 1979 decision finding the use of general prayers in the public schools constitutional, for example, the Constitutional Court based its decision on the concept of positive religious freedom: "To be sure, the state must balance this affirmative freedom to worship as expressed by permitting school prayer with the negative freedom of confession of other parents and pupils opposed to school prayer. Basically, [schools] may achieve this balance by guaranteeing that participation be voluntary for pupils and teachers."[22] The Constitutional Court saw allowing prayers in schools as making room for children who wanted to pray and disallowing such prayers as being a violation of their freedom to pray.

The prominence given to the free exercise of religion is rooted in the twin emphases on religious liberty as a positive right and the principle of neutrality. The Constitutional Court has frequently referred to neutrality as an important component of its free exercise decisions. Free exercise rights extend to people of all religious faiths and of none. In one of its decisions the Court declared: "The right to free exercise extends not only to Christian Churches but also to other religious creeds and ideological associations. This is a consequence of the ideological-religious neutrality to which the state is bound and the principle of equality with respect to churches and denominations."[23]

Religious freedom as a positive right is also important in free exercise protections since freedom is seen as including the opportunity to exercise that freedom. In an interview Gerhard Robbers of Trier University's law faculty made clear that positive religious freedom is fully in keeping with religious neutrality: "Positive religious freedom means that government actively creates room for religious behavior, for religious life. . . . This is not promoting religion. That would be against neutrality. It is just that there needs to be a basis, if people are religious, for them to practice their religion."[24] In the United States and France, neutrality is often seen as demanding a strict separation of church and state. In Germany, by contrast, neutrality requires the state actively to create space for the realization of a person's religious worldview. The Constitutional Court noted this distinction in a 2003 case when it wrote that the "duty of neutrality imposed on the state by the Basic Law was not a distancing neutrality of the nature of laicist non-identification with religions and ideologies, but a respectful neutrality. . . which imposed on the state a duty to safeguard a sphere of activity both for the individual and for religious and ideological communities."[25]

The expansive and strong concept of free exercise does not mean it is unlimited. The Constitutional Court and German commentators have frequently stressed that when the free exercise of religion infringes on human dignity or public health and safety a certain balancing or weighing process must take place. In one decision the Court wrote that the church-state provisions of the Constitution require the courts "to balance and weigh the different interests and values at stake in the relationship between the freedom of the churches and the limits imposed on this freedom."[26] Some of the principles discussed thus far can be illustrated by reference to a particularly dramatic free exercise case that came before the Constitutional Court. A married couple, both of whom were members of the Association of Evangelical Brotherhood, held to a religious faith that believed it was inappropriate to make use of blood transfusions to solve medical problems. The wife suffered complications in the birth of the couple's fourth child, and the doctors thought a blood transfusion was essential. The wife, with the support of her husband, refused the blood transfusion and died. The husband was subsequently prosecuted and convicted for failure to provide his wife with necessary assistance. On appeal, the Court overturned the decisions of the lower courts on the basis of the free exercise provision of Article 4 of the Basic Law.

In its decision, the Constitutional Court noted that in this case personal religious freedom was clashing with a person's obligation to obey the law, but the law must yield.

> The duty of all public authority to respect serious religious convictions, [as] contained in Article 4(1) of the Basic Law, must lead to a relaxation of criminal laws when an actual conflict between a generally accepted legal duty and a dictate of faith results in a spiritual crisis for the offender that, in view of the punishment labeling him a criminal, would represent an excessive social reaction violative of his human dignity.[27]

Thus the Court decided even a law that was not aimed at constricting certain religious practices, but was a law of general applicability that met certain legitimate, appropriate public purposes, was overruled by the free exercise protections of Article 4. This is a position that the U.S. Supreme Court, as seen in chapter 2, has largely abandoned over the past several decades.

This is not to suggest that there are no points of controversy on the scope of religious freedom in Germany. Probably the most contentious issue over the past decade has been the freedom of Muslim women who are teachers in government-run schools to wear the traditional Muslim headscarf or *hijab*.[28] In 2003, the Constitutional Court ruled that prohibiting teachers from wearing headscarves would require a specific law empowering authorities to make this prohibition. Over the next decade half of the German states, including four of the five most populous, passed laws banning public school teachers from wearing the *hijab*. The state laws differed on whether the prohibition applied only to headscarves or to all religious clothing. In 2015, however, the Court revisited the issue and reversed course. In this second headscarf decision, the Court ruled that a general ban on the headscarf is a violation of freedom of religion. This case demonstrates the strong German commitment to free exercise rights and its particular reading of religious neutrality. While the Court recognized that the state must be neutral among religions, it concluded that allowing teachers to wear religious symbols did not mean that the state was endorsing those symbols. As with other religious freedom cases, the Court defined neutrality in a way to encourage freedom of religion for all beliefs.[29]

STATE SUPPORT FOR CHURCHES

The concept of a church-state partnership has done much to frame questions related to various forms of state cooperation with or support for religion. A booklet put out by the Evangelical Church clearly makes this point: "State and Church, which consider themselves to bear responsibility for the same people in one and the same society, are thus obliged to strive for intelligent cooperation."[30] Robbers has expressed a similar outlook: "Once you accept that religion is something public, government should also have something to do with it, the community as such should have something to do with it."[31] Church and state—throne and altar—are seen as having different responsibilities, but they both have public responsibilities, they are both important for society as a whole and its welfare, and thus cooperation between the two works to the benefit of society as a whole. This is not to say that the state should favor any one religious group over another, or should even favor the religious over the nonreligious. One German observer after another whom we interviewed made this point. But it does mean that the state should cooperate with the church and should seek to create space or room for it to fulfill its responsibilities.

This perspective results in government supporting and helping the churches in a number of ways. One way it does this is by granting the three main, historical religious communities—Evangelical, Catholic, and Jewish—

status as a corporation under public law.[32] This status has both practical and philosophical repercussions. Practically speaking, it helps assure these religious bodies of their legal autonomy, gives them the right to levy taxes on their members, allows them to offer religious instruction in the public schools, and enables them to work with the government to appoint prison, hospital, and military chaplains. Just as important is the mind-set that it reveals, one that sees the major religious bodies as having a public, or societal, significance. Religion is seen as being more than a purely private concern. Public corporation status is granted by the state governments, and thus the religious bodies with that status vary somewhat from one state to another. The decision to grant PLC status is made at the state level based on certain requirements, including an assurance of permanence, the size of the organization, and an indication that the organization is not hostile to the constitutional order or fundamental rights. Twenty-eight religious communities in Germany have been granted this status in one or more of the states, including many of the free Protestant churches and as of 2006 in Berlin, under order of the Constitutional Court, the Jehovah's Witnesses.

Best known and most important of the privileges granted to churches that have qualified as public corporations is the church tax (*Kirchensteuer*).[33] Under the church tax all members of the Catholic and Evangelical churches and of Jewish congregations are assessed a fee set by the churches that amounts to about 8 or 9 percent of what is owed the federal government in income taxes. This money is added to one's income tax bill—in fact, it is deducted from one's paychecks by employers along with the income taxes that are owed—and is forwarded to the churches by the government, after the government deducts a small fee (about 4 percent of the money collected) for collection expenses. People who do not pay are subject to the same penalties and means of collection as are taxes that are owed.[34] In the case of Catholics and the Evangelical Protestant Church, membership comes automatically with baptism and follows that person the rest of his or her life. The only way a member can escape the church tax is to resign his or her membership in the church, which, due to the public corporation nature of the churches, involves a formal, legal process and an appearance before the civil authorities. In 2011 income from the church tax amounted to 9.2 billion euros (about $12 billion) to the Catholic and Evangelical churches, which amounted to about 70 percent of their total income. The money is used to finance both the pastoral activities of the churches and wide-ranging charitable and educational activities.[35]

The origins of the church tax system go back to the early nineteenth century, when the state confiscated church property in most areas of Germany, and as compensation, the civil governments agreed to make annual payments to the churches. In time these cash payments were transferred into the right of the churches to tax their members, with the civil authorities cooperating in collecting the taxes. The legal basis for the church tax is found in Article 137(6) of the Weimar Constitution, which has been incorporated into the current Constitution. It reads: "Religious communities that are public corporations shall be entitled to levy taxes in accordance with Land [state] law on the basis of the civil taxation." In a series of decisions the Constitutional Court has upheld the legality of the church tax system.

It is important to be clear on what the church tax is and is not. It is not simply a matter of general tax revenues being turned over to the churches. It is a cooperative venture by the churches and the civil authorities, in which the churches levy certain fees on their own members and the civil authorities collect those fees and are reimbursed for their expenses in doing so. Thus one can argue that the church tax does not violate the norm of governmental neutrality—funds are collected only from the church's own members with the amount set by the church, the government is reimbursed for its expenses, and one can avoid their payment by simply leaving the church. Jewish as well as Christian congregations are beneficiaries of it. On the other hand, one can argue that the principle of neutrality is being violated since the coercive power of the state is being put at the disposal of the churches, a service that is not available to most other organizations and religious groups who have not qualified for public corporation status. To an American observer the church tax system is highly unusual in at least two respects. First, the system establishes a formal contact between the church and state that would be unthinkable in the American context, and second, most Germans, who are at best sporadic in their church involvement, have nonetheless paid the church tax for decades with little complaint. More than anything else, the church tax demonstrated that the concept of church-state partnership had permeated German society and was not merely a theoretical or elite principle.

In recent years, however, more Germans are rethinking their passive support for the system. Over the past decade, more than two million Germans (Protestant and Catholic) have formally relinquished their membership in the church.[36] A Catholic journalist whom we interviewed and who has had his differences with the church hierarchy complained strongly that the church tax greatly strengthens the power of the central church hierarchy, since the money goes to the regional church offices, including the Vatican, and is distributed downward from there. Others have felt that the church tax has made the churches overly complacent. One person we interviewed compared the situation to one that is frequently alleged to occur when a developed nation gives too much money too freely to an underdeveloped nation: complacency, a strengthening of forces defending the status quo, and a sapping of initiative and creativity. When asked about his perception of the fairness of the church tax system, the pastor in the Protestant Old Reformed Church in Lower Saxony—which is a free Protestant church and not a part of the church tax system—replied that he was happy not to be a part of the church tax system, since he felt his church obtained more contributions by a voluntary system than the Evangelical and Catholic churches do by church taxes.[37]

As the system is premised on the assumption that the tax is paying for certain religious services, the Catholic Bishops' Conference in Germany issued an edict in 2012 that barred Catholics who had refused to pay the tax from receiving communion, making a confession, serving as a godparent, or holding any office in the church. The edict effectively made the refusal to pay the tax on par with the severest offenses against the church. Norbert Lüdecke, a professor of canon law at Bonn University, wryly noted that "refusing to pay the taxes is considered an offense only slightly less bad than denial that Jesus is the son of God."[38] Jochen Teuffel, a Protestant pastor from Bavaria, caused controversy when he administered communion to a woman who had refused to pay the tax. Far from being disaffected with the church, however, Teuffel indicated in an interview that the woman was an active member of his parish who contributed money directly to the congregation.[39]

It is difficult to say what the future holds for the church tax. On the one hand, more than 60 percent of Germans remain part of the system. The churches are generally seen as socially important institutions; they strengthen German society and ably provide many charitable and educational services. The church tax is one means by which one can relatively painlessly fulfill one's financial obligation to these all-important cultural, charitable, and educational institutions. Germany's largest party, the CDU/CSU, supports the current system, while many of the leaders of the second largest party, the SPD, want to expand it to include Muslims. On the other hand, the system is hardly sustainable if Germans continue to leave the churches at the current rate. Although they are minor parties, both the Greens and the Left have come out against the church tax. While it would be surprising given the history of partnership between church and state in Germany, and the mindset that it has established, it is also possible that a growing portion of the German population is adopting the voluntarist principles inherent in American religion.

The current system's most serious deficiency has been the inability of German states fully to recognize Muslim mosques and associations as a public corporation. There is but one German state, Hesse, which in 2013 formally recognized a single Muslim organization, Ahmadiyya Muslim Jamaat.[40] One factor that explains this discrepancy is that German Muslims lack a centralized organizational structure. Both the Catholic and Evangelical churches are hierarchical in nature and thus they have centralized councils and leaders who can deal with centralized governmental bureaucratic bodies and leaders. However, two scholars have noted that German "Muslims are divided less by that [federal] structure than by their differing ideologies and lack of a centralizing hierarchy." They go on to note the many ethnic divisions such as Turkish, Kurdish, and Arab, as well as others among German Muslims. These divisions "provide a formidable barrier to the cohesion of Islamic groups, preventing them from presenting a united front to the German state in their efforts to obtain the goals which they seek."[41] This has led to an impasse, with German authorities for the most part saying the Muslims need to organize themselves in such a way that they can qualify for public corporation status and other forms of cooperation with the government.

One problem with this argument is that the German state has shown greater flexibility in coordinating with Muslim organizations in other areas of public policy. In 2006, German policy makers, in consultation with Islamic leaders, formed the German Islam Conference (DIK). The purpose of the DIK was to provide a channel of communication between Muslim groups and the state, and thereby diminish the risk of Islamic extremism. While the DIK has come under fire for not being fully representative of the German Muslim community, in the past several years the group has successfully negotiated the sometimes contentious issue of mosque construction and Islamic burials in Germany, taken the lead in developing programs of civic education training programs for imams, and worked on the issue of Islamic education in public schools.[42] The government's willingness to organize a peak association representing the disparate streams of German Muslim groups suggests that it can and should do the same in the area of public corporation status for Muslims.

THE CHALLENGE OF MUSLIM INCORPORATION

The inability of the Muslim community to gain public corporation status on par with other religious communities is one of the more evident examples for how Muslims have not been fully integrated into German society. Islam is now the third-largest religion in Germany. As with the other European countries in our study, the Islamic population in Germany has grown rapidly over the past several decades, from an estimated 20,000 in 1950, to 1.7 million in 1980, and 4.2 million in 2010. The percentage of the German population that is Muslim has increased from under 1 percent of the population in 1950 to 5 percent in 2010. Over the next twenty years, the Muslim population is expected to grow to 5.5 million and to represent just over 7 percent of the total German population. Two-thirds of the Muslims in Germany are of Turkish origin, followed by smaller groups from Pakistan, countries of the former Yugoslavia, Arab countries, Iran, Afghanistan, and Syria.[43]

The Muslim story in Germany is inextricably bound to Turkey. In the midst of postwar labor shortages, Germany signed bilateral arrangements with Turkey, among other countries, that sent laborers to Germany as "guest workers." The policy assumed that these workers would stay for a period of time and then go back to Turkey, and were not seen as immigrants who had come to make Germany their home. Yet many of them did stay, their families joined them, and these migrant families had children. Germany lacked a strong tradition of immigration and of integrating new ethnic or religious groups into German society. Obtaining German citizenship was an arduous process, and children born to foreigners were not entitled to citizenship by birth. Changes to the law in 2000 made it easier for immigrants and their children to obtain citizenship, but it is still more difficult for German mi-grants to gain citizenship relative to those in France or England. Less than half of the Muslims living in Germany at present are citizens. [44]

There remains a mind-set among some Germans that sees Muslims as foreigners living in Germany, rather than as persons who have become Ger-mans and share in the economic and cultural life of Germany. More than half of the respondents (53 percent) in a 2011 Pew survey reported that there were too many immigrants in Germany and 54 percent said that immigration had a fairly or very negative effect on the country.[45] While Germany has been spared a particularly dramatic terrorist attack like that of Madrid, London, Paris, or Brussels, deep concerns remain at the mass level about Muslims. A 2014 poll commissioned by the Bertelsmann Foundation found that 40 per-cent of Germans agreed with the statement that "because of Muslims I felt like a stranger in my own country," nearly two-thirds (61 percent) said that Islam was incompatible with the western world, and 72 percent contended that Muslims living in Germany want to "remain distinct from society."[46]

And these surveys were conducted *before* Chancellor Merkel opened the German borders in 2015 to asylum seekers from war-torn Syria, Afghanistan, and Iraq. According to the German Federal Ministry, there were 1.1 million migrants, most of whom were Muslim, who came to Germany in 2015 and registered for asylum.[47] Merkel later rescinded the policy and helped nego-tiate a treaty that sent tens of thousands of refugees to Turkey. Nonetheless, popular opposition to immigration intensified in the aftermath of her wel-coming policy, including increasing support for the anti-immigrant party, Alternative for Germany (AfD). In its party manifesto, the AfD boldly an-nounces "Der Islam gehört nicht zu Deutschland" (Islam does not belong in Germany).[48] A 2015 poll found that 60 percent of the German public shared this view.[49] As the only party officially to oppose any Islamic immigration to Germany, it is perhaps not surprising that the AfD did particularly well in the 2016 state elections in Baden-Württemberg, Rhineland-Palatinate, and Saxo-ny-Anhalt, winning 15.1 percent, 12.6 percent, and 24.2 percent of the vote, respectively, in the three elections.[50]

Evidence about the success of the integration of German Muslims is mixed. On average, Muslims have lower educational attainment (particularly Turkish Muslims), higher levels of unemployment, and are more likely to live in highly segregated communities. They are also much more religious on average and have more socially conservative views on a series of moral issues. On the other hand, 90 percent of German Muslims view democracy as a desirable form of government, the same percentage reports that they have regular contact with people of other faiths outside of work hours, half are members of a German Association, and only 1 percent could be described as radical Islamists.[51] There is, of course, much debate about what causes these different outcomes. One study found that the media contributed an atmosphere of polarization among the German public by focusing primarily on the problems associated with migration and leaving out the positive aspects of immigrants' lives in Germany.[52] The situation facing the refugees is even more problematic. Efforts to incorporate this population into German society have been bumpy and uneven. The widely publicized 2016 New Year's Eve assaults in Cologne on women by groups of men described as "the general category of refugees" reinforced widespread concerns about refugee-related crime, even though official data from Germany's Federal Police Agency suggest that the influx of refugees into the country had a low impact on crime numbers overall. In such a highly charged context, it is not surprising that there were more than one thousand attacks on refugee shelters in 2015.[53]

As is true for much of Europe and the United States, there is growing debate about Islam in Germany. On the whole the German government appears to be making the sorts of adjustments it needs to assure that its Muslim population is able freely to practice its faith. Leaders of the main churches and the dominant political parties have been generally supportive of German Muslims. Popular opposition to Islam remains high in Germany, however, and recent years have seen a popular backlash against Muslims.

CHURCH, STATE, AND EDUCATION

The distinguishing mark of Germany regarding religion and education was, until recently, the domination of public education by confessional schools (that is, schools that were public in the sense of being financed, owned, and controlled by government, and confessional in the sense of being marked by either Catholic or Evangelical religious exercises and teachings). At the time of the writing of the Weimar Constitution there was a strong movement to develop secular schools that would be committed to teaching loyalty to the new liberal, political order, but the Catholic Center Party, with the help of conservative Protestants, was strong enough to force a compromise that made room for the continued existence of confessional schools.[54] As a result, confessional schools dominated public education in the interwar period.

There was a strong effort during the Nazi era to undermine the diversity of the school system in favor of schools uniformly supportive of the regime. As one Nazi leader bragged, "The curriculum of all categories in our schools has already been so far reformed in an anti-Christian and anti-Jewish spirit that the generation which is growing up will be protected from the black [that is, clerical] swindle."[55] Following World War II the occupying powers generally favored doing away with confessional schools in favor of unified, secular schools.[56] Again, this was resisted by church authorities, especially by the Catholic Church. In the western zone, therefore, the occupying authorities allowed local areas to decide whether they wished interdenominational schools or confessional schools. The 1949 Basic Law placed the responsibility for education with the state governments, not the national government. Initially, most Catholic areas opted for confessional schools and most Protestant areas for interdenominational schools. As recently as 1967, 40 percent of all schools in Germany were public Catholic schools, 17 percent were public Evangelical schools, 40 percent were interdenominational (or nonconfessional, sometimes referred to as "Christian") public schools, and 3 percent were private schools.[57]

But things have changed. Protestants had for some time not seen the need for separate confessional schools and many Catholic areas opted for interdenominational Christian schools. (The terminology here is confusing for Americans, since even the interdenominational or "Christian" schools are public schools.) In 1968, for example, Bavaria—a heavily Catholic area—voted by referendum to do away with Catholic schools in favor of interdenominational Christian schools. The religious nature of interdenominational schools is largely confined to prayers, separate voluntary classes in the religion of one's choice, and a general emphasis on the historical or cultural role of religion in German society. At present, there are three types of schools in Germany: governmental schools, governmental religious schools, and private religious schools.

The legal, constitutional basis for religion in public education—practices that would be clearly unconstitutional in the United States under current Supreme Court interpretations—is found in subsections 2 through 4 of Article 7 of the Basic Law:

> 2. Parents and guardians have the right to decide whether children receive religious instruction.
> 3. Religious instruction shall form part of the curriculum in state schools except non-denominational schools. Without prejudice to the state's right of supervision, religious instruction shall be given in accordance with the doctrine of the religious community concerned. Teachers may not be obligated to give religious instruction against their will.
> 4. The right to establish private schools shall be guaranteed. Private schools as alternatives to state schools shall require the approval of the state and be subject to Land [state] legislation.

A 1975 case decided by the Constitutional Court dealt directly with the issue of religious instruction in public schools. The state of Baden-Württemberg had decided in 1967 to establish interdenominational Christian schools. Some nonreligious parents objected to the religious education their children were receiving. The Court ruled in favor of the interdenominational school. Its reasoning in doing so reveals much about the German approach to this issue and how it differs from the American one. The Court first noted that "the complainants' request to keep the education of their children free from all religious influences . . . must inevitably conflict with the desire of other citizens to afford their children a religious education."[58] It then went on to make a crucial observation that the U.S. Supreme Court has never accepted: "The elimination of all ideological and religious references would not neutralize the existing ideological tensions and conflicts, but would disadvantage parents who desire a Christian education for their children and would result in compelling them to send their children to a lay school that would roughly correspond with the complainants' wishes."[59] The key point made by the Court is that a school stripped of all religious elements does not lie in a zone of neutrality between the religious and the secular, but is implicitly secular in nature. In such a school the children of the nonreligious parents would receive the exact sort of education their parents desire; the children of religious parents would not. Given this fact and the resulting necessity for compromise, the Court ruled that the state should be given the latitude to make the policy decision that it had.

Article 7(3) requires the government to assure the presence of religious instruction in state-run schools: "Religious instruction shall form part of the curriculum in state schools." The operative word here is "shall," not "may." Also important is the fact that religious instruction is to be a part of the standard curriculum, not an extracurricular or ancillary course of study. It is, however, to be voluntary. For children up to the age of fourteen, parents may choose the nature of the religious instruction they are to receive or decide they are to receive no religious instruction at all. At the age of fourteen, the decision rests with the students, not their parents. Thus the religious instruction made available in most German schools is similar to the in-school released time programs the U.S. Supreme Court rejected as violating the First Amendment in a 1948 decision.[60]

It is also important to note that the religious bodies themselves, not the public school authorities, control the content of the religious courses of study. Article 7(3) ("[R]eligious instruction shall be given in accordance with the doctrine of the religious community concerned") has been interpreted to mean that the religious authorities, not the schools, determine what is taught. The state neither assigns children to the religious instruction classes nor controls their content. In practice these classes are for two or three hours a week, and are taught by clergy specially appointed to this role or by regular public school teachers (although under Article 7(3) of the Constitution no teacher can be forced to teach a class in religion against his or her will).

Classes have always been available to members of the historically dominant Catholic or Evangelical churches, and most states have similarly accommodated the small but growing Jewish community. Until very recently, classes in Islam were not offered to the nine hundred thousand Muslim students enrolled in German schools. As with the debate on granting corporation status to Muslims, it was often said that the absence of a centralized, hierarchical organization among German Muslims made it hard for state officials to incorporate Muslims into the existing system. M. A. H. Hobohm, deputy chairman of the Central Council of Muslims in Germany and managing director of the King Fahd Academy in Bonn, made this point to us in an interview several years ago: "Very often we have to face a situation where the German authorities tell us, 'We do not know with whom to talk in such matters because there are so many Islamic communities and even Islamic faith organizations.' They either do not really understand that in Islam there is no hierarchical order, no organization with a center, or they don't want to understand it. Sometimes I have the feeling we have stated this to them so often that if they really don't understand it, it is because they lack the will to understand it."[61]

In recent years, however, there has been a dramatic shift in public policy. Starting in 2010 in the state of North Rhine Westphalia, where one-third of Germany's Muslims live, 150 schools offered Islamic studies classes to thirteen thousand children in grades 1 through 10.[62] Four years later, Islamic instruction was available in all the former Western German states, though none of the eastern ones, where relatively few Muslims live. After decades of foot-dragging by public officials, Islamic instruction in the schools is now on the same footing as Catholic and Protestant religious education in much of the country. The most important cause for this shift has been the realization among German authorities that Islamic religious instruction can be a way to counter radical teaching and to encourage the successful integration of the nation's growing Muslim minority into the values of the larger society. Working with Islamic leaders, educational officials have designed curriculums that emphasize Islamic teachings on tolerance and acceptance of differences.[63] The contrast with the United States is once again instructive. In the United States, religious instruction in public schools is seen as inherently divisive, while Germany has come to the conclusion that religious instruction can be a means of social integration.

In regard to religious exercises in the public schools, most interdenominational schools have prayers at the beginning of the school day and sometimes at the end. As Kommers has written, "The predominant German view is that such practices constitute an important aspect of religious liberty so long as freedom of choice prevails."[64] As seen earlier, in 1979 the Constitutional

Court considered the question of the constitutionality of such prayers and ruled in favor of their constitutionality based on the positive right of religious parents to have their children pray in school, as long as the voluntary nature of the prayers is maintained.

One of the church-state issues that stirred up the most controversy in Germany in recent years concerned a Bavarian law that required a crucifix to be displayed in every public school classroom. In 1995 the Constitutional Court ruled that if any student objected to having a crucifix in the classroom, it would have to be removed. At the heart of its decision was the Court's conclusion that "freedom of faith as guaranteed by Article 4(1) of the Basic Law requires the state to remain neutral in matters of faith and religion."[65] The Court then went on to weigh the positive freedom of religious parents to have a religious symbol such as a cross present in their children's classrooms against the negative freedom of nonreligious or non-Christian parents to have their children's classrooms free of a Christian religious symbol. It concluded: "Parents and pupils who adhere to the Christian faith cannot justify the display of the cross by invoking their positive freedom of religious liberty. All parents and pupils are equally entitled to the positive freedom of faith, not just Christian parents and pupils."[66]

This decision unleashed a storm of criticism throughout Germany. The then chancellor, Helmut Kohl, condemned it. Newspapers and radio call-in shows debated it, with the clear preponderance of opinion indicating opposition to it. In fact, the criticism grew so intense and the calls for ignoring the Court's decision so frequent that there were fears for the constitutional order and the legitimacy of the Court. Justice Dieter Grimm, one of the Constitutional Court justices who had been in the majority, felt compelled to write a major statement in which he argued for the rule of law and called for obedience to the Court's decision, even by those who strongly disagree with it.[67] The furor began to die down only when the Court made clear it had not ruled that all crucifixes in Bavarian classrooms must come down, but only that they must come down if students in a particular classroom register a complaint. The vast majority stay on the classroom walls.

This decision and the reactions to it illustrate several key points. First, to an American observer—coming from a political system where the posting of the Ten Commandments in classrooms and the presence of a cross in a city's seal have been held unconstitutional—it is surprising that the question of crucifixes in public school classrooms is even being debated. That this issue is part of church-state debate in Germany today illustrates the extent to which church and state are in a cooperative relationship. The uproar the decision created in the nation reveals the strong support that still exists for this relationship. Second, this case illustrates the broad acceptance of the concepts of neutrality and positive religious freedom. The reasoning of both the majority and dissenting justices revolved around these concepts. They were accepted by both sides in this case; they differed only on how they were to be applied in this instance. Both sides agreed the state should be neutral on matters of religion, neither favoring nor discriminating against any religious or ideological perspective, and in interpreting this neutrality, both agreed that a genuine neutrality sometimes requires the state to take certain positive steps in order to create the possibility or the space people of faith need to live their faith.

There are—compared to most of the other countries studied in this book—few private religious schools in Germany. Only about 5 percent of students attend private religious schools, a lower percentage than in Australia, Britain, the Netherlands, and the United States, although the demand for those schools is growing. The relatively small size of this sector no doubt reflects the German tradition of incorporating religious elements into the public schools. Private schools receive most of their current expenses—but not their capital expenses—from public funds, although the exact amount they receive can vary from 75 to 90 percent of their costs.[68] The vast majority of nongovernmental religious schools in Germany are Catholic or Protestant. There are, however nine Jewish primary schools and one Muslim school in Berlin that have been formally recognized and receive state funding.[69]

The Constitution assures in Article 7(4) the right to establish private schools, but they must be approved by the state government, and obtaining that approval can be a difficult, time-consuming process. The basic requirement for approval is a school's ability to demonstrate that it is equivalent to the public schools in terms of educational quality and that it does not discriminate in its acceptance of pupils on the basis of the economic means of their parents. But once such standards have been met, the Constitutional Court ruled in 1987, private schools must receive public funding. The Court did so largely on the basis that educational freedom requires that parents be able to choose for their children the school with the religious or ideological worldview with which they are in agreement. Once religiously based private schools receive official state recognition, they find few, if any, restrictions placed on their ability to integrate religious elements into their programs. They are free, for example, to appoint teachers on the basis of their church membership.[70] The key requirements are that they must meet the state-established curriculum standards and their students must be able to do well in the comprehensive exams that are an integral part of the German educational system. For example, nongovernmental religious schools may not omit the teaching of evolution, and students in those schools cannot opt out of required swimming lessons for religious reasons.[71]

The right to establish a private school does not, however, include a right to home schooling, which is illegal in Germany. The German courts have consistently ruled that students may be required to attend public schools or approved private schools, and German families who choose to home school their children anyway face legal action.[72] The difference with the United

States, where home schooling has expanded dramatically in recent decades, is quite stark and reflects very different perspectives about the rights and obligations of parents and of the government. In the United States, preference is given to the right of parents to educate their children, while in Germany the emphasis is put on the government's obligation to provide a good education for children.

One final note on private church-related education involves the widespread church-sponsored kindergartens. German children typically start school at the age of six, and the regular school system does not contain kindergartens as in the United States. A majority of families send their children from three to five years of age to kindergartens, which are sponsored by churches, other religious bodies, or independent societies created for that purpose. The expenses are covered by state and municipal funds, parental payments, and church or society funds.[73] There are no state-imposed limits on prayers, Bible stories, or other religious elements in the kindergarten programs. In addition to the many Protestant and Catholic kindergartens around the country, there are also a handful of Jewish and Islamic ones.

In summary, based on the constitutionally enshrined concept of parental control over the religious upbringing of one's children, the norm of governmental neutrality in matters of religion, and the concept of positive religious freedom, Germany allows various forms of religion into its public schools as long as the principle of voluntary participation is respected. It also permits widespread public financial support for religious schools without interference with their religious missions, as long as the educational quality of the schools—as determined by the state governments—is assured. The sizable Muslim minority in Germany has been included in the system of public funding of private religious schools at least in Berlin, and they have finally been incorporated into the system of religious instruction in the public schools.

CHURCH, STATE, AND NONPROFIT SERVICE ORGANIZATIONS

Germany has a long history of public-private partnerships between the state and nonprofit organizations, or what some have described as corporatism or neocorporatism.[74] The German government relies extensively on private nonprofit organizations to deliver most of the social services that are the hallmark of the German welfare state. The Catholic-inspired principle of subsidiarity, which we introduced in our discussions of France and the Netherlands, also plays a crucial role here.

> The doctrine of subsidiarity essentially holds that the responsibility for caring
> for individuals' needs should always be vested in the units of social life closest
> to the individual—the family, the parish, the community, the voluntary associ-

ation—and that larger, or higher level, units should be enlisted only when a problem clearly exceeds the capabilities of these primary units. . . . What is more, the doctrine holds that the higher units have an obligation not only to avoid usurping the position of the lower units, but to help the lower units perform their role.[75]

This concept has been explicitly incorporated into several laws that require the government not to take over and provide social services directly if there are private social service agencies able and willing to provide them. Section 4 of the Social Assistance Act states that "if assistance in individual cases is ensured by free welfare associations, the [public] social assistance bodies shall refrain from implementing their own measures."[76] The Youth Welfare Act contains the provision: "In so far as suitable establishments and arrangements provided by the free youth assistance associations are available or can be extended or provided, the [public] Youth Welfare Office shall not offer such establishments and arrangements on its own."[77] The practice of relying extensively on nonprofit private associations for the provision of social services has a historical as well as theoretical basis. A host of associations emerged in Germany in the nineteenth century and "became the elementary form of political opposition against the state; after the failed revolution of 1848, they also became a surrogate for the democracy that had not been achieved within the state order itself."[78] As a result, associations playing an intermediate role between the individual and the government gained a certain legitimacy. Germany's experience under the Nazis worked to reinforce this legitimacy, with private associations coming to be seen as a way to avoid a dangerous, overcentralized, dominant government.

There are six main associations of social service and health care organizations that are referred to as the free welfare associations. They carry out most of these privately delivered services. These associations are Diakonisches Werk, or Diakonie (the Evangelical Church's federation of social service and health agencies), Caritas (the Catholic counterpart to Diakonisches Werk), the Central Welfare Association for Jews in Germany (Zentralwohlfahrsstelle der Juden in Deutschland), the Workers' Welfare Association (Arbeiterwohlfahrt—an association of secular social agencies with ties to the Social Democratic Party), the German Equity Welfare Association (Deutscher Paritätischer Wohlfahrtsverband—an association of secular agencies not aligned with any political party), and the Red Cross (Deutsches Rotes Kreuz). The first three of these free welfare associations are all religious in nature. Grounding its mission on a "Christian view of mankind," for example, Diakonie strives to "fashion ourselves after God's unconditional love as embodied by Jesus Christ."[79]

With 559,000 and 465,000 full- and part-time employees, respectively, Caritas and Diakonisches Werk (Diakonie) are by far the largest among the free welfare associations. Diakonie operates 30,000 inpatient and outpatient care centers, from nursing homes and hospitals to community outreach and welfare centers, provides 165,431 places in elderly care, and 151,646 places in disabled care services. There are nearly 25,000 Caritas centers and institutions in Germany that offer support services for children and families, residential homes for the homeless and those with substance abuse, and immigration and asylum centers. In addition, Caritas runs nearly one-quarter of all of Germany's hospitals. Together, more than 1.2 million people volunteer annually with one of these two large organizations.[80]

The nonprofit sector is heavily financed by the government. Overall, 64 percent of the funds spent by the German nonprofit sector come from the government, with most of the remaining funds coming from fees charged for services, private grants, and fundraising.[81] The religious associations share fully in the receipt of public funds. Just under half (46 percent) of Caritas's 144 million euros ($165 million) budget in 2014 came from the government.[82] Through the Central Welfare Association for Jews in Germany the small Jewish community shares in the receipt of public funds, especially for the resettlement of Jewish immigrants from eastern European countries, Holocaust survivors' care, and social welfare for Jewish elderly.[83]

Robbers summarizes the difference between the American and German approaches to government funding of faith-based social service organizations: "it is generally acknowledged that, given a comprehensive support by the State of social activities, the religious communities may not be excluded from such support and so discriminated against."[84] As seen in chapter 2, in the United States President George W. Bush's faith-based initiative—which aimed to make government funds available to religiously based service organizations on the same basis as secular ones—was met by a storm of criticism on the basis that it would violate church-state separation. In Germany *not* to fund faith-based organizations while funding their secular counterparts is viewed as discriminating against the religious organizations.

There are a few nonprofit Muslim service organizations.[85] Many Muslims look to their local mosque and informal mosque-based services when in need. Some Muslim social service organizations have received funding from individual state and local governments, but they are generally not included in the cooperative funding schemes of the federal government. In theory they are eligible for such funding, but their small numbers and the lack of an organized, centralized push for such funds have thus far prevented them from sharing in national funding schemes as do the two large, well-established Christian communities and the Jewish community. We are again back to the dilemma posed by the organizational structure of the Muslims—or, better, the lack of a centralized organizational structure—combined with the German inability or unwillingness to develop ways to integrate splintered Muslim communities into its existing church-state practices.

Anheier and Seibel have made the additional important point that the nonprofit-government relationship goes beyond financial support by the government. "[A]s a result of both the principle of subsidiarity and the principle of self-governance, nonprofit organizations tend to be relatively well-integrated into the policy making function of government. In many areas of legislation, public authorities are required to consult nonprofit organizations in matters of economic, social and cultural policy."[86] There indeed is a non-profit-government partnership in providing important social and health services, a partnership that includes the major religiously based organizations as full partners.

The concept of church autonomy is important for understanding the degree of freedom religious nonprofit service organizations have in pursuing their religious missions, even when working as partners with the government in providing services. The concept of church autonomy includes religious service organizations. Robbers has made this point clearly:

> A church's right of self-determination is not restricted to a narrowly-drawn field of specifically "ecclesiastical" activities. The idea of freedom of religious practice extends to preserve the right of self-determination in other areas that are also based or founded upon religious objectives, such as the running of hospitals, kindergartens, retirement homes, private schools and universities. [87]

In an interview Robbers reemphasized this point: "Caritas, Diakonisches Werk, private schools, and kindergartens are a part of the church. They are ministries for the performance of persons' faith, for following Christ's example. They are the church being the church as much as saying prayers or lighting candles in a church. Therefore, the principle of self-determination applies to these ministries as fully as it does to the churches themselves."[88]

Article 137(3) of the Weimar Constitution, which was incorporated into Germany's current Constitution as Article 140, reads in part: "Every religious community shall regulate and administer its affairs independently within the limits of the law valid for all." This provision—when combined with the previously made point that religiously based service organizations are considered an integral part of the church—has resulted in general agreement on the right of nonprofit service organizations to make hiring decisions on the basis of religion, an issue that we saw in chapter 2 is under sharp debate in the United States. In the 1983 *Catholic Hospital Abortion Case* a Catholic hospital had dismissed a doctor after he had publicly stated he opposed the church's teaching on abortion. The Constitutional Court held that the hospital was an "affair" of the church and thus under church regulation. The Court argued that, given the fact that Catholic canon law views abortion as the killing of innocent human life, to require the church to retain on staff a doctor who rejects this teaching would undermine the church's religious mission as it has defined it.

The Federal Court reaffirmed this holding in a landmark 2014 case that once again dealt with an employee at a Catholic hospital.[89] In that case, a medical superintendent had been dismissed from his position following his civil divorce and remarriage, neither of which were recognized by the Church. The court upheld the right of churches and other religious institutions to require their employees to abide by their religious and moral ethos. In doing so, the court cited Article 4, sections 1 and 2 of the Basic Law that protects religious freedom, and Article 140 that guarantees the right of religious communities to regulate their internal affairs. The State was obliged to remain neutral, the court concluded, and respect the Church's right to enforce its norms. While pleased that the court had strengthened the religious freedom of the churches in its decision, the German bishops nonetheless voted the next year to adjust Church labor law so that employees would no longer automatically lose their jobs for remarrying without an annulment or for forming gay unions.[90] The principle of institutional autonomy remained important for the bishops, but they came to the reasonable conclusion that they had little interest in firing the scores of workers at Catholic institutions who were violating some church norm.

The contrast between Germany and the United States is again quite interesting. The U.S. Supreme Court has tended to see religiously based social service agencies as engaged in both religious and secular activities and to extend free exercise rights only to their religious activities. Religious freedom only goes so far, leaving the courts in the unenviable position of having always to find the balance between the religious rights of institutions and the rights of employees to equal protection. The German Constitutional Court, by contrast, has a more expansive understanding of religious freedom. The charitable activities of churches and other religious organizations, along with their hiring decisions, are interpreted within the scope of the religious freedom language of the Basic Law.

There are still frequent struggles between the various religiously based service organizations and government regulators. But as seen in the Netherlands in chapter 4, most of the struggles revolve around the issue of the cutback of government funds in a time of retrenchment and issues related to professional performance standards, not concerns of religion being integrated into the programs financed by the government. Our interviewees did not run into problems with governmental officials over such questions as requiring agency employees to be members of the sponsoring church and to meet expected behavior standards, having devotional exercises as a part of their programs, and having salaried chaplains or pastors conducting religious services. One official in the central office of the Evangelical Church told us the big problem was not government interference, but finding enough young people with a deep religious life who wished to work for church social agencies.

In short, Germany has an extensive system of public funding of a wide variety of religiously based social service and health care associations. The strong German commitment to providing basic services, not through centralized bureaucracies but through private nonprofit associations, and its commitment to religious pluralism implied by the principles of neutrality and positive religious freedom, come together to support this system. The Evangelical and Catholic churches, with their large, well-established social and health ministries, share fully in this partnership, as does the Jewish community. But the few Muslim nonprofit service organizations that there are have largely not been incorporated into this funding scheme.

CONCLUDING OBSERVATIONS

Germany does not have a formally established church as does England, yet the underlying mind-set that supports the concept of a church-state partnership has some similarities to England's partial establishment. Leopold Turowski, a Catholic Church representative, has written that "religious and secular responsibilities are essentially aspects of a single common good, meant to fulfill the needs of one and the same human person in unified societal existence."[91] Turowski gives expression to a concept at the heart of the German church-state perspective. Church and state—throne and altar—are seen as twin pillars for a strong, prosperous German society. Throne and altar are in a partnership. This means that most Germans see religion as having an important public role to play as a unifying, inspiring, educating, critiquing force in society.

As a result Germany supports a number of practices in which the state cooperates with, assists, and makes room for religion, such as the church tax and certain religious elements in public schools. The formal ties between church and state such as those found in England are not present in Germany, but there are various informal means of church-state cooperation and support for consensual religious beliefs and practices, as there are in England. To the extent this constitutes an informal establishment, it is a multiple establishment, in that the cooperation and support extend to Protestants and Catholics alike and to smaller religious groups to some extent.

But this is not the full story. German church-state practice also has some important parallels with the principled pluralism of the Netherlands and its embrace of the pluralist church-state model. Germany places a strong emphasis on church autonomy and explicitly articulates principles such as state neutrality on matters of religion and freedom of religion as a positive right. These principles are similar to the principles of pluralism espoused by the

Dutch and modify and qualify the German commitment to a church-state partnership. Germans see the partnership concept and the neutrality, autonomy, and positive religious freedom principles as complementing each other in such a way as to lead to greater religious freedom for all. Kommers has written that "the accommodationist stance of German constitutional law is often defended as a means of maintaining pluralism and diversity in the face of powerful secularizing trends toward social uniformity and moral rootlessness."[92] What many American observers would see as leftover elements of religious establishment that are subversive of religious pluralism and diversity, most Germans would insist are essential to religious pluralism and diversity.

The key to understanding these divergent perspectives is that the typical German observer has a concept of religious freedom as possessing both positive and negative aspects, while Americans tend to see religious freedom largely as a negative freedom. Rudolf Weth, the director of a federation of Evangelical social agencies in Neukirchen, referred, in an interview with us, to "positive religious neutrality."[93] This "positive religious neutrality" conceives of the state as not advancing any religious or philosophical viewpoint—it must be neutral. There was enough of that, he indicated, in the Nazi era and in the GDR. In that sense there is a separation of church and state. But, he argued, the state must also have a holistic view of human beings. People are religious, ideological beings. The state should not favor any one religion or ideology, but it must make room for the religious, ideological nature of humankind.

Under this perspective the state will be truly neutral only if it sometimes takes certain positive steps in order to make room for or to accommodate those who wish to live a religious life. Recall the Constitutional Court decision in the *Interdenominational School Case* that made the telling argument that "elimination of all ideological and religious references would not neutralize the existing ideological tensions and conflicts, but would disadvantage parents who desire a Christian education for their children."[94] A school that is made religiously "neutral" by removing all references to religion is neutral among contending religious traditions, but it is not neutral between religious and secular perspectives. Rather, it implicitly promotes a general secular "uniformity and moral rootlessness." German law—in contrast to American law—has recognized and sought to accommodate this perspective in its church-state stances.

There is a logic and an appeal to the German mind-set on church and state and especially to the principles of neutrality and positive religious freedom that underlie them. Germany is clearly and appropriately committed to religious freedom and pluralism. It has largely been successful in giving due recognition to the importance of religion in the life of the nation and in the lives of many of its citizens, and at the same time has assured the freedom of those without religious faith. It has an expansive concept of the free exercise of religion. Its efforts to integrate both religion and secular ideologies into the public schools and to fund both religiously and secularly based social service agencies and private schools are fully in keeping with religious pluralism and state religious neutrality. One can always question whether in specific instances—such as consensual prayers and crucifixes in the public schools—the German Constitutional Court has reached the conclusion most in keeping with religious neutrality and freedom for all. But the German emphasis on an expansive concept of the free exercise of religion, the commitment to governmental neutrality on matters of religion, and the concept of positive religious rights have led the German courts—at the very least—to frame issues such as these appropriately and to ask the right questions.

All this is not to say that the German approach to church-state questions is without challenges. As we noted earlier, an increasing number of Germans are opting out of the church tax system, which puts financial pressure on the current arrangement. This could be a short-term blip, or it could be the leading edge of a much larger secularization process that will lead to diminished public support for the close partnership between church and state and the various public works done by religious organizations in Germany. We do not want to oversell this point, however. A clear majority of Germans remain a part of the church tax system, and institutions once established are quite durable over time. There is, in short, every reason to conclude that while the German model of partnership and autonomy will adapt to new circumstances, it is not likely fundamentally to change.

This adaptation is particularly important in regard to the more than four million Muslims who have not been fully incorporated into the current arrangement. The German system evolved in a setting where there essentially were two religious bodies—the Catholic and Evangelical—and both of these thoroughly institutionalized, with regional and central administrative bodies. Thus the German church-state system assumed that there would be religious bodies that the government can recognize, accommodate, and negotiate with. German Muslims, however, are divided along ethnic, theological, and political lines, and they lack a unified, centralized religious organization. As related earlier, the person who is probably the foremost church-state German scholar said to us in an interview while describing the challenges in forging a cooperative relationship between the government and the Muslims that for there to be a partnership there must be a partner. In recent years, however, German officials have shown greater willingness to create such a partner. Working with Muslim leaders, the government established the German Islam Conference in 2006 to be a representative body with whom the government could negotiate. While far from perfect, the conference is nonetheless an example for how the German system can adapt to changing circumstances and is a step in the direction toward more equal treatment for all religious groups.

This effort has been made more urgent by recent Islamist terrorist attacks in Europe, which have aroused fears and suspicions on both sides, and by the influx of asylum seekers, most of whom are Muslim. By various measures, German Muslims are disadvantaged, and as noted, a sizable percentage of the German population seems hesitant to work at integrating Muslims into German society. There needs to be compromise and flexibility on the part of the civil authorities, the general public, as well as the Muslim population and its leaders. This remains the major challenge to the German church-state system that seeks a church-state partnership, while maintaining the autonomy of the religious bodies.

But the challenge of integrating the Muslim minority into the present church-state system ought not to deflect from the fact that Germany—building on the basic principles of neutrality, church autonomy, and positive religious rights and a strong emphasis on free exercise rights—has largely dealt successfully with issues of religious pluralism. It has done so while also paying deference to the traditional German sense of religion as a public force in society. It does not relegate religion to the private sphere as Enlightenment liberalism would do, but has created a public role, a public space for religion, and at the same time it allows for a plurality of religious and secular belief systems. This is what the liberal Enlightenment tradition in the United States has said cannot be done, which makes the fact that Germany has been largely successful in doing so all the more impressive.

NOTES

1. Rachael Pells, "German Bishop Calls for Islam to Be Taught in All State Schools," *Independent* (May 29, 2016). Available at http://www.independent.co.uk/news/world/europe/german-bishop-calls-for-islam-to-be-taught-in-all-state-schools-a7054906.html.

2. Gerhard Robbers, "State and Church in Germany," in Gerhard Robbers, ed., *State and Church in the European Union*, 2nd ed. (Baden-Baden, Germany: Nomos Verlagsgesellschaft, 2005), 80.

3. Donald P. Kommers, *The Constitutional Jurisprudence of the Federal Republic of Germany*, 3rd ed. (Durham, N.C.: Duke University Press, 2012), 461.

4. David P. Conradt and Eric Langenbacher, *The German Polity*, 10th ed. (Lanham, Md.: Rowman & Littlefield, 2013), chap. 4.

5. The terminology used to refer to the Protestant Church in Germany can be confusing to Americans. The *Evangelische Kirche in Deutschland* (EKD) is usually translated as the Evangelical Church, and we follow this customary practice in this book. But this term ought not to be confused with the way in which "evangelical" is often used the in American and British contexts to refer to the more theologically conservative, biblically oriented wing of Protestantism.

6. "The Evangelical Church in Germany: Facts and Figures," https://www.ekd.de/english/download/facts_and_figures_2016.pdf; "The Future of the Global Muslim Population," Pew Research Center for Religion and Public Life, http://www.pewforum.org/2011/01/27/the-future-of-the-global-muslim-population/.

7. World Values Survey Wave 6 2010–2014 OFFICIAL AGGREGATE v.20150418. World Values Survey Association (http://www.worldvaluessurvey.org). Aggregate File Producer: Asep/JDS, Madrid, Spain; Christof Wolf, "How Secularized Is Germany? Cohort and Comparative Perspectives," *Social Compass* 55, 2 (2008), 111–26.

8. "Freedom and Security: Principles for Germany. Party Manifesto of the Christian Democratic Union of Germany (CDU)," http://www.kas.de/wf/doc/kas_13533-544-2-30.pdf? 110509134343.

9. On the Constitutional Court see Kommers, *The Constitutional Jurisprudence of the Federal Republic of Germany*, 3–29, and Donald P. Kommers, *The Federal Constitutional Court* (Washington, D.C.: Institute for Contemporary German Studies, 1994).

10. For good overviews of this period, see Stathis N. Kalyvas, *The Rise of Christian Democracy in Europe* (Ithaca, N.Y.: Cornell University Press, 1996); and Andrew C. Gould, *Origins of Liberal Dominance: State, Church, and Party in Nineteenth Century Europe* (Ann Arbor: University of Michigan Press, 1999).

11. John S. Conway, "The Political Role of German Protestantism, 1870–1990," *Journal of Church and State* 34 (1992), 820. Also see Daniel R. Borg, "German National Protestantism as a Civil Religion," in Menachem Mor, ed., *International Perspectives on Church and State* (Omaha: Creighton University Press, 1993), 255–67.

12. Article 136. The outlawing of a state church was found in Article 137.

13. Frederic Spotts, *The Churches and Politics in Germany* (Middletown, Conn.: Wesleyan University Press, 1973), 9.

14. Spotts, *The Churches and Politics in Germany*, 9.

15. Quoted in Spotts, *The Churches and Politics in Germany*, 11.

16. Carolyn M. Warner, *Confessions of an Interest Group: The Catholic Church and Political Parties in Europe* (Princeton, N.J.: Princeton University Press, 2000), chap. 9; Brent F. Nelsen and James L. Guth, *Religion and the Struggle for European Union* (Washington, D.C.: Georgetown University Press, 2015).

17. The then West German authorities insisted on calling the Constitution a "Basic Law" (*Grundgesetz*), since it was seen as being of a provisional nature because of the Soviet zone (soon to become the German Democratic Republic, or East Germany) not being included in the government that was being created. In this book we will use Basic Law and Constitution interchangeably, since the Basic Law functions exactly as a Constitution.

18. All quotations from the Basic Law are taken from the English translation published by the Press and Information Office of the Federal Republic of Germany (1994).

19. Bernd Schaefer, *The East German State and the Catholic Church: 1945–1989*, trans. Jonathan Skolnik and Patricia C. Sutcliffe (New York and Oxford: Bergbahn Press, 2010); Wendy R. Tyndale, *Protestants in Communist East Germany: In the Storm of the World* (Burlington, Vt.: Ashgate, 2010).

20. Karl Cordell, "The Role of the Evangelical Church in the GDR," *Government and Opposition* 25 (1990), 48–59; Martin Elf and Sigrid Rossteutscher, "Stability or Decline? Class, Religion and the Vote in Germany," *German Politics* 20 (2011), 111–31.

21. *Religious Oath Case* (1972), 33 BVerfGE 23. Reprinted and translated in Kommers, *The Constitutional Jurisprudence of the Federal Republic of Germany*, 454.

22. *School Prayer Case* (1979), 52 BVerfGE 223. Reprinted and translated in Kommers, *The Constitutional Jurisprudence of the Federal Republic of Germany*, 464–65.

23. *Rumpelkammer Case* (1968), 24 BVerfGE 236. Reprinted and translated in Kommers, *The Constitutional Jurisprudence of the Federal Republic of Germany*, 446.

24. Interview with Gerhard Robbers (February 23, 1996).

25. *Headscarf Ruling* (2003), BVerfG, 2 BvR, 10. Available in translation at http://www.bundesverfassungsgericht.de/SharedDocs/Entscheidungen/EN/2003/09/rs20030924_2bvr143602en.html.

26. Quoted in Kommers, *The Constitutional Jurisprudence of the Federal Republic of Germany*, 494–95. The quotation is from the *Catholic Hospital Abortion Case* (1983), 70 BVerfGE 138.

27. *Blood Transfusion Case* (1971), 32 BVerfGE 98. Reprinted and translated in Kommers, *The Constitutional Jurisprudence of the Federal Republic of Germany*, 451.

28. A good summary of this controversy in Germany can be found in Jytte Klausen, *The Islamic Challenge: Politics and Religion in Western Europe* (New York: Oxford University Press, 2005), 177–79. For a review of the court's legal argument in the case, see Matthias Mahlmann, "Religious Tolerance, Pluralist Society and the Neutrality of the State: The Federal Constitutional Court's Decision in the *Headscarf* Case," *German Law Journal* 4 (2003), 1009–16.

29. Matthias Mahlmann, "Religious Symbolism and the Resilience of Liberal Constitutionalism: On the Federal German Constitutional Court's Second Head Scarf Decision," *German Law Journal* 16 (2015), 887–900.

30. *The Evangelical Church in Germany: An Introduction*, para. 6.1.

31. Interview with Gerhard Robbers (February 23, 1996).

32. On the public corporation status of religious communities and its significance, see Claus Hofhansel, "Recognition Regimes for Religious Minorities in Europe: Institutional Change and Reproduction," *Journal of Church and State* 57 (2013), 90–118; and "United States Department International Religious Freedom Report for 2014, Germany," available at http://www.state.gov/documents/organization/171696.pdf.

33. On the church tax see Robbers, "State and Church in Germany," 89–90, and Kommers, *The Constitutional Jurisprudence of the Federal Republic of Germany*, 484–89.

34. The churches have, however, opted out of the possibility of a taxpayer being imprisoned for nonpayment of the church tax.

35. For data on church taxes see "The Catholic Church in Germany: Facts & Figures 2010/2011," http://www.dbk.de/en/zahlen-fakten/ and "Evangelical Church in Germany: Facts and Figures 2013," https://www.ekd.de/english/download/facts_and_figures_2013.pdf.

36. Chase Gummer, "In Germany, Many Believers Balk at Tweak to Church Tax," *Wall Street Journal* (September 2, 2014); Conor Gaffey, "217,716 Leave German Catholic Church," *Newsweek* (July 21, 2015), http://europe.newsweek.com/217716-leave-german-catholic-church-330612.

37. Interview with Gerrit Jan Beuker (August 18, 2006).

38. Quoted in Melissa Eddyoct, "German Catholic Church Links Tax to Sacraments," *New York Times* (October 6, 2012), A9.

39. "Jochen Teuffel: Abendmahl für Ausgetretene: Pfarrer zeigt sich selbst an." Available at http://www.tz.de/bayern/abendmahl-ausgetretene-pfarrer-jochen-teuffel-zeigt-sich-selbst-3502579.html.

40. "Erste muslimische Gemeinde erhält Kirchenstatus," *Zeit Online* (June 13, 2013), http://www.zeit.de/gesellschaft/zeitgeschehen/2013-06/islam-kirche-hessen-koerperschaft.

41. Carolyn M. Warner and Manfred W. Wenner, "Religion and the Political Organization of Muslims in Europe," *Perspectives on Politics* 4 (2006), 465.

42. Jonathan Laurence, *The Emancipation of Europe's Muslims: The State's Role in Minority Integration* (Princeton, N.J.: Princeton University Press, 2012), 182–84.

43. Houssain Kettani, "Muslim Population in Europe: 1950–2020," *International Journal of Environmental Science and Development* 1, 2 (June 2010), 154–62; "The Future of the Global Muslim Population," Pew Research Center for Religion and Public Life, http://www.pewforum.org/2011/01/27/the-future-of-the-global-muslim-population/.

44. For good overviews of this history, see Jørgen Nielsen, *Towards a European Islam* (London: Macmillan, 1999); Klausen, *The Islamic Challenge: Politics and Religion in Western Europe;* Joel S. Fetzer and J. Christopher Soper, *Muslims and the State in Britain, France, and Germany* (Cambridge: Cambridge University Press, 2005), chap. 4.

45. "Muslim-Western Tensions Persist," Pew Research Center, http://www.pewglobal.org/2011/07/21/muslim-western-tensions-persist/.

46. Religion Monitor: Understanding Common Ground, Special Study of Islam, 2015. https://www.bertelsmann-stiftung.de/en/our-projects/religion-monitor.

47. Andrea Thomas, "Record Number of Asylum Seekers Flood Germany," *Wall Street Journal* (January 6, 2016), A4.

48. 2016 Programme für Deutschland: Das Grundsatzprogramm der Alternative für Deutschland. Available at https://www.alternativefuer.de/wp-content/uploads/sites/7/2016/06/2016-06-09_afd-grundsatzprogramm-stuttgart_web-version.pdf.

49. Matt Broomfield, "Majority of Germans Think Islam Does Not 'Belong' in Their Country," *Independent* (May 13, 2016). Available at http://www.independent.co.uk/news/world/europe/refugee-crisis-germany-islam-does-not-belong-in-country-a7027361.html.

50. Stefan Kuzmany, "Germany's Election Hangover: The Right Wing Takes Flight," *Spiegel Online International* (March 14, 2016). Available at http://www.spiegel.de/international/germany/right-wing-populist-afd-does-well-in-german-state-votes-a-1082254.html.

51. "Muslims in the EU: Germany." Open Society Institute, http://www.thegreatdebate.eu/pdf/Muslims%20in%20Germany/eumap%20muslims%20in%20%20germany.pdf.

52. Gualtiero Zambonini, "The Evolution of German Media Coverage of Migration," *Migration Policy Review* (2009). Available at http://www.migrationpolicy.org/research/evolution-german-media-coverage-migration.

53. Broomfield, "Majority of Germans Think Islam Does Not 'Belong' in Their Country."

54. See Charles L. Glenn, *Choice of Schools in Six Nations* (Washington, D.C.: U.S. Department of Education, 1989), 193–95.

55. The writer was Alfred Rosenberg, quoted in J. S. Conway, *The Nazi Persecution of the Churches, 1933–1945* (New York: Basic Books, 1968), 182.

56. See Glenn, *Choice of Schools in Six Nations*, 197–201, and Spotts, *The Churches and Politics in Germany*, 212–19.

57. Spotts, *The Churches and Politics in Germany*, 219.

58. *Interdenominational School Case* (1975), 41 BVerfGE 29. Reprinted and translated in Kommers, *The Constitutional Jurisprudence of the Federal Republic of Germany*, 469.

59. *Interdenominational School Case* (1975), 41 BVerfGE 29. Reprinted and translated in Kommers, *The Constitutional Jurisprudence of the Federal Republic of Germany*, 469.

60. The decision was *McCollum v. Board of Education*, 333 U.S. 203 (1948).

61. Interview with M. A. H. Hobohm (November 20, 1996).

62. Isabelle de Pommereau, "Why German Public Schools Now Teach Islam," *Christian Science Monitor* (January 20, 2010), A4.

63. Alison Smale, "Germany Adds Lessons in Islam to Better Blend Its Melting Pot," *New York Times* (January 6, 2014), A7.

64. Kommers, *The Constitutional Jurisprudence of the Federal Republic of Germany*, 472.

65. *Classroom Crucifix II Case* (1995), 93 BVerfGE 1. Reprinted and translated in Kommers, *The Constitutional Jurisprudence of the Federal Republic of Germany*, 474.

66. *Classroom Crucifix II Case* (1995), 93 BVerfGE 1. Reprinted and translated in Kommers, *The Constitutional Jurisprudence of the Federal Republic of Germany*, 478.

67. This statement, which appeared in the Frankfurter *Allgemeine Zeitung*, has been translated and reproduced in Kommers, *The Constitutional Jurisprudence of the Federal Republic of Germany*, 483–84.

68. Manfred Weiss, "Financing Private Schools: The West German Case," in William Lowe Boyd and James G. Cibulka, eds., *Private Schools and Public Policy: International Perspectives* (London: Falmer Press, 1989), 199. Also see John E. Coons, "Educational Choice and the Courts: U.S. and Germany," *American Journal of Contemporary Law* 34 (1986), 5–7.

69. For a helpful overview, see Annette Scheunpflug, "Non-governmental Religious Schools in Germany—Increasing Demand by Decreasing Religiosity?" *Comparative Education* 51, 1 (2015), 38–56.

70. Interview with Friedhelm Solms of Forschungsställe der Evangelischen Studiengemeinschaft (FEST) (February 22, 1996).

71. Scheunpflug, "Non-governmental Religious Schools in Germany," 43.

72. Charles L. Glenn and Jan de Groof, *Balancing Freedom, Autonomy and Accountability in Education*, vol. 2 (Nijmegen, the Netherlands: Wolf Legal Publishers, 2005), 163–85.

73. Heinz-Dieter Meyer, "Welfare between Charity and Bureaucracy: German Public and Church-Affiliated Pre-Schooling Compared" (unpublished paper, 1997), 6–7.

74. Rupert Strachwitz and Annette Zimmer, "The Third Sector and Political Ideologies: Unpacking Relations between Organized Civil Society and the State," *Journal of Political Ideologies* 15, 1 (2010), 273–87.

75. "The Third Route: Subsidiarity, Third Party Government and the Provision of Social Services in the United States and Germany," in Organization for Economic Cooperation and

Development, *Private Sector Involvement in the Delivery of Social Welfare Services: Mixed Models from OECD Countries* (Paris: OECD, 1994), 26.

76. Quoted in Helmut K. Anheier, "An Elaborate Network: Profiling the Third Sector in Germany," in Benjamin Gidron, Ralph M. Kramer, and Lester M. Salamon, eds., *Government and the Third Sector* (San Francisco: Jossey-Bass, 1992), 38.

77. Quoted in Anheier, "An Elaborate Network," 38.

78. Wolfgang Seibel, "Government-Nonprofit Relationships in a Comparative Perspective: The Cases of France and Germany," in Kathleen D. McCarthy, Virginia A. Hodgkinson, and Russy D. Sumariwalla, eds., *The Nonprofit Sector in the Global Community* (San Francisco: Jossey-Bass, 1992), 213. Anheier and Seibel have also written, "The early development of the modern German non-profit sector happened in antithesis to an autocratic state." Helmut K. Anheier and Wolfgang Seibel, "Defining the Nonprofit Sector: Germany," Working Papers of the Johns Hopkins Comparative Nonprofit Sector Project, no. 6 (Baltimore, Md.: Johns Hopkins Institute for Policy Studies, 1993), 29.

79. "Diakonie: The Social Welfare Organisation of Germany's Protestant Churches." Available at http://www.diakonie.de/the-social-welfare-organisation-of-the-protestant-church-in-9306.html.

80. For more information on these organizations see http://www.caritas-germany.org/home.aspx and http://www.diakonie.de/the-social-welfare-organisation-of-the-protestant-church-in-9306.html.

81. Lester M. Salamon, S. Wojciech Sokolwski, and associates, *Global Civil Society: Dimension of the Nonprofit Sector*, vol. 2 (Bloomfield, Conn.: Kurmarian Press, 2004), 32.

82. http://www.caritas-germany.org/germancaritasassociation/finances/finances.

83. https://www.aktion-deutschland-hilft.de/en/member-organisations/the-central-welfare-board-of-jews-in-germany-zwst/.

84. Robbers, "Religious Freedom in Europe," 3, http://home.lu.lv/~rbalodis/Publikacijas/Citu-raksti/Religious_Freedom_GR.pdf.

85. Kerstin Rosenow-Williams, *Organizing Muslims and Integrating Islam in Germany: New Developments in the 21st Century* (Leiden: Brill, 2012).

86. Anheier and Seibel, "Defining the Nonprofit Sector: Germany," 30.

87. Robbers, "State and Church in Germany," 83.

88. Interview with Gerhard Robbers (February 23, 1996).

89. Carl Gardner, "Constitutional complaint by C: Case no 2 BvR 661/12: German Federal Constitutional Court (Second Chamber)," Volume 4, Number 3 (2015), 538–39.

90. Tom Heneghan, "German Catholic Church Opens Labor Law More to Divorced and Gays," Reuters (May 6, 2015). See also Johan D. van der Vyver, "State Interference in the Internal Affairs of Religious Institutions," *Emory International Law Review* 26, 1 (2012), 1–9.

91. Leopold A. W. Turowski, "The Church and the European Community: Developments and Prospects," *European Vision* 10 (1990), 15.

92. Donald P. Kommers, "West German Constitutionalism and Church-State Relations," *German Politics and Society* 19 (Spring 1990), 11.

93. Interview with Rudolf Weth (February 14, 1996).

94. *Interdenominational School Case* (1975), 41 BVerfGE 29. Reprinted and translated in Kommers, *The Constitutional Jurisprudence of the Federal Republic of Germany*, 469.

Conclusion

Church and State in Pluralistic Democracies

Pluralism is both a fact and an aspiration. As we have used the term, it refers to the reality of religious diversity in democracies and a commitment to engaging that diversity in ways that support citizens' religious freedom and the common good. Our goal has been to guide democracies, and the United States in particular, about those realities and commitments of pluralism by learning from the rich opportunities for comparison across six democracies. We now consider what lessons and observations the experiences of these countries provide.

First, we summarize how each of the six countries has responded to the three questions we posed in our introduction.

- How far can a democratic polity go in permitting religiously motivated behavior that is contrary to societal welfare or norms?
- Should the state encourage and promote consensual religious beliefs and traditions in an attempt to support the common values and beliefs that bind a society together and make possible limited, democratic government?
- When religious groups and the state are both active in the same fields of endeavor, how can one ensure that the state does not advantage or disadvantage any one religious group or either religion or nonreligion over the other?

Second, we make four basic observations concerning what we believe can be gleaned from the experiences of the six countries whose church-state practices we have explored. Third, we respond to two objections that have sometimes been raised to religion playing a more fulsome role in the public life of nations.

A caveat is, however, in order. The material in our six country case studies shows that contemporary church-state practice has much to do with a nation's unique history and cultural assumptions. Practices that are largely unquestioned in one country, such as England's established church or Germany's church tax, are unimaginable in other countries, such as the United States or Australia. France's history of church-state separation contrasts fundamentally with the Dutch or British experience. Having said that, we believe that countries can learn from each other and that the distinct church-state policy of these six countries is fertile and largely untapped soil for resolving what have historically been and what promise in the future to be persistent tensions between religious and political institutions.[1] These six states face common challenges, particularly in light of the immigration and settlement of large numbers of Muslims and other religious minorities in recent decades, as they negotiate the boundaries between religion and politics.

SUMMARY CONCLUSIONS

Free Exercise Rights

The religious free exercise rights of the six countries vary a good deal in theory, but not as much as one might expect in practice. The pattern that emerges from our review of these democracies is that each basically protects religious liberty (which is no small achievement), but struggles with how to interpret that right in specific instances.

There are three principal mechanisms by which these countries secure religious freedom: constitutional provision, legislation, and cultural attitudes and assumptions. With the exception of England, a basic right to the free exercise of one's religion is enshrined in the constitutions of each of the countries in our study. Our review of the practices of the countries in our study has shown, however, that in many instances those rights are not consistently defended. Court cases from the United States and Australia demonstrate that constitutions do not always protect individuals and groups when their religious practice violates otherwise valid regulatory laws, irrespective of how important and deeply held are the religious beliefs that underlie their practice. The U.S. Supreme Court abandoned the compelling state interest test in its 1990 decision, *Employment Division v. Smith*, while the Australian High Court has never applied that standard in religious free exercise cases. The German Constitutional Court, by contrast, has been more aggressive in protecting religious liberty. While the Court does balance the religious rights of individuals and groups against the state's interest in public safety and health, it has been more likely than its judicial counterparts in Australia and the United States to overturn laws that conflict with religious belief and action.

Australia and the United States have gone the furthest with legislation to protect people against religious discrimination. Most of the Australian states have established antidiscrimination boards that defend people against religious discrimination; the United States also has a variety of laws against religious discrimination. The strongest legal protection for religious freedom in England is the 1998 Human Rights Act, which incorporated the European Convention on Human Rights (ECHR) into British law. The Convention includes a strong protection for religious freedom. The 2013 decision by the European Court of Human Rights in *Eweida and others v. United Kingdom*, which overturned the ruling of the British government on religious freedom grounds, indicated that England was moving closer to Germany and the Netherlands in having strong legal protection for religious free exercise rights. With the historic 2016 referendum vote that led the United Kingdom to leave the European Union, however, the decisions of a European court will presumably have less legal force going forward. The concern in France is not so much the absence of constitutional or legal protections for religious liberty, but how those protections have been balanced against other state interests. The 2004 legislation that prohibited the wearing of religious clothing in schools, the 2010 law that banned face coverings in public spaces, and various laws that restrict the practice of so-called cults are all examples of limits on religious freedom.

Constitutional and legal rights are significant, to be sure, but public opinion and the cultural assumptions underlying them seem just as important a safeguard for religious liberty. England does not have a constitutional protection for religious liberty, but the nation's practice is not far different from that of the United States, which does. The British protect religious liberty not so much because of the law, at least until recently, but because the British public has historically valued that right. The Netherlands also demonstrates the importance of cultural assumptions about religious freedom. The Dutch Constitution provides for religious liberty, but the judiciary does not have the power of judicial review over acts passed by the States-General. In theory, the States-General could pass laws that violate a person or group's right of religious free exercise, but in practice this rarely has happened because there is widespread public support for religious liberty and the Dutch may do a better job at securing religious rights than almost any other country in the world. Much as Americans revere the First Amendment protection for religious free exercise, the French embrace the values of the Declaration of the Rights of Man and the Citizen, which includes the right of religious freedom. The underlying values of each country help to explain why each consistently ranks very high on international measures of religious freedom.

Recent developments in each of these countries suggest, however, that societal values by themselves can be a thin reed on which to preserve religious freedom, particularly for minority religious groups. In its comparative survey of religious freedom around the globe, the Pew Research Center places Germany, France, and the United Kingdom in its second-highest category of religion-based social hostilities, that is, violence, intimidation, or abuse motivated by or perpetrated against religion by nonstate actors (e.g., terrorist groups, mobs). While the United States and the Netherlands are in the "moderate" category, the level of hostilities has been rising.[2] And we have a great deal of anecdotal evidence of the fraying of cultural acceptance of religious freedom as well. Donald Trump, during his campaign for the presidency, repeatedly called for a temporary ban on the immigration of all Muslims to the United States. The Brexit vote in the United Kingdom was driven in part by opposition to immigration, particularly Islamic immigration. Recent polls indicate that the anti-Islamic Freedom Party in the Netherlands and the National Front in France are at or near top of the polls in their respective country. The 2014 party platform of the Freedom Party affirms that "Islam is not a religion but a totalitarian political ideology" which "has no place in the Netherlands." In addition to her strong opposition to immigration, Marine Le Pen, the leader of the French National Front, has called for the closing of "radical" mosques in France and a ban on the building of new ones.[3]

In short, constitutional and legal protections for religious freedom are very important, particularly when those rights are under assault. They provide the opportunity for religious groups to litigate when they believe that the state has violated their rights, as many have done in the United States and Germany, and in some cases the constitutional courts have used that litigation to protect and/or extend religious free exercise rights. Ideally, the courts would interpret a constitutional protection of religious rights as a mandate to defend minority religious groups whose views are unpopular and for whom the political process is not consistently a sufficient safeguard.

The protection of free exercise rights, in whatever form it assumes, is an important expression of governmental neutrality on matters of religion. It sends a strong message that the government will not advantage or disadvantage people's religious choices by seeking to favor or burden any particular religion, but will instead ensure that there are no disabilities or advantages associated with adherence to any specific religion or secular belief system. This is particularly important for minority faiths whose religious free exercise rights the state might not otherwise secure.

There is one other significant pattern that emerges in these countries as it relates to free exercise rights. Germany and the Netherlands have a far more expansive and, we contend, appropriate understanding of religious liberty than England, the United States, France, or Australia. German practice recognizes that religious belief presupposes action based upon that belief; consequently the right to believe includes the right to act on one's beliefs. The German Constitutional Court explicitly acknowledged this point when it stated that religious freedom encompasses "the individual's right to align his behavior with the precepts of his faith and to act in accordance with his internal convictions." In Australia and the United States, by contrast, the courts have adopted an Enlightenment liberal understanding of religion that treats faith primarily as a private matter of individual conscience. Seen in this light, to secure religious liberty the state needs simply to protect an individual's right to believe what he or she will. The weakness of this idea is apparent in the failure of the U.S. Supreme Court to preserve the right of an Orthodox Jewish air force officer to wear a yarmulke as required by his faith, and the Australian High Court case that allowed the government to ban the Jehovah's Witnesses during World War II without any discussion of whether the church's teachings or practices threatened the state. Having abandoned or having never advocated a compelling state interest test, American and Australian courts lack a mechanism for discerning when people can legally act on the basis of their beliefs, which restricts religious free exercise rights for those people whose faith clashes with otherwise valid regulations.

A similar dynamic occurs in France around the eternally contested concept of *laïcité*. For many, this separation of religion from public life implies a positive commitment by the state to promote a secular public square denuded of any and all religious influence. This mind-set helps to explain why France, alone among the countries in our study, legislated a ban on the wearing of the headscarf in public schools. Even if the policy is evenhanded in that it supposedly applies to all "ostentatious" religious clothing and not simply to the wearing of the *hijab* the law nonetheless presumes that a sufficient guarantee for a robust religious liberty is to protect it in the private sphere alone.

The Dutch contribution to a more complete understanding of religious liberty is found in Article 6 of its Constitution, which protects religious belief whether one exercises it as an individual or "in community with others." This communitarian emphasis contrasts with the Enlightenment liberal idea that protecting individuals' right to religious worship guarantees their religious liberty. In liberal theory, the state protects religious rights indirectly, by guaranteeing freedom of worship without fear of state discrimination. Theorists as diverse as Michael Sandel, Will Kymlicka, Bhikhu Parekh, and Jürgen Habermas have noted, however, that the modern individual is a creation of community.[4] Individuals do not choose or live a religion in isolation from others, so the liberal attempt to elucidate the right of religious liberty apart from the community is insufficient. As we have demonstrated in the country chapters, religion has a public influence, and religious groups are actively involved in a wide variety of educational and social service activities. A more robust form of religious freedom requires the state to take positive measures aimed at protecting and promoting the religious expression of groups or communities in the public sphere in the same way that the state protects secular worldviews. As Habermas argues, neutrality in the public political arena means that "naturalistic world views do not enjoy a *prima facie* advantage over competing world views or religious understandings."[5]

This is precisely what the Dutch model of pillarization historically recognized, with policies geared toward the main Catholic, Reformed, and secular groups in society. As we have noted, pillarization in the Netherlands has changed radically in recent decades, but in their public policy the Dutch have retained the idea that it is appropriate for the state to accommodate both secular and religious organizations because people naturally want to express their principles, secular or religious, within and through groups. The Dutch view the issues of public support for religious schools and organizations as matters of the right of religious free exercise, and not an establishment of religion, as would be the case in the United States. The result is a cooperative arrangement between church and state, but the Netherlands still maintains the idea of governmental neutrality. It does so not by equating neutrality with the government withdrawing all support for religion, but by equally accommodating and supporting all communities' desire for education and social services within their religious or secular traditions. The state is thereby neutral among all religions and between religious and secular systems of belief.

In theory and in practice, each of the six countries recognizes that there are some values that are so fundamental to human existence and democratic society that religious freedom cannot be the basis for their violation. Chief among them are the public health, safety, and social welfare of citizens. On these grounds, none of the countries would tolerate human sacrifice, child sexual abuse, or violence even if it was part of a group's religious beliefs. These easy cases belie how difficult it is to draw a precise boundary between free exercise rights and the state's various interests, particularly in those cases when a religious group's teaching or practice violates social values but endangers no one. It does, however, establish the appropriate precedent that there are times when the government legitimately may regulate and even outlaw religious practices because they undermine the social norms that are the basis for social unity and democratic governance. The debate about the need for a democratic society to invest its citizens with certain key values leads us directly to the second question in our discussion.

Consensual Values

There is a strong impulse in each of the countries studied in this book to promote consensual values as a way of assimilating individuals and groups into democratic society. The norms often cited as being crucial for a democratic polity are tolerance, respect for the rule of law, public spiritedness, commitment to the democratic process, interpersonal trust, and the importance of diversity. The key places in which these issues are raised are citizenship and educational policies. In terms of citizenship norms, most of the countries in our study have introduced new tests for immigrants seeking citizenship. The impetus in each case was the enormous inflow of foreigners, particularly Muslims, and the fear that these newer immigrants were not successfully integrating into the values of the host country.[6] Citizenship tests are administered in the language of the country where the immigrants are seeking citizenship, sending a strong message about the link between competence in their new country's tongue and full membership in the political community. Immigrants are expected to learn the basic facts about the country's history, political institutions, and cultural values.

The issue is not whether the state should promote particular values. We believe that a democratic state must advance those norms that will help to sustain the polity, and support for the nation's political institutions and familiarity with its cultural practices are consonant with that purpose. The question, rather, is whether the tests should examine a candidate's moral and ethical views. The German state of Baden-Württemberg includes questions about the person's views on forced marriages, homosexuality, and women's rights, all designed with an eye toward the growing Islamic population. Other countries have similarly adopted citizenship norms meant to scrutinize a candidate's moral and ethical views.[7] While it is reasonable for the state to alert potential citizens to the fact that German or Dutch law recognizes same-sex partnerships and thereby affirms the legal equality of gay persons, the promotion of consensual values goes too far if the intent of this test is to deny citizenship to all persons who might be opposed to same-sex unions. A liberal state must be willing to tolerate the views of an illiberal minority.

The institution that has historically had the key role as the incubator of national values is the school. The common public schools in the United States were designed to be institutions of assimilation for the waves of newly arriving immigrants at the end of the nineteenth century. More recently, many of the countries in our study have refined their curricula for public schools to become much more explicit about defining and teaching national values. The national civics curriculum in Australia identifies commitment to parliamentary democracy, rule of law, compassion for those in need, freedom of expression, equality, accountability, common good, social justice, and sustainability.[8] Since 2002, secondary schools in England must meet statutory requirements in the area of citizenship, which include knowledge and understanding to become informed citizens, developing skills of inquiry and communication, and developing skills of participation and responsible action.[9] The goal of this citizenship education is cultural assimilation.

The six countries in our study differ, however, in the extent to which this goal of integration is the province of the public schools, as opposed to public and private schools, particularly religious ones. The United States is alone in providing virtually no aid to private religious schools, partly because of a belief that the common public schools should be the basic means by which children of all classes and religions are taught social and political values. There is a perception that private religious schools undermine this model because they segregate children on the basis of religion and allegedly on the basis of social class and race, and fail somehow to inculcate children with important democratic norms. There are two problems with this picture. First, it idealizes common schools as institutions that are inherently diverse. Due to the multiplicity of school districts in metropolitan areas, public schools in the United States are in fact segregated by race and social class. Second, the argument that separate religious schools do not promote key democratic values is an empirical claim, for which there is no supportive evidence of which we are aware and indeed a great deal of counterevidence. [10]

There will be some cases of religious or secular groups that do not support basic democratic norms, and they should properly be excluded from programs of public support. A private religious school that preaches hatred and violence toward others or does not provide an adequate education for children to function in the modern world has not signed on to the core consensual values of a democratic society and should not receive public support. If religious schools become nurseries of antisocial fundamentalism—which seems to be the implicit fear of them in many quarters—and they fail to reach their objectives in citizenship education, they should not receive state funding. The same is true for a religious counseling center that, for example, advises the female victims of violent domestic disputes to submit to the wishes of their abusive husbands.

As a general rule, however, religious schools and agencies do not undermine democratic values, but support them. Despite the concerns of liberals who stress the importance of the cultural assimilation of minority groups, there is very little evidence that religious schools or social service agencies fail to socialize citizens with the values necessary for life in a liberal democratic polity. There has been virtually no resistance among Muslims, as an example, to laws in each of these countries that ban polygamy, female circumcision, and arranged marriages if they are entered into under duress. The states that have gone the furthest to recognize group differences in their public policy—the Netherlands and Australia—seem not to have compromised their commitment to cultural assimilation or suffered any serious negative cultural effects for their policy. There is no necessary tension between the need for society to reach some consensus on key social values with a public policy that accommodates group identities. Bhikhu Parekh notes that "a multicultural society cannot be stable and last long without developing a common sense of belonging among its citizens . . . [but] commitment or belonging is reciprocal in nature. Citizens cannot be committed to their political community unless it is also committed to them, and they cannot belong to it unless it accepts them as belonging to it."[11] The problem with some of the states considered here is not so much that their public policies accommodate group differences, but that they fail to do so equitably. This is true in Germany, which has not met the religious instruction needs of Muslim students to the same degree it has for Protestant and Catholic students; in France, where Catholic schools are funded by the government but Islamic schools are not; and in the United States, which restricts tax-supported educational options to the state sector.

There is clearly much interest in Christian, Jewish, and Islamic schools in each of these six countries. With or without state aid these schools will attract students. The question then becomes what policy is most likely to ensure that those students will receive the kind of education necessary to assimilate them in key social and political values. We believe that bringing those schools into the state system with the promise of state aid is a better guarantee that they will promote consensual democratic values than consigning them to a status where they have little contact with state educational officials and are less beholden to state regulations. It is a compromise position in which the state supports separate schools, but with some common curriculum, particularly as it relates to the promotion of common values.

Having said that, we do not argue that the public schools can or should be the place for the inculcation of shared *religious* values. The experience of countries that include state-sponsored religious instruction and worship in public schools—as do England, Australia, and to a lesser degree, Germany— suggests that the pursuit of consensual religious beliefs in public institutions is doomed to failure. Each of these societies is religiously pluralistic and it is no longer possible, if it ever was, to discern consensual religious values that significant minorities of the population would not question. This myth is a legacy of nineteenth-century Enlightenment liberal educational reformers who mistakenly believed that one could suppress particularistic religious beliefs, but retain key values shared by all religious traditions. It is possible for a country to come up with guidelines for religious instruction and worship that satisfy the majority, of course, but this denies the rights of religious and secular minorities. The German Constitutional Court correctly recognized this fact in its 1995 decision that overturned a Bavarian law that required the display of a crucifix in every public school classroom, even when some students objected. Religious pluralism is a reality in each of the countries in our study, which makes it unfair for the state to promote a single religious worldview, and unlikely that it will succeed if it tries. A far better approach is for the state to allow separate, in-school religious education classes as the basic means for religious instruction, as both Germany and Australia do—and the United States Supreme Court has found unconstitutional.

The debate in England, where the law not only permits but actually requires Christian religious instruction and worship, demonstrates the problems that come when public schools attempt to promote a single religious vision. The religious education curriculum in England focuses as much as possible on consensual religious values and on the country's religious pluralism, but the results have dissatisfied non-Christians, nonbelievers, and many Christians as well. Non-Christians and nonbelievers fear that the schools will indoctrinate their children in the Christian religion, while many Christian groups contend that a focus on common religious values distorts and trivializes their faith. Not surprisingly, a majority of the schools have failed to meet the requirements of the Education Reform Act of 1988. The controversy illustrates that even when a majority of the people want religious instruction in the public schools, there is little agreement about what forms of religious worship and instruction the state should promote. The same is true for Australia's chaplaincy program, which rather naively assumes that a chaplain from a specific faith tradition can provide generic religious and pastoral advice to persons from diverse religious backgrounds. The program is not necessary for the promotion of shared values, and the fact that it is voluntary does not ensure that it can work in a way that is faithful to diverse religious beliefs or equitably between religious and nonreligious worldviews.

Public Aid to Religious Schools and Nonprofit Organizations

Religious organizations in each of the countries in our study provide a wide variety of educational and social services to the public similar to those the six governments provide. Each state is committed to governmental neutrality on matters of religion, but they differ on what that means in terms of public financial support when religious groups and the state are active in the same field of endeavor. The issue that crystallized the tension between state and church authorities was state provision of education in the nineteenth century. Religious communities traditionally provided education for group members, but the distribution of that service was so uneven that the state gradually began to provide education for all its citizens. Educational reformers believed that the state should not provide aid to religious schools because they encouraged sectarian disputes and worked against the assimilationist goal of the public schools. This position engendered conflict from many church leaders, particularly Roman Catholics in each of the countries and conservative Protestants in the Netherlands, who argued that this state action threatened the power and autonomy of religious communities. This was not an unfounded fear. Political theorist Michael Walzer has written: "State welfare undercuts private philanthropy, much of which was organized within ethnic communities; it makes it harder to sustain private and parochial schools; it erodes the strength of cultural institutions."[12]

The reformist ideal never took hold in Germany, where the government-sponsored schools originally were confessional in nature and most have gradually become schools that are broadly Christian in a nondenominational, nonsectarian sense and where provision is made for in-school religious instruction for the children of the major faith traditions. In the Netherlands, England, and France church leaders secured state funding for denominational schools on an equal basis with state-supported schools. Church schools received little or no state aid in the United States and Australia, largely because the dominant Protestant groups joined forces with liberal reformers to stop money going to Roman Catholic schools. In the early 1960s, Australia dramatically changed its policy and began offering substantial support to church schools, while at the same time the U.S. Supreme Court was articulating a policy of strict church-state separation that ruled government could not provide funding to religious schools. Neutrality in the United States came to mean that the state withdraws its financial support for religious schools because of a concern that this aid would demonstrate a preference for a religious over against a nonreligious perspective.

Religious schools have thrived in those countries where state aid is available; a higher percentage of citizens have attended religious schools in England, the Netherlands, France, and Australia than are active members of a church, mosque, or synagogue combined. The tension in those countries has come over the issue of which religious groups to include within the system. Australia and the Netherlands have gone the furthest and for the longest time to ensure that all religious groups are eligible for state aid, and there is a great diversity of religious as well as secular private schools in both countries. Because of its tradition of incorporating religious elements into public schools, Germany has relatively few religiously based private schools, but has provided state funding for those that exist and meet state standards. England has begun to support those schools outside the long-established system of aid to Christian and Jewish schools. France has been the most resistant to extending state funding to Islamic schools.

There was less conflict between church and state when each of these governments began to expand its social welfare role in the twentieth century. The fact that Enlightenment liberal thinking did not place as great an importance on the services these agencies offered as it did on public education, which involved issues of national unity and the inculcation of democratic values, no doubt made it easier to adopt public policies that included religious associations. As a result, five of the six countries rely extensively on religious agencies to provide social welfare services, and for the most part religious agencies in those countries have the autonomy to run their organizations as they see fit. France is the outlier on this issue as the French state has historically dominated civil society, including the provision of nonprofit social services. In recent years, however, the French state has been more willing to work with religious service organizations. What is somewhat surprising is that the United States funds religious agencies even though it does not fund religious schools. Because of the strict separation principles that led to the rejection of funding for religious schools, however, the religious autonomy of U.S. religious social service agencies is in more doubt in the United States than in the other countries. This can be seen in the controversy engendered by President George W. Bush's faith-based initiative, with many on the political left insisting that a nonprofit, religiously based social service organization that receives public funds loses its right to take religion into account in its hiring decisions.

OBSERVATIONS

We distill four key observations from the experiences of the democracies reviewed in this book. The basic norm of governmental neutrality on matters of religion we originally set out in the introductory chapter has been our guide in making these evaluative observations. This neutrality is substantive or positive in the sense of sometimes supporting positive governmental actions and sometimes governmental inaction. The basic, directing goal is that the state should neither favor nor disfavor any particular religion or religious belief structures as a whole or secularly based belief structures as a whole. Only in this way can the state ensure that people are neither advantaged or disadvantaged by their adherence to their secular or faith-based tradition.

Government Neutrality and the Free Exercise of Religion

We are convinced that governmental neutrality is gained, first, when free exercise rights are limited only because of compelling societal interests. When government imposes certain burdens on religious practices—even when it does so in pursuit of what in most circumstances are valid regulatory purposes—governmental policy disadvantages those religions whose practices are being burdened. In the nineteenth century U.S. laws against polygamy constricted the Mormons' free exercise of their religious beliefs. Australia effectively banned Jehovah's Witnesses during World War II. In recent years, France, the Netherlands, and parts of Germany have banned either the wearing of the *hijab* in public schools or of the *burqa* in public places.

We are not saying that neutrality demands that the claim of the religious group must always trump the broader society's need for order or other societal interests. What we do insist is that if governmental religious neutrality is to be maintained, the state must only restrict the practices of communities of religious or secular belief when it has a compelling, significant societal purpose. It is more important that this be the standard that is fairly and honestly applied than any particular outcome in specific instances. Given the grave danger from foreign invasion the Australians were facing in World War II and given the clear antigovernment beliefs of the Jehovah's Witnesses at that time, the government justifiably sought to protect itself against organizations that actively sought to overthrow the state. A compelling state interest of the highest order—survival of the state itself—was at stake. The problem with the action taken by the Australian High Court lies in its failure to justify its decision on the basis of whether or not the Jehovah's Witnesses did, in fact, threaten a vital state interest. Similarly, our concern with the U.S. Supreme Court's decision in regard to Mormon polygamy in the nineteenth century lies less in the outcome of the decision than in its basis (that the free exercise protection encompass only religious beliefs, not religiously inspired actions). If France, Germany, or the Netherlands continue to limit the wearing of Muslim headscarves or other distinctive Muslim attire, they should only do so on the basis of protecting key society-wide interests, not out of fear or prejudice.

Our purpose is not to say how other countries—whose specific conditions and circumstances we can only know in general terms—should decide these sensitive, often difficult issues. We do, however, insist that they should not be decided on the basis of conventional, majoritarian practice or the political and social power of long-dominant religious groups. They should be decided in a fair, honest attempt to allow the maximum amount of religious freedom congruent with societal order, health, and safety. Anything less would put the adherents of those religions at a disadvantage without there being a compensating societal advantage. Government's religious neutrality would be violated.

Government Neutrality and the Promotion of Consensual Religious Beliefs

Our second observation is that it is extremely difficult for states to promote consensual religious values and still maintain their religious neutrality. England and Germany have sought to do the most along these lines, and in the case of Germany it has self-consciously sought to do so in a manner respectful of differing religious traditions. Yet in reviewing their practices we came away convinced that their success in doing so, while maintaining governmental religious neutrality, is less than complete. Most efforts to inculcate consensual religious values have been directed at public elementary and secondary schoolchildren. (We are thinking here of religious or worship experiences that are made a part of the school day or—as is the case in some German schools—the presence of religious symbols in public school classrooms, not released time programs where schoolchildren receive religious instruction in the faith or secular beliefs of their families.) The fact that many British schools do not follow the clear legal mandate to include prayers and worship experiences of a "broadly Christian character" reveals the difficulty many school officials feel they have in doing so in a manner fair to all students in a society that is increasingly religiously pluralistic. The provisions that the German Constitutional Court has insisted upon for the right of children to be excused from public prayers in the schools or to insist that a crucifix be removed from their classroom have put a large burden on these children and their parents. Such children must choose between living in an atmosphere that goes against their religious beliefs and distinguishing themselves as being different from other students. The problem inherent in all such efforts is that religion and secular belief structures are particular and concrete in nature, not general or vague. It is simply not possible to find religious common ground that has enough content to be at all meaningful. Pluralism requires accommodation of diverse and sometimes incommensurable perspectives, not homogenization or privatization. Those who dissent from whatever religious common ground the state seeks to identify and then promote find themselves being put at a state-created disadvantage.

Government Neutrality and Church-State Separation

Our third observation is that efforts at the strict separation of church and state—in which the United States engaged for a time and which still exerts a strong influence today—also invariably violate state religious neutrality. The state violates religious neutrality when under the auspices of strict separation public schools ban released time programs, schools sponsored by religious groups are denied funds, and religious social and health service agencies must downplay or put at risk their religious character in order to receive public funds all other agencies are receiving. Government is no longer treating religious and nonreligious viewpoints and groups in an evenhanded manner. It collects taxes from citizens who are adherents of a wide range of religious and secular viewpoints and from members of a wide range of religious communities (and, for some, secularly based communities of belief), and then distributes those tax funds in support of only some of them. Strict separation policies advantage those whose implicit or explicit beliefs lead them to be comfortable with public schools stripped of religion or with social service agencies whose religious character is left in question. But those who desire their children to receive religious instruction in keeping with their particularistic beliefs (especially when the state compels education, as nearly every western democracy does) or wish to support or receive services from religiously based service agencies are put at a competitive disadvantage.

Strict separation was born in the context of eighteenth-century debates over the appropriateness of public funding for churches and their clergy. In that situation strict separation properly says the state should strictly separate itself from the church, not funding any or all churches. Even funding all religions equally would still discriminate against or disadvantage those citizens who are adherents of no religious faith. In addition, when the issue is direct government funding of churches and clergy, for the government not to do so does not disadvantage religion generally, since the state would not be funding competing secular belief structures. The state is being neutral. That, however, is not the issue today. None of the six democracies included in this study directly funds churches or clergy to any significant extent. It is no longer even an issue.

Instead the issue has shifted to the arena of schools and social and health service organizations. Here the state, religiously based organizations, and secularly based organizations—all three—are providing the same services. Under strict separation the state may, of course, fund its own secularized services and presumably could fund and otherwise cooperate with private secularly based organizations, but could not fund or cooperate too closely with religiously based organizations (or at least could not fund them if they integrate their religious aspects into the services they render). But this is not neutrality. The state is favoring schools and organizations of a nonreligious nature over those of a religious nature. All of the democracies considered in this book except the United States have recognized this. Time and again in our interviews, and especially in the Netherlands, Australia, and Germany, people made reference to the fact that funding religiously based schools or social service agencies or making provision for released time religious classes in public schools constitutes an attempt at fairness or neutrality.

We would argue that public policies that expand opportunities for religious understanding (and even instruction, such as released time programs) in public schools or that provide equally for public funding of private religiously and secularly based schools (e.g., vouchers) and social service organizations are fully in keeping with state religious neutrality, and may sometimes be required by the neutrality norm. This is a counterpart to the point we made in our first observation, dealing with free exercise protections. We argued there that if in the absence of a compelling societal interest the government were to limit the rights or practices of certain religious groups it would be putting them at a disadvantage in a way that other religious or nonreligious groups were not. Similarly, if government were to fund a variety of schools (either public or private) but not fund religious schools, it would be putting the religious schools at a state-created disadvantage. Or if government were to fund its own social and health services and private secular social and health services, but not fund religious social and health services, it would be putting those religious service organizations at a state-created disadvantage.

Government Neutrality and Funding for Religious Schools and Service Organizations

Our fourth observation is that government funding of religious schools and organizations is not only in keeping with the norm of state religious neutrality, but that it also actively promotes three key values often associated with liberal democracy: choice, societal pluralism, and participatory democracy. We want to elaborate at some length on how state aid promotes these social norms.

Public funding makes religious education more affordable for low- and middle-income parents who choose to exercise that option. Parents who want a religious education for their children have less choice in the United States than in the other countries in our study. Similarly, without public finance of religious social service organizations there would be less diversity in those services. Citizens in each nation have access to services that have a specific philosophical basis in such key areas as mental health, drug and alcohol rehabilitation, residential aged care, and marriage services. The current policies being followed by all these countries—with the exception of schools in the United States—encourage greater citizen choice and are broadly neutral among religions and between a religious and a nonreligious perspective. To the extent that choice is a value (and we do not suggest that it is the only value in a liberal democracy) public funding of religious schools and agencies is preferable.

Genuine choice is only possible, however, if the state grants nongovernment schools and welfare organizations a significant degree of autonomy. To be sure, nongovernmental organizations should be accountable to the government for the funds they receive and that they must meet standards in the services they offer. But nongovernment organizations must also have autonomy, the freedom to operate according to their own convictions. There are limits to that freedom. The state should not allow religious or secular associations to engage in or advocate illegal actions that would undermine public order, health, and safety. Nor should they be allowed to foment hatred and the violation of norms of civility and respect for the rights of others. The government should not, however, seek to impose a standardized model into which, say, Muslim, Catholic, Jewish, and secular child care or marital counseling services would be forced. The imposition of common rules and standardized services onto such agencies would threaten the diversity that is a virtue of contemporary policy. To the extent that there are groups of citizens who want services tailored to a specific value system, schools and agencies must be free to retain their specific character with policies on hiring, admissions, and service delivery.

State funding for religious schools and service agencies also promotes social pluralism and respects the diversity of cultural identities. Religious schools enable groups to maintain and instill the tenets of their faith and relate them to the contemporary world. This is particularly true for immigrants who do not necessarily support assimilation if this implies that they must absorb all of the values, ethos, and practices of that society. Since government schools and agencies typically support consensual religious or secularized perspectives, people who belong to religious communities with distinctive and often nonmajoritarian religious beliefs will tend to find themselves disadvantaged. Pluralism asserts that the state should tolerate competing educational and social service ideas because the diverse religious and secular communities that make up a nation have a right to exist in the context of freedom to live out their beliefs uncoerced by the state. Pluralism challenges the idea that the intent of public education or social services is to unify a diverse polity by supplanting particularistic identities through cultural assimilation. [13]

As each of these societies becomes more pluralistic, the demand for particularistic services grows and the issue becomes whether or not each state will accommodate group differences through public finance of religious schools and social service organizations. So long as there is a clear demand for services to be organized through ethnic and religious communities, we believe that it makes sense for the state to finance those organizations. Public aid reinforces group identities, which gives greater recognition to the fact that religious and ethnic life is lived out through community organizations like the school. While we recognize that the state has an interest in ensuring that these organizations meet certain minimal levels of service by establishing uniform standards, centralized service provision is economically inefficient and potentially dangerous, particularly for those groups that want to retain a distinctive perspective. We argue that genuine pluralism is preferable because it demonstrates public recognition and support of the religious group differences that are a part of each of these societies. There is also evidence that services provided through faith-based groups are as efficient, cost-effective, and successful as those provided by the government. [14]

Public aid to religious schools and welfare organizations also strengthens participatory democracy and localized decision making. Public aid to religious schools and agencies empowers groups at local levels to participate in the decisions that are most important to them. It reinforces what Paul Hirst describes as "associative democracy." [15] Associationalism claims that "individual liberty and human welfare are both best served when as many of the affairs of society as possible are managed by voluntary and democratically self-governing associations." [16] In an associational democracy, the state provides the finance for public goods, such as education or social welfare, but allows local associations to administer them. These groups are accountable to the government for use of the funds, but are more responsive to those for whom the service is provided. The idea is that the state encourages groups to organize themselves by assigning to them rights and political power.[17]

The Dutch corporatist arrangement is the clearest indication of this policy in practice. We do not suggest that corporatism is the appropriate model for any one of these states, but we do argue that there are legitimate ways for the state to step in to structure and encourage religious group life. With the exception of the United States, and to a lesser extent France, the countries in our study have taken positive and, in our view, legitimate steps to ensure that religious groups can live out their faith in what is probably the most important public institution, the school. Each of the states has allowed group life to flourish in social welfare services, although the autonomy and status of those organizations are in some question in some of the countries. It is our conviction that governmental neutrality demands public finance for all religious groups, as long as they support basic democratic norms. We also contend that state aid promotes the socially beneficial goals of choice, social pluralism, and participatory democracy.

Two Objections

In this book we have made clear the extent to which the U.S. church-state practices—especially as they relate to establishment of religion issues such as state funding of religious schools and social and health service organizations—differ from those followed in the other democracies considered here. We have also argued that this strict separationist approach of the United States—which, although weakening, still exerts an influence—has led it to violate the norm of state neutrality toward religion. Clearly, the other democracies considered here—especially the Netherlands and Australia—have done a better job of meeting the norm of state religious neutrality and thereby of assuring the full religious freedom of all than has the United States.

It is appropriate for us to close this book by briefly considering two objections often raised in the United States to the practices and principles followed by other democracies and advocated by us. One key point that opponents of public funds going to religious schools and service organizations often make is that doing so leads to invidious distinctions in society along religious lines and undermines key goals of a liberal polity, including societal unity, tolerance, and respect for women.[18] According to this argument it is a mistake to recognize and accommodate group differences, and especially religious group differences, because doing so leads to dangerous divisions in society and encourages the kinds of social demarcations that are unhealthy for democracy. Brian Barry, as an example, argues that "a situation in which groups live in parallel universes is not one well calculated to advance mutual understanding or encourage the cultivation of habits of cooperation and sentiments of trust."[19] A successful democracy, the argument goes, assumes a minimum of consensus that a truly pluralistic society cannot achieve. A policy of public funding for the educational and social service efforts of separate religious groups is unacceptable because doing so reinforces the tendency of people to separate along ethnic, class, gender, and religious lines. Sectarian conflicts such as what Northern Ireland and the former Yugoslavia experienced, and what Syria and Iraq are experiencing today, illustrate the dangers one courts when religion and politics are allowed to mix. What is preferable is a model of strict church-state separation, in which religion is privatized, and of liberal egalitarianism that evaluates people on the basis of their individual achievements, and not according to their membership in groups. A commitment to these liberal values provides the common bond for the nation's citizens and overcomes the problems inherent in a more pluralistic system.

This is a powerful and, in some cases, persuasive argument. The former Yugoslavia, Syria, and Iraq are indeed terrifying examples of what can happen when a polity makes invidious distinctions between people based solely upon their group membership. Liberal individualism rightly calls attention to the horrors that can result when group identity defines our politics. Even more concerning and relevant to our study, each of our six countries has experienced violence committed by a small cadre of Islamic extremists, and in virtually all of those instances the violent acts were committed by people who were born and/or raised in that country. We recognize the grave dangers in a rigid, extreme form of separatism that elevates group loyalty—whether based on religion, ethnicity, language, or other considerations—to a position of preeminence over all other loyalties. Loyalty to one's religious or other group then becomes all-consuming and is not balanced by loyalties to the nation-state or to the community. In such a circumstance, people might fail to embrace the liberal values that make possible a peaceful co-existence in a pluralistic society. This kind of separatism is clearly not the democratic ideal, either for society as a whole or for the minority groups in question. Moreover, we acknowledge that there are legitimate grounds for restricting the practices of religious groups or individuals, so long as there is some overriding societal interest in doing so.

Two facts need to be recognized, however. One is that religion does not pose a *unique* danger of being the source of an extreme separatism that threatens societal unity. One has only to think of the American Civil War, the breakup of the Soviet Union, and the ongoing, sometimes violent struggle of the Kurds in Iraq and Turkey for a separate nation-state to realize that many forces other than religion can lie behind societal disunity and actual or threatened civil war. Indeed, some scholars have argued that what we often call "wars of religion" in Europe had less to do with religion and more to do with other factors, including secular ideology itself.[20] Identity can pose a dangerous source of societal division; religion, however, is only one source of identity, and therefore it does not necessarily pose a uniquely dangerous source of societal division. Second, religion has historically become a dangerous, divisive force in society when one or more religious groups asserted monopolistic claims. It is when political elites attempt to use specific religions to assert their power that tensions and possibly violent conflict arise. This was true in the case of Europe's so-called religious wars in the seventeenth century and the civil war in Bosnia-Herzegovina in the 1990s. Those in the United States who advocate a constitutional amendment that would declare the United States a Christian nation or who seek to reinstate organized prayer in the public schools err in a similar way. The problem in these cases lies with the idea that the government should promote or endorse a particular faith over other religious and secular worldviews. This naturally leads to bitter social and political disputes among people who are not of the preferred faith.

A key question at the heart of this debate is the following: What are the likely effects of the type of group recognition policies that we advocate? Will aid to religious schools and social service agencies, and perhaps other positive actions to recognize or accommodate the whole range of religious and secular belief structures, intensify cultural differences in unhealthy ways? Are such policies likely to nurture dangerous social values or practices among religious groups? We believe that the answer to these questions is clearly no.

The most compelling challenge faced by the countries in our study has been the violence done by Islamic extremists in the name of their religion. It is important to note that only a tiny percentage of the Muslim population in the United States, France, the Netherlands, Australia, England, and Germany have extremist tendencies, and there is no evidence that state recognition of Islamic schools or associations is the cause for that radicalism. Australia is likely the most generous among our countries in financing Muslim schools, yet as we noted in our country chapter, nearly all of the Australian jihadists who had traveled overseas to fight in Iraq or Syria attended government-run schools, not Islamic ones. France does not finance many Muslim schools, but it arguably has a more serious problem with Islamic extremism than other countries in our study that do. There clearly are a small number of people in each of these countries who are not assimilating to key social values. The reasons for that extremism are complex and hard to isolate, but a pluralistic policy of recognizing group rights is not the cause.

We argue, further, that state aid to religious and ethnic organizations' educational or social efforts can promote the state's goal of integrating immigrant groups into society while at the same time encouraging social pluralism.[21] Surveys of Jewish and Muslim communities in Australia, for example, indicate that involvement with ethnic or religious organizations has helped, not restricted, the assimilation process for immigrant groups. One way that this integrative process has worked is that it has encouraged religious groups to work together for a common end. The countries in our study with the most pluralistic system of state aid to religious schools and organizations—the Netherlands and Australia—have witnessed the formation of a political coalition among the various faiths—Catholic, Protestant, Jewish, Islamic—to protect their shared status. In a curious twist of fate, British Muslims have arguably become the most vocal advocates for retaining the Established Church of England. The pluralistic policy of aid to religious schools and organizations gives them a common stake in the political system, which has helped to domesticate religious disputes in these countries. This is no small accomplishment, and it challenges the assumption that recognition of group rights will necessarily exacerbate tensions based on religion. A pluralistic policy of funding for religious schools and social agencies has not intensified social divisiveness in those countries that have adopted this policy, and there is no reason to believe that it would engender greater conflict among religious groups if the United States followed this example.

A second basic concern often expressed by American strict separationists goes in the opposite direction by suggesting that a strict separation, no-aid-to-religion approach is necessary to safeguard the welfare of religion. This argument harkens to the concerns of Baptists and others that separationism is primarily about protection of religion from the state, not vice versa. The argument is that state support for religion—even its educational and social service activities—inevitably leads to a weakening of religion as government imposes regulations along with its support and religion becomes fat and complacent. In fact, American strict separationists often point to the experience of European countries such as England, Germany, and the Netherlands to make their case. In these countries religion receives much public aid of one type or another, but the churches are moribund; in the United States religion does not receive public aid and the churches are alive and active. If churches and their respective schools and service agencies are receiving ample government funds, what purpose is served in people committing their own time and money to the work of those religious organizations? Scholarship by Roger Finke, Rodney Stark, and Anthony Gill that has applied a supply side economic theory to religious activism makes a similar point. [22]

There is, however, no reason to conclude that a neutral governmental policy of aiding religious and secular schools and social agencies weakens religion, nor is there evidence linking the secularization—or diminishing church activism—of the British, French, Australian, Dutch, and German societies with state aid to religious schools and organizations. In the Netherlands, for example, there was a clear secularization trend that swept through Dutch society in the 1960s and 1970s. [23] If government funding of religious schools and social service organizations caused this trend, however, it was a long time coming, since there had been significant public funding of such organizations since the end of the nineteenth century. In addition, the Dutch secularization trend started not so much in the schools and religious social service agencies, but in the churches themselves. And the churches receive no governmental support or aid. If government support and recognition of religion is a causative factor in the secularization of Dutch society, one would expect it to be most advanced where the most aid is found—the schools and social service organizations—and the least advanced in the churches themselves that do not receive aid. But that relationship does not hold up. Similar points can be made in regard to all of the countries studied where the state has made public provision of funds available to religious schools and social service agencies. In all six of these countries, for example, we interviewed people from religious schools or social service organizations whose religious commitments were strong, vigorous, and up-front. Yet they all also received public funding. At the very least this demonstrates that there is not a *necessary* causative link between public funds and the atrophy of distinctive religious commitments. The same point can be made by noting that France has largely followed a strict church-state separation model. If in fact strict separation policies lead to large, active religious congregations, the churches of France should be overflowing with worshippers. This, however, is hardly the case. A causative link between an absence of significant governmental support for religiously based schools and social service agencies—or for religion more generally—and vigorous religion simply does not exist.

At the close of this book we return to the theme of religious freedom for all—the freedom to believe and follow the eternal truths one's conscience dictates without the involvement of government either to favor or to hinder. This becomes an ever more elusive goal in an era marked by increasing levels of religious pluralism, and with the growth of the modern welfare state that involves the government in almost all aspects of society. There is much that liberal democracies can learn from each other. We are convinced there is especially much to be learned from those practices rooted in an acceptance and even celebration of religious diversity. Those practices seek to attain religious neutrality, not by a blanket, no-aid-to-religion standard nor by seeking and supporting consensual religious beliefs, but by treating all faiths and secular systems of belief in a manner that accepts them for what they are, protects them to the extent vital societal interests allow, and in programs of governmental support and cooperation, treats them in an evenhanded manner. There is much wisdom in such a course.

NOTES

1. This was a point rather ironically raised by Justice Scalia in his dissenting opinion in the case of *Roper v. Simmons,* 543 U.S. 551 (2005). In that case, the Court held that it is unconstitutional to impose capital punishment for crimes committed by persons under the age of

eighteen. The Court's opinion relied in part on international law and the practices of other western democracies to support the holding. The United States, Justice Kennedy noted, stood alone in allowing juveniles to be executed. In his dissenting opinion, Justice Scalia, citing an earlier edition of this book as a source, noted that the Court is oblivious to international norms when it comes to religious establishment issues such as public funding for religious schools. He argued that the Court should similarly reject international norms when it came to directing American practices regarding executions. In our view, a more consistent and reasonable standard would be for democratic states to learn from each other on issues as diverse as funding for religious schools and executions for juveniles.

2. See Pew Research Center, *Latest Trends in Religious Restrictions and Hostilities* (Washington, D.C.: Pew Research Center, 2015), 54–55.

3. "The Party for Freedom Election Program, 2012," available at http://www.pvv.nl/index.php/visie/verkiezingsprogramma-2012.html; Nick Robins-Early, "A Field Guide to Europe's Radical Right Political Parties," *Huffington Post* (February 2, 2015), available at http://www.huffingtonpost.com/2015/02/12/europe-far-right_n_6511022.html.

4. Michael Sandel, *Liberalism and the Limits of Justice* (Cambridge: Cambridge University Press, 1982); Will Kymlicka, *Liberalism, Community, and Culture* (Oxford: Clarendon Press, 1989); Bhikhu Parekh, *Rethinking Multiculturalism: Cultural Diversity and Political Theory* (London: Macmillan, 2000); and Jürgen Habermas and Joseph Ratzinger, *The Dialectics of Secularization: On Reason and Religion*, trans. Brian McNeil, C.R.V. (San Francisco: Ignatius Press, 2006).

5. Habermas and Ratzinger, *The Dialectics of Secularization*, 51.

6. Rainer Bauböck, Bernhard Perchinig, and Wiebke Sievers, eds., *Citizenship Policies in the New Europe*, 2nd ed. (Amsterdam: Amsterdam University Press, 2009).

7. Christian Joppke, "Through the European Looking Glass: Citizenship Tests in the USA, Australia, and Canada," *Citizenship Studies* 17, 1 (2013), 10.

8. Australian Curriculum, Assessment and Reporting Authority, *The Shape of the Australian Curriculum: Civics and Citizenship* (Sydney: Australian Curriculum, Assessment, and Reporting Authority, 2012). Available at http://www.acara.edu.au/verve/_resources/Shape_of_the_Australian_Curriculum__Civics_and_Citizenship_251012.pdf.

9. England Department of Education, *Citizenship Programmes of Study: Key Stages 3 and 4: National Curriculum in England* (London: Crown, 2014). Available at http://www.gov.uk.

10. See Jonathan Hill and Kevin R. den Dulk, "Religion, Volunteering, and Educational Setting: The Effect of Youth Schooling Type on Civic Engagement," *Journal for the Scientific Study of Religion* 52 (2013), 179–97; and Ray Pennings et al., *Private Schools for the Public Good* (Hamilton, Ont.: Cardus, 2014).

11. Parekh, *Rethinking Multiculturalism: Cultural Diversity and Political Theory*, 341–42.

12. Michael Walzer, "Pluralism: A Political Perspective," in Will Kymlicka, ed., *The Rights of Minority Cultures* (New York: Oxford University Press, 1995), 153.

13. For a more general argument for this assertion in the U.S. context, see also John Inazu, *Confident Pluralism: Surviving and Thriving through Deep Difference* (Chicago: University of Chicago Press, 2016).

14. See Stephen V. Monsma and J. Christopher Soper, *Faith, Hope, and Jobs: Welfare-to-Work in Los Angeles* (Washington, D.C.: Georgetown University Press, 2006).

15. Paul Hirst, *Associative Democracy: New Forms of Economic and Social Governance* (Amherst: University of Massachusetts Press, 1994).

16. Hirst, *Associative Democracy*, 19.

17. Veit Bader, *Secularism or Democracy? Associational Governance of Religious Diversity* (Amsterdam: Amsterdam University Press, 2007).

18. See, for example, Amy Gutman, *Democratic Education*, rev. ed. (Princeton, N.J.: Princeton University Press, 1999); Susan Moller Okin, *Is Multiculturalism Bad for Women?* (Princeton, N.J.: Princeton University Press, 1999); Brian Barry, *Culture and Equality* (Cambridge: Polity Press, 2001); and Francis Fukuyama, "Identity, Immigration, and Liberal Democracy," *Journal of Democracy* 17, 2 (2006), 5–20.

19. Barry, *Culture and Equality*, 88.

20. William T. Cavanaugh, *The Myth of Religious Violence: Secular Ideology and the Roots of Modern Conflict* (New York: Oxford University Press, 2009).

21. For a good analysis of this position, see Iris Marion Young, "Together in Difference: Transforming the Logic of Group Political Conflict," in Kymlicka, ed., *The Rights of Minority Cultures*, 155–78.

22. Rodney Stark and Laurence R. Iannoccone, "A Supply-Side Reinterpretation of the 'Secularization' of Europe," *Journal for the Social Scientific Study of Religion* 33 (1994), 230–52; Rodney Stark, *The Rise of Christianity: A Sociologist Reconsiders History* (Princeton, N.J.: Princeton University Press, 1996); Roger Finke and Rodney Stark, *The Churching of America: Winners and Losers in Our Religious Economy* (New Brunswick, N.J.: Rutgers University Press, 2005); and Anthony Gill, *The Political Origins of Religious Liberty* (Cambridge: Cambridge University Press, 2008).

23. One historian who has carefully studied the Dutch secularization trend of the 1960s sees the chief causative factor lying not in the Dutch pluralistic system of recognition of and aid to religious and secular schools and social agencies, but in the religious, political, and social elites' response to the cultural changes moving through western societies in the 1960s. That response emphasized accommodating and accepting rather than resisting these changes. See James C. Kennedy, *Building New Babylon: Cultural Change in the Netherlands during the 1960s* (Ph.D. dissertation, University of Iowa, 1995).

Selected Bibliography

Alley, Robert S., ed. *The Supreme Court on Church and State*. New York: Oxford University Press, 1988.

Andeweg, Rudy B. and Galen A. Irwin. *Dutch Government and Politics*. New York: St. Martin's Press, 1993.

Bader, Veit. *Secularism or Democracy? Associational Governance of Religious Diversity*. Amsterdam: Amsterdam University Press, 2007.

Bakvis, Herman. *Catholic Power in the Netherlands*. Kingston, Ont.: McGill-Queen's University Press, 1981.

Barry, Brian. *Culture and Equality*. Cambridge: Polity Press, 2001.

Bax, Erik H. *Modernization and Cleavage in Dutch Society*. Aldershot, U.K.: Avebury, 1990.

Bebbington, D. W. *Evangelicalism in Modern Britain*. London: Unwin Hyman, 1989.

Beckford, James A. and Sophie Gilliat. *Religion in Prison: Equal Rites in a Multi-Faith Society*. Cambridge: Cambridge University Press, 1998.

Bijsterveld, Sophie C. van. *The Empty Throne: Democracy and the Rule of Law in Transition*. West Lafayette, Ind.: Purdue University Press, 2002.

Black, Amy E., Douglas L. Koopman, and David K. Ryden. *Of Little Faith: The Politics of George W. Bush's Faith-Based Initiative*. Washington, D.C.: Georgetown University Press, 2004.

Bolt, John. *A Free Church, a Holy Nation: Abraham Kuyper's American Public Theology*. Grand Rapids, Mich.: Eerdmans, 2001.

Bouma, Gary D. *Being Faithful in Diversity: Religions and Social Policy in Multifaith Societies*. Adelaide: ATF Press, 2011.

Bowen, John. *Why the French Don't Like Headscarves: Islam, State, and Public Space*. Princeton, N.J.: Princeton University Press, 2007.

Bratt, James D. *Abraham Kuyper: Modern Calvinist, Christian Democrat*. Grand Rapids, Mich.: Eerdmans, 2013.

Breward, Ian. *A History of the Australian Churches*. Sydney: Allen and Unwin, 1993.

Burleigh, Michael. *Earthly Powers: The Clash of Religion and Politics in Europe, from the French Revolution to the Great War*. New York: Harper, 2005.

Campbell, Tom, Jeffrey Goldsworthy, and Adrienne Stone, eds. *Protecting Rights without a Bill of Rights: Institutional Performance and Reform in Australia*. Aldershot, U.K.: 2006.

Carlson-Thies, Stanley. *Democracy in the Netherlands: Consociational or Pluriform?* Ph.D. dissertation, University of Toronto, 1993.

Cavanaugh, William T. *The Myth of Religious Violence: Secular Ideology and the Roots of Modern Conflict*. New York: Oxford University Press, 2009.

Chapman, Mark, Judith Maltby, and William Whyte, eds. *The Established Church: Past, Present and Future.* London: T&T Clark International, 2011.

Conradt, David P. and Eric Langenbacher. *The German Polity*, 10th ed. Lanham, Md.: Rowman & Littlefield, 2013.

Currie, David P. *The Constitution of the Federal Republic of Germany.* Chicago: University of Chicago Press, 1994.

Daalder, Hans and Galen Irwin, eds. *Politics in the Netherlands: How Much Change?* Totowa, N.J.: Cass, 1989.

Davie, Grace. *Religion in Modern Europe: A Memory Mutates.* Oxford: Oxford University Press, 2000.

———. *Religion in Britain: A Persistent Paradox.* Hoboken, N.J.: John Wiley and Sons, 2015.

DiIulio, John Jr. *Godly Republic: A Centrist Blueprint for America's Faith-Based Future.* Berkeley: University of California Press, 2007.

Dreisbach, Daniel L. and Mark David Hall. *The Sacred Rights of Conscience: Selected Readings on Religious Liberty and Church-State Relations in the American Founding.* Indianapolis: Liberty Fund, 2009.

Eck, Diana. *A New Religious America: How a "Christian Country" Has Become the World's Most Diverse Nation.* New York: HarperOne, 2002.

Fetzer, Joel S. and J. Christopher Soper. *Muslims and the State in Britain, France, and Germany.* Cambridge: Cambridge University Press, 2005.

Finke, Roger and Rodney Stark. *The Churching of America: Winners and Losers in Our Religious Economy.* New Brunswick, N.J.: Rutgers University Press, 2005.

Fowler, Robert Booth, Allen Hertzke, Laura Olson, and Kevin R. den Dulk. *Religion and Politics in America: Faith, Culture, and Strategic Choices.* Boulder, Colo.: Westview, 2014.

Gay, Peter. *The Enlightenment: An Interpretation.* New York: Knopf, 1966.

Gill, Anthony. *The Political Origins of Religious Liberty.* Cambridge: Cambridge University Press, 2008.

Glenn, Charles Leslie Jr. *The Myth of the Common School.* Amherst: University of Massachusetts Press, 1987.

Glenn, Charles Leslie Jr. and Jan de Groof. *Balancing Freedom, Autonomy and Accountability in Education,* vol. 2. Nijmegen, the Netherlands: Wolf Legal Publishers, 2005.

Green, Steven K. *The Bible, the School, and the Constitution: The Clash That Shaped Modern Church-State Doctrine.* New York: Oxford University Press, 2012.

Gutman, Amy. *Democratic Education,* rev. ed. Princeton, N.J.: Princeton University Press, 1999.

Habermas, Jürgen and Joseph Ratzinger. *The Dialectics of Secularization: On Reason and Religion,* trans. Brian McNeil, C.R.V. San Francisco: Ignatius Press, 2006.

Hamburger, Philip. *Separation of Church and State.* Cambridge, Mass.: Harvard University Press, 2002.

Hatch, Nathan. *The Democratization of American Christianity.* New Haven, Conn.: Yale University Press, 1989.

Hogan, Michael. *The Sectarian Strand.* New York: Penguin Books, 1987.

Inazu, John. *Confident Pluralism: Surviving and Thriving through Deep Difference.* Chicago: University of Chicago Press, 2016.

Jupp, James, ed. *The Australian People: An Encyclopedia of the Australian Nation, Its People and Their Origins.* Cambridge: Cambridge University Press, 2002.

Kaye, Richard, ed. *Anglicanism in Australia: A History.* Melbourne: Melbourne University Press, 2002.

Klausen, Jytte. *The Islamic Challenge: Politics and Religion in Western Europe.* New York: Oxford University Press, 2005.

Kommers, Donald P. *The Federal Constitutional Court.* Washington, D.C.: Institute for Contemporary German Studies, 1994.

———. *The Constitutional Jurisprudence of the Federal Republic of Germany,* 3rd ed. Durham, N.C.: Duke University Press, 2012.

Kuru, Ahmet T. *Secularism and State Policies toward Religion: The United States, France, and Turkey.* New York: Cambridge University Press, 2009.

Kuyper, Abraham. *Calvinism: Six Stone Foundation Lectures.* Grand Rapids, Mich.: Eerdmans, 1931.

Kymlicka, Will. *Liberalism, Community, and Culture.* Oxford: Clarendon Press, 1989.

Laurence, Jonathan. *The Emancipation of Europe's Muslims: The State's Role in Minority Integration.* Princeton, N.J.: Princeton University Press, 2012.

Laycock, Douglas. *Religious Liberty: Vol. 1.* Grand Rapids, Mich.: Eerdmans, 2010.

Levy, Jonah. *Tocqueville's Revenge: State, Society, and Economy in Contemporary France.* Cambridge, Mass.: Harvard University Press, 1999.

Levy, Leonard W. *The Establishment Clause: Religion and the First Amendment,* 2nd ed. Chapel Hill: University of North Carolina Press, 1994.

Lewis, Philip. *Islamic Britain: Religion, Politics and Identity among British Muslims.* London: I.B. Taurus, 1994.

Lyons, Mark. *Third Sector: The Contribution of Nonprofit and Cooperative Enterprise in Australia.* Sydney: Allen and Unwin, 2001.

Maddox, Marion. *God under Howard: The Rise of the Religious Right in Australian Politics.* Sydney: Allen and Unwin, 2005.

Marsden, George M. and Bradley J. Longfield, eds. *The Secularization of the Academy.* New York: Oxford University Press, 1992.

May, Henry A. *The Enlightenment in America.* New York: Oxford University Press, 1976.

Mead, Sidney E. *The Lively Experiment.* New York: Harper & Row, 1963.

Means, Paul Banwell. *Things That Are Caesar's: The Genesis of the German Church Conflict.* New York: Round Table Press, 1935.

Monsma, Stephen V. *Positive Neutrality.* Westport, Conn.: Greenwood, 1993.

———. *When Sacred and Secular Mix: Religious Nonprofit Organizations and Public Money.* Lanham, Md.: Rowman & Littlefield, 1996.

———. *Putting Faith in Partnerships: Welfare-to-Work in Four Cities.* Ann Arbor: University of Michigan Press, 2004.

Monsma, Stephen V. and J. Christopher Soper. *Faith, Hope, and Jobs: Welfare-to-Work in Los Angeles.* Washington, D.C.: Georgetown University Press, 2006.

Monsma, Stephen V. and Stanley Carlson-Thies. *Protecting the Religious Freedom of Faith-Based Organizations.* Grand Rapids, Mich.: Baker, 2015.

Moon, Jeremy and Campbell Sharman, eds. *Australian Politics and Government: The Commonwealth, the States, and the Territories.* New York: Cambridge University Press, 2003.

Nelsen, Brent F. and James L. Guth. *Religion and the Struggle for European Union.* Washington, D.C.: Georgetown University Press, 2015.

Nielsen, Jørgen. *Muslims in Western Europe,* 2nd ed. Edinburgh, U.K.: Edinburgh University Press, 1995.

Norton, Philip. *The British Polity,* 5th ed. New York: Routledge, 2010.

Oomen, Barbara. *Rights for Others: The Slow Home-Coming of Human Rights in the Netherlands.* New York: Cambridge University Press, 2013.

Organization for Economic Cooperation and Development. *Private Sector Involvement in the Delivery of Social Welfare Services: Mixed Models from OECD Countries.* Paris: OECD, 1994.

———. *School: A Matter of Choice.* Paris: OECD, 1994.

Parekh, Bhikhu. *Rethinking Multiculturalism: Cultural Diversity and Political Theory.* London: Macmillan, 2000.

Ploeg, Tymen J. van der and John W. Sap, eds. *Rethinking the Balance: Government and Nongovernmental Organizations in the Netherlands.* Amsterdam: VU University Press, 1995.

Post, Harry. *Pillarization: An Analysis of Dutch and Belgian Society.* Aldershot, Netherlands: Avebury, 1989.

Prochaska, Frank. *Christianity and Social Service in Modern Britain: The Disinherited Spirit.* New York, Oxford: Oxford University Press, 2006.

Putnam, Robert D. and David E. Campbell. *American Grace: How Religion Unites and Divides Us.* New York: Simon & Schuster, 2010.

Ramadan, Tariq. *To Be a European Muslim.* Leicester, England: Islamic Foundation, 1999.

Reichley, A. James. *Faith in Politics.* Washington, D.C.: Brookings Institution, 2002.

Robbers, Gerhard, ed. *Church Autonomy: A Comparative Survey.* Frankfurt am Main, Germany: Peter Land, 2001.

———. *State and Church in the European Union,* 2nd ed. Baden-Baden, Germany: Nomos Verlagsgesellschaft, 2005.

Rossiter, Clinton. *Seedbed of the Republic.* New York: Harcourt, Brace & World, 1953.

Sachs, W. L. *The Transformation of Anglicanism from State Church to Global Communion.* Cambridge: Cambridge University Press, 1993.

Saeed, Abdullah and Shahram Adkbarzadeh, eds. *Muslim Communities in Australia.* Sydney: UNSW Press, 2001.

Salamon, Lester M. and Helmut K. Anheier, eds. *Working Paper of the Johns Hopkins Comparative Nonprofit Sector Project,* no. 35. Baltimore, Md.: Johns Hopkins Institute for Policy Studies, 1999.

Salamon, Lester M., S. Wojciech Sokolowski, and associates. *Global Civil Society: Dimension of the Nonprofit Sector,* vol. 2. Bloomfield, Conn.: Kurmarian Press, 2004.

Seligman, Adam B., ed. *Religious Education and the Challenge of Pluralism.* New York: Oxford University Press, 2014.

Smidt, Corwin et al. *Pews, Prayers, and Participation: Religion and Civic Responsibility in America.* Washington, D.C.: Georgetown University Press, 2008.

Sniderman, Paul M. and Louk Hagendoorn. *When Ways of Life Collide: Multiculturalism and Its Discontents in the Netherlands.* Princeton, N.J.: Princeton University Press, 2007.

Spotts, Frederic. *The Churches and Politics in Germany.* Middletown, Conn.: Wesleyan University Press, 1973.

Stark, Rodney. *The Rise of Christianity: A Sociologist Reconsiders History.* Princeton, N.J.: Princeton University Press, 1996.

Tash, Robert C. *Dutch Pluralism.* New York: Lang, 1991.

Van Kley, Dale K. *The Religious Origins of the French Revolution.* New Haven, Conn.: Yale University Press, 1996.

Wald, Kenneth and Allison Calhoun-Brown. *Religion and Politics in the United States,* 7th ed. Lanham, Md.: Rowman & Littlefield, 2014.

Witte, John, Jr. and Joel A. Nichols. *Religion and the American Constitutional Experiment: Essential Rights and Liberties,* 4th ed. Boulder, Colo.: Westview Press, 2016.

Index

About the Authors

Chris Soper is a Distinguished Professor of Political Science at Pepperdine University in Malibu, California. He is coauthor of *Confucianism, Democratization, and Human Rights in Taiwan* (2013), *Faith, Hope, and Jobs: Welfare-to-Work in Los Angeles* (2006), *Muslims and the State in Britain, France, and Germany* (2005), and *The Challenge of Pluralism: Church and State in Five Western Democracies* (first edition, 1997); coeditor of *Equal Treatment of Religion in a Pluralistic Society* (1998); and author of *Religious Beliefs and Political Choices: Evangelical Christianity in the United States and Great Britain* (1994), as well as numerous essays and articles in scholarly journals.

Kevin R. den Dulk is the Paul B. Henry Professor of Political Science and the executive director of the Henry Institute for the Study of Christianity and Politics at Calvin College (Grand Rapids, Michigan). An award-winning teacher, his scholarly work focuses especially on how religion works through civil society to foster democratic citizenship. He has coauthored or coedited several books, including Religion and Politics in America (2013), *Pews, Prayers, and Participation* (2008), *A Disappearing God Gap?* (2010), *Christianity in Chinese Public Life* (2014), *Mediating Religion and Government* (2014), and *The Church and Religious Persecution* (2015).

Stephen V. Monsma is a research fellow at the Henry Institute for the Study of Christianity and Politics, Calvin College (Grand Rapids, Michigan) and a professor emeritus of political science at Pepperdine University (Malibu, California). He has published widely in the fields of church-state relations and faith-based nonprofit organizations. In addition to the first edition of *The Challenge of Pluralism: Church and State in Five Democracies*, his best-known works are *Free to Serve* (2016, with Stanley Carlson-Thies), *Faith, Hope and Jobs: Welfare-to-Work in Los Angeles* (2006, with J. Christopher Soper), *Putting Faith in Partnerships: Welfare-to-Work in Four Cities* (2004), *When Sacred and Secular Mix: Religious Nonprofit Organizations and Public Money* (1996), and *Positive Neutrality* (1993).

Lightning Source UK Ltd.
Milton Keynes UK
UKHW012337270819
348691UK00004B/1069/P